T0213521

Lecture Notes in Computer Science 10481

Commenced Publication in 1973
Founding and Former Series Editors:
Gerhard Goos, Juris Hartmanis, and Jan van Leeuwen

More information about this series at http://www.springer.com/series/7412

Snehasis Mukherjee · Suvadip Mukherjee
Dipti Prasad Mukherjee · Jayanthi Sivaswamy
Suyash Awate · Srirangaraj Setlur
Anoop M. Namboodiri · Santanu Chaudhury (Eds.)

Computer Vision, Graphics, and Image Processing

ICVGIP 2016 Satellite Workshops, WCVA, DAR, and MedImage
Guwahati, India, December 19, 2016
Revised Selected Papers

 Springer

Editors
Snehasis Mukherjee
Indian Institute of Information Technology
SriCity
India

Suvadip Mukherjee
GE Global Research
Bangalore
India

Dipti Prasad Mukherjee
Indian Statistical Institute
Kolkata
India

Jayanthi Sivaswamy
International Institute of Information
   Technology
Hyderabad
India

Suyash Awate
Indian Institute of Technology Bombay
Mumbai
India

Srirangaraj Setlur
CEDAR
Buffalo, NY
USA

Anoop M. Namboodiri
International Institute of Information
   Technology
Hyderabad
India

Santanu Chaudhury
CSIR-CEERI
Pilani, Rajasthan
India

ISSN 0302-9743   ISSN 1611-3349 (electronic)
Lecture Notes in Computer Science
ISBN 978-3-319-68123-8   ISBN 978-3-319-68124-5 (eBook)
https://doi.org/10.1007/978-3-319-68124-5

Library of Congress Control Number: 2017956086

LNCS Sublibrary: SL6 – Image Processing, Computer Vision, Pattern Recognition, and Graphics

This Springer imprint is published by Springer Nature
The registered company is Springer International Publishing AG
The registered company address is: Gewerbestrasse 11, 6330 Cham, Switzerland

Preface

The tenth version of the Indian Conference on Vision, Graphics and Image Processing (ICVGIP) was held at IIT Guwahati in December 2016. ICVGIP already taken a unique position within the scientific community in India. Starting with the ninth version of ICVGIP, workshops on contemporary topics have become an integral part of the conference. The most recent in this series of ICVGIP workshops were held on December 19, 2016, at the IIT Guwahati. Four tracks on Computer Vision Applications, Medical Image Processing, Document Analysis and Recognition, and Digital Heritage were part of the workshop program this year. The collection of papers in this edited volume is extended versions of papers presented in the first three of the four above mentioned tracks. The authors of the papers presented in this workshop had submitted an extended version of the paper keeping in mind the feedback received at the workshop.

Overall 52 papers were submitted in the Computer Vision Applications track and after a rigorous double-blind review process, we could accept 18 papers keeping the quality and time-frame of a single-day workshop. This track mainly focused on industrial applications of computer vision and related technologies.

The Medimage Workshop focused on problems in medical image computing and invited original contributions to address these problems. The workshop received 14 papers and after a double-blind review process, 7 were accepted for presentation as poster or oral.

The DAR Workshop was organized to bring together people working in the field of Document Analysis and Recognition. The workshop received 10 submissions of which 7 papers were accepted for presentation, through a double-blind review process.

We would like to thank the Technical Program Committee members and the reviewers for their time and dedication. We acknowledge support and guidance from the dynamic Organizing Committee of ICVGIP 2016. In particular we appreciate support received from Dr. Prithwijit Guha and Mathew Francis.

We hope that our efforts and the contributions presented in this collection will encourage new ideas and further collaborative efforts between computer vision researchers in industry and academia.

August 2017

Snehasis Mukherjee
Suvadip Mukherjee
Dipti Prasad Mukherjee
Jayanthi Sivaswamy
Suyash Awate
Srirangaraj Setlur
Anoop M. Namboodiri
Santanu Chaudhury

Organization

Editors

Snehasis Mukherjee	IIIT SriCity, India
Suvadip Mukherjee	GE Global Research, India
Dipti Prasad Mukherjee	Indian Statistical Institute, India
Jayanthi Sivaswamy	IIIT Hyderabad, India
Suyash Awate	IIT Bombay, India
Srirangaraj Setlur	CEDAR, SUNY Buffalo, USA
Anoop M. Namboodiri	IIIT Hyderabad, India
Santanu Chaudhury	CSIR-CEERI Pilani, India

Technical Program Committee for WCVA

Aditya Nigam	IIT Mandi, India
Afzal Godil	National Institute of Standards and Technology, USA
Andrea Vaccari	University of Virginia, USA
Balasubramanian Raman	IIT Roorkee, India
Chetan Arora	IIIT Delhi, India
Chiranjoy Chattopadhyay	IIT Jodhpur, India
Devi Prasad Dogra	IIT Bhubaneswar, India
Nilanjan Ray	University of Alberta, Canada
Pratik Shah	IIIT Vadodora, India
Rituparna Sarkar	University of Virginia, USA
Sanmuganathan Raman	IIT Gandhinagar, India
Shiv Ram Dubey	IIIT SriCity, India
Soumitra Samanta	University of Liverpool, UK
Swapna Agarwal	TCS Innovation Lab, India
Angshuman Paul	Indian Statistical Institute, India
Prithwijit Guha	IIT Guwahati, India
Vineet Gandhi	IIIT Hyderabad, India
P. Viswanath	IIIT SriCity, India
Rajiv Ranjan Sahay	IIT Kharagpur, India
Sanjoy Kumar Saha	Jadavpur University, India

Technical Program Committee for MedImage

Jayanta Mukhopadhyay	IIT Kharagpur, India
Niranjan Joshi	BIRAC Regional entrepreneurship centre, Bangalore, India
Ananda Shankar Chowdhury	Jadavpur University, India

Gopal Joshi	Noodle Analytics, India
Ajit Rajwade	IIT Bombay, India
Anubha Gupta	IIIT Delhi, India
Debdoot Sheet	IIT Kharagpur, India
Bipul Das	GE Global Research, India
Amit Kale	Bosch Corporate Research, India
Arnav Bhavsar	IIT Mandi, India

Technical Program Committee for DAR

Srinivasa Chakravarthy	IIT Madras, India
Utpal Garain	Indian Statistical Institute, India
Gaurav Harit	IIT Jodhpur, India
C.V. Jawahar	IIIT Hyderabad, India
Anoop M. Namboodiri	IIIT Hyderabad, India
Atul Negi	University of Hyderabad, India
Swapan Kumar Parui	Indian Statistical Institute, India
A.G. Ramakrishnan	IISc, India
Srirangaraj Setlur	CEDAR, SUNY Buffalo, USA

Contents

WCVA

A Novel Intelligent Multiple Watermarking Schemes for the Protection
of the Information Content of a Document Image 3
   K.R. Chetan and S. Nirmala

Experimental Evaluation of 3D Kinect Face Database 15
   A.A. Gaonkar, M.D. Gad, N.T. Vetrekar, Vithal Shet Tilve, and R.S. Gad

Photometric Normalization Techniques for Extended Multi-spectral Face
Recognition: A Comparative Analysis 27
   N.T. Vetrekar, R. Raghavendra, R.S. Gad, and G.M. Naik

Dictionary Based Approach for Facial Expression Recognition
from Static Images 39
   Krishan Sharma and Renu Rameshan

Vision Based Pose Estimation of Multiple Peg-in-Hole
for Robotic Assembly 50
   Pitchandi Nagarajan, S. Saravana Perumaal, and B. Yogameena

A Spatio Temporal Texture Saliency Approach for Object
Detection in Videos....................................... 63
   A. Sasithradevi, S. Mohamed Mansoor Roomi, and I. Sanofer

Simultaneous Reconstruction of Multiple Hand Shredded Content-Less
Pages Using Graph-Based Global Reassembly 75
   K.S. Lalitha, Sukhendu Das, Arun Menon, and Koshy Varghese

Super Resolution Mapping of Trees for Urban Forest Monitoring
in Madurai City Using Remote Sensing......................... 88
   D. Synthiya Vinothini, B. Sathyabama, and S. Karthikeyan

Scale-Invariant Image Inpainting Using Gradient-Based
Image Composition 97
   Mrinmoy Ghorai, Soumitra Samanta, and Bhabatosh Chanda

Recursive Structure from Motion 109
   M. Chebiyyam, S. Chaudhury, and I.N. Kar

A Hybrid Deep Architecture for Face Recognition in Real-Life Scenario 120
   A. Sanyal, U. Bhattacharya, and S.K. Parui

Brain Tumor Segmentation from Multimodal MR Images Using
Rough Sets.   133
   Rupsa Saha, Ashish Phophalia, and Suman K. Mitra

A Text Recognition Augmented Deep Learning Approach
for Logo Identification.   145
   Moushumi Medhi, Shubham Sinha, and Rajiv Ranjan Sahay

High Frame Rate Real-Time Scene Change Detection System.   157
   Sanjay Singh, Ravi Saini, Sumeet Saurav, Pramod Tanwar,
   Kota S. Raju, Anil K. Saini, Santanu Chaudhury, and Idaku Ishii

Painting Classification Using a Pre-trained Convolutional Neural Network . . .   168
   Sugata Banerji and Atreyee Sinha

Eigen Domain Transformation for Soft-Margin Multiple Feature-Kernel
Learning for Surveillance Face Recognition   180
   Samik Banerjee and Sukhendu Das

A Beta Distribution Based Novel Scheme for Detection of Changes
in Crowd Motion   192
   Soumyajit Pal, Sounak Mondal, Sanjoy Kumar Saha,
   and Bhabatosh Chanda

Reconstruction of Sparse-View Tomography via Banded Matrices.   204
   T. Prasad, P.U. Praveen Kumar, C.S. Sastry, and P.V. Jampana

DAR

SPODS: A Dataset of Color-Official Documents and Detection of Logo,
Stamp, and Signature.   219
   Amit Vijay Nandedkar, Jayanta Mukherjee, and Shamik Sural

Text and Non-text Separation in Scanned Color-Official Documents   231
   Amit Vijay Nandedkar, Jayanta Mukherjee, and Shamik Sural

Multi-font Telugu Text Recognition Using Hidden Markov Models
and Akshara Bi-grams   243
   Koteswara Rao Devarapalli and Atul Negi

Anveshak - A Groundtruth Generation Tool for Foreground Regions
of Document Images   255
   Soumyadeep Dey, Jayanta Mukherjee, Shamik Sural,
   and Amit Vijay Nandedkar

Writer Identification for Handwritten Words.   265
   Shilpa Pandey and Gaurav Harit

Kalanjiyam: Unconstrained Offline Tamil Handwritten Database   277
  Faizal Hajamohideen and S. Noushath

Info-Graphics Retrieval: A Multi-kernel Distance Based Hashing Scheme . . .   288
  Ritu Garg and Santanu Chaudhury

MedImage

Neovascularization Detection on Retinal Images   301
  Sudeshna Sil Kar, Santi P. Maity, and Seba Maity

Distribution Based EEG Baseline Classification   314
  Gopika Gopan K., Neelam Sinha, and Dinesh Babu J.

Texture Based Person Identification Using Dental Radiographs
and Photographs in Forensic Odontology   322
  G. Jaffino, A. Banumathi, Ulaganathan Gurunathan, and J. Prabin Jose

Shearlet Based Medical Image Fusion Using Pulse-Coupled Neural
Network with Fuzzy Memberships   337
  Niladri Shekhar Mishra, Sudeb Das, and Amlan Chakrabarti

MR Imaging via Reduced Generalized Autocalibrating Partially Parallel
Acquisition Compressed Sensing.   345
  Sheikh Rafiul Islam, Seba Maity, Santi P. Maity, and Ajoy Kumar Ray

Tracking of Retinal Microsurgery Tools Using Late Fusion of
Responses from Convolutional Neural Network over Pyramidally
Decomposed Frames   358
  Kaustuv Mishra, Rachana Sathish, and Debdoot Sheet

Cardiac Ultrasound Image Enhancement Using Tissue Selective Total
Variation Regularization.   367
  *Deepak Mishra, Santanu Chaudhury, Mukul Sarkar,
  and Arvinder Singh Soin*

Methods and System for Segmentation of Isolated Nuclei in Microscopic
Breast Fine Needle Aspiration Cytology Images   380
  *Hrushikesh Garud, Sri Phani Krishna Karri, Debdoot Sheet,
  Ashok Kumar Maity, Jyotirmoy Chatterjee, Manjunatha Mahadevappa,
  and Ajoy Kumar Ray*

Segmentation of Lumen and External Elastic Laminae in Intravascular
Ultrasound Images Using Ultrasonic Backscattering Physics Initialized
Multiscale Random Walks   393
  Debarghya China, Pabitra Mitra, and Debdoot Sheet

Author Index   405

WCVA

A Novel Intelligent Multiple Watermarking Schemes for the Protection of the Information Content of a Document Image

K.R. Chetan[(⊠)] and S. Nirmala

Department of CSE, JNN College of Engineering, Shimoga, Karnataka, India
chetankr@jnnce.ac.in, nir_shiv_2002@yahoo.co.in

Abstract. Most of the past document image watermarking schemes focus on providing same level of integrity and copyright protection for information present in the source document image. However, in a document image the information contents possess various levels of sensitivity. Each level of sensitivity needs different type of protection and this demands multiple watermarking techniques. In this paper, a novel intelligent multiple watermarking techniques are proposed. The sensitivity of the information content of a block is based on the homogeneity and relative energy contribution parameters. Appropriate watermarking scheme is applied based on sensitivity classification of the block. Experiments are conducted exhaustively on documents. Experimental results reveal the accurate identification of the sensitivity of information content in the block. The results reveal that multiple watermarking schemes has reduced the amount of data to be embedded and consequently improved perceptual quality of the watermarked image.

Keywords: Multiple watermarking · Intelligent watermarking · Fragile watermarking · Robust watermarking · Integer wavelets · Contourlets · Gradient binarized blocks · GLCM

1 Introduction

Document images are used as proof for authentication and business transactions. Traditionally digital watermarking has been used as a primary technique for copyright protection and integrity management of document images [1–3]. The document image consists of information with various levels of sensitivity. For instance, in a cheque image, the signature and amount are dynamically changing information for each cheque and thus possess highest level of sensitivity. The bank name, logo, cheque number contain regeneratable information content and hence constitute lower level of sensitivity. There also exists many empty areas in a cheque which can be classified as insensitive areas. Each sensitivity level needs different type of protection. Therefore, there is a need to use multiple watermarking techniques on the different areas of the same document image. The multiple watermarking schemes have two fold objectives: improve the perceptual quality of the watermarked image by reducing embedding capacity; perform tamper detection and recovery with better accuracy.

S. Mukherjee et al. (Eds.): ICVGIP 2016, LNCS 10481, pp. 3–14, 2017.
https://doi.org/10.1007/978-3-319-68124-5_1

This paper is organized as follows: Sect. 2 provides a literature review of the existing works in intelligent and multiple watermarking schemes. The proposed model is explored in Sect. 3. Section 4 presents experimental results of the proposed multiple watermarking scheme. Conclusions of the proposed work are summarized in the last section.

2 Literature Review

Digital watermarking is classified as robust, fragile and semi-fragile based on the robustness to incidental and intentional attacks [4]. A detailed survey of the works on robust, fragile and semi-fragile watermarking techniques can be found in [5–10]. Most of the past efforts on watermarking schemes apply single type of watermarking technique on the entire document image. Houmansadr et al. [11] proposed a watermarking technique based on the entropy masking feature of the Human Visual System (HVS). Kankanhalli and Ramakrishnan [12] developed a watermarking technique by embedding just noticeable watermarks. Radharani et al. [13] designed a content based watermarking scheme in which watermark is generated using Independent Component Analysis (ICA) for each block of the input image. In [14–16], few works on the segmentation of the image into objects using image statistics and subsequently applying the robust watermarking schemes for each objects are described. Shieh et al. [17] proposed the use of genetic algorithm (GA) [18] to compute the optimal frequency bands for watermark embedding into a Discrete Cosine Transform (DCT) based watermarking system, which can simultaneously improve security, robustness, and image quality of the watermarked image. A novel idea was put forward in [19] to embed multiple watermarks with different compression domains into the same source. Lu et al. [19] developed an algorithm for embedding multiple watermarks into the Vector Quantization (VQ) domain, as well as for hiding the secret keys associated with the watermarks in the transform domain to enhance the robustness of the watermarked image. Sheppard et al. [20] discussed the different ways of multiple watermarking like rewatermarking, segmented watermarking and composite watermarking [20]. They explored different attack scenarios [21, 22] and level of robustness that could be provided by each category of multiple watermarking.

The literature reviews on the content based multiple watermarking techniques reveals that most of the existing works lack intelligent classification of information content of a document image based on sensitivity to the attacks. In the existing techniques, authors attempted to apply multiple watermarks of the same type to each block of the document image and it is not based on the appropriateness of the watermarking for the information content present in the block. In addition, the existing schemes also incur tradeoff between robustness and fragility of the watermarking multiple times. These issues motivate towards an intelligent classification of the different areas of a document image and application of different types of watermark schemes appropriate to the sensitivity requirement of each area of the document image. In this paper, a new model for intelligent multiple watermarking is designed that automatically computes desired type of watermarking for each block of the document image.

3 Proposed Model

The proposed model for the novel intelligent multiple watermarking system consists of two processes namely Embedding and Extraction. The Embedding process divides the input document image into blocks and intelligently determines the type of watermarking to be applied for each block. The watermarking algorithm depends on the information content of the image. This is primarily available through the energy component and hence luminance component in transformation is used. Further image is converted back to color after watermarking to produce watermarked image. The embedding technique depends on the type of watermarking. Robust watermarking is implemented using integer wavelet embedding [23] and fragile watermarking is accomplished using contourlet based embedding [24]. Extraction process is carried on the blocks of the watermarked image. The result of the watermark extraction depends on the type of the watermarking. The outcome of the robust watermark extraction on the block of the watermarked image is content authentication of the block. The outcome of fragile watermark extraction on the block of the watermarked image results in tamper detection and recovery of information content in the block. The following subsection explores the embedding process and extraction process in detail.

3.1 Multiple Watermark Embedding

The multiple watermark embedding process is shown in Fig. 1. It is an intelligent and adaptive embedding scheme which depends on the information content of the

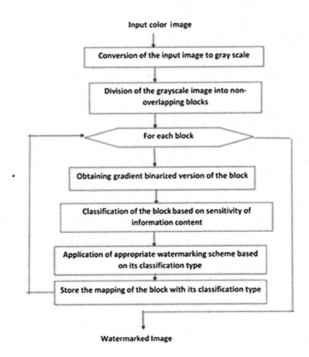

Fig. 1. Multiple watermark embedding process

document image. Experiments have been conducted on all document images corpus to analyze the effect of size of the block on accuracy in identification of the type of the block and processing time. For each block, gradient binarized version of the information content in the block is obtained. Further, the sensitivity level of each block and type of watermarking required is found automatically. Subsequently, appropriate watermark embedding algorithm is applied for each block.

The gradient binarized version of the information content in the block is computed using the following algorithm:

Algorithm : *Gradient_Binarized_Block(B)*
Input: *An image block B of size 128X128 with pixel values containing gray levels (0-255)*
Output: *Gradient Binarized block of B*
   1. for every pixel p at location (i, j) in the block,
   2.   **do** find its gradient value

$$g_p(i,j) = \sum_{x=-1}^{1}\sum_{y=-1}^{1} p(x+i, y+j) \tag{1}$$

   3.   compute maximum gradient value in the block

$$g_{max} = max_{i=1}^{128X128}\left(g_p(i,j)\right) \tag{2}$$

   4.   Set gradient threshold g_{thresh} to $(g_{max})/2$
   5.   Convert all the pixel values from gray levels to binary using g_{thresh}. The values of the pixels having gray levels above g_{thresh} is set to 1 and values of the rest of the pixels is set to 0.
   6.   Let $n1$ denote the total number of pixels having value 1 and $n0$ denote total number of pixels with value 0.
   7.   Compute new gradient threshold as

$$g_{thresh1} = round(n1 * w1 + n0 * w2) \tag{3}$$

   8.   **if** $g_{thresh1} = g_{thresh}$
            then return
         else
            $g_{thresh} = g_{thresh1}$
   9.   **return** gradient_binarized_block of B

In this algorithm, the values of the weights $w1$ and $w2$ is empirically set to 0.5. The number of iterations required for termination of this algorithm depends on the distribution of the information content in the block. The outcome of this algorithm is a binary version of the block that gives segmentation of foreground and background information contents in the block.

Algorithm: Classification_of_sensitivity_level*(B)*

Input: Gradient_binarized_block *B*

Output: *Sensitivity_level* of *B*

1. Computation of the energy distribution of the block using median of the pixel values in gradient binarized block *B*

$$ED_b = median(g_b) \qquad (4)$$

2. Computation of the relative energy distribution RED_b of binarized block b using:

$$RED_b = \frac{ED_b}{max_{n=1}^{nb}(ED\ )} \qquad (5)$$

   where, nb denotes the total number of blocks in the source document image.

3. Computing gray level cooccurence matrix (GLCM) of gradient binarized block b and designate it as $GLCM_b$
4. Compute value of homogeneity parameter HM_b
5. Compute sensitivity levels of block as follows:

$$sensitivity\_levels = \begin{cases} 0, & HM_b < 0.5 \ and \ RED_b > 0.7 \\ 1, & 0.5 \leq HM_b < 0.85 \ and \ RED_b \geq 0.3 \\ 2, & otherwise \end{cases} \qquad (6)$$

6. **return** *sensitivity_level*

Experiments have been conducted on the document image corpus to decide on the appropriate range to relative energy distribution and homogeneity values for determining the sensitivity levels of the blocks. The average RED_b and HM_b values for different types of information content in these document images is calculated and values are recorded in Table 1. It can be observed from the values in Table 1 that RED values for blocks of document image containing dynamically changing information content are in the range 0.7–0.85 and HM values lie between 0.29–0.50. Thus, sensitivity level of the block with HM less than 0.5 and RED above 0.7 is set to 0. Similarly, it can see in Table 1 that blocks of the document image containing preprinted information content has RED values above 0.3 and HM values in between 0.5 to 0.85. Therefore, sensitivity level of these blocks is set to 1. For all the other blocks, sensitivity level is set to 2.

The type of watermarking used depends on the sensitivity levels of the information content in the block. Highly sensitive blocks are protected using fragile watermarking technique. In this paper an effective fragile watermarking technique based on contourlets [24] is used. Partially sensitive blocks are protected using robust watermarking technique [23]. The size of the block is decided based on two factors: effectiveness in the identification of the sensitivity of the block and processing time for identification.

Table 1. Computation of *RED* and *HM* values for different classes of document images in the corpus

Document image class	Preprinted information		Dynamically changing information	
	RED	HM	RED	HM
Cheques	0.33	0.67	0.72	0.50
Bills	0.36	0.82	0.79	0.35
Identity cards	0.62	0.85	0.76	0.39
Marks cards	0.30	0.79	0.85	0.29
Certificates	0.54	0.51	0.70	0.36

Experiments have been conducted exhaustively on all the document images to measure the impact of size of the block against accuracy in identifying sensitivity level of the block. The average number of blocks expected for each sensitivity level and number of blocks being accurately identified is recorded in Table 2. It can be observed from average accuracy in identification values that the blocks of lesser size exhibits higher accuracy.

Table 2. Impact of size of the blocks of a document image on accuracy in identification of its sensitivity level and processing time for identification

Block size	Type-0		Type-1		Type-2		IA (in %)	Processing time (in secs)
	EB	IB	EB	IB	EB	IB		
32 × 32	348	339	210	204	466	466	98.53	102.12
64 × 364	83	75	57	52	116	116	94.92	78.7
128 × 3128	22	20	17	15	25	25	93.75	32.11
256 × 3256	5	4	4	3	7	7	87.50	21.16

Where, EB-Expected no. of blocks evaluated manually by an expert, IB-Identified No. of blocks from the proposed approach, IA-Identification Accuracy of a block, which is calculated as the ratio of sum of IB of all block types over sum of EB of all the block types. Considering the values of the accuracy in identification of sensitivity level of a block and processing time incurred for identification, size of the block is set to 128 × 128.

3.2 Multiple Watermark Extraction

Multiple watermark extraction process has two fold objectives based on the of watermark extraction process involved. Robust watermark extraction aims at content authentication of the block. This is implemented using robust watermarking scheme [23]. Fragile watermark extraction involves tamper detection and recovery of the information content of a document image. The fragile watermark extraction is performed using contourlets [24]. Multiple watermark extraction has similar steps as in multiple watermark embedding process discussed in Sect. 3.1 until the identification of the type of the gradient binarized block. Subsequently, the type of the block extracted and generated is compared and if there is a mismatch, the corresponding block of the document image is declared "inauthentic". However, if there is a match, then watermark extraction is carried out based on the type of the block. The extracted and generated watermarks are compared for similarity using Feature Similarity Index [24] and based on the comparison, the tamper detection of the block is decided. If the block is tampered, recovery of information content is made by extracting watermark embedded at robust locations [24]. During robust watermark extraction, the watermark is extracted from the LL-band of the integer wavelet transformation performed on the block of a document image. The extracted watermark is decoded using binary block coding technique [23]. The decoded watermark is compared with original watermark and decision of content authentication of the block is performed [23].

4 Results

We have created a corpus of document images. All the images in the corpus are scanned document images. The classes of document image corpus considered are Cheques, Bills, Identity Cards, Marks cards and Certificates. Each class of document image consists of 30 images. The results of the identification of type of the blocks of a sample document image in the corpus are shown in Fig. 2.

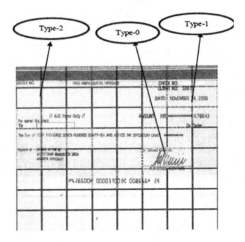

Fig. 2. Results of identification of the type of the block of a sample Cheque image

It can be observed in Fig. 2, that there are three types of blocks in the sample Cheque image. The blocks with dashed border are Type-0 blocks. They are highly sensitive blocks containing large variations in the information content and distribution of the information. The blocks with dotted border are Type-1 blocks i.e. partially sensitive blocks which contain preprinted information. They have moderate homogeneity in distribution of the information content. Remaining type of blocks in the document image are the insensitive blocks (Type-2) which contain less energy and higher homogeneity of information. We have tested the accuracy of the identification for all the classes of document images in the corpus.

Once the blocks are identified, appropriate type of watermarking has been applied based on the type of the block to obtain watermarked image. Subsequently multiple watermark extraction has been applied on the watermarked image and incidental and intentional attacks have been applied on the watermarked image. The results of multiple watermark embedding and extraction are shown in Fig. 3. Figure 3 shows that watermarked image is perceptually similar to source document image in the corpus. An example of incidental attack on partially sensitive block and intentional attack on a highly sensitive block of the watermarked image is demonstrated in Fig. 3. Further, one could also observe there is great degree of accuracy in tamper detection and recovery of the highly sensitive block.

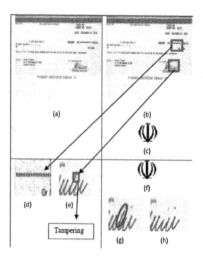

Fig. 3. Results of proposed multiple watermarking system (a) source document image (b) watermarked image (c) original watermark for robust watermarking (d) zoomed up Partially sensitive block with salt and pepper noise attack (e) zoomed up Highly sensitive tampered block (f) extracted robust watermark (g) tamper detection results (h) tamper recovery result

5   Analysis

The performance of the proposed watermarking system is measured in terms of the following parameters: (i) Performance analysis using Peak Signal to Noise Ratio (PSNR) (ii) Robustness Analysis using Normalized Correlation Coefficient (NCC) (iii) Fragility Analysis using accuracy of Tamper detection and recovery.

5.1   Performance Analysis

The performance of the proposed multiple watermarking scheme is evaluated in terms of PSNR. The perceptual quality of the watermarked image of size NXN is measured using Peak Signal to Noise Ratio (PSNR) [25]. A graph of PSNR values is depicted in Fig. 4 for different classes of the document images. The graph shown in Fig. 4 reveals that PSNR values of the multiple watermarking schemes are better than robust and fragile watermarking schemes when applied separately. This increase in PSNR and subsequently the perceptual quality of the watermarked image is due to the fact that all the blocks of the document image are not watermarked. The quantity of the watermark to be embedded depends on the type of the block. Hence, the noise induced due to watermarking is reduced to some extent and this result in the better fidelity of the watermarked image.

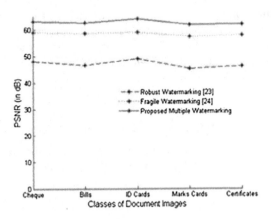

Fig. 4. Effect of watermarking schemes on PSNR values of different classes of document images in the corpus

5.2   Robustness Analysis

The robustness of the proposed multiple watermarking scheme is tested by applying various attacks such as horizontal cropping, vertical cropping, resizing, noise and JPEG compression on all the document images in the corpus. The degree of robustness obtained is evaluated in terms of NCC: [26]. The NCC values obtained by the application of proposed watermarking scheme only on partially sensitive blocks and robust watermarking scheme applied on the entire document image is recorded in Table 3. The NCC values in Table 3 show that there is a slight improvement in the robustness of the watermarked image. The increase in robustness is due to the localization of robustness to the blocks that are partially sensitive.

Table 3.   Average NCC values for different incidental attacks

Incidental attack	Existing Robust watermarking scheme [23]	Proposed multiple watermarking scheme
Salt and pepper noise	0.93	0.96
Cropping	0.97	0.97
Resizing	0.94	0.95
JPEG compression	0.94	0.96

5.3   Fragility Analysis

The fragility capability of any watermarking scheme is evaluated in terms of accuracy of tamper detection and tamper recovery parameters. Accuracy of tamper detection is evaluated as follows:

$$TDA = 1 - \frac{\sum_{i=1}^{n}(ta_i \oplus td_i)}{n} \tag{7}$$

where, n – total number of bits in the fragile watermarked blocks, ta – tampered bit, td – tamper detection bit. The average values of TDA and TRA are computed for all document images in the corpus under different intentional attacks for proposed fragile watermarking scheme and contourlet based scheme [24] separately. These values are tabulated in Table 4. It can be observed that proposed multiple watermarking schemes has a slight improvement capability in detection and recovering from tampering of information content of document image.

Table 4.   Average TDA and TRA values for different intentional attacks

Intentional attacks	Existing Fragile water marking scheme [24]		Proposed multiple watermarking scheme	
	TDA	TRA	TDA	TRA
Insertion	0.9	0.87	0.91	0.90
Deletion	0.92	0.91	0.92	0.92
Modification	0.87	0.87	0.90	0.89

6   Conclusions

A novel intelligent multiple watermarking schemes are proposed in this paper. The blocks of a document image have been automatically classified into various sensitivity levels with greater accuracy. The performance analysis of the proposed approach reveals improvement in the perceptual quality of the watermarked image. The proposed scheme also outperforms the existing methods [23, 24] in providing robustness, tamper detection and recovery capabilities. Improvement on the accuracy of identification of type of block is taken up as future work of the current study.

References

1. Wu, M., Liu, B.: Watermarking for image authentication. In: Proceedings of the IEEE International Conference on Image Processing, pp. 437–441 (1998)
2. Cox, I., Miller, M., Bloom, J., Fridrich, J., Kalker, T.: Digital Watermarking And Steganography. Morgan Kaufmann Publishers Inc., San Francisco (2007)
3. Hartung, F., Kutter, M.: Mutimedia Watermarking Techniques. Proc. IEEE 87(7), 1079–1107 (2002)

4. Potdar, V.M., Han, S., Chang, E.: A survey of digital image watermarking techniques. In: 3rd IEEE International Conference on Industrial Informatics, pp. 709–716 (2005). doi:10.1109/Indin.2005.1560462

5. Mirza, H., Thai, H., Nakao, Z.: Color image watermarking and self-recovery based on independent component analysis. In: Rutkowski, L., Tadeusiewicz, R., Zadeh, L.A., Zurada, J.M. (eds.) ICAISC 2008. LNCS, vol. 5097, pp. 839–849. Springer, Heidelberg (2008). doi:10.1007/978-3-540-69731-2_80

6. Wang, M.S., Chen, W.C.: A majority-voting based watermarking scheme for color image tamper detection and recovery. Comput. Stand. Interfaces **29**, 561–571 (2007)

7. Bas, P., Chassery, J.M., Macq, B.: Geometrically invariant watermarking using feature points. IEEE Trans. Image Process. **11**(9), 1014–1028 (2002)

8. Qi, W., Li, X., Yang, B., Cheng, D.: Document watermarking scheme for information tracking. J. Commun. **29**(10), 183–190 (2008)

9. Dawei, Z., Guanrong, C., Wenbo, L.: A chaos-based robust wavelet-domain watermarking algorithm. Chaos, Solitons Fractals **22**(1), 47–54 (2004)

10. Schirripa, G., Simonetti, C., Cozzella, L.: Fragile digital watermarking by synthetic holograms. In: Proceedings of the European Symposium on Optics/Fotonics in Security & Defence, London, pp. 173–182 (2004)

11. Houmansadr, A., et al.: Robust content-based video watermarking exploiting motion entropy masking effect. In: Proceedings of the International Conference on Signal Processing and Multimedia Applications, pp. 252–259 (2006)

12. Kankanhalli, M.S., Ramakrishnan, K.R.: Adaptive visible watermarking of images. In: IEEE International Conference on Multimedia Computing and Systems, vol. 1, pp. 568–573 (1999)

13. Radharani, S., et al.: A study on watermarking schemes for image authentication. Int. J. Comput. Appl. (0975 – 8887) **2**(4), 24–32 (2010)

14. Kay, S., Izquierdo, E.: Robust content based image watermarking. In: Proceedings of the Workshop on Image Analysis for Multimedia Interactive Services (2001)

15. Kim, M.-A., Lee, W.-H.: A content-based fragile watermarking scheme for image authentication. In: Chi, C.-H., Lam, K.-Y. (eds.) AWCC 2004. LNCS, vol. 3309, pp. 258–265. Springer, Heidelberg (2004). doi:10.1007/978-3-540-30483-8_31

16. Habib, M., Sarhan, S., Rajab, L.: A Robust-Fragile dual watermarking system in the DCT domain. In: Khosla, R., Howlett, R.J., Jain, L.C. (eds.) KES 2005. LNCS, vol. 3682, pp. 548–553. Springer, Heidelberg (2005). doi:10.1007/11552451_74

17. Shieh, C.-S., et al.: Genetic watermarking based on transform-domain techniques. J. Pattern Recogn. **37**, 555–565 (2004)

18. Goldberg, D.E.: Genetic Algorithms in Search Optimization and Machine Learning. Addison-Wesley, Reading (1992)

19. Lu, Z.-M., Xu, D.-G., Sun, S.-H.: Multipurpose image watermarking algorithm based on multistage vector quantization. IEEE Trans. Image Process. **14**(6), 822–831 (2005). doi:10.1109/Tip.2005.847324

20. Sheppard, N.P., Safavi-Naini, R., Ogunbona, P.: On multiple watermarking. In: Dittmann, J., Nahrstedt, K., Wohlmacher, D. (eds.) Multimedia and Security: New Challenges Workshop, p. 38871 (2001)

21. Voloshynovskiy, S., Pereira, S., Pun, T., Eggers, J.J., Su, J.K.: Attacks on digital watermarks: classification, estimation based attacks, and benchmarks. IEEE Commun. Mag. **39**(8), 118–126 (2001)

22. Wang, S., Zhang, X.: Watermarking scheme capable of resisting sensitivity attack. IEEE Signal Process. Lett. **14**(2), 125–128 (2007)

23. Chetan, K.R., Nirmala, S.: An efficient and secure robust watermarking scheme for document images using integer wavelets and block coding of binary watermarks. J. Inf. Secur. Appl. **24–25**, 13–24 (2015)
24. Chetan, K.R., Nirmala, S.: A novel fragile watermarking scheme based on contourlets for effective tamper detection, localization and recovery of handwritten document images. IEEE Signal Process. Lett. (Communicated)
25. Aggarwal, E.D.: An efficient watermarking algorithm to improve payload and robustness without affecting image perceptual quality. J. Comput. **2**(4) (2010). ISSN 2151-9617
26. Zhu, X., et al.: Normalized correlation-based quantization modulation for robust watermarking. IEEE Trans. Multimed. **16**(7), 1888–1904 (2014)

Experimental Evaluation of 3D Kinect Face Database

A.A. Gaonkar[1(✉)], M.D. Gad[2], N.T. Vetrekar[1], Vithal Shet Tilve[3],
and R.S. Gad[1]

[1] Department of Electronics, Goa University, Taleigao Plateau, Goa, India
{elect.aagaonkar,elect.ntvetrekar,rsgad}@unigoa.ac.in
[2] Goa Engineering College, Farmagudi, Goa, India
miteshgad92@gmail.com
[3] School of Earth and Space Exploration Arizona State University, Tempe, USA
tilvi@asu.edu

Abstract. 3D face recognition has gain a paramount importance over 2D due to its potential to address the limitations of 2D face recognition against the variation in facial poses, angles, occlusions etc. Research in 3D face recognition has accelerated in recent years due to the development of low cost 3D Kinect camera sensor. This has leads to the development of few RGB-D database across the world. Here in this paper we introduce the base results of our 3D facial database (GU-RGBD database) comprising variation in pose ($0°$, $45°$, $90°$, $-45°$, $-90°$), expression (smile, eyes closed), occlusion (half face covered with paper) and illumination variation using Kinect. We present a proposed noise removal non-linear interpolation filter for the patches present in the depth images. The results were obtained on three face recognition algorithms and fusion at matching score level for recognition and verification rate. The obtained results indicated that the performance with our proposed filter shows improvement over pose with score level fusion using sum rule.

1 Introduction

Facial expressions, poses and variations have attracted the research world since long, as it is easily obtainable and convenient biometric trait as compared to the iris, voice, gait etc. 2D facial images has well defined roots in the world of biometric research due to low cost of its acquisition system and wide availability [1]. But 2D face recognition system faces its limitations when it comes to mostly illumination and pose variation [2]. In order to overcome these short comings of 2D recognition, 3D recognition system captured the market as security concern has increased from local to the defense level. Research in 3D biometric was an expensive task as the expense of system requirement for acquiring 3D images was very high and time consuming [3] until the development of efficient, low-cost RGB-D Kinect camera. This system provides 2D RGB image as well as depth information i.e. distance from each pixel to the sensor [4].

Images captured by Kinect camera has low resolution and noisy yet it has more spatial information compared to 2D in form of depth which is a robust inherent property associated for 3D face recognition against uncontrolled environment.

© Springer International Publishing AG 2017
S. Mukherjee et al. (Eds.): ICVGIP 2016, LNCS 10481, pp. 15–26, 2017.
https://doi.org/10.1007/978-3-319-68124-5_2

Ekenel et al. obtained 3-D face recognition approach using the discrete cosine transform (DCT) which is a local appearance-based model at feature level [5]. Huynh et al. has proposed a new LBP based descriptor namely Gradient-LBP (G-LBP) for gender recognition task on EURECOM and Texas database [6]. Vezzetti et al. proposed a new 3D face recognition algorithm, whose framework based on extracting facial landmarks using the geometrical properties of facial shape [7]. Min et al. have generated a 3D database based on the Kinect sensor having 52 subjects over two sessions for 2D, 2.5D, 3D and video. Here recognition rates are calculated for 2D, 2.5D, and 3D-based face data using standard face recognition techniques like PCA, LBP, SIFT, LGBP, ICP, and TPS and also RGB and Depth images were fused using score-level fusion [8]. Ajmera et al. has computed CRR based on modified SURF descriptors and image enhancement techniques and filters like adaptive histogram equalization, NLM filter etc. for their internal database and has compared it with Eurecom and Curtin face database and also has performed scored level fusion [9]. Hg et al. had proposed RGB-D Face dataset (VAP database) of 31 subjects containing 1581 images and have developed a face detection protocol using curvature analysis technique and tested for VAP database [10]. Goswami et al. had generated IIIT-D RGB-D face database of 106 subjects with multiple Images per subject. Authors has also proposed an algorithm for 3D face recognition which involves computation of entropy map and visual saliency map followed by HOG descriptor for feature extraction and finally the use of Random Decision Forest (RDF) classifier for establishing identity. The algorithm was tested for IIIT-D and Eurecom Database [4, 11]. Table 1 is giving the brief idea about existing Kinect base 3d facial databases.

Table 1. Existing 3D facial databases

Database	No. of subjects	Variations			
		Angles/poses	Occlusion	Expressions	Illumination
Eurecom [8]	52	Neutral face, right, left	Paper and hand on face, sunglasses	Smile, mouth open	Single pose
VAP [10]	31	Combination of 17 vertical and horizontal face poses	–	Smile, sad, yawn, anger	–
Curtin face [3]	100	Various poses	–	Various expressions	Yes
IIIT-D [11]	106	Various poses	–	Various expressions	Yes
IIT-K [9]	100	0°, 15°, 30°, 45°, 60°, 75°, 90°	–		Yes
VT-KFER [20]	32	Frontal, right, left	–	6 facial expressions	–
GU-RGBD	64	0°, 45°, 90°, −45°, −90°	Paper on face	Smile, eyes close	Full session 2

Mao et al. has work on identification and filling of expansion holes. Here the holes are identified based on depth histogram and the filling of holes is done using linear interpolation and graph based interpolation method [13]. Solh and AlRegib has proposed two approaches for dis-occlusion removal in Depth Image-Based Rendering (DIBR): hierarchical hole-filling (HHF) and depth adaptive hierarchical hole-filling. The said approaches follows pyramid like approach from lower resolution estimate of 3D wrapped image to estimate the said hole pixels [14]. Wang et al. have propose a hole filling algorithm to improve image quality of DIBR. Here to determine the order of hole filling the depth information is added to the priority calculation function. Next when searching for the best matching block the gradient information is used as auxiliary information [15, 16]. Feng et al. has proposed an adaptive background biased depth map hole-filling method [17]. Based on this literature survey we are proposing simple weighted average nonlinear interpolation hole/patch removal algorithm for the 3D database generated at our laboratory. We are presenting our GU-RGBD facial database having variation in pose, expressions and occlusion; collected over two sessions for 64 subjects. This database will be made available in public domain for research purpose. Extensive experimental evaluation is performed for the State of the Art face recognition algorithm in the form of identification and verification rate.

The rest of the paper is organized as follows: Sect. 2 describes the GU-RGBD data generation setup and protocol. Section 3 is giving the detail explanation of the proposed filter. Section 4 explains the experimental evaluation protocol for database. Section 5 comprises of results and discussion and the final conclusion is given in Sect. 6.

2   3D Database Generation

2.1   3D Imaging Setup

3D biometric imaging laboratory having controlled and uncontrolled environmental conditions was setup at our work place. This setup was comprised of RGBD camera, light sources, and a computer system. RGBD images were captured using Xbox 360 Kinect depth camera from Microsoft, which consists of two parts, RGB camera to capture 2D image information and depth sensor which acquires depth information.

The depth sensor has an infrared projector combined with a monochrome CMOS sensor, which captures 3rd dimension (distance between subject and sensor) i.e. depth. The sensor placement was at the height of 1.5 mts from the floor and approximately at the distance of 1.25 mts from the subject. To set the controlled condition two QTH light sources of 600 W were kept at an angle 45° normal to the subject position. In order to maintain the uniform background and equal illumination on all sides white muslin cloth backdrop was mounted behind the subject. The direct projection of light on the subject was avoided with white muslin cloth umbrellas in front of light sources. To set uncontrolled environmental condition the subject was exposed to the ambient light by opening the windows while capturing the images.

2.2   3D Image Acquisition Protocol

The image acquisition was performed after proper calibration of camera to confirm the constant parameters throughout the experiment. Here the highest resolution for Kinect color sensor (1280 × 960) and Kinect depth sensor (640 × 480) was selected. Database was collected in two sessions (controlled and un-controlled) for the students and staff of our organization. The image capturing protocol was designed as shown in Fig. 1. We have introduced eight variations per individual in the image acquisition process, having variation in pose (−90°, −45°, 0°, +45°, +90°), expressions (smile, eyes closed) and occlusion (paper was covering half part of the face).

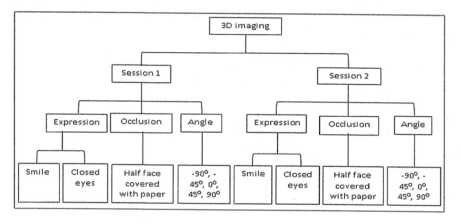

Fig. 1. 3D image acquisition protocol

For every subject, eight RGB and eight depth images were captured to form total of 16 in every session. The session 1 consists 16 images captured in controlled environmental condition and session 2 consist of 16 images captured in uncontrolled environmental condition by keeping window open for ambient light to enter the lab and the QTH sources were off. Thus total of 32 images captured per subject. The GU-RGBD database has the enrollment of 64 subjects out of which 49 are males and 15 are females from various age group. The size of database is 64(subjects) * 32 (images per subject) = 2048 images. The sample images of database are shown in Fig. 2.

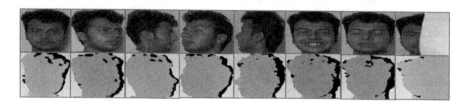

Fig. 2. 3D image acquisition protocol

3   Proposed Patch Removal Filter

The images captured by Kinect are noisy and inaccurate [8]. The presence of patches (zero value pixels present on the depth face) degrade the captured information and thus affects the recognition rate and hence it has to be enhanced in the pre-processing stage. We are using the interpolation method to replace the patch with the neighboring pixels. There are various scenarios of the characteristics of patch like localized position on facial triangle, size of patch and patch position on the boundaries. Hence sometimes surrounding information if not available in such scenarios especially when patch is placed at boundary positions. Hence, there is a need to allocate the weightage for the populace of surrounding pixels in the form of some constants i.e. a_1, a_2. The proposed filter acts as the solution for patches present on depth faces.

The depth images of M × N dimensions usually having the 4:3 aspect ratio are extended by adding M/4 dummy rows and column pixels respectively for the higher dimensions of aspect ratio as shown in Fig. 3(a). This is extended so as to avoid the occurrence of computational errors for the pixels at the outer boundary as window of filter expands. Then 'NaN' values are assigned to the dummy rows and column pixels so as to avoid filling of false information for patches in vicinity of boundary. The proposed filter scan image by initially setting a $l \times l$ kernel i.e. '$u_{(l,l)}$' to locate zero value pixel (which is a patch) to be replaced.

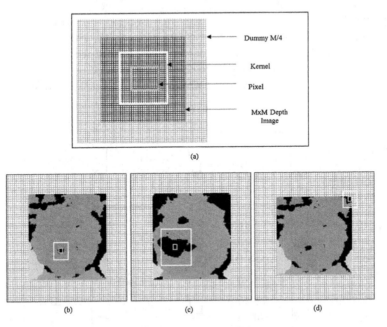

Fig. 3. Filter implementation: (a) schematic view of filter, (b)–(d) patches of different sizes

The mathematical expression for the Kernel function is given below in Eq. 1.

$$u_{(l,l)} = \sum_{k_1=0}^{l} \sum_{k_2=0}^{l} u_{(i \mp k_1, j \mp k_2)} \qquad (1)$$

Where $l = 0, 1, 2, \ldots\ldots$ M/2. Equation 1 is combination of zero and non-zero terms and hence we can write the same equation in the form of Eq. 2.

$$u_{(l,l)} = \bar{u}_{(i,j)_o} + \bar{u}_{(i,j)_{\bar{o}}} \qquad (2)$$

Further we select values of $a_1 = \bar{u}_{(i,j)o} = 5\%$ and $a_2 = \bar{u}_{(i,j)\bar{o}} = 95\%$ so that we give more importance to populace of non-zero value as compared to populace of zero values to interpolate the pixel. So for a said kernel size verify if the condition: $0.05 * nos(\bar{u}_{(i,j)o})$ $\leq 0.95 * nos(\bar{u}_{(i,j)\bar{o}})$, if not satisfied then increase the kernel size till the condition is satisfied. Once the condition is satisfied one can generate the average value of the kernel Eq. 2 and further interpolate value $y'_{(i,j)}$ as described in Eq. 3.

$$y'_{(i,j)} = y_{(i,j)} + u_{(i,l)} \quad \forall y_{(i,j)} = 0 \qquad (3)$$

Here $\bar{u}_{(i,j)o}$ is average value of zero depth pixels and $\bar{u}_{(i,j)\bar{o}}$ is average value of non-zero depth pixel values after proper populace factor of 5% and 95%. The proposed filter is followed by median filter for smoothening the image.

Figures 3(b)–(d) are the pictorial view for the working of the filter. Assume the region marked as pixel in Fig. 4 to be a single pixel. In Fig. 3(b) the patch is surrounded by high population of non-zero depth values. In such scenarios, a window of 3×3 is much capable of removing the patch. In case of Fig. 3(c), the population of zeroes is dominant around the marked pixel (a patch), so the window has to be

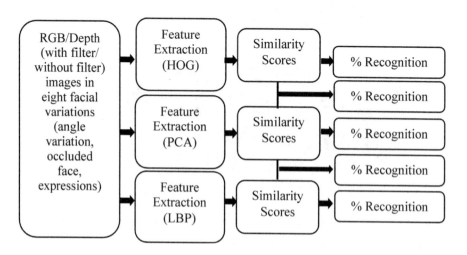

Fig. 4. Database evaluation protocol

expanded until the 95% and 5% of contribution comes from the non-zero depth values and zero depth values respectively. The case of patch located at one of the corner is shown in Fig. 3(d), here it can be seen that the window is expanding out of the image boundaries, where the contribution of the dummy rows and column pixels is neglected this is because the dummy elements are assigned to NaN, hence there is no contribution from them towards the new value of the pixel.

4   Database Evaluation Protocol and Methodology

The generated GU-RGBD database is having variation in pose, occlusion, expressions and illumination variation over two sessions out of which the images with 0° pose (i.e. neutral face) from session 1 (controlled condition) is used as gallery images and rest of the database was tested against it for computation of recognition rate.

The experimental evaluation protocol for database is as described in Fig. 4. The captured RGB and depth images were cropped manually to 256 × 256 dimensions using Matlab script. In most of the variation of the database only partial faces are visible thus it restricted the use of existing face detection algorithms for cropping. The cropping of RGB and depth images was followed by resizing them to 96 × 96 dimension to enhance the computational time. The proposed filtering technique was than implemented on depth images in order to remove the patches present in them. The process of feature Extraction was performed on the RGB images and depth images (with filter and without filter) separately by using techniques like Principle Component Analysis (PCA), histogram of oriented gradients (HOG) and Local binary patterns (LBP).

Similarity scores were computed using 'sum rule' for the extracted features of gallery images against the features of test dataset for respective algorithms and the recognition rates were obtained for RGB, depth (unfiltered) and depth filtered images using HOG [18], PCA [19] and LBP [12]. The evaluation of fusion performance for PCA + HOG and PCA + LBP was done by obtaining the recognition rates at matching score level.

5   Results and Discussion

The experimental evaluation of proposed GU-RGBD database for various poses, occlusion and expressions was carried out using PCA, HOG, LBP and their fusion at matching score level as protocol described in previous section. The recognition rates for RGB and Depth images were obtained separately at Rank 5. As mentioned earlier all the images 0° pose variation (neutral images) from session 1 is set as Gallery dataset for testing all other datasets. Variations from session 1 and session 2 are tested against it, to obtain performance in form of recognition rates.

Table 2 shows the recognition rates obtained for RGD images using various algorithms. It's clear from above table that for both session 1 and session 2 variations like smile, eyes closed and 0° pose variation (session 2) gives high level of recognition as compared to other existing variations. This is because the full face geometry is

Table 2. Recognition rates of RGB images using PCA, HOG, LBP and their fusion

RANK 5	Variation	PCA	HOG	LBP	PCA + HOG	PCA + LBP
Session 1	0°	–	–	–	–	–
	45°	34.375	21.875	20.3125	35.9375	28.125
	90°	14.0625	10.9375	7.8125	15.625	7.8125
	−45°	20.3125	23.4375	14.0625	37.5	12.5
	−90°	10.9375	12.5	7.8125	12.5	7.8125
	Smile	79.6875	92.1875	81.25	92.1875	85.9375
	Eyes closed	82.8125	95.3125	89.0625	90.625	92.1875
	Paper occlusion	20.3125	75	12.5	59.375	14.0625
Session 2	0°	76.5625	92.1875	42.1875	93.75	68.75
	45°	21.875	26.5625	14.0625	31.25	21.875
	90°	14.0625	10.9375	7.8125	15.625	7.8125
	−45°	15.625	21.875	10.9375	25	10.9375
	−90°	6.25	14.0625	7.8125	9.375	7.8125
	Smile	78.125	90.625	50	92.1875	60.9375
	Eyes closed	76.5625	92.1875	51.5625	93.75	65.625
	Paper occlusion	15.625	62.5	14.0625	51.5625	15.625

visible and available for computation. 45° and −45° variation is having higher performance compared to 90° and −90° variation in both the sessions, since facial area under computation is more in 45° and −45° variation as compared to that of 90° and −90° variation. As compared to the various algorithms used the overall performance of HOG for session 1 and session 2 is at the higher level. As an example the computed recognition rate using HOG is 95% for eye close and 92% for smile on other hand it is 82% for eyes close and 79% for smile using PCA and 89% for eyes close and 81% for smile using LBP. The performance for paper occlusion mode is high using HOG 75% in session 1 and 62% in session 2 compared to other algorithms.

The computed recognition rates for depth images with filter and without filter are listed in Table 3. For variations like smile and eyes close (in both sessions) and 0° pose variation (session 2) a similar trend is seen as that of recognition rate for RGB images i.e. they generate the higher recognition rate compared to other facial variations in the table. In case of depth images also the recognition rate for 45° and −45° pose variation is dominant over 90° and −90° pose variation as the face triangle region under computation is larger in 45° and −45° pose variation. It is further observed that the filter is improvising the recognition rates as compared to base results in most of the cases for all the algorithms. Example for smile variation in session 1 recognition rates using PCA is 89.0625% (without filter) and 90.625% (with filter), using HOG 93.75% (without filter) and 95.3125% (with filter) and using LBP 48.4375% (without filter) and 50% (with filter).

Further the recognition rates are computed by using score level fusion methodology for HOG + PCA scores and PCA + LBP scores for both RGB and Depth images as shown in Tables 2 and 3 respectively. PCA + HOG columns in both the tables shows

Table 3. Recognition rates of depth images using PCA, HOG, LBP and their fusion

RANK 5	Variations	Image type	PCA	HOG	LBP	PCA + HOG	PCA + LBP
Session 1	0°	With filter	–	–	–	–	–
		Without filter	–	–	–	–	–
	45°	With filter	21.875	10.9375	20.3125	28.125	23.4375
		Without filter	21.875	17.1875	18.75	26.5625	23.4375
	90°	With filter	15.625	14.0625	17.1875	17.1875	23.4375
		Without filter	15.625	14.0625	14.0625	17.1875	18.75
	−45°	With filter	17.1875	10.9375	25	21.875	25
		Without filter	17.1875	18.75	17.1875	15.625	17.1875
	−90°	With filter	15.625	9.375	20.3125	12.5	15.625
		Without filter	12.5	14.0625	14.0625	12.5	15.625
	Smile	With filter	90.625	95.3125	50	98.4375	78.125
		Without filter	89.0625	93.75	48.4375	93.75	70.3125
	Eyes closed	With filter	89.0625	92.1875	54.6875	92.1875	79.6875
		Without filter	89.0625	89.0625	34.375	92.1875	57.8125
	Paper occlusion	With filter	29.6875	25	14.0625	37.5	21.875
		Without filter	32.8125	46.875	7.8125	35.9375	10.9375
Session 2	0°	With filter	73.4375	71.875	25	76.5625	35.9375
		Without filter	73.4375	65.625	18.75	71.875	28.125
	45°	With filter	23.4375	20.3125	14.0625	23.4375	17.1875
		Without filter	23.4375	17.1875	12.5	25	12.5
	90°	With filter	17.1875	12.5	14.0625	14.0625	18.75
		Without filter	17.1875	10.9375	10.9375	15.625	10.9375
	−45°	With filter	14.0625	10.9375	17.1875	10.9375	20.3125
		Without filter	14.0625	15.625	10.9375	9.375	14.0625
	−90°	With filter	10.9375	12.5	12.5	9.375	15.625
		Without filter	10.9375	7.8125	10.9375	9.375	6.25
	Smile	With filter	71.875	68.75	32.8125	78.125	50
		Without filter	73.4375	62.5	14.0625	78.125	23.4375
	Eyes closed	With filter	76.5625	67.1875	28.125	81.25	53.125
		Without filter	78.125	60.9375	15.625	76.5625	21.875
	Paper occlusion	With filter	37.5	34.375	4.6875	51.5625	9.375
		Without filter	37.5	45.3125	17.1875	48.4375	29.6875

marginal improvement in most of the cases due to fusion technique. In Session 2 (Table 2) for smile pose recognition rate using PCA is 78.125%, with HOG is 90.625% and PCA + HOG is 92.1875%. Similarly session 2 (Table 3) for smile pose in depth mode the recognition rate using PCA is 73.43%, with HOG is 62.5% and PCA + HOG is 78.125%. The proposed filter gives the improvement in recognition rate at Rank 5 for almost all poses with fusion methodology using PCA + HOG and PCA + LBP over both the sessions. It may be noted that the published results also indicates the poor performance i.e. below 50% for the pose like various angular and occlusion poses. Hence the base results obtained are unison with the published results in literature [8].

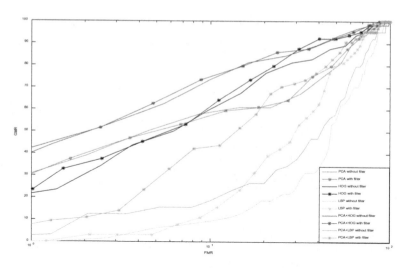

Fig. 5. ROC curves for different algorithms with and without filter for 0° pose variation in session 2 (depth)

The graphical view of verification rates for various algorithms and their fusion are shown in Fig. 5. It indicates that the verification rates at 10° FMR for different algorithms using filter is higher as compared to without filter. Also it can be seen that the highest verification rate is obtained due to fusion of PCA + HOG with application of the filter. Thus filter performs reasonably well as compared to the without filter.

6 Conclusion

Kinect based GU-RGBD database is presented in this paper. The database was generated over two session's i.e. controlled and uncontrolled environmental conditions, with each session having variations like variation in pose (−90°, −45°, 0°, +45°, +90°), expressions (smile, eyes closed) and occlusion (paper was covering half part of the face). We have also proposed a nonlinear interpolation filter for removal of patches present in depth images. Experimental evaluation of proposed database is done to obtain the recognition rates using PCA, HOG and LBP and also the score level fusion of PCA + HOG and PCA + LBP was performed. From the obtained results it is observed that, recognition rates obtain for RGB using HOG is higher than other algorithms. Also fusion has improved the performance of RGB to some extent. The proposed patch removal filter was applied to the RGBD database and it is found that the recognition rate of depth images is enhanced. The score level fusion of PCA + HOG has also given the improved. The proposed filter can be further extended using weighted average mean. As the kernel expand the interpolation can be implemented with dominant contribution from intermediate neighbors.

Acknowledgment. Authors would like to acknowledge the financial assistance from Minister of Electronics and Information Technology (MeitY) under Visvesvaraya PhD Scheme for carrying out research work at Goa University. Authors are also thankful to Ms. Bhagyada Pai Kane, Ms. Shweta Sawal Desai and Mr. Saurabh Vernekar (Post graduate students, Department of Electronics, 2015 batch) for their support in the RGBD database collection and to all the subjects for their valuable participation.

References

1. Zhao, W., Chellappa, R., Rosenfeld, A., Phillips, P.: Face recognition - a literature survey. ACM Comput. Surv. **35**(44), 399–458 (2003)
2. Sharma, P.B., Goyani, M.M.: 3D face recognition techniques - a review. Int. J. Eng. Res. Appl. (IJERA) **2**(1), 787–793 (2012)
3. Li, B.Y.L., Mian, A.S., Liu, W., Krishna, A.: Using Kinect for face recognition under varying poses, expressions, illumination and disguise. In: Applications of Computer Vision (WACV) IEEE Workshop, pp. 15–17 (2013)
4. Goswami, G., Vatsa, M., Singh, R.: RGB-D face recognition with texture and attribute features. IEEE Trans. Inf. Forensics Secur. **9**, 1629–1640 (2014)
5. Ekenel, H.K., Gao, H., Stiefelhagen, R.: 3-D face recognition using local appearance-based models. IEEE Trans. Inf. Forensics Secur. **2**(3), 630–636 (2007)
6. Huynh, T., Min, R., Dugelay, J.-L.: An efficient LBP-based descriptor for facial depth images applied to gender recognition using RGB-D face data. In: ACCV 2012, Workshop on Computer Vision with Local Binary Pattern Variants, Daejeon, Korea, pp. 5–9 (2012)
7. Vezzetti, E., Marcolin, F., Fracastoro, G.: 3D face recognition - an automatic strategy based on geometrical descriptors and landmarks. Robot. Auton. Syst. **62**, 1768–1776 (2014)
8. Min, R., Kose, N., Dugelay, J.-L.: KinectFaceDB - a Kinect database for face recognition. IEEE Trans. Syst. Man Cybern.: Syst. **44**, 1534–1548 (2014)
9. Ajmera, R., Nigam, A., Gupta, P.: 3D face recognition using Kinect. In: ICVGIP 2014, Bangalore, India, pp. 14–18 (2014)
10. Hg, R.I., Jasek, P., Rofidal, C., Nasrollahi, K., Moeslund, T.B., Tranchet, G.: An RGB-D database using Microsoft's Kinect for windows for face detection. In: IEEE 8th International Conference on Signal Image Technology and Internet Based Systems (2012)
11. Goswami, G., Bharadwaj, S., Vatsa, M., Singh, R.: On RGB-D face recognition using Kinect. In: 2013 IEEE Sixth International Conference on Biometrics: Theory, Applications and Systems (BTAS) (2013)
12. Ahonen, T., Hadid, A., Pietikainen, M.: Face description with local binary patterns: application to face recognition. IEEE Trans. Pattern Anal. Mach. Intell. **28**(12), 2037–2041 (2006)
13. Mao, Y., Cheung, G., Ortega, A., Ji, Y.: Expansion hole filling in depth-image-based rendering using graph-based interpolation. In: IEEE International Conference on Acoustics, Speech and Signal Processing, pp. 26–31 (2013)
14. Solh, M., AlRegib, G.: Hierarchical hole-filling for depth-based view synthesis in FTV and 3D video. IEEE J. Sel. Top. Sig. Process. **6**(5), 495–504 (2012)
15. Wang, D., Zhao, Y., Wang, J., Wang, Z.: A hole filling algorithm for depth image based rendering based on gradient information. In: 2013 Ninth International Conference on Natural Computation (ICNC) (2013)
16. Wang, D., Zhao, Y., Wang, Z., Chen, H.: Hole-filling for DIBR based on depth and gradient information. Int. J. Adv. Robot. Syst. **12**(2) (2015)

17. Feng, L., Po, L.-M., Xu, X., Ng, K.-H., Cheung, C.-H., Cheung, K.-W.: An adaptive background biased depth map hole-filling method for Kinect. In: Industrial Electronics Society, IECON 2013 - 39th Annual Conference of the IEEE (2013)
18. Dalal, N., Triggs, B.: Histograms of oriented gradients for human detection. In: 2005 IEEE Computer Society Conference on Computer Vision and Pattern Recognition (CVPR 2005) (2005)
19. Turk, M., Pentland, A.: Eigenfaces for recognition. J. Cognit. Neurosci. 3(1), 71–86 (1991)
20. Aly, S., Abbott, L., White, S., Youssef, A.: VT-KFER - a Kinect-based RGBD+ time dataset for spontaneous and non-spontaneous facial expression recognition. In: 2015 International Conference on Biometrics (ICB) (2015)

Photometric Normalization Techniques for Extended Multi-spectral Face Recognition: A Comparative Analysis

N.T. Vetrekar[1(✉)], R. Raghavendra[2], R.S. Gad[1], and G.M. Naik[1]

[1] Department of Electronics, Goa University, Goa, India
{elect.ntvetrekar,rsgad,gmnaik}@unigoa.ac.in
[2] Norwegian Biometrics Laboratory, NTNU, Gjøvik, Norway
raghavendra.ramachandra@ntnu.no
https://www.unigoa.ac.in/
https://nislab.no/

Abstract. Biometric authentication based on face recognition acquired enormous attention due to its non-intrusive nature of image capture. Recently, with the advancement in sensor technology, face recognition based on Multi-spectral imaging has gained lot of popularity due to its potential of capturing discrete spatio-spectral images across the electromagnetic spectrum. Our contribution here is to study empirically, the extensive comparative performance analysis of 22 photometric illumination normalization techniques for robust Multi-spectral face recognition. To evaluate this study, we developed a Multi-spectral imaging sensor that can capture Multi-spectral facial images across nine different spectral band in the wavelength range from 530 nm to 1000 nm. With the developed sensor we captured Multi-spectral facial database for 231 individuals, which will be made available in the public domain for the researcher community. Further, quantitative experimental performance analysis in the form of identification rate at rank 1, was conducted on 22 photometric normalization techniques using four state-of-the-art face recognition algorithms. The performance analysis indicates outstanding results with utmost all of the photometric normalization techniques for six spectral bands such as 650 nm, 710 nm, 770 nm, 830 nm, 890 nm, 950 nm.

Keywords: Face recognition · Multi-spectral face imaging · Photometric normalization · Feature extraction · Feature classifier

1 Introduction

Biometric authentication based on face recognition is one of the most popular authentication system among the other physiological or behavioral modes of biometric. Various reforms such as algorithm, sensor development, etc. have been taken place since its (face mode) introduction to authentication. The advantage of using facial biometric trait is that; it is non-intrusive which finds its potential in the surveillance applications. In spite of these advantages, the performance

© Springer International Publishing AG 2017
S. Mukherjee et al. (Eds.): ICVGIP 2016, LNCS 10481, pp. 27–38, 2017.
https://doi.org/10.1007/978-3-319-68124-5_3

of traditional face recognition has been affected by spoofing (example, use of mask on face), intra-class variations such as illumination variation, pose, expressions [10] etc. One of these issue mainly illumination variation is addressed by Multi-spectral imaging, that captures the images at specific frequencies across the spectrum. The potential of Multi-spectral imaging is very well utilized in the literature by considering more than one broad spectral bands such as visible and near infrared [11], visible and SWIR [12], visible and MWIR [13], visible and thermal [14] etc., or hyper-spectral imaging (uses large overlapping bands across the spectrum) [20], for robust illumination invariant face recognition. The idea of using Multi-spectral imaging technology is to obtain complementary spatio-spectral information (example, visible sensor captures only reflectance data where as thermal image sensor capture heat energy radiated from the object i.e. remittance energy) to improve the accuracy of authentication system.

Further, Multi-spectral imaging obtains complementary image information, therefore the straight forward utilization of these raw sample images to the algorithm may not be feasible for the robust performance. Especially in heterogeneous or cross spectral facial matching [15] where images placed in the gallery and probe set are from different spectrum having different appearance due to the optical properties of facial skin. Photometric normalization techniques on the other hand have shown great potential in compensating the above problem by extracting most common dominant features from the heterogeneous bands before facial matching [16,17]. Further, the significance of few photometric normalization techniques have been tested by Han et al. [2] on the publicly available visible image (RGB) database having large illumination variation (such as shadow on one side) in his analysis study for face recognition. As per our understanding, comparative analysis study of large photometric normalization algorithms have not been addressed yet on Multi-spectral facial database in the literature, that will give handle for selecting the best photometric normalization method for robust performance.

Photometric normalization algorithms basically employed to compensate large variations in illuminations such as strong shadow, saturation of image region due to over exposure [18] etc. Further, Photometric normalization techniques helps to limit the noise, at the same time it preserves the facial feature (such as edges) for face recognition. There are plenty of photometric normalization methods, proposed in the literature as an noise reduction and enhancement techniques and obtained promising results in the literature [2]. But not all methods perform equally well (for example some methods can perform for constrained lighting variation and cannot perform in large lighting variations [19]). However it has also been found that the better visualization of image after photometric normalization does not always mean higher recognition accuracy [2]. All these facts certainly accelerated us to conduct extensive comparative performance analysis study on the large set of photometric normalization techniques to understand its significance of performance across different state-of-the-art face recognition algorithms using Multi-spectral imaging dataset.

Thus in this paper we employ 22 photometric normalization techniques [21] including: Single Scale Retinex (SSR), Multi Scale Retinex (MSR), Adaptive Single Scale Retinex (ASR), Homomorphic Filtering Based Normalization (HOMO), Single Scale Self Quotient (SSQ), Multi-scale self Quotient (MSQ), DCT-based normalization (DCT), Retina Modeling based normalization (RET), Wavelet based normalization (WA), Wavelet Denoising based normalization (WD), Isotropic diffusion based normalization (IS), Anisotropic diffusion based normalization (AS), Steerable Filter based normalization (SF), Non-Local Means based normalization (NLM), Adaptive Non-Local Means based normalization (ANL), Modified anisotropic diffusion normalization (MAS), Gradient faces normalization (GRF), Single scale weberfaces normalization (WEB), Multi-scale weberfaces normalization (MSW), Large- and small-scale features normalization (LSSF), Tan and Triggs normalization (TT), and DoG Filtering-based normalization (DOG). The evaluation of these photometric normalization technique have been conducted on our captured Multi-spectral facial database across nine narrow spectral bands (530 nm, 590 nm, 650 nm, 710 nm, 770 nm, 830 nm, 890 nm, 950 nm, 1000 nm) in 530 nm to 1000 nm wavelength range using our developed Multi-spectral imaging sensor. The Multi-spectral facial database captured comprises of 231 individuals that will be made available in the public domain for research. This will be the first time that Multi-spectral face database will be evaluate across large set of photometric normalization techniques. Following are our major contributions:

1. Development of Multi-spectral imaging sensor to capture facial database across nine spatial-spectral bands in 530 nm to 1000 nm wavelength range.
2. Quantitative empirical evaluation in the form of identification rate for 22 photometric normalization techniques.
3. Use of Multi-spectral facial database for evaluating 22 photometric normalization techniques. The Multi-spectral database captured for 231 individuals will be made available in public domain for the research.

The rest of the paper is organized as follows: Sect. 2 gives the details of various optical equipment involved in developing Multi-spectral imaging setup and description of database, Sect. 3 illustrates the pre-processing of Multi-spectral facial database and visual illustration of 22 photometric normalization techniques across nine spectral bands, Sect. 4 explains briefly four feature extraction methodologies and a feature classifier involved in face recognition, Sect. 5 gives the comparative performance analysis of 22 photometric normalization techniques in the form of identification rate, and Sect. 6 illustrates the final conclusion.

2   Multi-spectral Imaging Sensor and Database

The development of multi-spectral imaging sensor to capture facial images across nine different narrow band spectrum in the range 530 nm to 1000 nm, involve the use of various optical equipment. In the following subsection we describe briefly the details of various optical equipment involved in the developed sensor.

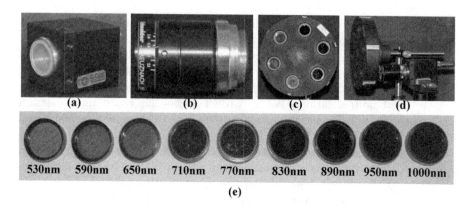

Fig. 1. Multi-spectral imaging equipments: (a) Sensor, (b) Lens, (c) Filter wheel equipped with optical filters (d) Developed Multi-spectral imaging sensor, (e) Nine optical filters involved in imaging

2.1 Equipments

- **Camera**: We used BCi5 CMOS camera (Fig. 1(a)) from C-Cam Technologies for the sensor development. The camera has 1.3 megapixel CMOS sensor with an active image area of 8.58 mm (H) × 6.86 mm (V) that can capture image from 400 nm to 1000 nm spectral range. The CMOS sensor provides support for multi-slope exposure mode that allows to prevent over exposure of brighter regions of the image with excellent signal-to-noise ratio. The camera is controlled by SDK (Software Development Kit) provided by the C-cam Technologies.
- **Lens**: We used a compatible c-mount lens (Fig. 1(b)) (model: Xenoplan 2.8/50-0902) for our CMOS camera in the visible and near infrared range. The lens with 2.8 f-number provides excellent speed and the special optical design allows it to prevent any unwanted shading on the sensor array.
- **Optical filters**: The narrow bandpass filter (Interference filter) were obtained from CVI Melles Griot (Fig. 1(e)). These bandpass filter provides excellent isolation of wavelengths in a few nanometer or less in width. The optical filters used in this setup includes 530 nm, 590 nm, 650 nm, 710 nm, 770 nm, 830 nm, 890 nm, 950 nm, 1000 nm. The filters are attached with filter wheel to provides easier spectral band selection as shown in Fig. 1(c).

All these optical equipments led to the development of our final customized Multi-spectral imaging sensor as shown in the Fig. 1(d).

2.2 Multi-spectral Face Database

The developed Multi-spectral imaging sensor was used to build Multi-spectral facial database across nine different spectral bands. The data collected in two sessions: session one involves training samples, the samples obtained across the

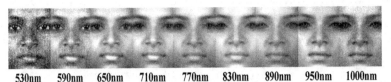 

530nm   590nm   650nm   710nm   770nm   830nm   890nm   950nm   1000nm   Whole light Image

Fig. 2. Sample images from our Multi-spectral face database

Table 1. Multi-spectral face database description

Database			
No. of class	Bands	Whole light	Total images
231	9	1	$231 \times (9 + 1) = 2{,}310$

full range of camera (400 nm to 1000 nm) without the use of filter wheel and we call this sample image as whole light image. The session two consists of probe samples, captured across nine narrow spectral bands namely 530 nm, 590 nm, 650 nm, 710 nm, 770 nm, 830 nm, 890 nm, 950 nm, 1000 nm. The sample images of our Multi-spectral facial database is shown in Fig. 2.

The total of 231 individuals participated in the data collection that consists of 158 male and 73 female. About 95% of the individuals were in the age group 22–30 and remaining 5% were above 35 years of age. The detail description of the database captured is given in the Table 1. Further, our entire Multi-spectral facial database captured, have single instance per individual (Table 1). Therefore, for experimental evaluation we finalized a protocol which involves whole light image as training sample and individual spectral bands as probe sample images. The experimental evaluation in the form of identification rate was performed independently across all nine spectral bands on 22 photometric normalization techniques using four state-of-the-art face recognition algorithm for the comparison.

3   Pre-processing

The pre-processing of an images are required for the efficient performance of face recognition algorithms. This involves facial region extraction, geometric alignment and photometric normalization.

Facial region extraction involves manual location of center of eye co-ordinates which is used by a software to obtain the facial region and determine its boundaries. The extracted facial region was usually used to reduces the computation time involved in processing algorithm and performance enhancement.

Geometric alignment is required for the detected facial region to compensate for any perturbation in the frontal pose using eye co-ordinates. This involves image rotation and translation correction before cropping image to 120×120 spatial dimension.

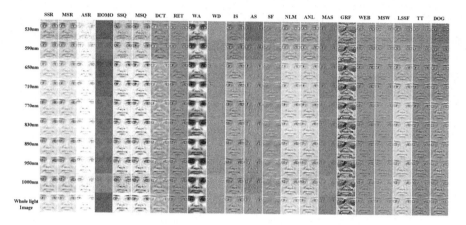

Fig. 3. Spectral band images after 22 photometric normalization techniques

Photometric Normalization technique was further used in our study for image enhancement before feature extraction algorithm. The resultant enhanced image obtained after the photometric normalization exhibit most of the predefined characteristic features required for robust performance. We employed 22 photometric normalization techniques that are based on Retinex theory [1] and are mainly fit for noise invariant feature description algorithms [2]. The performance of face recognition algorithm was tested on each of the 22 photometric normalization methods involved in this paper. The visual illustration of images after 22 photometric normalization algorithm across nine spectral band is shown in the Fig. 3.

4   Feature Descriptor and Classifier

This section of paper present four different state-of-the-art feature descriptor algorithm involved in paper. These algorithms includes: Histogram of Oriented Gradient (HoG) [3], Local Phase Quantization (LPQ) [4], GIST [5] and Log-Gabor transform [6]. These algorithms have proven its accuracy based on their ability to extract local and global features of an image in the literature. Further for efficient classification of the features, we introduced Collaborative Representation Classifier (CRC) [7] that has been developed recently for robust face recognition in the literature. The proposed face recognition scheme employed here in this paper is illustrated in Fig. 4. Further, in the next, we describe each of these methodologies in short.

Histogram of Oriented Gradients (HOG): HOG is a feature description method introduced in the literature for detection of humans [3]. HOG descriptor basically depends on the magnitude of gradient vectors, that characterize the local objects shape and appearance in the image. The contribution of each gradient vector to histogram depends on its magnitude. The magnitude of gradient vectors are

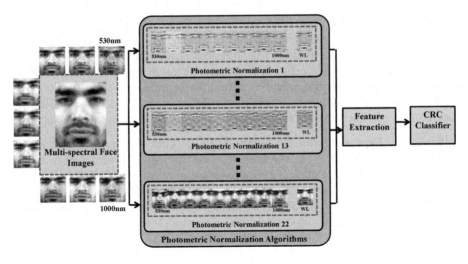

Fig. 4. Proposed scheme (Here, WL corresponds to whole light image)

placed in any one of the nine bins of histogram based on its occurrence. The size of each bins are 20° ranging from 0 to 180°. In practice this method is performed by dividing image in to uniform blocks and obtaining the histogram of gradient vector for each of the blocks. The final descriptor will be the concatenation of histograms from each these blocks. In our experiment, for the image size of 120×120 we obtained 196 blocks with 50% overlap. The final HOG descriptor after concatenation of histogram (196 blocks $\times$ (4 histogram for each blocks $\times$ 9 bins per histogram)), obtained to have 7056×1 dimension.

Local Phase Quantization (LPQ): LPQ was first proposed by Ojansivu and Heikkilä [8] as a texture descriptor for blurred image and latter this method was further used by Ahonen et al. [4] for blurred face recognition. The method provides excellent robustness against image blurring by making use of quantized phase for discrete Fourier transform (DFT). In practice, LPQ operator identifies the texture information by locally computing descriptor at every pixel location to give 256×1 histogram dimensions for texture classification.

GIST: Oliva and Torralba [5] introduced GIST for scene recognition from an image based on local and global descriptor. For efficient description of scene, GIST concentrate on the shape of scene that is based on the relationship of surface outline and properties which further discard the possible use of local objects and relationship among these local objects. Ideally this method first transforms the image into 32 feature maps using 32 gabor filters (4 scales $\times$ 8 orientation $= 32$ gabor filters). Further dividing each feature map into 16 region to obtain 16 averaged value for each feature map. Final descriptor is obtained by concatenating each 32 feature maps to get (16 averaged values $\times$ 32 feature maps) to give 512×1 GIST descriptor dimension.

Log-Gabor transform: This method obtains high frequency components of image i.e. edge information to describe the feature matrix. In practice, this approach make use of several banks of filters with different orientation and scale. However, in this work for efficient description we employed 8 different orientations and 4 different scales on 120×120 image to obtain feature matrix of size 460800×1. Further, to avoid the computation time and memory usage we down-sampled the feature matrix by factor of six to get final feature vector of dimension 76800×1.

Collaborative Representation Classifier (CRC): This method is introduced recently by Zhang et al. [7] in the literature for efficient face recognition. CRC algorithm is an extension of Sparse Representation classifier (SRC) [9] which is very complex and expensive. CRC make use of regularized least square parameters to represent the probe samples as linear combination of gallery set. Thus, obtains outstanding recognition rate with minimum classification error.

5   Results

In this section of paper, we discuss the quantitative results obtained for 22 photometric normalization methods using four state-of-the-art face recognition algorithms. The obtained results include, the identification rate across nine narrow spectral bands as shown in Table 2. However, the Multi-spectral facial database captured under individual class contains single instance (Table 1) across nine bands. Therefore, we developed a protocol for experimental evaluation of results that includes wholelight image as training dataset and all individual nine spectral bands as prob dataset as explained in the Sect. 2. The performance evaluated are obtained for individual spectral bands to know the accuracy of each bands using face recognition algorithms across 22 photometric normalization techniques. The empirical results in the form of identification rate at rank 1 for 22 photometric normalization algorithm is illustrate in Table 2. Further, based on the empirical results we make our following analysis.

Analysis I: Here we discuss about the overall performance of 22 photometric normalization algorithms (Table 2). Following are the major observations:

a. Out of 22 photometric normalization algorithms DOG obtains the highest Identification rate for HOG-CRC, GIST-CRC and Log-Gabor-CRC multi-spectral face recognition algorithms.
b. The least performance is obtained by WD method for all four recognition algorithms.
c. DOG, LSSF, MSW, WEB, GRF, SF, WA, are the only methods that obtained 100% identification rate at rank 1 for some of these bands. However, SSQ, WD, IS, AS, SF, GRF, LSSF, obtains 0% recognition rate (It may be noted that the 0% rate obtained only for 530 nm and 1000 nm spectral band which are least performing bands for all four face recognition algorithms).

Table 2. Performance analysis in terms of identification rate

Algorithm	Bands nm	SSR	MSR	ASR	HOMO	SSQ	MSQ	DCT	RET	WA	WD	IS	AS	SF	NLM	ANL	MAS	GRF	WEB	MSW	LSSF	TT	DOG
HOG-CRC	530	3.98	3.98	7.52	7.08	8.41	7.96	15.49	12.83	10.18	7.08	3.54	8.41	9.29	11.06	6.64	10.62	15.49	15.93	15.49	15.49	12.83	29.2
	590	56.2	54.87	30.09	32.3	40.71	44.25	69.47	63.27	48.67	32.3	34.51	33.19	32.3	50.44	44.69	35.84	61.06	64.16	66.81	50	61.5	81.42
	650	99.56	99.12	97.79	99.12	99.12	98.67	98.23	99.12	99.12	97.34	99.56	99.12	99.56	99.56	99.56	98.67	99.12	99.56	99.56	99.56	98.67	99.56
	710	98.67	99.12	96.46	99.12	97.79	97.34	97.79	99.56	98.23	96.9	99.12	98.67	100	99.56	99.56	99.56	99.79	99.12	100	100	100	99.56
	770	97.79	97.79	97.79	99.12	98.23	98.67	98.23	97.79	98.23	96.9	98.23	97.79	98.67	97.79	98.23	98.67	98.23	99.12	99.12	99.12	98.67	99.12
	830	99.12	99.12	98.67	98.67	97.79	99.12	98.23	99.12	98.23	97.79	99.12	98.23	98.67	99.12	99.12	97.79	98.23	99.12	99.12	99.12	98.67	99.12
	890	97.79	97.79	95.13	97.79	97.34	97.34	97.34	98.67	97.34	96.02	98.23	95.13	97.34	98.23	98.23	96.9	97.34	98.67	98.67	97.79	98.67	99.12
	950	97.34	97.34	94.69	97.34	97.34	96.46	97.34	98.23	98.67	94.69	97.79	95.58	96.02	98.23	98.23	96.9	98.23	98.67	98.23	97.79	98.23	99.12
	1000	63.27	59.29	27.88	26.55	25.22	33.19	73.89	62.83	55.31	29.2	32.3	20.8	31.86	55.75	44.69	30.09	57.08	52.66	54.42	48.67	46.9	73.89
LPQ-CRC	530	2.66	0.44	0.44	0.44	0	0.88	1.33	0.88	3.54	2.21	0	0	0	0.44	1.33	0.88	0	1.33	1.33	0	1.77	1.33
	590	12.39	7.96	0.88	2.21	2.21	3.98	7.08	5.76	9.74	1.33	3.98	1.33	3.98	9.29	10.62	0.44	0.44	1.77	2.66	4.42	2.21	4.87
	650	85.4	84.96	27.88	47.79	39.38	56.64	73.89	69.03	69.47	3.98	67.26	19.03	63.72	79.65	75.22	35.85	26.55	52.21	51.33	73.45	42.48	64.6
	710	93.8	90.71	27.88	52.66	44.69	64.6	80.09	81.42	79.2	5.31	71.68	23.45	71.68	88.94	83.19	39.82	39.38	51.77	56.2	80.53	51.77	73.89
	770	95.13	93.8	49.56	61.06	52.66	69.47	82.74	89.82	84.07	7.52	81.42	30.09	77.88	94.25	90.71	42.04	47.79	67.7	65.93	87.17	66.37	80.09
	830	96.46	95.13	49.12	67.7	56.64	74.78	84.96	87.61	82.3	7.08	81.86	38.05	86.28	90.71	92.04	50.88	46.46	66.37	70.35	84.07	62.39	81.86
	890	83.63	79.65	23.01	34.51	30.01	45.58	70.8	65.49	61.5	5.75	61.95	15.04	60.18	75.22	71.68	26.55	23.89	37.17	42.04	64.16	36.73	56.64
	950	74.34	65.49	11.5	24.34	21.24	30.97	57.08	50.44	50.88	5.31	38.94	10.62	39.38	61.5	56.64	16.81	11.95	25.66	27.43	50	26.55	40.27
	1000	5.75	4.42	1.77	9.29	6.2	3.98	0	1.77	0	4.87	6.2	3.1	2.21	0.88	0.88	1.77	3.98	1.77	3.98			
GIST-CRC	530	16.37	14.16	3.1	5.31	10.18	3.54	11.95	3.98	28.76	2.21	7.08	1.77	7.52	14.16	4.87	2.66	9.29	7.52	7.52	12.39	4.42	31.42
	590	64.6	59.74	14.6	38.94	36.73	29.65	64.16	41.59	69.03	4.87	52.21	21.24	42.48	61.06	47.34	21.24	35.4	46.02	53.1	65.04	40.71	77.88
	650	96.9	97.79	96.9	98.23	98.23	98.67	98.67	99.12	99.12	61.5	99.12	98.23	99.56	98.23	97.79	99.12	98.67	99.56	99.12	99.56	99.56	100
	710	97.34	97.79	96.02	99.56	99.56	99.12	98.67	98.23	99.12	100	72.57	99.12	98.23	99.12	98.23	99.12	100	99.56	99.12	99.56	99.56	100
	770	97.34	97.79	97.34	98.67	99.12	98.23	98.67	98.67	99.12	76.11	98.67	99.12	99.12	98.23	98.67	99.12	100	100	98.67	98.67	99.12	100
	830	97.79	97.79	97.79	98.67	99.12	99.56	98.67	98.67	99.12	76.11	98.67	98.67	99.56	97.79	99.12	98.67	99.56	99.12	99.56	98.67	99.12	99.12
	890	96.46	97.34	96.46	97.79	97.34	98.67	98.23	98.67	98.23	65.49	98.23	97.79	99.12	99.56	98.67	99.12	100	98.67	99.12	98.67	97.79	99.12
	950	97.34	97.79	94.69	97.79	97.34	97.34	98.67	99.12	99.56	61.06	99.12	94.25	98.67	98.67	98.67	97.79	97.34	99.12	98.23	99.12	98.67	100
	1000	74.34	73.01	28.76	42.48	38.5	31.86	76.11	60.62	72.57	7.96	62.39	17.26	40.71	73.89	61.95	25.66	33.19	54.42	61.95	72.57	47.79	75.66
LogGabor-CRC	530	77.43	76.11	41.15	37.17	36.28	52.66	85.4	79.65	95.58	33.63	66.37	34.07	74.78	83.63	75.66	40.27	51.77	64.16	65.49	80.09	75.22	90.27
	590	92.48	92.48	80.97	86.73	80.38	96.46	96.9	96.46	99.12	65.49	96.02	73.45	95.58	96.9	96.9	83.63	94.25	96.46	96.46	97.34	96.9	98.23
	650	99.12	99.12	97.79	99.79	99.56	99.56	98.67	98.67	100	91.59	98.67	98.23	98.67	99.12	99.56	98.67	99.56	99.12	99.12	98.67	98.67	100
	710	99.12	98.67	97.34	96.9	98.67	99.12	97.79	99.79	100	92.04	99.12	97.34	98.23	99.56	98.67	97.79	99.56	99.79	97.79	99.12	98.23	99.56
	770	99.12	98.67	96.9	96.02	98.67	98.67	98.67	98.23	98.23	94.25	98.67	97.34	98.67	98.67	97.79	97.79	98.67	98.67	98.67	98.23	99.12	99.56
	830	98.67	98.67	96.9	98.67	99.56	99.56	98.23	99.12	99.56	93.36	98.67	97.79	99.56	98.67	98.67	97.97	100	99.12	99.12	99.12	99.12	99.56
	890	98.23	97.79	94.69	95.13	97.79	98.23	98.67	98.23	99.56	90.27	99.12	95.58	97.79	97.34	98.67	95.58	99.12	97.79	97.34	98.67	98.23	98.67
	950	98.67	98.67	97.34	96.46	98.67	99.12	97.79	98.23	100	91.15	97.79	96.02	99.12	97.79	99.56	55.58	99.56	98.67	98.67	99.12	98.67	99.12
	1000	96.02	96.02	84.96	89.38	92.04	95.58	95.58	96.46	97.34	76.55	93.81	79.65	94.69	95.58	95.58	90.27	93.36	94.69	94.69	97.79	96.02	97.79

Analysis II: This section will talk about performance of four face recognition algorithms on 22 photometric normalization algorithms. Empirically, we observe that:

a. Out of four face recognition algorithms employed in the empirical study, Log-Gabor-CRC obtains consistently higher performance for all 22 photometric normalization methods as compared to other face recognition algorithms.

b. Very poor performance is observed in the case of LPQ-CRC proposed approach for all 22 photometric normalization methods.

c. 100% identification rate is observed for HOG-CRC (for 710 nm band), GIST-CRC (for 650 nm, 710 nm, 770 nm, 890 nm and 950 nm bands) and Log-Gabor-CRC (for 650 nm, 710 nm, 830 nm and 950 nm bands).

Analysis III: In this section we describe the performance of nine Multi-spectral bands with respect to 22 photometric normalization algorithms. Following are our observations:

a. Spectral bands such as 650 nm, 710 nm, 770 nm, 830 nm, 890 nm, 950 nm obtains above 90% identification rate at rank1.

b. The performance of 530 nm spectral band is poor in all 22 photometric normalization methods.

c. 100% identification rate has been observed in 650 nm, 710 nm, 770 nm, 830 nm, 890 nm, 950 nm spectral bands for one or more individual photometric normalization algorithm out of 22 methods.

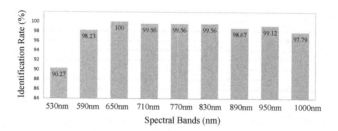

Fig. 5. Identification rate of spectral bands at rank 1 for DOG using LogGabor-CRC algorithm (Best results are demonstrated)

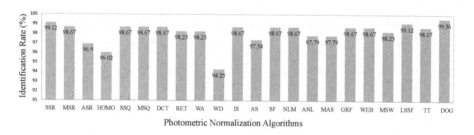

Fig. 6. Identification rate for 22 photometric normalization algorithms using LogGabor-CRC algorithm (Best results with 770 nm spectral bands are illustrated)

Figure 5 illustrate the performance of nine spectral bands using LogGabor-CRC for DOG photometric normalization method (best results are illustrated). Further, the variation in identification rate at rank 1 for all 22 photometric normalization algorithm is shown in Fig. 6 (best results are illustrated). However, the extensive comparative analysis (Table 2) across 22 photometric normalization algorithm will provide an handle to select the best performing normalization methods for robust face recognition.

6   Conclusions

For robust performance of any face recognition algorithm requires proper selection of image enhancement technique. In this paper we empirically evaluated the comparative performance analysis of 22 photometric normalization techniques for Multi-spectral face recognition. To evaluate this study we developed Multi-spectral sensor to capture face database for 231 individuals across nine spectral band covering 530 nm to 1000 nm wavelength range. We performed quantitative empirical evaluation in the form of identification rate at rank 1 to understand the significance of all photometric normalization methods using four state-of-the-art face recognition algorithms. The outstanding results with varying performance is obtained with all photometric normalization methods.

References

1. Land, E.H., McCann, J.J.: Lightness and retinex theory. J. Opt. Soc. Am. **61**(1), 1–11 (1971)
2. Han, H., Shan, S., Chen, X., Gao, W.: A comparative study on illumination preprocessing in face recognition. Pattern Recogn. **46**(6), 1691–1699 (2013)
3. Dalal, N., Triggs, B.: Histograms of oriented gradients for human detection. In: IEEE Computer Society Conference on Computer Vision and Pattern Recognition (CVPR 2005), vol. 1, pp. 886–893. IEEE Computer Society, Washington, D.C. (2005)
4. Ahonen, T., Rahtu, E., Ojansivu, V., Heikkila, J.: Recognition of blurred faces using local phase quantization. In: 19th International Conference on Pattern Recognition, pp. 1–4. IEEE, Tampa (2008)
5. Oliva, A., Torralba, A.: Modeling the shape of the scene: a holistic representation of the spatial envelope. Int. J. Comput. Vis. **42**(3), 145–175 (2001)
6. Xiao, Z., Guo, C., Ming, Y., Qiang, L.: Research on log Gabor wavelet and its application in image edge detection. In: 6th International Conference on Signal Processing, vol. 1, pp. 592–595 (2002)
7. Zhang, L., Yang, M., Feng, X.: Sparse representation or collaborative representation: which helps face recognition? In: IEEE International Conference on Computer Vision (ICCV), pp. 471–478 (2011)
8. Ojansivu, V., Heikkilä, J.: Blur insensitive texture classification using local phase quantization. In: Elmoataz, A., Lezoray, O., Nouboud, F., Mammass, D. (eds.) ICISP 2008. LNCS, vol. 5099, pp. 236–243. Springer, Heidelberg (2008). doi:10.1007/978-3-540-69905-7_27
9. Wright, J., Yang, A.Y., Ganesh, A., Sastry, S.S., Ma, Y.: Robust face recognition via sparse representation. IEEE Trans. Pattern Anal. Mach. Intell. **31**(2), 210–227 (2009)
10. Schroff, F., Treibitz, T., Kriegman, D., Belongie, S.: Pose, illumination and expression invariant pairwise face-similarity measure via Doppelganger list comparison. In: International Conference on Computer Vision (ICCV 2011), pp. 2494–2501 (2011)
11. Zhang, Z., Wang, Y., Zhang, Z.: Face synthesis from near-infrared to visual light via sparse representation. In: International Joint Conference on Biometrics (IJCB), pp. 1–6 (2011)
12. Bourlai, T., Kalka, N., Ross, A., Cukic, B., Hornak, L.: Cross-spectral face verification in the short wave infrared (SWIR) band. In: 20th International Conference on Pattern Recognition (ICPR 2010), pp. 1343–1347. IEEE Computer Society, Washington, D.C. (2010)

13. Bourlai, T., Cukic, B.: Multi-spectral face recognition: identification of people in difficult environments. In: IEEE International Conference on Intelligence and Security Informatics (ISI), pp. 196–201 (2012)

14. Hu, S., Choi, J., Chan, A.L., Schwartz, W.R.: Thermal-to-visible face recognition using partial least squares. J. Opt. Soc. Am. A **32**(3), 431–442 (2015)

15. Liao, S., Yi, D., Lei, Z., Qin, R., Li, S.Z.: Heterogeneous face recognition from local structures of normalized appearance. In: Tistarelli, M., Nixon, M.S. (eds.) ICB 2009. LNCS, vol. 5558, pp. 209–218. Springer, Heidelberg (2009). doi:10.1007/978-3-642-01793-3_22

16. Kalka, N.D., Bourlai, T., Cukic, B., Hornak, L.: Cross-spectral face recognition in heterogeneous environments: a case study on matching visible to short-wave infrared imagery. In: International Joint Conference on Biometrics (IJCB), pp. 1–8 (2011)

17. Kang, D., Han, H., Jain, A.K., Lee, S.: Nighttime face recognition at large standoff: cross-distance and cross-spectral matching. Pattern Recogn. **47**(12), 3750–3766 (2014)

18. Short, J., Kittler, J., Messer, K.: A comparison of photometric normalisation algorithms for face verification. In: Sixth IEEE International Conference on Automatic Face and Gesture Recognition, pp. 254–259 (2004)

19. Du, B., Shan, S., Qing, L., Gao, W.: Empirical comparisons of several preprocessing methods for illumination insensitive face recognition. In: IEEE International Conference on Acoustics, Speech, and Signal Processing (ICASSP 2005), vol. 2, pp. ii/981–ii/984 (2005)

20. Uzair, M., Mahmood, A., Mian, A.: Hyperspectral face recognition with spatiospectral information fusion and PLS regression. IEEE Trans. Image Process. **24**(3), 1127–1137 (2015)

21. Štruc, V., Vitomir, Š., Nikola, P., Nikola, P.: Photometric normalization techniques for illumination invariance. In: Advances in Face Image Analysis: Techniques and Technologies, pp. 279–300. IGI Global (2011)

Dictionary Based Approach for Facial Expression Recognition from Static Images

Krishan Sharma$^{(\boxtimes)}$ and Renu Rameshan

School of Computing and Electrical Engineering, Indian Institute of Technology,
Mandi, Himachal Pradesh, India
krishan_sharma@students.iitmandi.ac.in, renumr@iitmandi.ac.in

Abstract. We present a simple approach for facial expression recognition from images using the principle of sparse representation using a learned dictionary. Visual appearance based feature descriptors like histogram of oriented gradients (HOG), local binary patterns (LBP) and eigenfaces are used. We use Fisher discrimination dictionary which has discrimination capability in addition to being reconstructive. The classification is based on the fact that each expression class with in the dictionary spans a subspace and these subspaces have non-overlapping directions so that they are widely separated. Each test feature point has a sparse representation in the union of subspaces of dictionary formed by labeled training points. To check recognition performance of the proposed approach, extensive experimentation is done over Jaffee and CK databases. Results show that the proposed approach has better classification accuracy than state-of-the-art techniques.

Keywords: Histogram of oriented gradient · Local binary pattern · Eigenfaces · Dictionary learning · Sparse representation · Facial expression recognition

1 Introduction

Facial expressions play an important role in human communication. Mehrabian's [1] study of non verbal communication shows that 55% of information transfers through facial expressions. Ekman [2] linked facial expressions to basic emotions (disgust, happy, sad, fear, surprise, anger).

An automatic facial expression recognition system can be used for human computer interaction by making computers more receptive to human needs but it has always been a difficult and challenging task for the computer vision community researcher from past several years. Recently many researchers are working on this problem and fast growth is seen. In fact many digital cameras in market now uses facial expression recognition algorithms but recognition error rate is still high due to large pose, scale and rotation variation, different lighting condition and occlusion.

© Springer International Publishing AG 2017
S. Mukherjee et al. (Eds.): ICVGIP 2016, LNCS 10481, pp. 39–49, 2017.
https://doi.org/10.1007/978-3-319-68124-5_4

Sparse representation and dictionary learning techniques are successfully applied to various image processing and computer vision tasks like compression, denoising, super-resolution and classification etc. Mairal et al. [3] proposed a method to learn separate dictionaries for different classes and classification performed is based on reconstruction error, however this is a very inefficient and time consuming process when number of training classes are large.

Aharon et al. [4] proposed KSVD based method to learn an overcomplete dictionary that is purely reconstructive but lacks discrimination capabilities hence not suitable for classification. The discriminative KSVD (DKSVD) [5] learns a dictionary that is based on extending the KSVD algorithm by incorporating the classification error into the objective function, discrimination is obtained by iteratively updating dictionary atoms based on linear predictive classifier. Liu et al. [6] combined Gabor features with DKSVD for facial expression recognition. Sparse coding trees [7] are supervised classification trees for expression recognition that use node-specific dictionaries and classifiers to direct input based on classification results in the feature space at each node. Guo [8] proposed a smile expression classification technique based on biologically inspired feature and patched based dictionary learning. Cottor [9] also proposed a region based weighted voting of sparse representation classifiers for facial expression recognition.

The aim of this paper is to develop a new approach which uses appearance based features along with Fisher discrimination dictionary [10] for classification. Appearance based features include histogram of oriented gradients (HOG) [11], local binary patterns (LBP) [12] and eigenfaces [13] that encode visual variations of the face images. The idea behind using the Fisher discrimination dictionary is that each expression class with in the dictionary forms a class specific subdictionary that spans a subspace and these subspaces for all different classes are widely separated and each test feature point has a sparse representation in the union of subspaces of dictionary formed by labeled training feature points.

Our contribution is using Fisher discrimination dictionary in feature space for achieving facial expression classification with an improved performance. The proposed classifier has a performance superior to the state of the art techniques. The dictionary is learned in such a way that subspaces formed by each subdictionary are orthogonal to each other. Each test image is then classified by finding the maximum projection of its feature point in these subspaces. Result shows that HOG features perform best with Fisher discrimination dictionary. The paper is structured as follows. Section 2 describes the proposed approach. Experimental analysis and results are given in Sect. 3. Section 4 describes the conclusion and future work.

2   The Proposed Approach

The proposed facial expression recognition algorithm as shown in Fig. 2 consists of the following steps, *viz.* Region of interest and reference point detection (Sect. 2.1), face normalization (Sect. 2.2), feature extraction (Sect. 2.3), learning dictionary from training data (Sect. 2.4), classification through dictionary

(a) original image

(b) reference point detection

(c) face normalization

(d) face ROI detection

Fig. 1. Face image registration

(Sect. 2.5). The face region of interest (ROI) from any input profile face image is detected using the Viola & Jones face detection algorithm proposed in [14]. The detected face is normalized by first detecting two reference points for image registration. Center of both eyes are chosen as the reference points for image registration. After normalization, appearance based image features are extracted and classification is performed with learned dictionary.

2.1 Reference Point Detection

The major problems which occur in expression recognition from face images are affine (scaling, translation and rotation) variations. To overcome these problems, face images are normalized first by detecting two reference points *viz* e1 and e2. e1 and e2 are denoted as left eye and right eye center respectively which are detected automatically using template matching (Fig. 1b). Five different templates for each eye are made and co-ordinates to the reference points are assigned based on maximum voting strategy over correlation values.

2.2 Face Normalization

Face normalization (Fig. 1c) is required to overcome the issues caused by affine transformation such as rotation and scaling. It is required that all the face images

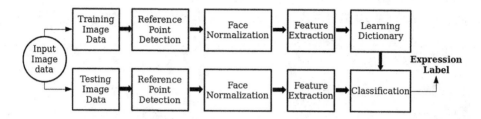

Fig. 2. Flow diagram of proposed approach

in the database should be of same size and properly registered around the given reference points i.e. reference points in all the database images should lie at same co-ordinate locations.

Let (a_1^0, b_1^0) and (a_2^0, b_2^0) denotes the co-ordinates of reference points e1 and e2 respectively in the original image I_0. Reference point co-ordinates $e1'$ and $e2'$ in the registered image template I_1 are (a_1^1, b_1^1) and (a_2^1, b_1^1) respectively. Image I_0 is scaled to Image I_s with respect to reference point e1 by a scaling factor $K = \frac{d_0}{dist(e1,e2)}$, where d_0 is a predefined distance between the reference points $(e1'$ and $e2')$ of the reference image template obtained by scaling matrix $[T_s]$. Image I_s is rotated to Image I_r with respect to e1 using rotation matrix $[T_r]$ by an angle $\theta = \frac{b_2^0 - b_1^0}{a_2^0 - a_1^0}$, where θ is the angle between horizontal axis and line joining e1 and e2. Image I_r is translated to I_t by $t_x = a_1^1 - a_1^0$ and $t_y = b_1^1 - b_1^0$ in x and y direction respectively using translation matrix $[I_t]$. The image transformation matrix from original image I_0 to the register image I_1 is given as:

$$T = \underbrace{\begin{bmatrix} cos\theta & -sin\theta & a_1^o \cdot (1 - cos\theta) + b_1^o \cdot sin\theta \\ sin\theta & cos\theta & b_1^o \cdot (1 - cos\theta) - a_1^o \cdot sin\theta \\ 0 & 0 & 1 \end{bmatrix}}_{\text{Rotation Matrix } [T_r] \ w.r.t. \ \text{point } e_1} \underbrace{\begin{bmatrix} K & 0 & a_1^o \cdot (1 - K) \\ 0 & K & b_1^o \cdot (1 - K) \\ 0 & 0 & 1 \end{bmatrix}}_{\text{Scaling Matrix } [T_s] \ w.r.t. \ \text{point } e_1} \underbrace{\begin{bmatrix} 1 & 0 & t_x \\ 0 & 1 & t_y \\ 0 & 0 & 1 \end{bmatrix}}_{\text{Translation } [T_t]}$$

$$(1)$$

2.3 Feature Extraction

In this work, three different types of feature extraction methods are used which exploit different key properties of facial expressions. All of them are discussed here in detail.

Histogram of Oriented Gradients: The well known HOG descriptor [11] is used to extract the facial expression features. The prime advantage of using the HOG representation is that it captures edge or gradient structure that is a very good characteristic of facial expressions. HOG features are also invariant to geometric and photometric transformations. Contrast normalization in HOG makes it invariant to shadowing and illumination changes.

Local Binary Patterns: LBP features [12] are used to encode spatial variations from face image which is the effective representation of facial features as it is robust to rotation and illumination variations. The binary patterns are generated at a pixel by thresholding its neighboring pixels and the threshold is selected based on the value at the center pixel. Histograms of these patterns represent an image as the feature vector.

Eigenfaces: Eigenfaces [13] are the set of eigenvectors obtained from the covariance matrix of training data. Face images can be represented in a low dimension subspaces of original face space by projecting the face image over eigenvectors (eigenfaces) sorted by their eigenvalue.

2.4 Learning Dictionary from Training Data

Fisher discrimination dictionary proposed by Yang et al. [10] is used for classification purpose due to its high discrimination and reconstruction capabilities. We are giving a brief overview of Fisher discrimination dictionary in this section. Unlike the previous dictionary learning methods which learn either the shared dictionary or different class specific dictionaries, this method learns a structured dictionary $\mathbf{D} = [\mathbf{D}_1, \mathbf{D}_2, \ldots, \mathbf{D}_j, \ldots \mathbf{D}_c] \in \mathbb{R}^{n*p}$, where c, n and p denotes the total number of classes, feature vector dimension and total number of dictionary atoms respectively. $\mathbf{D}_j \in \mathbb{R}^{n*p_j}$ is the class specific sub-dictionary for j^{th} class with p_j dictionary atoms.

While learning the Fisher dictionary, three constraints are enforced. First constraint is that each class specific sub-dictionary should have well representation of training data belong to that class and poor representation belong to other classes. Second constraint is that representation coefficients should have large between class scatter and small within class scatter and third constraint is the high sparsity of representation coefficients.

Let $\mathbf{Y} = [\ \mathbf{Y}_1, \mathbf{Y}_2, \ldots, \mathbf{Y}_j, \ldots \mathbf{Y}_c] \in \mathbb{R}^{n*N}$ denotes the input training data with N examples, where $\mathbf{Y}_j \in \mathbb{R}^{n*N_i}$ are the data samples belongs to j^{th} class. Similarly, sparse coefficients are defined as $\mathbf{X} = [\mathbf{X}_1, \mathbf{X}_2, \ldots, \mathbf{X}_j, \ldots \mathbf{X}_c] \in \mathbb{R}^{p*N}$ such that $\mathbf{Y} \approx \mathbf{DX}$. It is desirable that dictionary $\mathbf{D}$ should be discriminative and reconstructive simultaneously along with sparse coding coefficients. Therefore, cost function can be defined as:

$$J_{\{\mathbf{D},\mathbf{X}\}} = \min_{\mathbf{D},\mathbf{X}} \underbrace{\sum_{j=1}^{K}(||\mathbf{Y}_j - \mathbf{DX}_j||_F^2 + ||\mathbf{Y}_j - \mathbf{D}_j\mathbf{X}_j^j||_F^2)}_{\text{reconstruction term}}$$

$$+ \underbrace{\lambda_1(tr(S_w(\mathbf{X})) - tr(S_b(\mathbf{X})) + \eta||\mathbf{X}||_F^2)}_{\text{discrimination term}} \tag{2}$$

$$+ \underbrace{\lambda_2||\mathbf{X}||_1}_{\text{sparsity constraint}} \quad s.t. \quad ||\mathbf{D}_i\mathbf{X}_j^i||_F^2 \leq \epsilon_f \quad \forall j \neq i$$

where $S_w(\mathbf{X})$ and $S_b(\mathbf{X})$ are within and between class scatter respectively. λ_1, λ_2 and η are parameters. $||\mathbf{X}||_F^2$ is added to make the discriminative term convex.

This cost function is non-convex jointly with $\mathbf{D}$ and $\mathbf{X}$. To make it convex, this is optimized with respect to one variable keeping other fixed. Thus the optimization method is an iterative algorithm with alternate sparse coding and dictionary update stages. More details can be found in [10].

2.5 Classification Through Dictionary

Let a test sample $\mathbf{y}$ belongs to class $\mathbf{Y}_j$ is represented sparsely as $\mathbf{x}$ over learned dictionary $\mathbf{D}$. Let $\boldsymbol{\mu}_j$ denotes the mean vector of representation coefficients $\mathbf{X}_j$ which is the sparse representation of $\mathbf{Y}_j$ over the dictionary $\mathbf{D}$. For test sample $\mathbf{y}$ to belong to $\mathbf{Y}_j$, it should be represented well by class specific sub-dictionary $\mathbf{D}_j$ i.e. representation residual error should be least with $\mathbf{D}_j$ and simultaneously representation coefficient should be closest to $\boldsymbol{\mu}_j$. Sparse representation $\hat{\mathbf{x}}$ of test sample $\mathbf{y}$ over dictionary $\mathbf{D}$ can be solved as:

$$\hat{\mathbf{x}} = \arg\min_{\mathbf{x}}\{||\mathbf{y} - \mathbf{D}\mathbf{x}||_2^2 + \gamma||\mathbf{x}||_1\} \tag{3}$$

where γ is a regularization parameter between reconstruction term and sparsity constraint term. $||.||_p$ is p^{th} norm where $p = 1$ or 2.

$\hat{\mathbf{x}} = [\hat{\mathbf{x}_1}, \hat{\mathbf{x}_2}, \ldots, \hat{\mathbf{x}_c}]$; where $\hat{\mathbf{x}_j}$ denotes the representation coefficient over class specific sub-dictionary $\mathbf{D}_j$. If test sample $\mathbf{y}$ belongs to j^{th} class then representation residual error $||\mathbf{y} - \mathbf{D}\hat{\mathbf{x}_j}||_2^2$ will be less than $||\mathbf{y} - \mathbf{D}\hat{\mathbf{x}_i}||_2^2$ for $j \neq i$ and also $\hat{\mathbf{x}_j}$ will be near to mean vector $\boldsymbol{\mu}_j$ than $\boldsymbol{\mu}_i$ for $j \neq i$. By incorporating both the representation residual error and representation coefficient term in classification, metric for classification can be defined as:

$$e_j = ||\mathbf{y} - \mathbf{D}_j\hat{\mathbf{x}_j}||_2^2 + \alpha.||\hat{\mathbf{x}} - \boldsymbol{\mu}_j||_2^2 \tag{4}$$

where α is the weight balance term. Class label for test sample y is given as:

$$classlabel\{y\} = argmin_j\{e_j\} \tag{5}$$

2.6 Subspace Analysis of Learned Dictionary

Fisher dictionary can be seen as structural combination of different class specific sub-dictionaries where each sub-dictionary is spanning a subspace within dictionary space. It is desirable that each pair of sub-dictionaries should be maximally incoherent making each pair of subspaces orthogonal to each other. To make each sub-dictionary more discriminative and to promote the incoherence between sub-dictionaries, Yang et al. added $(||D_i X_j^i||_F^2 \leq \epsilon_f \ \forall j \neq i)$ as a penalty term to the cost function. This constraint enforces that j^{th} class data can not be represented by i^{th} class sub-dictionary hence should make each sub-dictionary maximally incoherent with each other i.e. subspaces should be mutually orthogonal. Definition of principal angles is given in Definition 1. Definition shows that subspaces are orthogonal if any of the principal angle is $\pi/2$.

Definition 1 [15]. *Let S_i and S_j are the subspaces spanned by sub-dictionaries D_i and D_j respectively. Let columns of $Q_{Si} \in \mathbb{R}^{n*k}$ and $Q_{Sj} \in \mathbb{R}^{n*k}$ are the orthonormal bases for these subspaces. The principal angles ($\theta_l \in [0, \pi/2]$; $l=1,\ldots,k$) between these subspaces can be defined as*

$$\cos \theta_l = \max_{u_l \in span(Q_{Si})} \max_{v_l \in span(Q_{Sj})} u_l^T v_l$$
$$s.t.: \quad ||u_l||_2 = ||v_l||_2 = 1$$
$$u_l^T u_m = 0; \quad m = 1, 2, \ldots, l-1 \qquad (6)$$
$$v_l^T v_m = 0; \quad m = 1, 2, \ldots, l-1$$

Total angle between subspaces S_i and S_j is defined as

$$\theta_T = \cos^{-1}(\prod_{l=1}^{k} \cos \theta_l) \qquad (7)$$

The principal angles (in degree) in HOG feature space between 13-dimensional subspaces for sad and neutral expressions in Jaffee Database are [20.45 33.77 40.51 44.43 50.46 51.83 55.93 61.81 68.66 70.97 76.82 82.80 84.36]. These angles show that though the two subspaces are not exactly orthogonal, yet they do not have any common direction i.e. these subspaces are widely separated but not maximally separated.

3   Experimental Analysis

3.1   Databases

The Japanese Female Facial Expression (JAFFEE) Database. This database [16] consists of 213 grayscale images with seven different facial expression (happy, sad, surprise, fear, disgust, anger, neutral) posed by 10 Japanese female models. Each expression image has been rated on 6 emotion adjectives by 60 Japanese subjects (Fig. 3).

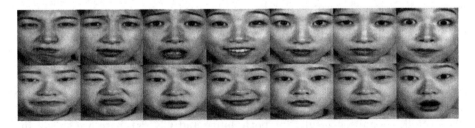

Fig. 3. Jaffee database [16] sample images of anger, disgust, fear, happy, neutral, sad and surprise emotion respectively

Cohn-Kanade AU-Coded Expression Database. This database [17] includes 486 sequences from 97 posers. Each sequence begins with a neutral expression and proceeds to a peak expression. The peak expression for each sequence in fully FACS coded and given an emotion label. The emotion label refers to what expression was requested rather than what may actually have been performed. Subjects in the released portion of the Cohn-Kanade AU-coded facial expression database are 97 university students. They ranged in age from 18 to 30 years. Sixty-five percent were female, fifteen percent were African-American, and three percent were Asian or Latino. Image sequences from neutral to target display were digitized into 640 by 480 or 490 pixel arrays with 8-bit precision for grayscale values (Fig. 4).

Fig. 4. CK database [17] sample images of anger, disgust, fear, happy, sad and surprise emotion respectively

3.2   Testing Strategy

The image database is divided into two parts, one-third data is used for testing and rest for training. First we extract the face from raw image data using Viola & Jones face detection algorithm then each face is register by two reference points which are center of both the eyes and image is normalized to 120*96 pixel size. Fisher dictionary is learned by feature extracted from training data. For testing, 3-fold cross validation is performed over both datasets.

Anger	Disgust	Fear	Happy	Neutral	Sad	Surprise
AN	DI	FE	HA	NE	SA	SU

3.3   Results and Discussion

The overall recognition results for both Jaffee and CK database are shown in Tables 1 and 2 respectively. Three different features are used to learn Fisher discrimination dictionary. Experimentation results show that HOG features with Fisher dictionary gives best recognition results. This is due to the fact that

HOG captures edges or gradient structures. These structures represent the characteristics of facial expressions. Recognition performance of eigenface features over CK database is poor due to large variation in face skin color of individual subject varying from very dark to fair. Tables 3 and 4 show the comparison of our approach with the state of art techniques and hence we can conclude that our results are comparable with previous approaches.

Table 1. Recognition Performance (%) over Jaffee database

	LBP Features							Eigenface Features							HOG Features						
	AN	DI	FE	HA	NE	SA	SU	AN	DI	FE	HA	NE	SA	SU	AN	DI	FE	HA	NE	SA	SU
AN	93.33	6.67	0	0	0	0	0	93.34	0	0	3.33	3.33	0	0	96.67	3.33	0	0	0	0	0
DI	10	90	0	0	0	0	0	3.33	80	6.67	0	0	6.67	3.33	6.67	90	0	0	0	3.33	0
FE	0	3.33	96.67	0	0	0	0	0	6.67	83.33	3.33	0	6.67	0	0	0	100	0	0	0	0
HA	0	0	0	96.67	0	0	3.33	0	0	3.33	66.7	23.33	6.67	0	0	0	0	96.67	0	3.33	0
NE	3.33	0	0	0	93.33	0	3.33	0	0	3.33	6.67	90	0	0	0	0	0	0	100	0	0
SA	6.67	3.33	13.33	0	0	76.67	0	6.67	3.33	6.67	0	3.33	76.67	3.33	0	3.33	3.33	3.33	0	90	0
SU	0	0	0	0	3.33	0	96.67	0	6.67	3.33	0	0	3.33	86.67	0	0	3.33	3.33	0	0	93.34
Rec. Rate	91.90							82.38							95.23						

Table 2. Recognition performance (%) over CK database

	LBP Features							Eigenface Features							HOG Features						
	AN	DI	FE	HA	NE	SA	SU	AN	DI	FE	HA	NE	SA	SU	AN	DI	FE	HA	NE	SA	SU
AN	93.33	6.67	0	0	0	0	0	93.34	0	0	3.33	3.33	0	0	96.67	3.33	0	0	0	0	0
DI	10	90	0	0	0	0	0	3.33	80	6.67	0	0	6.67	3.33	6.67	90	0	0	0	3.33	0
FE	0	3.33	96.67	0	0	0	0	0	6.67	83.33	3.33	0	6.67	0	0	0	100	0	0	0	0
HA	0	0	0	96.67	0	0	3.33	0	0	3.33	66.7	23.33	6.67	0	0	0	0	96.67	0	3.33	0
NE	3.33	0	0	0	93.33	0	3.33	0	0	3.33	6.67	90	0	0	0	0	0	0	100	0	0
SA	6.67	3.33	13.33	0	0	76.67	0	6.67	3.33	6.67	0	3.33	76.67	3.33	0	3.33	3.33	3.33	0	90	0
SU	0	0	0	0	3.33	0	96.67	0	6.67	3.33	0	0	3.33	86.67	0	0	3.33	3.33	0	0	93.34
Rec. Rate	91.90							82.38							95.23						

Table 3. Recognition performance (%) of state-of-the-art techniques over JAFFEE database

Method	Recognition accuracy
Optical flow + SVM [18]	87.5
Gabor + DKSVD [5]	94.3
2DPCA + SVM [19]	94
LBP + DKSVD [5]	78.6
2D locality preserving projections [20]	95
LGIP + SVM [21]	92.4
Proposed approach (HOG + FDD)	**95.23**

Table 4. Recognition performance (%) of state of art techniques over CK database

Method	Recognition accuracy(%)
Optical flow + SVM [18]	89.2
Muscle based feature + SVM [22]	85.9
Differential AAM + KNNS [23]	86.5
Rankboost with l1 regularization [24]	88
AU Dictionary + Sparse coding [25]	88.2
Proposed approach (HOG + FDD)	**93.33**

4   Conclusion and Future Work

In this paper, we have described a Fisher discrimination dictionary based approach to recognize facial expressions from static images. Various appearance based descriptors like histogram of oriented gradient (HOG), local binary pattern (LBP) and eigenfaces are used and results show that HOG features along with Fisher discrimination dictionary gives the best recognition performance. For future, this work can be extended to recognize facial expression from videos using temporal information.

References

1. Mehrabian, A.: Nonverbal Communication. Transaction Publishers, Piscataway (1972)
2. Ekman, P., Rolls, E., Perrett, D., Ellis, H.: Facial expressions of emotion: an old controversy and new findings [and discussion]. Philos. Trans. R. Soc. B: Biol. Sci. **335**(1273), 63–69 (1992)
3. Mairal, J., Bach, F., Ponce, J., Sapiro, G., Zisserman, A.: Discriminative learned dictionaries for local image analysis. In: IEEE Conference on Computer Vision and Pattern Recognition, CVPR 2008. IEEE, pp. 1–8 (2008)
4. Aharon, M., Elad, M., Bruckstein, A.: K-SVD: an algorithm for designing overcomplete dictionaries for sparse representation. IEEE Trans. Sig. Process. **54**(11), 4311 (2006)
5. Zhang, Q., Li, B.: Discriminative K-SVD for dictionary learning in face recognition. In: 2010 IEEE Conference on Computer Vision and Pattern Recognition (CVPR). IEEE, pp. 2691–2698 (2010)
6. Liu, W., Song, C., Wang, Y.: Facial expression recognition based on discriminative dictionary learning. In: 2012 21st International Conference on Pattern Recognition (ICPR). IEEE, pp. 1839–1842 (2012)
7. Chen, H.C., Comiter, M.Z., Kung, H.T., McDanel, B.: Sparse coding trees with application to emotion classification. In: 2015 IEEE Conference on Computer Vision and Pattern Recognition Workshops (CVPRW), pp. 77–86, June 2015
8. Guo, L.: Smile expression classification using the improved BIF feature. In: 2011 Sixth International Conference on Image and Graphics (ICIG), pp. 783–788, August 2011

9. Cotter, S.F.: Weighted voting of sparse representation classifiers for facial expression recognition. In: 2010 18th European Signal Processing Conference. IEEE, pp. 1164–1168 (2010)

10. Yang, M., Zhang, L., Feng, X., Zhang, D.: Fisher discrimination dictionary learning for sparse representation. In: 2011 International Conference on Computer Vision. IEEE, pp. 543–550 (2011)

11. Dalal, N., Triggs, B.: Histograms of oriented gradients for human detection. In: 2005 IEEE Computer Society Conference on Computer Vision and Pattern Recognition (CVPR 2005), vol. 1, pp. 886–893. IEEE (2005)

12. Ojala, T., Pietikainen, M., Maenpaa, T.: Multiresolution gray-scale and rotation invariant texture classification with local binary patterns. IEEE Trans. Pattern Anal. Mach. Intell. **24**(7), 971–987 (2002)

13. Turk, M.A., Pentland, A.P.: Face recognition using eigenfaces. In: IEEE Computer Society Conference on Computer Vision and Pattern Recognition, Proceedings CVPR 1991. IEEE, pp. 586–591 (1991)

14. Viola, P., Jones, M.J.: Robust real-time face detection. Int. J. Comput. Vis. **57**(2), 137–154 (2004)

15. Harandi, M., Sanderson, C., Shen, C., Lovell, B.C.: Dictionary learning and sparse coding on Grassmann manifolds: an extrinsic solution. In: Proceedings of the IEEE International Conference on Computer Vision, pp. 3120–3127 (2013)

16. Lyons, M.J., Akamatsu, S., Kamachi, M., Gyoba, J., Budynek, J.: The Japanese Female Facial Expression (JAFFE) Database (1998)

17. Lucey, P., Cohn, J.F., Kanade, T., Saragih, J., Ambadar, Z., Matthews, I.: The extended Cohn-Kanade dataset (CK+): a complete dataset for action unit and emotion-specified expression. In: 2010 IEEE Computer Society Conference on Computer Vision and Pattern Recognition-Workshops. IEEE, pp. 94–101 (2010)

18. Liao, C.-T., Chuang, H.-J., Duan, C.-H., Lai, S.-H.: Learning spatial weighting via quadratic programming for facial expression analysis. In: 2010 IEEE Computer Society Conference on Computer Vision and Pattern Recognition-Workshops. IEEE, pp. 86–93 (2010)

19. Oliveira, L., Mansano, M., Koerich, A., de Souza Britto Jr., A.: 2D principal component analysis for face and facial-expression recognition. Comput. Sci. Eng. **13**(3), 9–13 (2011)

20. Cheng, F., Yu, J., Xiong, H.: Facial expression recognition in Jaffe dataset based on Gaussian process classification. IEEE Trans. Neural Netw. **21**(10), 1685–1690 (2010)

21. Lubing, Z., Han, W.: Local gradient increasing pattern for facial expression recognition. In: 19th IEEE International Conference on Image Processing (ICIP) (2012)

22. Benli, K.S., Eskil, M.T.: Extraction and selection of muscle based features for facial expression recognition. In: 2014 22nd International Conference on Pattern Recognition (ICPR), pp. 1651–1656, August 2014

23. Cheon, Y., Kim, D.: Natural facial expression recognition using differential-aam and manifold learning. Pattern Recogn. **42**(7), 1340–1350 (2009)

24. Yang, P., Liu, Q., Metaxas, D.N.: Rankboost with L1 regularization for facial expression recognition and intensity estimation (2009)

25. Taheri, S., Qiu, Q., Chellappa, R.: Structure-preserving sparse decomposition for facial expression analysis. IEEE Trans. Image Process. **23**(8), 3590–3603 (2014)

Vision Based Pose Estimation of Multiple Peg-in-Hole for Robotic Assembly

Pitchandi Nagarajan[1](✉), S. Saravana Perumaal[1], and B. Yogameena[2]

[1] Department of Mechanical Engineering, Thiagarajar College of Engineering,
Madurai 625015, India
{pnmech, sspmech}@tce.edu
[2] Department of Electronics and Communication Engineering,
Thiagarajar College of Engineering, Madurai 625015, India
ymece@tce.edu

Abstract. Vision sensors are used to estimate the pose (position and orientation) of mating components in a vision assisted robotic peg-in-hole assembly which is a crucial step in aligning the mating hole-component with the corresponding moving peg-component. The accuracy of this estimation decides the performance of peg-in-hole robotic assembly with an appropriate mapping between the image and task environment using a fixed overhead camera or camera on robot arm. The wheel and hub assembly in automobile has multiple holes and pegs in their mating parts which lead to more complex pose estimation procedure. The success rate of the assembly process (without jamming) is affected by an inaccurate pose estimation which leads to lateral and/or axial misalignment between the mating components during its insertion phase. On this consideration, this work proposes a pose estimation algorithm for a multiple peg-in-hole assembly with the use of genetic algorithm based two-stage camera calibration procedure. The proposed algorithm has also been tested for its performance in estimating the pose of the multiple pegs in wheel-hub of a car. The result reveals that the proposed method estimates the pose of the pegs accurately with minimum re-projection error.

Keywords: Pose estimation · Multiple peg-in-hole · Camera calibration · Genetic algorithm · Robot assembly

1 Introduction

Vision sensors are the predominantly used sensors in a robotic assembly system to align, manipulate and assemble the mating component in the robot end-effector with the other mating part of the assembly. The feedback of the vision sensor is used to sense the dynamic mating component in working environment and to improve the alignment of mating components. An assembly has two components: (a) protruded part on the component often termed as peg and (b) hollow part on the mating component named as hole. Often the assembly task is horizontal or vertical insertion of peg component into the hole component to establish a permanent contact. The wheel and wheel-hub assembly of an automobile has multiple pegs and multiple-holes. In these assemblies, the wheel-hub is fixed with the automobile and the hole component (wheel)

© Springer International Publishing AG 2017
S. Mukherjee et al. (Eds.): ICVGIP 2016, LNCS 10481, pp. 50–62, 2017.
https://doi.org/10.1007/978-3-319-68124-5_5

is inserted over the multiple pegs. The success rate of the assembly without jamming or wedging is affected by the presence of lateral or angular misalignment of the components. The precision and speed of alignment is influenced by the estimation of position and orientation (pose) of the multiple-peg component [4].

The process of controlling the robotic manipulators using the feedback of the vision sensors is named as Visual servoing. Main shortcomings of a visual servoing system are poor accuracy as well as stability, due to even small pose estimation error [2], and retaining the considered object always in the field of view [3]. Pose of the object cannot be accurately estimated due to non-trackability of the object, roughly calibrated camera and error in 3D model of the target [9].

An object tracking or recognition system depends on the efficiency of the feature extraction system for faster and accurate position estimation in pixel coordinates. Scale Invariant Feature Transform (SIFT) [6, 13] and Speed Up Robust Feature (SURF) [1] are commonly adopted to extract the target features from the video frames. Based on the geometrical features of the object, few researchers [10, 18] have used morphological image processing operations like boundary extraction and gradient operations like edge detection, circle detection, ellipse detection algorithms for feature tracking. The object of interest in this work is a wheel-hub which has four pegs (cylindrical rods) and screws on its surface. These features make the feature tracking based on gradient operations adaptable in this work.

Camera calibration is the process of determining the relationship between real world (metric) information and the 2D image information [19]. The properties of the camera used (intrinsic parameters) for acquisition and parameter set describing the geometric relation between the Cartesian world space coordinate system and the image coordinate system (extrinsic parameters) are determined using this calibration techniques. The presence of the lens distortion in the camera displaces the coordinates non-linearly. The distortion in the lenses is due to the errors in assembly of lens and the geometric features of the lens [15]. Various distortions like radial, tangential and thin prism distortion are possible in images [16]. Radial distortion is common in machine vision cameras which causes pincushion and barrel effect on the images [15]. Direct linear Transformation (DLT) of camera parameters lack the capability to incorporate non-linear distortion in the camera model. Therefore, direct non-linear transformation or two-stage camera calibration [5, 14, 17] is advantageous to include distortion and estimate the camera parameters. The performance of the direct non-linear transformation requires precise initial guess which is crucial. This makes the two-stage camera calibration technique suitable for the proposed work. Hence, a genetic algorithm based two stage camera calibration is adopted in this work.

On the consideration of above said issues, this work is aimed at developing an accurate pose estimation algorithm for determining the pose of the multiple pegs with minimum re-projection errors. This paper is organized as follows: Sect. 2 presents the vision assisted multiple peg-in-hole robot assembly environment, Sect. 3 explains the proposed pose estimation algorithm, Sect. 4 depicts the experimentation of the proposed calibration and pose estimation algorithm, Sect. 5 presents the results and discussion of the performance of the proposed work and Sect. 6 provides the conclusion of this work.

2 Vision Assisted Multiple Peg-in-Hole Robot Assembly Environment

Vision sensors are used to perceive the changes in the assembly environment and to control the manipulator in performing the assembly operation in accordance to the changes. Figure 1, shows a vision assisted robotic assembly environment considered in this work to perform a multiple peg-in-hole assembly. In the considered environment, the multiple-peg component is mounted on a shaft which rotates about its center axis. The camera (vision sensor) is mounted at a fixed position in the robotic assembly environment such that the multiple-peg components lie in the field of view of the camera at all instances. The camera and the peg-component are mounted such that the optical axis of the camera and the z-axis of the component lies in the same plane. Hence, the distance between the peg component and the camera remains same because only rotation about the z-axis is allowed. Since the distance remains same, monocular camera is sufficient and adopted in this work to estimate the coordinates of the peg centers. The robotic manipulator has the mating multiple-hole component in its end-effector. In order to assemble the mating components, the co-ordinate frames of the hole and peg components have to be aligned and then the insertion task has to be executed. Pose of the multiple-peg component $^{C}T_{P}$ is required to align the manipulator with axes of the mating components. $^{C}T_{E}$ represents the transformation matrix of end effector with respect to camera. The current pose of the end-effector with respect to the robot base is given as:

$$^{R}T_{E} = {}^{R}T_{C}{}^{C}T_{P}{}^{P}T_{E} \tag{1}$$

Where,

$^{R}T_{C}$ is the pose of the camera with respect to robot base (known).
$^{C}T_{P}$ denotes the pose of the multiple-peg part in the table with respect to the camera in the current position.

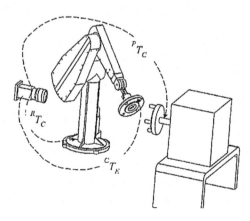

Fig. 1. Vision assisted multiple peg-in-hole robotic assembly environment

^PT_E represents the pose of the end-effector with respect to the hole part in the current frame and is given by (2)

$$^PT_E = \left[^CT_P\right]^{-1}{}^CT_E \tag{2}$$

In visual servoing, ^CT_P is computed through pose estimation algorithm and compared with the target $^CT_P^*$ at every instant to minimize the error and to generate the ^RT_E for robot manipulation. Precise camera calibration procedure is required to compute the ^CT_P accurately in the Cartesian space which enables the accurate alignment of mating components.

3 Proposed Pose Estimation Algorithm

The proposed pose estimation algorithm is divided into two modules: position estimation module and orientation estimation module. In the position estimation module, the multiple-pegs are tracked and the pixel coordinates of the wheel-hub and the peg centers are estimated using the feedback from the monocular camera. The pixel coordinates are fed to genetic algorithm based camera calibration to estimate the camera parameters and the position of centers in metric coordinates. Using the position of the centers in metric, the orientation estimation module estimates the pose of the wheel-hub with respect to the camera. Figure 2, shows the overview of the proposed pose estimation algorithm.

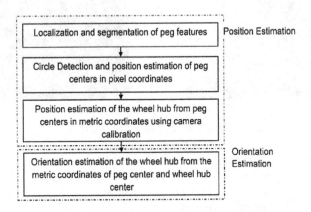

Fig. 2. Overview of the proposed pose estimation algorithm

3.1 Position Estimation Module

The wheel-hub used in this work has four pegs. Determining the centers of each peg gives the position of the wheel-hub in pixels at tracking stage followed by metric position in calibration stage.

Multiple-pegs Tracking. In this module, each peg on the wheel-hub is tracked using the monocular camera frames. Since the top surface of the pegs and the component base area of the wheel-hub are at different planes, there is a significant change in their intensity values. This intensity difference aids segmenting the pegs from the background by estimating a global threshold value using the Otsu's thresholding method. The segmentation process replaces all pixels in the input image with intensity greater than threshold value by 1 (white) and replaces all other pixels with 0 (black). Pegs are having higher intensity than the component base of the wheel-hub and hence they are shown as 'white' in Fig. 3. Further, the noise present in the binary image after the segmentation process is removed by area based filtering. An 8-connectivity neighborhood is used to create the connected components in the binary image. The area properties of the connected components are calculated. The areas of interest are the pegs and the wheel-hub center hole and the screw portion area. The area of the noise components present in the image are comparatively lesser than the area of screw. Hence the connected components with the area property less than that of the screw area are removed on this filtering. In case of noise components with higher area, they are removed in the circle detection stage as they are non-circular objects.

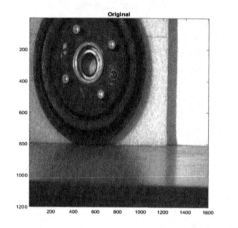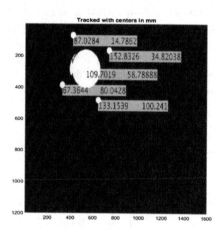

Fig. 3. Tracked peg and wheel-hub center

The circles in the segmented image are identified by a two stage Circular Hough Transform (CHT) method [11]. In this CHT, a circle is drawn for each edge point with a radius 'r'. This method adopts an (3D) accumulator array computation technique in which the first two dimensions represent the coordinates of the circle and the last specify the radii. The values in the accumulator (array) are increased every time whenever a circle is drawn with the desired radii over every edge point. The accumulator, which keeps count of the circles passing through coordinates of each edge point, and makes a vote to find the highest count. The coordinates of the center of the circles in the images are the coordinates with the highest count. The details pertaining on this method related to matlab function is cited in reference [11]. There are four pegs in the wheel-hub and two screws present between the pegs labelled 1&4 and pegs 2&3. Taking the first screw as reference, the first peg could be labeled as 1 and other pegs are labelled sequentially in anticlockwise direction. Figure 3, shows the pegs detected in a frame using the multiple-peg tracking module.

Genetic Algorithm Based Camera Calibration. The estimated coordinates in pixel values are to be converted to metric coordinates to calculate the pose of the multiple-peg object in Cartesian space. The precise calculation of the 3D coordinates and pose of the object depends on the accuracy of the calibration procedure. In this regard, a genetic algorithm based two-stage camera calibration procedure is adapted in this work. In the first stage, a linear solution is computed by considering distortion-free camera model and in the second stage, genetic algorithm is used to compute the optimal camera parameters including distortion by using the closed form solution as an initial guess [12].

A pin-hole model with lens distortion as shown in Fig. 4, is adopted in this work. Considering (X_w, Y_w, Z_w) as the 3D world coordinate system, and (X_c, Y_c, Z_c) as camera coordinate system, (X_i, Y_i) represents the image coordinate system. Further, O_i and O_c represent the center of the image coordinate system and the optical center of the camera coordinate system, respectively. O_i and O_c are collinear and aligned with the Z_c axis of the camera coordinate system. (x_i, y_i) be the image coordinates measured through any point extraction algorithm. Let P be the test point (x_w, y_w, z_w) as the world coordinate and (x_u, y_u) be the estimated undistorted image coordinate (x_c, y_c, z_c) point. Focal length i.e. the distance between the image plane and the camera plane is denoted as f.

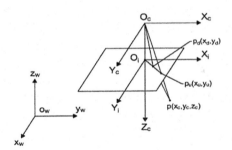

Fig. 4. Complete camera model with radial distortion

On considering the radial distortion, the image coordinate (x_u, y_u) of the distortion-free model is subtracted with the distortion factor D_x to estimate the distorted image coordinate (x_d, y_d). The distortion is modelled as a second order polynomial [15].

$$x_d + D_x = x_u$$
$$y_d + D_y = y_u \tag{3}$$

$$D_x = x_d(k_1 r^2)$$
$$D_y = y_d(k_1 r^2)$$
$$r = \sqrt{x_d^2 + y_d^2}$$

k_1 is the distortion coefficient.

The distorted image coordinates (x_d, y_d) are transformed to computer image coordinates (x_f, y_f) by multiplying with the uncertainty scaling factor and by adding the center of the frame. In the first stage, a linear approximation method as described by Tsai [7, 15] is used to determine the camera parameters by considering a distortion-free camera model which forms the bounds for the second nonlinear genetic algorithm stage.

Genetic Algorithm is adopted to identify the optimal intrinsic and extrinsic parameters of the camera incorporating the radial distortion in the camera model. Linear approximation stage estimates the rotation matrix, translation vector in x and y direction. Therefore, the proposed GA has focal length and translation about z-axis as the genes in the chromosome which enables the proposed method to have faster convergence to optimal results. P_1 represents the initial population of the 1st generation, f and T_z represent the genes (parameters) present in a chromosome, j represents the chromosomes in the population of a generation, k represents the generations and n & m are the number of chromosomes in the population and number of generations, respectively. The initial population for the genetic algorithm is

$$\left(f^j\right)_k = f_{linear}; \forall \ 1 \leq j \leq n \text{ and } k = 1$$

$$\left(T_z^j\right)_k = T_{zlinear}; \forall \ 1 \leq j \leq n \text{ and } k = 1$$

$$\left(q^j\right)_k = \left\{ \left(f^j\right)_k, \left(T_z^j\right)_k \right\} \forall \ 1 \leq j \leq n \text{ and } k = 1$$

$$P_1 = \left(q_i^j\right)_1 \tag{4}$$

where $f_{linearr}$, $T_{linearr}$ are the focal length and translation about z-axis estimated in first stage. The bounds on the parameters f and T_z are taken as $\pm 25\%$ of the linearly estimated values (stage 1 results).

$$\left(q_{1 \ bound}^j\right)_k = f_{linear} \pm \left(0.25^* f_{linear}\right)$$

$$\left(q_{2 \ bound}^j\right)_k = T_{zlinear} \pm \left(0.25^* T_{zlinear}\right)$$

$$\left(q_{max}^j\right)_k = \{f_{max}, T_{zmax}\} \ \forall \ 1 \leq j \leq n \text{ and } 1 \leq k \leq m$$
$$\left(q_{min}^j\right)_k = \{f_{min}, T_{zmin}\} \ \forall \ 1 \leq j \leq n \text{ and } 1 \leq k \leq m \tag{5}$$

As lens distortion is considered in this camera model, the distortion coefficient k_1 for each chromosome is calculated as:

$$\left(k_1^j\right)_k = \frac{C_3(f^j)_k}{C_1\left(C_2 + \left(T_z^j\right)_k\right)} - \frac{C_4}{C_1} \ \forall \ 1 \leq j \leq n \text{ and } 1 \leq k \leq m \tag{6}$$

$$c_1 = d_y y_i r^2$$

$$c_2 = r_7 x_w + r_8 y_w$$

$$c_3 = r_4 x_w + r_5 y_w + T_y$$

$$c_4 = d'_y y_i \text{ and } r = \sqrt{x_d^2 + y_d^2}$$

The variation between the actual image coordinates and the calculated coordinates using the estimated camera parameters is termed as re-projection error [8] which is the common performance measure of any camera calibration technique.

$$E_{rms} = \frac{1}{n} \sum_{l=1}^{n} \sqrt{(x_f - x_i)^2 + (y_f - y_i)^2} \qquad (7)$$

Hence the objective of this proposed genetic algorithm based calibration technique is to determine the optimal values of f and T_z for minimum re-projection error (E_{rms}).

$$\left(q^j\right)^*_k = \min(E_{rms}) \qquad (8)$$

Subject to $f_{min} \leq f^* \leq f_{max}$ and $T_{zmin} \leq T_z^* \leq T_{zmax}$

GA Operators. The convergence of a genetic algorithm depends on the selection of the mutation and cross over operators employed in the algorithm. The genes are encoded as real numbers to have understanding in the computation. The best chromosomes among the population are selected for reproduction using the proportionate reproduction method. Crossover operation creates new children in the population. The off-springs of the crossover operation have better fitness than the parent chromosomes. Even though if bad off-springs are created in the crossover phase, they will be eliminated by the subsequent reproduction phase in the next generation and thus off springs with better fitness than their parents are retained in the subsequent generation. A blend over crossover operation is adopted in this work, since they prevent the algorithm from getting trapped in the local optimal solution.

Two parents from the initial population $(q_i^j)_k$ and $\left(q_i^{j+1}\right)_k$ are selected and the off-springs $(o1_i^j)_k$ and $(o2_i^j)_k$ are generated by

$$(o1_i^j)_k = \left(\min\left((q_i^j)_k, \left(q_i^{j+1}\right)_k \right) \right) - \alpha \left((q_i^j)_k - \left(q_i^{j+1}\right)_k \right)$$

$$(o2_i^j)_k = \left(\max\left((q_i^j)_k, \left(q_i^{j+1}\right)_k \right) \right) + \alpha \left((q_i^j)_k - \left(q_i^{j+1}\right)_k \right)$$

$$(q^{j})_{k+1} = \left((o2_i^j)_k - (o1_i^j)_k \right) * rand + (o1_i^j)_k \qquad (9)$$

where $i = 1, 2, j = 1, 2, \ldots n$ and $k = 1, 2, \ldots m$ and the value of α is taken as 0.75.

Mutation operation increases the diversity in the population which improves the convergence to global optimal solution. A power mutation operator is adopted in this work using the following expressions.

$$\left(q_i^j\right)_{k+1} = \begin{cases} \left(q_i^j\right)_k - s\left(\left(q_i^j\right)_k - \left(q_{i\,min}^j\right)_k\right) & \text{if } u < r \\ \left(q_i^j\right)_k - s\left(\left(q_{i\,max}^j\right)_k - \left(q_i^j\right)_k\right) & \text{if } u \geq r \end{cases} \tag{10}$$

Where $u = \left(\left(q_i^j\right)_k - \left(q_{i\,min}^j\right)_k\right) \Big/ \left(q_{i\,max}^j\right)_k - \left(\left(q_{i\,min}^j\right)_k\right)$ and r is a uniformly distributed random value between 0 and 1.

$$s = p^* s_r^{p-1}, \quad 0 \leq s_r \leq 1$$

Where p is the index of distribution and s_r is a uniform distributed random number between 0 and 1.

3.2 Orientation Estimation

After obtaining the image coordinates of the centers of pegs from tracking stage and the camera parameters from calibration stage, the metric coordinates of each pegs are determined. The wheel-hub is allowed to rotate about z-axis and/or to translate along x-axis only by constraining the translation along z-axis and rotation about X&Y axes. The linear displacement along x-axis (position of the peg) is estimated using the metric information of the peg centers. The orientation of the wheel-hub about z-axis is estimated by calculating the angle between the line1 connecting the peg1 center and wheel-hub center, and the horizontal line (line2) passing through wheel hub center as shown in Fig. 5 and (11).

$$\tan \theta = \left[\frac{m_1 - m_2}{1 + (m_1 \circ m_2)} \right] \tag{11}$$

m_1, m_2 are the slopes of the line1 and line2 respectively.

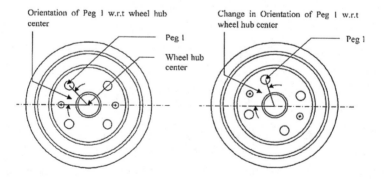

Fig. 5. Orientation estimation from the peg1 center and wheel-hub center

4 Experimental Arrangement

This section explains the experiments performed with the wheel-hub to evaluate the performance of the proposed pose estimation algorithm in terms of its accuracy. The experimental environment has the target object wheel-hub placed at a distance of 0.27 m from a fixed camera. DNV 3001 CCD camera with f50 lens is used to capture the wheel-hub images in this experiment at 10 fps. As discussed, the accuracy of the pose estimation algorithm is influenced by the accuracy of the camera calibration procedure and the feature tracking procedure. To ensure the performance of the proposed camera calibration procedure and to estimate the camera parameters, the algorithm is tested with the checker board images placed at the same location of the wheel-hub. The chess board pattern of 6 × 8 corner points with an interval of 29 mm is captured from five various orientations at an image resolution of 1600 × 1200 with the DNV camera. The camera parameters estimated by the proposed work is listed in Table 1. The image coordinates of the peg centers and the metric coordinates after the camera calibration are listed in Table 2. The accuracy of the pose estimated could be ensured only when the pose is fed to the manipulator to align the end-effector with respect to the object. In order to ensure the performance of the proposed pose estimation algorithm, the accuracy of tracking module is tested by comparing the metric values of radii of pegs at each instant with their corresponding true values.

Table 1. Camera parameters estimated by proposed work

Stages	Focal length f(mm)	Translation T_z	Rotation matrix $[R]$			Distortion coefficient k_1 (pixel^{-2})
Linear (stage1)	54.74	$\begin{bmatrix} -945.2 \\ 663.51 \\ 308.52 \end{bmatrix}$	$\begin{bmatrix} 0.999 & 0.004 & 0.034 \\ -0.011 & 0.979 & 0.203 \\ -0.032 & -0.203 & 0.978 \end{bmatrix}$			0
Genetic algorithm (stage2)	47.95	$\begin{bmatrix} -945.2 \\ 663.51 \\ 267.38 \end{bmatrix}$	$\begin{bmatrix} 0.999 & 0.004 & 0.034 \\ -0.011 & 0.979 & 0.203 \\ -0.032 & -0.203 & 0.978 \end{bmatrix}$			1.097 E−5

Table 2. Image and metric coordinates of pegs at frame 1

Peg no.	Image coordinates (Pixels)	Metric coordinates (mm)
1	(140.064, 127.673)	(28.993, 26.428)
2	(470.513, 93.238)	(97.396, 19.300)
3	(506.212, 421.383)	(104.785, 87.226)
4	(175.285, 456.696)	(36.284, 94.536)

5   Results and Discussion

Each peg's center in pixels is estimated using the multiple-peg tracking and the camera parameters from the genetic algorithm based camera calibration technique. The metric coordinates of the centers are obtained from the estimated camera parameters. The results of our proposed calibration algorithm are compared with Zhang's (2001) camera calibration algorithm based matlab camera calibration toolbox. The obtained root mean square re-projection error of toolbox is 0.37 pixels whereas that of the proposed algorithm is 0.0310 pixels. The results also show that our proposed algorithm has better accuracy in estimating the camera parameters than the matlab calibration toolbox which in turn ensures minimum pose estimation error. It is evident from Fig. 6, that 57% of re-projected points has less than 0.03 pixel distance error which proves the measurement accuracy of the proposed calibration technique. It is observed from Fig. 7, that the proposed method is able to estimate a point and re-project a point within an error range of 0.5 pixels. Table 3 represents the mean and standard deviation of the error between the true value and the estimated metric value of the radius of peg1 for specific interval of frames. The tracking and calibration stages of the proposed pose estimation technique are capable to estimate the pose within an error range of less than 1 mm.

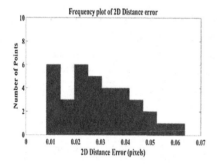

Fig. 6. Frequency plot of 2D measurement error for checkerboard calibration.

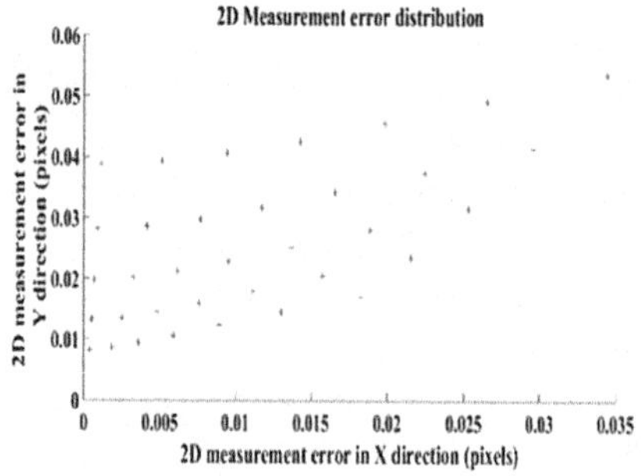

Fig. 7. 2D measurement error distribution for checkerboard calibration.

Table 3. Mean and standard deviation of the errors between true and estimated radius of peg1

Frame range	True metric value of peg-1 (mm)	Mean error	Standard deviation
1–10	10.1	0.677	0.689
11–20	10.1	0.206	0.333
21–30	10.1	−0.171	0.259
31–45	10.1	−0.431	0.463

6 Conclusion

Vision sensors offer flexibility in perceiving the multiple hole component in a dynamic environment. Pose of the mating components in an assembly are determined using the feedback of vision sensor. The successful attainment of assembly action is influenced by the accuracy of estimated pose of the hole component and alignment between each peg and the corresponding hole in the wheel-hub. In this regard, a pose estimation algorithm has been proposed to determine the position and orientation of the multiple-pegs in the wheel-hub. Each peg in the wheel-hub is tracked for its center using the circle detection algorithm. With the use of pixel coordinates of tracked centers the position of the pegs with respect to the camera in metric values are determined by a two-stage genetic algorithm based camera calibration technique. The change in orientation is also obtained by calculating the angle of line connecting the centers of peg and wheel-hub, with the horizontal axis. The proposed pose estimation algorithm is experimented to validate its performance in terms of accuracy. Experimental results show that the calibration technique used in the proposed pose estimation algorithm has capability to re-project the peg with an accuracy of 0.0310 pixels. Besides, the proposed algorithm is suitable for a vision assisted robot assembly system with the positioning accuracy of 1 mm.

References

1. Bay, H., Tuytelaars, T., Van Gool, L.: SURF: speeded up robust features. In: Leonardis, A., Bischof, H., Pinz, A. (eds.) ECCV 2006. LNCS, vol. 3951, pp. 404–417. Springer, Heidelberg (2006). doi:10.1007/11744023_32
2. Chaumette, F., Hutchinson, S.: Visual servo control part I: basic approaches. IEEE Robot. Autom. Mag. **13**, 82–90 (2006)
3. Chaumette, F.: Potential problems of stability and convergence in image based and position based visual servoing. In: Kriegman, D.J., Hager, G.D., Morse, A.S. (eds.) The Confluence of Vision and Control. LNCIS, vol. 237, pp. 66–78. Springer, London (1998). doi:10.1007/BFb0109663
4. Dong, G., Zhu, Z.: Position based visual servo control of autonomous robotic manipulators. Acta Astronaut. **115**, 291–302 (2015)
5. Ji, Q., Zhang, Y.: Camera calibration with genetic algorithms. IEEE Trans. Syst. Man. Cybern. Part A: Syst. Hum. **31**, 120–130 (2001)
6. Lee, S., Kim, E., Park, Y.: 3D object recognition using multiple features for robotic manipulation. In: Proceedings of IEEE International Conference on Robotics and Automation, USA, pp. 3768–3774 (2006)
7. Lenz, R., Tsai, R.: Techniques for calibration of the scale factor and image center for high accuracy 3D machine vision metrology. In: Proceedings of IEEE International Conference on Robotics and Automation, pp. 68–75 (1987)
8. Li, W., Gee, T., Friedrich, H., Delmas, P.: A practical comparison between Zhang's and Tsai's calibration approaches. In: Proceedings of International Conference on Image and Vision Computing (IVCNZ), New Zealand, pp. 166–171, November 2014
9. Mallis, E.: Survey of vision based robot control. In: Proceedings of European Naval Ship Design, Captain Computer IV Forum, Brest, France, pp. 1–16 (2002)

10. Marchand, E., Boutherny, P., Chaumette, F., Moreau, V.: Robust real time visual tracking using a 2D-3D model based approach. In: Proceedings of the 1999 IEEE International Conference on Computer Vision, pp. 262–268 (1999)
11. Mathworks Circle Detection Algorithm, June 2016. http://in.mathworks.com/help/images/examples/detect-and-measure-circular-objects-in-an-image.htmlaccessed
12. Nagarajan, P., Saravana Perumaal, S.: GA based camera calibration for vision assisted robotic assembly system. IET Comput. Vision (2016). doi:10.1049/iet-cvi.2016.0004
13. Song, K.T., Chang, C.H.: Object pose estimation for grasping based on robust center point detection. In: proceedings of 8th Asian Control Conference, Taiwan , pp. 305–310 (2011)
14. Song, X., Yang, B., Feng, Z., et al.: Camera calibration based on particle swarm optimization. In: Proceedings of IEEE International Conference on Image and Signal Processing, Tianjin, pp. 1–5 (2009)
15. Tsai, R.: A versatile camera calibration technique for high accuracy 3D machine vision metrology using off the shelf TV cameras and Lenses. IEEE J. Robot. Autom. 3(4), 323–344 (1987)
16. Weng, J., Cohen, P., Herniou, M.: Camera calibration with distortion models and accuracy evaluation. IEEE Trans. Pattern Anal. Mach. Intell. 14, 965–980 (1992)
17. Yang, Z., Chen, F., Zhao, J., et al.: A novel camera calibration method based on genetic algorithm. IEEE Conference on Industrial Electronics and Applications, Singapore, pp. 2222–2227, June 2008
18. Youngrock, Y., DeSouza, G.N., Avinash Kak, C.: Real-time tracking and pose estimation for Industrial objects using geometric features. In: Proceedings of IEEE International Conference on Robotics and Automation, Taiwan, pp. 3473–3478 (2003)
19. Zhang, Z.: A flexible new technique for camera calibration. IEEE Trans. Pattern Anal. Mach. Intell. 22, 1330–1334 (2000)

A Spatio Temporal Texture Saliency Approach for Object Detection in Videos

A. Sasithradevi[(✉)], S. Mohamed Mansoor Roomi, and I. Sanofer

Thiagrajar College of Engineering, Madurai, Tamilnadu, India
devisasithra@gmail.com, smmroomi@gmail.com,
sanofer@gmail.com

Abstract. Detecting what attracts human attention is one of the vital tasks for visual processing. Saliency detection finds out the location of foci of attention on an outstanding object in image/video sequences. However, temporal information in videos play major role in human visual perception in locating salient objects. This paper presents a novel approach to detect salient object in a video using spatio-temporal textural saliency which also includes temporal information, an important aspect in videos. In this work, the context driven static saliency extracted from Lab color space in XY plane is combined with the local phase quantization on three orthogonal planes (LPQ-TOP) driven dynamic saliency to detect the spatio-temporal saliency in videos. The dynamic saliency is obtained by fusing two temporal saliencies extracted from XT-plane and YT-plane using LPQ texture feature, which extracts the temporal salient region. This approach is evaluated on Benchmark dataset and the result shows that the proposed saliency approach yields promising performance.

Keywords: Local phase quantization · Orthogonal plane · Spatio-temporal saliency · Static saliency · Dynamic saliency

1 Introduction

The huge volume of video data highly needs the simplification of the tasks involved in video processing by first identifying the salient region of interest. The salient object detection from image and video acts as an interesting and challenging work, since it gives saliency map that highlights the object of interest and suppresses the background. Such salient object detection is an essential step in applications like video retrieval, video analysis, video summarization, video annotation and adaptive image and video compression.

The mechanism of Human Visual system's ability to identify salient region in visual scene has been resembled with many models in the recent years. Gray [1] proposed an algorithm that assumes the object of interest to be large in size and to be in motion for a considerable period of time under slowly varying or constant motion parameter. The approach used in [2] integrates both patch level and region level abstractions in a unified way. The spatial saliency has been obtained by estimating color contrast cue and color distribution cue. The patch level motion abstraction extracts optical flow of a video frame that supports temporal saliency then both are

© Springer International Publishing AG 2017
S. Mukherjee et al. (Eds.): ICVGIP 2016, LNCS 10481, pp. 63–74, 2017.
https://doi.org/10.1007/978-3-319-68124-5_6

integrated to obtain spatio-temporal saliency. In [3], Hyper complex Fourier Transform is applied to the current video frame to obtain static salient region, then three frame difference algorithm is used to extract motion salient region and both are combined with dynamic fusion strategy. The work proposed in [4] expresses the object detection in video as an optimal salient path discovery problem. In this method, Instead of detecting salient object in individual frames separately, the salient object of interest is detected and tracked simultaneously by computing the spatio-temporal path having the maximum saliency density in the video. Mahapatra [5] proposed a method that use spatio-temporal coherency information for segmenting the salient object in video. The spatial coherency map gives the regular object region but the temporal coherency map gives the high coherent motion region, then both are fused to obtain salient object. The method suggested in [6] uses Gestalt theory and creates encoding vectors to estimate the feature channel joint distribution. It gives local saliency scores by using integral histograms and the salient regions of different sizes can be preserved by applying figure-ground segregation on individual scales. An exhaustive survey on saliency detection is done in [7] which compares the existing salient object detection approaches and evaluates their pros and cons. It suggests that the integration of more sophisticated techniques enhance accuracy. Muthuswamy [8] proposes a method to find salient object using particle filters, which are guided by spatio-temporal saliencies and color feature. It generates spatial and motion saliencies by comparing local feature with dominant feature in frame. A hierarchy associated rich feature (HARF) construction frame work is proposed in [9], which works based on integrating the elementary features from multilevel regions in hierarchy. These elementary features can be enriched by incorporating multi-layered deep learning features. Regional Saliency scores are predicted based on HARF representation using a boosted predictor. In [10], salient object is detected using eigenvalue analysis of a graph Laplacian which is defined over color similarity in image superpixels with the assumption that the most of the image boundary pixel are covered by non-salient background. It yields a continuously-valued solution to salient foreground detection and segmentation using Fiedler vector. Even though there exists few studies on the use of visual saliency in video, accounting temporal nature of the video is still an issue. Hence, in this work, salient object detection on videos using spatio-temporal Local Phase Quantization (LPQ) [18] is addressed. As illustrated in Fig. 1, a video data can be partitioned into three orthogonal planes viz, XY plane, XT plane and YT plane along spatial and temporal axis. The spatial (S_{XY}) saliency is determined using context aware saliency in XY plane and temporal saliencies (T_{XT} and T_{YT}) are computed by Temporal-LPQ features along XT and YT planes. Finally, S_{XY}, T_{XT} and T_{YT} are fused together using Dynamic Fusion strategy to obtain the final saliency map for the video data.

The main contributions of this work are:

- Modeling saliency of dynamic scenes with temporal LPQ texture features.
- Extracting temporal saliency by applying center surround technique and deriving dynamic saliency by fusing the temporal LPQ textures using statistical strategy.
- Computing spatial saliency using context saliency features and to attain the final Spatio temporal saliency by fusing the spatial and dynamic saliencies.

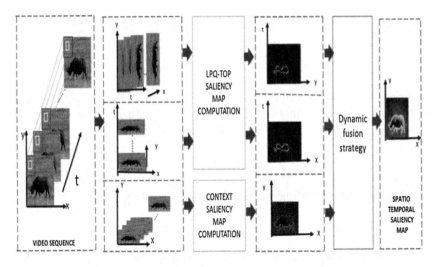

Fig. 1. Proposed spatio-temporal saliency approach

Organization of this paper, in nutshell: Sect. 2 briefly describes the Local Phase Quantization (LPQ). The proposed spatiotemporal saliency approach is presented in Sect. 3. Section 4 validates the proposed algorithm's ability and Sect. 5 concludes this saliency detection work.

2   Local Phase Quantization

The local phase quantization [18] is based on the Fourier phase computed at every pixel position on a local window. The details of the local phase have been computed using Short Time Fourier transform (STFT) at each pixel position 'i' of an image/frame over the neighborhood 'N_i' is given by:

$$X(w, i) = \sum_{k \in N_i} x(i - k) e^{-j2\pi w^T k} = w_v^T x_i. \tag{1}$$

where 'w_v' is the kernel vector of the 2D-Discrete Fourier transform at v^{th} frequency and 'x_i' is the vector of neighborhood 'N_i'. From (1), it is evident that STFT of an image/frame can be computed using convolution operation. The separable property of kernel functions makes the computation of STFT simpler by convolving the rows and columns consecutively. The complex coefficients used in LPQ computation are: $v_1 = [a, 0]^T$, $v_2 = [0, a]^T$, $v_3 = [a, a]^T$, $v_4 = [a, -a]^T$ where 'a' is the scalar frequency. Employing these kernel vectors, the frequency response is given by

$$X_i^c = [X(v_1, i), X(v_2, i), X(v_3, i), X(v_4, i)]. \tag{2}$$

$$X_i = [\text{Re}\{X_i^c\}, \text{Im}\{X_i^c\}]^T. \tag{3}$$

Considering the real and imaginary parts of the complex coefficients, the transformation matrix is:

$$W = [\text{Re}\{w_{v_1}, w_{v2}, w_{v_3}, w_{v_4}\}, \text{Im}\{w_{v_1}, w_{v2}, w_{v_3}, w_{v_4}\}]^T. \tag{4}$$

Assuming the frame as a function of first order Markov process, 'ρ' as the correlation coefficient between adjacent pixels and 'σ_2' as the variance of each sample, the covariance between pixel positions 'x_i' and 'x_j' is given by

$$\sigma_{ij} = \rho^{\|x_i - x_j\|}. \tag{5}$$

The covariance matrix of the kernel matrix is obtained by,

$$\boldsymbol{D} = \boldsymbol{WCW}^{\mathrm{T}}. \tag{6}$$

where 'C' is the covariance matrix of the samples in neighborhood. The Singular Value Decomposition (SVD) of the covariance matrix 'D' is

$$D = U \sum V^T. \tag{7}$$

The G_i is computed at all positions as $G_i = V_{X_i}^T$ and quantized as

$$q_j = \begin{cases} 1, & g_j \geq 0 \\ 0, & \text{otherwise} \end{cases} \tag{8}$$

where 'g_j' is the jth component of G_i. The binary coefficients 'q_j' are represented between 0 and 255 using,

$$B = \sum_{k=1}^{8} q_k 2^{k-1} \tag{9}$$

The histogram of B at all positions of the image is used as 256 dimensional feature vector.

3   Proposed Saliency Approach

The proposed method is based on the modeling of dynamic scenes in video using LPQ in three orthogonal planes (TOP) and the spatial saliency computed using center surround mechanism. The final Spatio temporal saliency is computed by fusing the color saliency in XY plane with the temporal saliency computed by LPQ-TOP as shown in Fig. 1.

3.1   Dynamic Attention Modelling by LPQ-TOP

Dynamic textures can model varying complex scenes with time like waving trees, snow, fog and waterfall. In this work, the LPQ-TOP approach, which is an extension of LPQ that combines both motion and static features, is applied. It has been used in various applications like expression recognitions [12] and action unit detection [13]. The LPQ-TOP models the dynamic information in videos by extending the conventional LPQ in two directions in addition to XY viz. XT and YT planes. LPQ-XT and LPQ-YT provide varying textural information across space-time transition, whereas LPQ-XY provides the static information about the appearance texture of the objects in the spatial domain. The common intersection of these three planes is the center pixel, hence the each pixel in a video clip is modeled by LPQ-TOP by considering the phase distribution in each plane separately.

3.2   Center Surround Saliency Detection

Center Surround (CS) [19] mechanism relates the visual stimuli of the center region with the visual stimuli of the surrounding region by comparing the feature distributions in both regions using distance measure. The center region 'r_c' enclosed by the surrounding region 'r_s', both centered at pixel location as (i_c, j_c) is used to extract the LPQ feature distribution as histograms 'H_c' and 'H_s' in the center and surrounding region respectively. The saliency value of the pixel at center $P = (r_c, r_s)$ is computed by the Chi-square dissimilarity value as:

$$Sal(p) = \sum_k \frac{(H_c(k) - H_s(k))^2}{(H_c(k) + H_s(k)/2)}. \tag{10}$$

where 'k' denotes the number of bins in the histogram. The saliency computed separately on the three planes using center surround mechanism. These three saliencies are combined using dynamic fusion strategy [14]. The dynamic fusion strategy weights the saliencies to combine them by the ratio of their statistical mean. Thus the motion saliency is obtained by fusing the saliency in XT and YT plane using the dynamic fusion. Likewise, the spatial/appearance saliency is combined with motion/temporal saliency to derive the LPQ-TOP based Spatio-temporal saliency.

3.3   Proposed Saliency Computation

The performance of the proposed approach is compared with contrast based LPQ-TOP, LPQ-TOP (only), and the phase discrepancy method. As shown in Table 1, the performance of LPQ-TOP saliency is not satisfactory. The poor performance is due to the absence of color feature in computing the spatial saliency. Hence, the contrast based saliency derived from Lab color space is used for computing the appearance saliency. In [15], the contrast of the pixels in a frame/image are weighted by providing higher

Table 1. Characteristics of videos in NTT Dataset

Video	Number of frames	Characteristics
Rhino	100	Moving object and background
Bird1	115	Waving background and moving object
Bird2	84	Waving background and fast moving object
Horse	89	Slowly moving object
Fox	101	Slowly moving object and background
Sunflower	101	Waving object
Skiing1	63	Moving object and snow background
Skiing2	83	Moving object and snow background
Airplane	72	Moving object on uniform background
Tiger	107	Moving object on complex background

values to the center of the frame, but it is not usual in any video that the salient object to be present in the center of the frame. Hence, pixel weighting is eliminated and the contrast value is computed as Euclidean distance between the frame patches. A pixel 'j' is said to be salient if and only if the mein of the patch Pj centered at pixel 'j' is different compared to all other patches in the frame. Consider $d_{ec}(P_j, P_k)$ as the Euclidean distance between the normalized Lab color space patch vectors P_j and P_k. Then the contrast difference value $C_{j,\alpha}$ of a pixel 'j' at scale 'α' is the sum of the Euclidean distance between each other pixel in its defined neighborhood along individual channels, given by:

$$C_{j,\alpha} = \sum_{z \in w} d_{ec}(p_{j,\alpha}, P_z).$$ (11)

where 'z' is the neighborhood of the pixel 'j' at scale 'α', $P_{j,\alpha}$ is the color value of the pixel at position 'j' and P_z is the color value of the pixel in its neighborhood.

The temporal saliency obtained from the dynamic texture features is combined with the contrast based spatial using dynamic fusion strategy to obtain the spatio-temporal saliency. Even though this saliency approach produces better performance than LPQ-TOP, the performance is still improved by combining the context aware spatial saliency [16] with the temporal LPQ-TOP saliency. In context aware saliency detection approach, the dissimilarity measure between two patches is

$$d(p_i, p_j) = \frac{d_{color}(p_i, p_j)}{1 + c.d_{position}(p_i, p_j)}.$$ (12)

$d_{color}(P_i, P_j)$ is the Euclidean distance between the patches and 'j' is the number of most similar patches. The value of c is chosen as three [16]. The saliency of the pixel 'i' is given by:

$$S_i^r = 1 - \exp(-\frac{1}{j}\sum_{j=1}^{J} d(p_i^r, p_j^r)). \tag{13}$$

The saliency which includes the context information:

$$S_i = \frac{1}{M}\sum s_i^r(1 - d_{foci}^r(i)). \tag{14}$$

'M' denotes the number of scales and $d_{foci}(i)$ is the positional distance between pixel i and closest foci of attention pixel. The final Spatio-temporal saliency map is the combination of spatial context aware saliency and temporal LPQ-TOP.

4 Performance Evaluation

This section demonstrates the performance of the proposed approach using LPQ-TOP features on the NTT dataset [17]. As illustrated in Table 1, the dataset consists of ten video sequences having complex background scenes like running water, waving grass and trees, fog. The performance of the proposed method is evaluated by comparing it with the saliency method using LPQ-TOP (only), LBP-TOP [20] the combination of spatial contrast-LPQTOP and saliency detection based on phased discrepancy [11]. Table 1 summarizes the visual of comparison of results obtained by different methods. The motion saliency is extracted from LPQ-TOP plane using the center surround mechanism with $r_c = 17$ and $r_s = 97$. From Table 2, it is evident that the phased discrepancy method produces poor performance compared to other techniques in comparison. Analyzing the performance of the proposed Spatio-temporal saliency approach on the test video sequence independently, bird1 sequence results show that our method produces unsatisfactory results, as the sequence is composed of highly complex background like fast waving tree branches. For the same bird1 sequence, other comparison methods also provide poor detection results than the proposed approach. Referring to the results of contrast-LPQTOP, it depicts that this method performs well along the boundaries but fails to detect the entire object. LPQ-TOP method's performance individually in detecting salient objects of the video is limited compared to its combination with color feature. Observing the results of phased discrepancy method, the method works somewhat better in Leopard sequence only.

To evaluate any segmentation algorithm, Benchmark measures are vital in validating the algorithm. Hence to validate the proposed spatio-temporal textural saliency approach, the well-known benchmark measures like Precision and Recall measures are computed as:

$$\text{Precision} = \text{tp}/(\text{tp} + \text{fp}). \tag{15}$$

$$\text{Recall} = \text{tp}/(\text{tp} + \text{fn}). \tag{16}$$

Table 2. Visual comparison of the proposed approach with [11, 20]

Original frame	Contrast+ LPQ-TOP	LPQ-TOP	PD [11]	LBP-TOP [20]	Proposed

where 'tp' is true positives, 'fp' is false positives and 'fn' is false negatives obtained from ground truth. Fewer 'fp' and misses results in high precision and recall respectively. The final saliency map for every frame in a video sequence which reflects over 6 units in temporal axis is normalized. A value of threshold is chosen between 0 and 1 to obtain the binary map in steps of 0.1. The highest precision and recall value that results in varying the threshold in each frame is averaged over the entire video data. From the experimental results shown in Figs. 2 and 3, it is clear that the proposed Spatio-temporal salient detection technique yields superior performance compared to other related techniques in [2]. Experimental results for different frames in the NTT Dataset using the proposed technique is shown in Table 3.

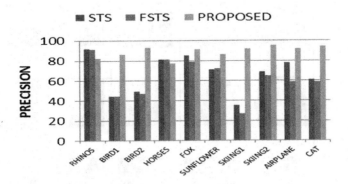

Fig. 2. Precision comparison of proposed method on NTT dataset

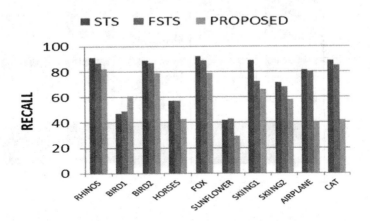

Fig. 3. Recall comparison of proposed method on NTT dataset

Table 3. Results of proposed methodology on different frames in video

Video	#10	#20	#30	#40	#50
Rhino					
Bird1					
Bird2					
Horse					
Fox					
Sun flower					
Skiing1					

5 Conclusion

In this paper, a Spatio-temporal saliency approach which combines the context aware spatial saliency and temporal LPQ-TOP saliency is presented. The spatial and temporal saliencies are computed separately for the videos. For the temporal saliency, the LPQ-TOP features in the XT and YT plane are extracted and combined using dynamic statistical fusion technique. Likewise, spatial saliency derived from the context aware saliency is fused with the motion saliency. Dynamic weighting on the individual saliencies are controlled by the statistical mean of the temporal saliencies. Experimentation on the benchmark video sequence demonstrates the effectiveness of the proposed Spatio-temporal saliency approach.

References

1. Gray, C., James, S., Collomosse, J.: A particle filtering approach to salient video object localization. In: IEEE International Conference on Image Processing, Paris, pp. 194–198 (2014)
2. Kannan, R., Ghinea, G., Swaminathan, S.: Discovering salient object from videos using spatio temporal salient region detection. Sig. Process. Image Commun. **36**, 154–178 (2015)
3. Li, H., Wang, Y., Liu, W.: Moving object detection based on HFT and dynamic fusion. In: Proceedings of the International Conference on Signal Processing, China, pp. 895–899 (2014)
4. Luo, Y., Yua, J.: Salient object detection in videos by optimal spatio-temporal path discovery. In: 21st ACM International Conference on Multimedia, Newyork, USA, pp. 509–512 (2013)
5. Mahapatra, D., Gilani, S.O., Saini, M.K.: Coherency based spatio-temporal saliency detection for video object segmentation. IEEE J. Sel. Top. Sig. Process. **8**(3), 454–462 (2014)
6. Mauthner, T., Possegger, H., Waltner, G., Bischof, H.: Encoding based saliency detection for videos and images. In: 28th International Conference on Computer Vision and Pattern Recognition, Bosto, MA, pp. 2494–2502 (2015)
7. Borji, A., Sihite, D.N., Itti, L.: Salient object detection: a benchmark. In: Fitzgibbon, A., Lazebnik, S., Perona, P., Sato, Y., Schmid, C. (eds.) ECCV 2012. LNCS, pp. 414–429. Springer, Heidelberg (2012). doi:10.1007/978-3-642-33709-3_30
8. Muthuswamy, K., Rajan, D.: Particle filter framework for salient object detection in videos. IET Comput. Vis. **9**, 428–438 (2015)
9. Zou, W., Komodakis, N.: HARF: hierarchy associated rich features for salient object detection. In: International Conference on Computer Vision, Santiago, Chile, pp. 406–414 (2015)
10. Perazzi, F., Sorkine Hornung, O., Sorkine-Hornung, A.: Efficient salient foreground detection for images and video using fiedler vector. In: Workshop on Intelligent Cinematography and Editing, vol. 34, no. 2, pp. 21–29 (2015)
11. Zhou, B., Hou, X., Zhang, L.: A phase discrepancy analysis of object motion. In: Kimmel, R., Klette, R., Sugimoto, A. (eds.) ACCV 2010. LNCS, vol. 6494, pp. 225–238. Springer, Heidelberg (2011). doi:10.1007/978-3-642-19318-7_18
12. Jiang, B., Valstar, M.F., Pantic, M.: Action unit detection using sparse appearance descriptors in space-time video volumes. In: IEEE International Conference on Automatic Face & Gesture Recognition and Workshops, USA, pp. 314–321 (2011)
13. Zhen, Q., Huang, D., Wang, Y., Chen, L.: LPQ based static and dynamic modeling of facial expressions in 3D videos. In: Sun, Z., Shan, S., Yang, G., Zhou, J., Wang, Y., Yin, Y. (eds.) CCBR 2013. LNCS, vol. 8232, pp. 122–129. Springer, Cham (2013). doi:10.1007/978-3-319-02961-0_15
14. Muddamsetty, S.M., Sidibe, D., Tremeau, A., Meriaudeau, F.: A performance evaluation of fusion techniques for spatio-temporal saliency detection in dynamic scenes. In: Proceedings of IEEE International Conference on Image Processing, Australia, pp. 1–5 (2013)

15. Liu, F., Gleicher, M.: Automatic image retargeting with fish eye-view warping. In: 18th Annual ACM Symposium on User Interface Software and Technology, USA, pp. 153–162 (2005)
16. Goferman, S., Zelnik-manor, L., Tal, A.: Context-aware saliency detection. In: IEEE Conference on Computer Vision and Pattern Recognition, San Francisco, CA, pp. 1915–1926 (2010)
17. Website for NTT Dataset. www.kecl.ntt.co.jp/
18. Ojansivu, V., Heikkilä, J.: Blur insensitive texture classification using local phase quantization. In: Elmoataz, A., Lezoray, O., Nouboud, F., Mammass, D. (eds.) ICISP 2008. LNCS, vol. 5099, pp. 236–243. Springer, Heidelberg (2008). doi:10.1007/978-3-540-69905-7_27
19. Lin, L., Zhou, W.: LGOH-based discriminant centre-surround saliency detection. Int. J. Adv. Rob. Syst. **10**, 1–8 (2013)
20. Muddamsetty, S.M., Sidibé, D., Trémeau, A., Mériaudeau, F.: Spatio-temporal saliency detection in dynamic scenes using local binary patterns. In: ICPR, Sweden, pp. 2353–2358 (2014)

Simultaneous Reconstruction of Multiple Hand Shredded Content-Less Pages Using Graph-Based Global Reassembly

K.S. Lalitha[1]($\boxtimes$), Sukhendu Das[1], Arun Menon[2], and Koshy Varghese[2]

[1] Department of Computer Science and Engineering, IIT Madras, Chennai, India
kslalitha@cse.iitm.ac.in, sdas@iitm.ac.in
[2] Department of Civil Engineering, IIT Madras, Chennai, India
{arunmenon,koshy}@iitm.ac.in

Abstract. Hand shredded content-less pages reassembly is a challenging task. This has applications in forensics and fun games. The process is even more tedious when the number of pages from which the fragments are obtained is unknown. An iterative framework to solve the jigsaw puzzles of multiple hand shredded content-less pages has been proposed in this paper. This framework makes use of the shape-based information alone to solve the puzzle. All pairs of fragments are matched using the normalized shape-based features. Then, incorrect matches between the fragments are pruned using three scores that measure the goodness of the alignment. Finally, a graph-based technique is used to densely arrange the fragments for the global reassembly of the page(s). Experimental evaluation of our proposed framework on an annotated dataset of shredded documents shows the efficiency in the reconstruction of multiple content-less pages from arbitrarily torn fragments and performance metrics have been proposed to numerically evaluate the reassembly.

Keywords: Content-less page reassembly · Partial contour matching · Shape features · Agglomerative Clustering · Multiple page reassembly

1 Introduction

Environmental conditions, like fire and weathering, and human activities cause damages to the paper documents. These may result in the shredding of the paper documents. In fields like forensics, gaming, and archaeology, deciphering the content in shredded paper documents is a task of great importance. The process becomes even more complex when the shredded fragments have no content in it and the number of documents from which the fragments are obtained is unknown. Typically, features of fragments based on shape, color, texture or combinations of these, are used in reassembly. We solve the problem of reassembly using the shape (contour) information alone as the apictorial puzzles have no content in them. In this paper, we propose an approach to automatically reassemble hand shredded fragments from multiple content-less pages and we also propose performance metrics to measure the quality of the reassembly.

© Springer International Publishing AG 2017
S. Mukherjee et al. (Eds.): ICVGIP 2016, LNCS 10481, pp. 75–87, 2017.
https://doi.org/10.1007/978-3-319-68124-5_7

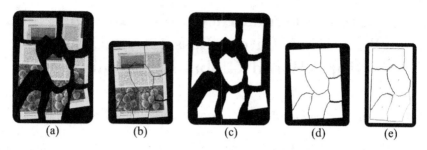

(a)   (b)   (c)   (d)   (e)

Fig. 1. Example page from dataset [11]. (a) Eight hand shredded paper fragments with content. (b) Reassembled page with content (ground-truth). (c) Binary masks (content-less) of the paper fragments, used as input for our problem. (d) Page reassembled using the binary masks in (c), by our proposed method. (e) Result generated by the method proposed in [6], when the features are extracted from the smoothed contours of the fragments in (c).

In our work, we use the *bdw082010* dataset [11], which has 48 double sided sheets, shredded by hand into 8 fragments each. Since, these sheets have information on both front and back sides, the dataset contains 96 pages. The fragments in this dataset have almost arbitrary shapes. For reassembly, only the binary segmentation mask of each of the fragments is used. Figure 1(a–b) shows eight fragments (with contents) from a page and the original document itself. Figure 1(c) shows the binary masks of the fragments. Our work reassembles the eight fragments in Fig. 1(c) into Fig. 1(d). Figure 1(e) shows the failure of method proposed in [6], one of the state of art methods to solve apictorial jigsaw puzzle.

The main contributions of our work are as follows:

1. We propose performance metrics to evaluate the reassembly numerically.
2. We propose an efficient framework to reassemble multiple content-less pages using graph-based clustering algorithm.
3. Our approach is unsupervised, that is, it does not require any prior information about the final reassembled shape and the number of pages to which the input fragments belongs to.

The rest of the paper is organized as follows: Sect. 2 discusses the related work. Section 3 gives a detailed overview of the framework proposed for reassembly of hand shredded content-less pages. Section 4 describes the experimental results. Section 5 concludes the work.

2   Related Works

The problem of reassembly of fragmented sheets is solved by considering shape-related features in [4–8,10,16,19], color/texture-related features in [14,17] and combination of shape-related & color-related features in [9,11,18]. In some works, as in [16], the contours are divided into contour segments, delimited by the corners, which are matched. Generally, distance metrics are used to measure the similarity of the features of the boundary points. In [11], Richter *et al.* proposed a supervised approach using an SVM classifier, to find points in the boundary with similar features. Most of the recent methods rely on texture features in the fragments to align globally and locally.

Global reassembly algorithms use a greedy approach to iteratively merge fragments. In [2], methods for global reassembly includes global relaxation to reduce the error in the final reconstruction. In [18], a graph-based algorithm that performs better groupwise matching and a variational graph optimization to minimize the error in final reconstruction are proposed. In [19], the candidate disambiguation problem has been formulated to define the compatibility between the neighboring matches and the global consistency is defined as the global criterion. In [9], Liu *et al.* proposed a spectral clustering based approach to reassemble multiple photos simultaneously.

The algorithms developed in [4–6,8,10] solve apictorial jigsaw puzzles. In [5], the "indents" and "outdents" are matched using ellipses fitted into them. In [10], the curve fitting is done using polar coordinate systems centered around the local extrema of the curvature. In [8], dynamic programming methods are used to match the curvature and arc length invariants. Once the matches are known, the robust relative transformations between the fragments are estimated using variants of ICP [13] or variants of MLESAC [12]. Incorrect matches are eliminated by locally verifying the transformation between fragments as in [12] or by checking the global compatibility between matches as in [18].

Recent work in [6], efficiently solves apictorial jigsaw puzzles. Here, the contours are decomposed into smaller arcs by *bivertex decomposition* and the arcs are then matched to fit the fragments. Also, an efficient algorithm to minimize the local error in alignment of fragments is proposed. However, as shown in 1(e), the method does not reassemble the hand shredded pages, as this method does not consider the overlap between fragments and the global placement of fragments during the reassembly. Our paper bridges the gap by reassembling shredded content-less pages.

3   Reassembly Framework

The main aim of the paper is to reassemble multiple hand shredded content-less pages using shape information alone. The iterative framework, shown in Fig. 2, is used in the reassembly process. The stages are discussed below:

3.1   Feature Extraction

The contours of the input fragments are approximated using the Douglas-Peucker algorithm [3], with parameter σ, to reduce the processing complexity. Given N input fragments from the shredded pages, $\widehat{\mathcal{U}} = \{U^1, U^2, \ldots, U^N\}$ and $\widehat{\mathcal{V}} = \{V^1, V^2, \ldots, V^N\}$ are the sets containing the actual contours and approximated

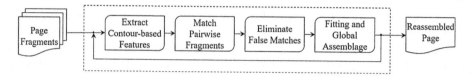

Fig. 2. The proposed iterative framework with various processing stages, for hand shredded content-less page reassembly.

contours, respectively. Each $V^i = \{v_1^i, v_2^i, \ldots, v_{n_i}^i\} \subseteq U^i$ describes the ith fragment, where, n_i is the number of points in the approximated i^{th} contour.

The following shape-based features are extracted from the vertices of the approximated contours:

- *Log of Absolute value of Signed Curvature* (κ) - assume, fragments' boundaries are *Jordan curves* of class C^2.
- *Log of Mean of Edge Lengths* (μ), from current vertex to the two adjacent vertices.
- *Angle between two vectors* (θ), one joining previous vertex & current vertex and other joining current vertex & next vertex.

The skewness measures of the distributions of the above features are close to 0, resulting in a equally weighted 3-dimensional feature vector at a vertex, $f = [\kappa, \mu, \theta]$. *Min-Max Normalization* is used to normalize features. The matrices containing the normalized feature vectors of the ith fragment are $FV_c^i, FV_a^i \in \mathbb{R}^{n_i \times 3}$, obtained by traversing in clockwise and anti-clockwise direction, respectively.

3.2 Pairwise Matching of Fragments

In this phase, all the possible alignment between two fragments are found out and the transformation corresponding to the alignments are estimated. Then, three scores are computed to evaluate the goodness of each of the alignments numerically. The process is repeated for all the pairs of fragments.

Similar Contour Segments Discovery. Using a modified version of Smith-Waterman (SW) algorithm [15], similar contour segments between two randomly chosen fragments, say i and j, are found out. A feature vector in FV_c^i is considered to be similar to another feature vector in FV_a^j, if the Euclidean distance between the feature vectors is less than ζ. Based on this, the common sub-sequences between FV_c^i and FV_a^j are found out. If M is the number of common sub-sequences between FV_c^i and FV_a^j, then there M possible ways in which fragments i and j can be aligned. For every $m \in 1, \ldots, M$, let $sp_m^i \subseteq V^i$ and $sp_m^j \subseteq V^j$ denote the sets containing contour points in fragment i that are similar to contour points in fragment j. Thus, the set $\mathbf{SP}^{i,j} = \{\{sp_1^i, sp_1^j\}, \{sp_2^i, sp_2^j\}, \ldots, \{sp_M^i, sp_M^j\}\}$ contains all the matched contour segments pairs. Matching using FV_a^i and FV_c^j also gives rise to the same set of matches, but the ordering (traversal direction) of points in the contour segments are reversed.

Estimation of Transformation and Scores. For every matched contour segments pair in $\mathbf{SP}^{i,j}$, a transformation is estimated. Unlike the prior works [12,13], we find a pair of points $\alpha, \alpha' \in sp_m^i$ and the corresponding points $\beta, \beta' \in sp_m^j$, such that $|\text{Len}(\alpha, \alpha') - \text{Len}(\beta, \beta')| \leq \delta$, where $\text{Len}(\alpha, \alpha')$ is the arc length between α and α', and δ is a parameter. A translation vector, $\boldsymbol{\lambda}$, is computed from the offset between α and β, as $\boldsymbol{\lambda} = \alpha - \beta$. The rotation angle, ϕ, is the angle between vectors $\overrightarrow{\alpha\alpha'}$ and $\overrightarrow{\beta\beta'}$. The Euclidean transformation, $A_m^{i,j} \in \text{SE}(2)$, applied to fragment j to align it with fragment i, is thus represented using its parameters as $A_m^{i,j} = (\phi, \boldsymbol{\lambda}) \in S^1 \times \mathbb{R}^2$ and the set containing the transformations between i and j is $\mathbf{A}^{i,j} = \{A_1^{i,j}, A_2^{i,j}, \ldots, A_M^{i,j}\}$. For each $A_m^{i,j} \in \mathbf{A}^{i,j}$, we calculate three scores, which are commonly used as topological features for 2-D shapes:

1. **_Connectivity_** _between fragments_ is the ratio of the length of the common sub-sequence between the fragments to the minimum of the two perimeters.

$$CNS_m^{i,j} = \frac{\text{Len}(sp_m^i)}{\min(\text{Perimeter}(V^i), \text{Perimeter}(V^j))}, \begin{cases} i, j \in 1, \ldots, N, \ i \neq j, \\ m = 1, \ldots, M. \end{cases} \quad (1)$$

2. _Relative_ **_Fitness_** _value_ is the ratio of the sum of the areas of overlap and gap between fragments to the mean of areas of the two fragments.

$$FTS_m^{i,j} = 2\frac{|OA^{i,j}| + |GA^{i,j}|}{\text{Area}(V^i) + \text{Area}(V^j)}, \begin{cases} i, j \in 1, \ldots, N, \ i \neq j, \\ m = 1, \ldots, M. \end{cases},$$

where, $OA^{i,j} = \text{Area}(V^i \cap AV^j)$, $\qquad(2)$

$GA^{i,j} = \text{Area}(V_m^{i,j}) - \text{Area}(V^i \cup AV^j)$,

$V_m^{i,j} = \text{Boundary}(V^i \cup AV^j)$, where $AV^j = A_m^{i,j} \star V^j$.

Operator '$\star$' denotes the transformation for all points in a fragment.

3. **_Compactness_** _of the merged Fragment_ is the ratio of the square of the perimeter of the merged fragment to the area of the merged fragment.

$$CMS_m^{i,j} = \frac{[\text{Perimeter}(V_m^{i,j})]^2}{\text{Area}(V_m^{i,j})}, \begin{cases} i, j \in 1, \ldots, N, \ i \neq j, \\ m = 1, \ldots, M. \end{cases} \quad (3)$$

The longer the common sub-sequence between the fragments, the better is the alignment. Thus, the _Connectivity_ score should have larger values. The lesser the area of overlap and gap between the fragments, the better is the alignment. Thus, the _Fitness_ score should have smaller values. The denser the fragments are arranged, the better is the alignment. Thus, the _Compactness_ score should also have smaller values.

3.3 Elimination of Incorrect Matches and Graph Generation

This phase eliminates the incorrect matches between two fragments based on the associated scores and finds the best possible alignment between two fragments. This is a four step process. First, we eliminate the matches that have *Connectivity* scores less than th_{CON} and *Fitness* scores greater than th_{FIT}, and the remaining transformations form a set of $\widetilde{\mathbf{A}}^{i,j} \subseteq \mathbf{A}^{i,j}$, $\forall i,j \in 1,\ldots,N$ and $i \neq j$, such that the cardinality of the set is $\left|\widetilde{\mathbf{A}}^{i,j}\right| = M' \leq M$.

Then, the Locking algorithm proposed in [6] is used to reduce the errors in the transformations. The parameters values of $K_1,\ldots,K_4$, ϵ, ν, ρ and j_{max} used are same as that given in [6]. Let, $\widetilde{\mathbf{LA}}^{i,j} = \text{Locking}(\widetilde{\mathbf{A}}^{i,j})$, $\left|\widetilde{\mathbf{LA}}^{i,j}\right| = M'$, be the set of error-corrected transformations. Application of this algorithm leads to increase in the *Connectivity* score and decrease in the *Fitness* score (recomputed).

Then, based on the *Connectivity* score, we again eliminate transformations and form a set $\widetilde{\mathbf{BA}}^{i,j} = \{\widetilde{BA}_1^{i,j},\ldots,\widetilde{BA}_{M''}^{i,j}\} \subseteq \widetilde{\mathbf{LA}}^{i,j}$ and $\left|\widetilde{\mathbf{BA}}^{i,j}\right| = M'' \leq M'$.

Finally, Single Best Transformation that align j with i, $SBA^{i,j}$, is estimated based on the *Compactness* (Cms) score of the transformations in $\widetilde{\mathbf{BA}}^{i,j}$ as:

$$SBA^{i,j} = \begin{cases} \underset{\substack{\widetilde{BA}_k^{i,j} \\ k=1,2,\ldots,M''}}{\arg\min} \ \text{Cms}(\widetilde{BA}_k^{i,j}), & \text{if } \left|\widetilde{\mathbf{BA}}^{i,j}\right| \neq 0, \\ null, & \text{Otherwise} \end{cases} \quad \begin{array}{c} \forall i,j \in 1,\ldots,N, \\ i \neq j. \end{array} \quad (4)$$

From Eq. (4), the single best transformation to align i with j is:

$$SBA^{j,i} = \begin{cases} (SBA^{i,j})^{-1}, & \text{if } SBA^{i,j} \neq null \\ null, & \text{Otherwise} \end{cases} \quad \begin{array}{c} \forall i,j \in 1,\ldots,N, \\ i \neq j. \end{array} \quad (5)$$

The above two transformations are appended to the set **SBA**, containing all the Single Best Transformations, $\mathbf{SBA} = \mathbf{SBA} \cup \{SBA^{i,j}, SBA^{j,i}\}$. If $SBA^{i,j} \neq null$ and $SBA^{j,i} \neq null$, we then add an edge, e_{ij}, between nodes i and j in the undirected graph, $G(\mathbf{V}, \mathbf{E})$, formed with input fragments as its nodes. Weight of the edge e_{ij} is:

$$w(e_{ij}) = \text{Cms}(SBA^{i,j}), \qquad i,j \in 1,\ldots,N, \ i \neq j. \quad (6)$$

Figure 3(a)–(e) shows an example of the process of elimination of incorrect pairwise matches of fragments. The final match in Fig. 3(e) is the best of all the matches identified by the Pairwise Fragment Matching phase in Fig. 3(b). Locking reduces the error in the alignment. The above steps are applied to all the possible pairings.

To increase the robustness during multiple pages reassembly, top 70 to 100 percent of the best matches are alone considered to be the input for the global reassembly phase.

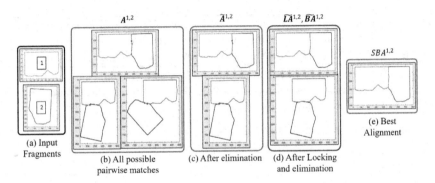

Fig. 3. Elimination of incorrect matches between fragments 1 and 2, for the example shown in Fig. 1(c). The fragment indices are given in rectangular boxes. (a) Pair of input fragment contours 1 and 2. (b) All possible pairwise matches between the fragments. (c) Pruned matches after elimination, based on transformation scores (Eqs. (1)–(3)). (d) Matches retained after locking the fragments and again eliminating matches based on transformation scores. (e) Best alignment between the pair.

3.4   Global Reassembly

In this phase, transformations are applied to approximately align the fragments. Unlike other methods that start from a seed fragment and then greedily aligns other fragments, the method proposed in this paper follows a Modified Agglomerative Clustering Algorithm to align the fragments together. Initially, consider each fragment as a cluster. Then, detect clusters corresponding to the best alignment, based on the edge weights of the graph G. Here, lesser the edge weight better is the alignment. Merge the pair of clusters, if the alignment of fragments in the participating clusters do not lead to overlap of fragments in the reassembled page. Choose the next best alignment and repeat the steps until there are no more clusters that can be merged without overlapping.

When fragments are clustered together, it implies that fragments can be assembled without any overlap, by applying the appropriate transformations. The proposed method for global reassembly is similar to an algorithm proposed in [11]. However, in the proposed method, the weight matrix need not be updated after every iteration. This reduces the computational overhead significantly.

The steps of the proposed method for global reassembly are given in Algorithm 1. We start by considering N singleton clusters as an initial set of clusters $\mathcal{C}^{(0)} = \{c_1, \ldots, c_N\}$. Each cluster contains a fragment index, $c_i = \{i\}$, $i \in 1, \ldots, N$. The transformations to be applied to the fragments corresponding to the elements of cluster c_k is stored in the set $\tau_k \in \mathrm{SE}(2)$. Initialize $\tau_k = \{I\}, \forall k = 1, \ldots, N$, where $I = (0, 0, 0) \in S^1 \times \mathbb{R}^2$ represents the identity transformation. Define a set containing all the initial transformations of the clusters as $\Gamma^{(0)} = \{\tau_1, \ldots, \tau_N\}$. The sets $\mathcal{C}^{(0)}$ and $\Gamma^{(0)}$, along with set of fragments $(\widehat{\mathcal{U}})$, graph (G) and set of single best transformations (**SBA**), are input to Algorithm 1.

Algorithm 1. *Algorithm for global reassembly:* initial set of fragments are given as input. Output contains clusters of fragments, that are aligned together without overlap, and their transformations.

Input: $\widehat{\mathcal{U}} = \{U^1, \ldots, U^N\}$: Set of fragments, $G(\mathbf{V}, \mathbf{E})$: Graph,
$\mathcal{C}^{(0)}$: Initial set of clusters, $\Gamma^{(0)}$: Initial set of cluster transformations,
SBA: Set of Single Best Transformations

Output: $\mathcal{C}^{(size(\mathbf{E}))}$: Final set of clusters,
$\Gamma^{(size(\mathbf{E}))}$: Final set of cluster transformations

---

1 Sort $\mathbf{E}$ in increasing order of weights
2 Set $iter \leftarrow 1$
3 **while** $iter \leq$ size($\mathbf{E}$) **do**
4 $\quad$ Assign a and b to the nodes connected by edge $\mathbf{E}(iter)$
5 $\quad$ Find the clusters c_A and c_B to which a and b belong to, respectively
6 $\quad$ Set $flag \leftarrow 0$
7 $\quad$ **if** c_A and c_B are not same **then**
8 $\quad\quad$ $(\widehat{c_A}, \widehat{\tau_A}) \leftarrow$ NewCluster$(a, b, c_A, c_B, \tau_A, \tau_B, SBA^{a,b})$ /* See Algorithm 2   */
9 $\quad\quad$ **if** fragments in $\widehat{c_A}$ do not overlap **then**
10 $\quad\quad\quad$ $\mathcal{C}^{(t)} = \{\mathcal{C}^{(t-1)} \setminus \{c_A, c_B\}\} \cup \widehat{c_A}; \Gamma^{(t)} = \{\Gamma^{(t-1)} \setminus \{\tau_A, \tau_B\}\} \cup \widehat{\tau_A}$
11 $\quad\quad\quad$ Set $flag \leftarrow 1$
12 $\quad\quad$ **end**
13 $\quad$ **end**
14 $\quad$ **if** $flag = 0$ **then**
15 $\quad\quad$ $\mathcal{C}^{(t)} = \mathcal{C}^{(t-1)}; \Gamma^{(t)} = \Gamma^{(t-1)}$
16 $\quad$ **end**
17 $\quad$ Increment $iter$ by 1
18 **end**
19 **return** $\left(\mathcal{C}^{(size(\mathbf{E}))}, \Gamma^{(size(\mathbf{E}))} \right)$

Algorithm 2 shows the steps of the function used to combine clusters and to compute the transformations for elements in the new cluster. Figure 4 shows examples of new valid clusters formed at the end of Algorithm 1. Figure 4(h) shows the page reassembled by the proposed method.

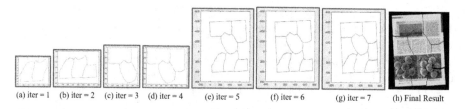

(a) iter = 1 (b) iter = 2 (c) iter = 3 (d) iter = 4   (e) iter = 5   (f) iter = 6   (g) iter = 7   (h) Final Result

Fig. 4. (a)–(g) New clusters formed at the end of every iteration in the global reassembly phase, for the example shown in Fig. 1(c). Here, *iter* indicates the iteration number in Algorithm 1. (h) The final reassembly result with content.

Algorithm 2. *Function to combine clusters:* two clusters (c_A, c_B) along with their transformations (τ_A, τ_B) are the input. Output is a new cluster $(\widehat{c_A})$ formed by combining the input clusters and transformations $(\widehat{\tau_A})$ to be applied to the elements in the new cluster.

```
1  Function NewCluster(a, b, cₐ, c_B, τₐ, τ_B, SBAᵃ'ᵇ)
2  |   New cluster, ĉₐ = {cₐ ∪ {b} ∪ {c_B \ {b}}}
3  |   Initialize τ̂ₐ = ∅
4  |   for each l in cₐ do
5  |   |   τ̂ₐ = τ̂ₐ ∪ {tran(A, l)}
   |   |   /* tran(A, l) ∈ τₐ represents the transformation applied to
   |   |      fragment corresponding to element l in cluster cₐ        */
6  |   end
7  |   Append transformation for element b as τ̂ₐ = τ̂ₐ ∪ {tran(A, a) * SBAᵃ'ᵇ}
   |      /* Operator '*' denotes multiplication of transformations     */
8  |   temp = (tran(A, a) * SBAᵃ'ᵇ) * Inverse(tran(B, b))
9  |   for each l in {c_B \ {b}} do
10 |   |   τ̂ₐ = τ̂ₐ ∪ {temp * tran(B, l)}
11 |   end
12 return (ĉₐ, τ̂ₐ)
```

4   Experiments and Results

Experiments are done to evaluate the reassembly accuracy numerically and to evaluate the contributions of the method in reassembling multiple documents.

The empirical values of the parameters used in all the experiments are follows:

$$\sigma : 1.4\text{–}3.1, \qquad \zeta : 0.06\text{–}0.10, \qquad \epsilon = 0.0001, \qquad \nu = 3,$$

$$K_1 = 15, \qquad K_2 = 4, \qquad K_3 = 1, \qquad K_4 = 0.5, \qquad \delta = 5,$$

$$th_{CON} : 0.10\text{–}0.15, \qquad th_{FIT} : 0.009\text{–}0.03, \qquad \rho = 1/3, \qquad j_{max} = 50.$$

The performance of the proposed algorithm solely depends on the choice of the above parameters. The reassembly approach discussed reassembles all the 96 distinct sheets available from the dataset [11] in at most 2 iterations.

Figure 5(a) shows that the *bivertex decomposition* method, proposed in [6] to find the initial set of possible matches, returns a larger set of hypotheses than our proposed method. Thus, the running time of the proposed method is comparatively less. According to [1], the worst-case lower bound on the number of iterations performed by ICP algorithm in order to converge is $\Omega(n/d)^{d+1}$, where n is the size of the input data point set and d is the dimensionality of the input data. In this work $d = 2$ and thus, if ICP algorithm is used to estimate the transformation, given n pairs of matched points, the worst-case lower bound on the number of iterations performed by ICP algorithm in order to converge is $\Omega(n^3)$. However, the running time complexity of the method proposed in this paper, in Pairwise Matching of Fragments phase, to estimate the transformation

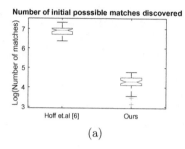
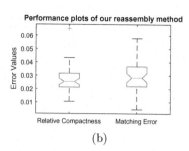

(a)   (b)

Fig. 5. (a) Number of initial possible matches discovered. (b) Performance plots of our reassembly method showing the distribution of the two error values. Box plots shows the median value (red line) as well as the 25th and 75th percentiles. The '+' symbols indicate the outliers (Color figure online).

is $O(n^2)$. Hence, the proposed work is much faster than the prior works, in estimating the transformation.

Performance Evaluation: To evaluate the performance of the reassembly framework numerically, we use the following two error measures:

1. **Relative Compactness Error:** It is the ratio of the difference in the *Compactness* scores of the final reassembled page and the minimum boundary rectangle, which encompasses the final reassembled page, to the *Compactness* score of the final reassembled page. Since in our case we know that the fragments should be reassembled into a rectangle, we are comparing the compactness score of the reassembly output of our method with the compactness score of the minimum bounding rectangle, and using the relative difference value as a performance metric.
2. **Matching Error:** This error measure, proposed in [18], is the ratio of the average distance between matching segments of the fragments to the diagonal of the minimum bounding rectangle encompassing the reassembled page.

Figure 5(b) shows the box plots of the two error values obtained by our method for the 96 distinct pages. It can be seen from the plot that the maximum value of the *Matching Error* obtained using our method is around 0.06, which is at least 40 percent less than the error values of the reassembly approach proposed in [18]. The least *Matching Error* value reported in [18] is 0.10.

Multiple Pages Reassembly: In a content-less fragment, generally, it is hard to find which side (front or back) of the fragment is to be used in the reassembly process. We evaluate our method by inputting both sides of the fragments simultaneously. Figure 6 shows the reconstruction of one such sheet. It is observed that the method is capable of reconstructing both front and back sides of the sheet simultaneously.

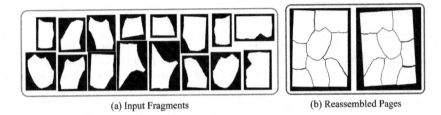

(a) Input Fragments   (b) Reassembled Pages

Fig. 6. Simultaneous reassembly of front and back of sheet 2, from dataset [11]. (a) Input: 8 fragments, both front and back sides scans. (b) Reassembled pages.

Simultaneous reassembly of fragments from multiple pages is challenging. When the number of sheets that has been shredded is unknown, the task becomes even more difficult. Figure 7(b) shows the result of the proposed method, when the 32 input fragments, shown in Fig. 7(a), are from four different pages. The method took 2 iterations to give output shown in Fig. 7(b). Figure 8(b) shows the result of one failure case of the proposed method, for the input in Fig. 8(a). The failure is due to an error in the matching of fragments.

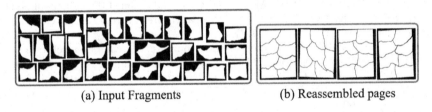

(a) Input Fragments   (b) Reassembled pages

Fig. 7. Simultaneous reassembly of four pages, from dataset [11]. (a) 32 input fragments. (b) Four correctly reassembled pages.

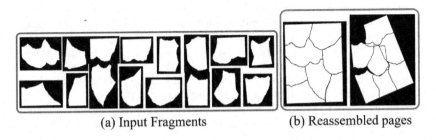

(a) Input Fragments   (b) Reassembled pages

Fig. 8. Simultaneous reassembly of two pages, from dataset [11]. (a) 16 input fragments. (b) Two reassembled pages, with one failure case.

5   Conclusion

A novel iterative framework for shape features based automatic reassembly of multiple hand shredded content-less pages has been proposed. Experiments are done to show the effectiveness of the proposed approach. The reassembly has been evaluated numerically using the performance metrics and experiments show that our method has less error than the existing approaches.

In future work, the difficulties introduced due to material loss will be handled. Exploration for extending the framework to reassemble 3-D broken objects would be an appropriate scope of future work.

References

1. Arthur, D., Vassilvitskii, S.: Worst-case and Smoothed Analysis of the ICP algorithm, with an application to the K-means method. In: 47th Annual IEEE Symposium on Foundations of Computer Science, pp. 153–164 (2006)
2. Castañeda, A.G., Brown, B.J., Rusinkiewicz, S., Funkhouser, T.A., Weyrich, T.: Global consistency in the automatic assembly of fragmented artefacts. In: The 12th International Symposium on Virtual Reality, Archaeology and Cultural Heritage, pp. 73–80 (2011)
3. Douglas, D.H., Peucker, T.K.: Algorithms for the reduction of the number of points required to represent a digitized line or its caricature. Cartogr. Int. J. Geogr. Inf. Geovisualization **10**, 112–122 (1973)
4. Freeman, H., Garder, L.: Apictorial jigsaw puzzles: the computer solution of a problem in pattern recognition. IEEE Trans. Electron. Comput. **13**, 118–127 (1964)
5. Goldberg, D., Malon, C., Bern, M.: A global approach to automatic solution of jigsaw puzzles. In: Eighteenth Annual Symposium on Computational Geometry, pp. 82–87 (2002)
6. Hoff, D.J., Olver, P.J.: Automatic solution of jigsaw puzzles. J. Math. Imaging Vis. **49**, 234–250 (2014)
7. Justino, E., Oliveira, L.S., Freitas, C.: Reconstructing shredded documents through feature matching. Forensic Sci. Int. **160**, 140–147 (2006)
8. Kong, W., Kimia, B.B.: On solving 2D and 3D puzzles using curve matching. In: 2001 IEEE Computer Society Conference on Computer Vision and Pattern Recognition, vol. 2, pp. 583–590 (2001)
9. Liu, H., Cao, S., Yan, S.: Automated assembly of shredded pieces from multiple photos. IEEE Trans. Multimedia **13**, 1154–1162 (2011)
10. Radack, G.M., Badler, N.I.: Jigsaw puzzle matching using a boundary-centered polar encoding. Comput. Graph. Image Process. **19**, 1–17 (1982)
11. Richter, F., Ries, C.X., Cebron, N., Lienhart, R.: Learning to reassemble shredded documents. IEEE Trans. Multimedia **15**, 582–593 (2013)
12. Richter, F., Ries, C.X., Romberg, S., Lienhart, R.: Partial contour matching for document pieces with content-based prior. In: 2014 IEEE International Conference on Multimedia & Expo, pp. 1–6 (2014)
13. Rusinkiewicz, S., Levoy, M.: Efficient variants of the ICP algorithm. In: Third International Conference on 3-D Digital Imaging and Modeling, pp. 145–152 (2001)
14. Sağiroğlu, M.Ş., Erçil, A.: A texture based matching approach for automated assembly of puzzles. In: The 18th International Conference on Pattern Recognition, vol. 3, pp. 1036–1041 (2006)

15. Smith, T.F., Waterman, M.S.: Identification of common molecular subsequences. J. Mol. Biol. **147**, 195–197 (1981)
16. Stieber, A., Schneider, J., Nickolay, B., Krüger, J.: A contour matching algorithm to reconstruct ruptured documents. In: Goesele, M., Roth, S., Kuijper, A., Schiele, B., Schindler, K. (eds.) DAGM 2010. LNCS, vol. 6376, pp. 121–130. Springer, Heidelberg (2010). doi:10.1007/978-3-642-15986-2_13
17. Tsamoura, E., Pitas, I.: Automatic color based reassembly of fragmented images and paintings. IEEE Trans. Image Process. **19**, 680–690 (2010)
18. Zhang, K., Li, X.: A graph-based optimization algorithm for fragmented image reassembly. Graph. Models **76**, 484–495 (2014)
19. Zhu, L., Zhou, Z., Hu, D.: Globally consistent reconstruction of ripped-up documents. IEEE Trans. Pattern Anal. Mach. Intell. **30**, 1–13 (2008)

Super Resolution Mapping of Trees for Urban Forest Monitoring in Madurai City Using Remote Sensing

D. Synthiya Vinothini$^{(\boxtimes)}$, B. Sathyabama, and S. Karthikeyan

Thiagarajar College of Engineering, Madurai, India
{synthiya, sbece, skarthikeyanlme}@tce.edu

Abstract. This paper proposes a super resolution mapping of trees pixel swapping method in Madurai city. Identifying and mapping the vegetation specifically trees is a significant issue in remote sensing applications where the lack of height information becomes a hard monocular recognition task. The density and shape of the trees gets affected by other man-made objects which gives rise to an erroneous recognition. The quality of recognition may be affected by various terms like resolution, visibility, sizes or scale. Predicting trees when they are partially blocked from view is also a challenging task. A common problem associated with the application of satellite images is the frequent occurrence of mixed pixels. The motivation of this work is to extract trees using pixel swapping method. Pixel-swapping algorithm is a simple and efficient technique for super resolution mapping to change the spatial arrangement of sub-pixels in such a way that the spatial correlation between neighboring sub-pixels would be maximized. Soft classification techniques were introduced to avoid the loss of information by assigning a pixel to multiple land-use/land-cover classes according to the area represented within the pixel. This soft classification technique generates a number of fractional images equal to the number of classes. Super resolution mapping was then used to know where each class is located within the pixel, in order to obtain detailed spatial patterns. The aim of supper resolution mapping is to determine a fine resolution map of the trees from the soft classification result. The experiment is conducted with images of Madurai city obtained from WorldView2 satellite. The accuracy of the pixel swapping algorithm was 98.74%.

Keywords: Super resolution mapping · Pixel swapping · Fuzzy C Means · Remote sensing · High resolution panchromatic image · Low resolution multispectral image · Urban forest

1 Introduction

The benefits of maintaining urban forests is of vital importance in terms of health, aesthetic and recreational benefits in industrialized cities. Well managed urban forests provide renewable resources for biological organisms and are also a vital source for maintaining environmental stability and ecological biodiversity. The groundwork of urban forest management is procuring detailed forest inventory information, but for

© Springer International Publishing AG 2017
S. Mukherjee et al. (Eds.): ICVGIP 2016, LNCS 10481, pp. 88–96, 2017.
https://doi.org/10.1007/978-3-319-68124-5_8

sustainable forest management, more information is needed on planning for future trees management in contrast with the status of the forested area [1].

Furthermore, single tree level forest information has been essential for various forest applications, such as monitoring urban forest regeneration, forest inventory, and evaluating forest damage. Field measurement and monitoring of urban trees are labor intensive and cost intensive. Remote sensing technology has become the alternative solution, cost effectively. Photogrammetrical method mainly depends on the quality of the image data, and the physiognomy of the stand. This growth provides viable sources of data and opportunities for automated forest interpretation at the tree level, which requires identification and delineation of individual tree crowns.

Very High Resolution Satellite images provide valuable information, for detecting objects like trees and buildings which is necessary in the field of Photogrammetry, Remote Sensing and GIS communities to show the features of land cover classes in urban or rural areas [2]. Dependent on the data source employed, object detection techniques can be classified in three groups: (i) using satellite imagery; (ii) using three-dimensional information; and (iii) combining both data sources [3]. Object detection techniques using high resolution imagery can be considered: low-level and high-level vision techniques. Low-level vision techniques are mainly based on edge detection and extraction from images, followed by processes of definition of rules and hypothesis in order to identify the objects [4]. High-level vision techniques try to imitate the human cognition process and decision making skills which are based on the analysis of the information. Pattern and object recognition, and image classification are common high-level vision techniques [3].

Object recognition by means of high resolution satellite imagery presents difficulties due to geometric and photometric reasons; other objects can constitute complex structures that create abrupt height discontinuities, occlusions, shadows, and radiometric reasons. The quality of the recognition is also affected by terms like resolution and visibility, sizes or scale. So identifying and mapping trees in such environment is a challenging task [2].

Initially, Kim and Muller [4] introduced graph theory to detect objects using aerial images. They used linear features and shadow information to validate the objects emergence. Sirmacek and Unsalan [4] developed graphical tools and Scale Invariant Transform (SIFT) to detect urban areas from satellite images and the accuracy in detecting objects using the above methods are not automatic and much accurate. Later, a fully automatic method is proposed by Ghaffarian and Ghaffarian[5] to detect objects from single high resolution Google Earth images. But, satellite images that offer RGB band shows poor accuracy because of the shadow detection results. Haala [6] employed a DSM segmentation technique based on local surface normal. However, most of the available methods are per pixel based which is accurate for ideal situation with high resolution imagery but it does not consider the critical issue of the satellite imagery which is of coarse resolution. It consists of mixed pixels where heterogeneous land cover classes are present within a single pixel. Different techniques like Linear optimization, Feed-forward neural network, Hopfield neural network, Markov random field, Support Vector Machine maps the sub-pixel information effectively. One important method among them is pixel swapping, where the sub-pixel classes are swapped to increase the spatial correlation among them. Optimized pixel swapping is presented in [9], in which the non-random initialization is performed by sorting the attractiveness between the subpixels and then iterating the swapping procedure until every sub-pixel is allotted to a single class. The computational burden of the algorithm can further be reduced by the proposed method which allocates a single class to each sub-pixel at non-random initialization such that the attractiveness score between the sub-pixels within a pixel is maximum. Then swapping is performed if it increases inter-pixel correlation and thus overall attractiveness. The goal of this work is to map trees at sub-pixel level using pixel swapping algorithm. This work proposes to initialize the subpixel classes with spatial correlation thereby decreasing computational burden for the algorithm. Swapping is mainly concentrated at the mixed pixels and skips the pure pixels to decrease run time and however maintaining the accuracy.

2   Proposed Methodology

This session proposes a super resolution mapping of tree cover for urban forest monitoring. The schematic diagram of the proposed method is given in Fig. 1. It is implemented under two stages namely super resolution mapping of trees, accuracy assessment using High Resolution Panchromatic (HRP) image.

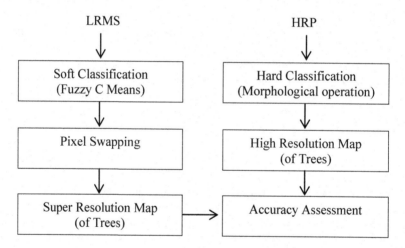

Fig. 1. Proposed super resolution based tree cover estimation using satellite image for urban forest monitoring.

2.1   Super Resolution Mapping of Trees

The input image for the present work is obtained from the WorldView2 satellite imagery. The super resolution mapping of trees comprises of soft classification performed by Fuzzy C Means (FCM) and Pixel Swapping.

2.1.1 Soft Classification by Fuzzy C Means Classification

Classification is the task of assigning a set of given data elements to a given set of labels or classes. Soft Classification estimates the class conditional probabilities explicitly and makes the class prediction based on the largest estimated probability. The soft classification method identifies only the proportion of the mixed pixel distribution in a low resolution image. For images having limited spatial resolution, overlapping intensities, poor contrast, noise and intensity inhomogeneity variation make the segmentation process, a difficult task [7]. Fuzzy C Means [8] method has robust characteristics for ambiguity and retains more information comparitively.

In fuzzy membership concept each pixel can belong to several land cover classes partially. Each pixel is assigned a membership vector representing each class with the range between 0 and 1. Thus, a pixel can belong to class to a certain degree and may belong to other classes in a certain degree and this degree of belongingness is indicated by fuzzy membership values. In the feature space if any point lies closer to the center of a cluster, then its membership grade is also higher (closer to 1) for that cluster.

2.1.2 Pixel Swapping

This section is devoted to explain the pixel swapping algorithm [9] which follows an initialization with spatial correlation such that the attractiveness within the pixel is high. The input to the algorithm is the land cover proportions of each pixel from the soft classifier. The labels of the sub-pixels are allocated initially in the HR grid by maintaining the proportion and the spatial correlation within the pixel. The non-random initialization is performed to reduce the number of computation which allocates a single class to each sub-pixel such that the attractiveness score (given by Eq. (1)) between the sub-pixels within a pixel is maximum. Then swapping is performed if it increases inter-pixel correlation and thus overall attractiveness *i.e.*, the labels are rearranged such that it increases the inter-pixel and intra-pixel spatial correlation. The spatial arrangements are updated by following the scoring, ranking and swapping steps:

Pixel Swapping Algorithm:

1. Perform non-random initialization within a pixel such that $\sum \alpha_i$ is maximum where α_i is the attractiveness score for each sub-pixel inside a pixel.
2. The attractiveness score (α_i) of each sub-pixel for a particular class 'c' is estimated as a distance weighted function of its neighbors:

$$\alpha_i = \alpha_c(p_i) = \sum_{j=1}^{n} \rho_{ij} z_c(p_i) \tag{1}$$

where n is the number of neighbors, $z_c(p_i)$ is the class belonging value and it is 1 for the class c and 0 other classes, ρ_{ij} is the weight dependent on the distance d_{ij} between the pixel p_i in the ith location and the neighbor pixel p_j in the jth location given by

$$\rho_{ij} = \exp\left(\frac{-d_{ij}}{\beta}\right) \qquad (2)$$

β is a non-linear parameter for the exponential decay model.

3. The attractiveness of each pixel is calculated, by summing the attractiveness score of all its sub-pixel.
4. Within each pixel the sub-pixel is ranked based on their attractiveness scores.
5. The two sub-pixels with least score is swapped and attractiveness is calculated. If there is an increase in the total attractiveness score, then the swap is saved else no swap.
6. Stop: if no further swaps are made.

2.2 Accuracy Assessment Using High Resolution Panchromatic (HRP) Image

Many earth observation satellites like WorldView, IKONOS, QUICKBIRD provide LRMS and HRP images of same scene. The availability of low resolution and high resolution images of a same scene are utilized in this work for accuracy assessment. The pixel swapping algorithm generates a Super Resolution Map (SRM) for the low resolution image. The SRM is generated to the size of the available high resolution image. Now the high resolution image is classified using a hard classification scheme described below to generate a High Resolution classified Map (HRM). Now both the SRM from a low resolution image and the HRM from the high resolution image are of same size and the accuracy assessment for SRM is performed by the using the HRM as a reference. The accuracy assessment is performed on two fold, one for HRM using ground truth and the other for SRM using HRM. The accuracy for SRM is the ratio of the number of pixels that are correctly classified with HRM as a reference map to the total number of pixels in the map. Further the accuracy assessment for the HRM from the HRP image is performed by ground truth analysis. The ground truth information is discussed in the experimental results and discussion section.

The following section deals with the generation of the HRM from HRP. In the context of remote sensing, morphological features have proved to be useful for the discrimination of objects in high spatial images [10, 11]. The algorithm for tree extraction is described as follows. First step is to read the high resolution panchromatic image since morphological operations are applied on each band separately. Next step is to mark the foreground objects, which must be connected blobs of pixels inside each of the foreground objects. Next opening is computed followed by opening-by-reconstruction. Following the opening with a closing can remove the dark spots and stem marks. Reconstruction-based opening and closing are more effective than standard opening and closing at removing small blemishes without affecting the overall shapes of the objects. Opening-closing by reconstruction removes features smaller than the structuring element, without altering the shape; reconstruct connected components from the preserved features. Thus the High Resolution (HR) map can be extracted using morphological operation. This HR map is used as a reference to verify the accuracy of the SR map. The algorithm for generating high resolution map is described below

Tree Cover Estimation from High Resolution Imagery:

1. Read the High Resolution Panchromatic image, X
2. Perform morphological erosion on the high resolution image.

$$Y_{Erode} = f_{erosion}(X, f_{SE}) \tag{3}$$

where f_{SE} is the structuring element, and $f_{erosion}$ is the morphological erosion function

3. Perform opening by reconstruction (obr) on the eroded image.

$$Y_{obr} = f_{\text{reconstruction}}(Y_{Erode}, f_{SE}) \tag{4}$$

where $f_{reconstruction}$ is the morphological reconstruction function.

4. Extract the connected components.

High resolution map of trees are extracted using morphological operations. The accuracy of the classified map depends on the selection of the right structural element which is involved in extracting the required morphological object. Disk shaped structuring element is selected for extracting trees. The high resolution map of trees extracted by the aforementioned algorithm is used as a reference for comparing the super resolution map of trees based on pixel swapping.

3 Experimental Results and Discussion

In this work, the urban forest is monitored in the Madurai city (Longitude 78.12°E, Latitude 9.92°N). Two different study areas are selected for experimental analysis which comprises of the Sellur region (Longitude 78.12275833°E, Latitude 9.94002778°N) and Thanakangulam area (Longitude 78.04655302°E, Latitude 9.88716387°N). The WorldView2 satellite provides HRP and LRMS images of the study areas with a scaling ratio of 4. The LRMS image and the HRP image is displayed Fig. 2. LRMS image is classified by FCM soft classifier and then super resolution mapping is performed on the class proportion result of FCM. The pixel swapping uses a magnification factor 4 *i.e.*, 4 × 4 subpixels for each pixel, so that the size of the SR map generated will comply with that of the HR map. The LRMS and HRP images are classified using hard classifier and the portion of the classified result is shown in Fig. 3.

The SRM and HRM is of same size and the number of pixels that are correctly classified in SRM is determined with HRM as a reference map. The classification accuracy of the pixel swapping is tabulated in Table 1 which is determined as a ratio of the number of correctly classified pixels to the total number of pixels in the map. Further the accuracy assessment for the HR Map has been conducted by field survey where 100 ground points has been selected and visited for verifying the results. Out of 100 points selected randomly 45 were selected to be trees and 55 points belongs to other class and the accuracy assessment is tabulated in Table 2.

The area covered by trees in an image is estimated by the following equations. The area is estimated from the super resolved maps. This study area consists of

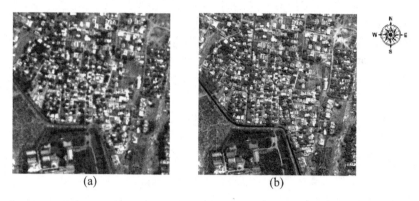

Fig. 2. Super resolution map of Urban area –study area 1 of Madurai, India (a) LRMS image (b) HRP image

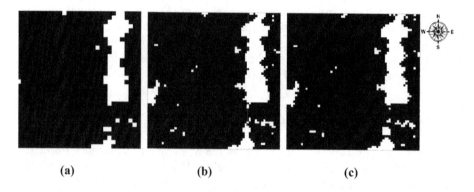

(a)   (b)   (c)

Fig. 3. A portion of classified image–study area 1 of Madurai, India (a) LR map using morphological feature (b) High Resolution map from HRP (c) Super resolution map

Table 1. Tree cover percentage in the geographical area of the study area

Study area	Total area (sq.km)	Area covered by trees (sq.km)	Tree cover percentage of geographical area	Accuracy of pixel swapping
1	16.3×10^{-3}	1.41×10^{-3}	8.62%	98.33
3	16.3×10^{-3}	0.28×10^{-3}	1.71%	98.61

8.62% and 1.71% of trees in the geographical area; the results are estimated and tabulated in Table 1 for all the study area considered. The accuracy of the pixel swapping algorithm is compared by the high resolution map generated using HRP and summarized in Table 1 and the average accuracy was 98.74%.

$$\text{Total area covered in image} = (\text{no. of Pixels}) * (\text{pixel resolution})^2 \quad (5)$$

$$\text{Tree cover area} = (\text{no. of Pixels classified as trees}) * \text{pixel resolution}^2 \quad (6)$$

$$\text{Tree cover percentage of geographical area} = \frac{TreeCoverArea}{TotalArea} * 100 \quad (7)$$

Table 2. Accuracy assessment of the hard classifier

Features	Trees	Others	User accuracy	Producer's accuracy
Trees	43	2	43/45 = 0.955	43/47 = 0.915
Others	4	51	51/55 = 0.927	51/53 = 0.962

Overall accuracy = (43 + 51)/100 = 94%

4 Conclusion

In this work, super resolution mapping of trees is implemented for urban forest monitoring. The low resolution multispectral satellite image is initially classified using soft classifier Fuzzy C Means to obtain the class proportion of each pixel. The sub-pixel mapping is performed by pixel swapping algorithm which increases the spatial correlation within the labels of the sub-pixels. The obtained super resolved map is then checked for accuracy using the high resolution panchromatic image available. The hard classification is performed by extracting morphological features for tree in the HRP image. Based on the classified results the tree cover region is estimated and thus the percentage of tree occupied in a given geographical area. It gives the total area occupied by the trees in a region covered by the image. The experiment was analysed on two different study areas in Madurai. As per the experiment, it was estimated that the tree cover percentage in the first area, is 8.62%, and that near study area 2 is 1.71%. The accuracy of the pixel swapping algorithm is compared by the high resolution map generated using HRP.

References

1. Miller, R.W., Hauer, R.J., Werner, L.P.: Urban Forestry: Planning and Managing Urban Greenspaces. Waveland Press, Long Grove (2015)
2. Sohn, G., Dowman, I.J.: Extraction of buildings from high resolution satellite data (2001)
3. Hermosilla, T., Ruiz, L.A., Recio, J.A., Estornell, J.: Evaluation of automatic building detection approaches combining high resolution images and lidar data. ISSN 2072-4292 (2011)
4. Kim, T., Muller, J.: Development of a graph based approach for building detection. Image Vis. Comput. **17**, 3–14 (1999)
5. Ghaffarian, S., Ghaffarian, S.: Automatic building detection based on supervised classification using high resolution Google earth images. In: The International Archives of the Photogrammetry, Remote Sensing and Spatial Information Sciences, 2014 ISPRS Technical Commission III Symposium, vol. Xl-3, 5–7 September 2014

6. Kim, J.R., Muller, J.P.: 3D reconstruction from very high resolution satellite stereo and its application to object identification. In: Symposium on Geospatial Theory, Processing and Applications, Ottawa (2002)
7. Bezdek, J.C., Ehrlich, R., Full, W.: FCM: the Fuzzy C-Means clustering algorithm. Comput. Geosci. **10**, 191–203 (1984)
8. Nayak, J., Naik, B., Behera, H.S.: Fuzzy C-Means (FCM) clustering algorithm: a decade review from 2000 to 2014. In: Jain, L.C., Behera, H.S., Mandal, J.K., Mohapatra, D.P. (eds.) Computational Intelligence in Data Mining - Volume 2. SIST, vol. 32, pp. 133–149. Springer, New Delhi (2015). doi:10.1007/978-81-322-2208-8_14
9. Niroumand Jadidi, M., et al.: A novel approach to super resolution mapping of multispectral imagery based on pixel swapping technique. ISPRS Ann. Photogrammetry Remote Sen. Spat. Inf. Sci. **1**, 159–164 (2012)
10. Huang, X., Zhang, L., Wang, L.: Evaluation of morphological texture features for mangrove forest mapping and species discrimination using multispectral IKONOS imagery. IEEE Geosci. Remote Sen. Lett. **6**(3), 393–397 (2009)
11. Aptoula, E.: Remote sensing image retrieval with global morphological texture descriptors. IEEE Trans. Geosci. Remote Sen. **52**(5), 3023–3034 (2014)

Scale-Invariant Image Inpainting Using Gradient-Based Image Composition

Mrinmoy Ghorai$^{(\boxtimes)}$, Soumitra Samanta, and Bhabatosh Chanda

Indian Statistical Institute, Kolkata, India
mgre04@gmail.com

Abstract. In this paper, we propose a novel scale-invariant image inpainting algorithm that combines several inpainted images obtained from multiple pyramids of different coarsest scales. To achieve this, first we build the pyramids and then we run an image inpainting algorithm individually on each of the pyramids to obtain different inpainted images. Finally, we combine those inpainted images by a gradient based approach to obtain the final inpainted image. The motivation of this approach is to solve the problem of appearing artifacts in traditional single pyramid-based approach since the results depend on the starting scale of the pyramid. Here we assume that most of the inpainted images produced by the pyramids are quite good. However, some of them may have artifacts and these artifacts are eliminated by gradient based image composition. We test the proposed algorithm on a large number of natural images and compare the results with some of the existing methods to demonstrate the efficacy and superiority of the proposed method.

Keywords: Inpainting · Scale-invariant · Multiple pyramid · Image composition

1 Introduction

In image inpainting, the problem is to fill a target (also known as missing or unknown) region by some visual information in order to obtain a visually pleasant and undetectable inpainted image. The information is copied either from the source (also called known) region of the input image or from a database of images similar to the input image. Image inpainting becomes a popular area in the field of image processing and computer vision as it is applied for several application like restoration (scratch removal) and image editing (text or object removal). The most difficult task is object removal since the target region is considered as a large blob. Among the various image inpainting methods, exemplar (patch) based method become most popular to handle the problem of object removal.

In the exemplar (patch) based methods, the texture and structure information is propagated from the source region into the inside of the target region. The concept is to copy the best matched patch from the source region and paste to the selected partially known target patch. This idea was proposed mainly for

© Springer International Publishing AG 2017
S. Mukherjee et al. (Eds.): ICVGIP 2016, LNCS 10481, pp. 97–108, 2017.
https://doi.org/10.1007/978-3-319-68124-5_9

texture synthesis [4]. To propagate the structure information, Criminisi et al. [2] first proposed an exemplar-based inpainting method which gives equal importance on the structure filling and the texture synthesis. For this, they compute a priority term depending on isophote strength for the ordering of filling of the target patches. The patch with highest priority is selected for patch inpainting. To improve the method proposed in [2] some other inpainting methods are introduced by changing the priority term and the dissimilarity measure [15,17,19]. These methods usually select a single patch from a set of candidate patches to infer the target patch. Recently, some authors [1,8,9,18] propose a linear combination of candidate patches to infer the target patch. Besides these methods, sparse representation is widely used in image inpainting [5,16,20], where the target patch is inferred by the sparse linear combination of a set of pre-defined patches (dictionary) or candidate patches. In [20], structure sparsity and patch sparse representation are introduced to provide a good solution of priority estimation and patch inference. Further, Li et al. [12] incorporate a Curvelet based multi direction feature in the constraint of sparse representation to maintain structure consistency and texture clarity in the unknown region. To incorporate *coherence* property of natural images some authors [1] suggest to inpaint the target region by the weighted average of the candidates of neighbor patches. Komodakis and Tziritas [10] propose MRF-based image inpainting, namely priority belief propagation (p-BP), by favoring the similarity with the overlapping region of the neighboring patches. Liu and Caselles [13] formulate inpainting as a global energy optimization problem using multiscale graph cuts algorithm. Darabi et al. [3] proposed *image melding* to improve PatchMatch [1] by incorporating geometric and photometric transformations.

Some of the previous methods [1,3,10,13] use pyramid-based technique as the basic framework to capture features in different scales. These methods start from the coarsest level and inpaint each sub-level to reach the finest level. So the quality of the resulted image depends on the inpainted image in the coarsest level. If the coarsest level produce unsatisfactory result then this information is propagated in the finest level, resulting a visually unpleasant inpainted image. Also if we do inpainting at each level of the pyramid individually, it is difficult to say which resolution is perfect for inpainting. For different images the resolution in the coarsest level may not be same to obtain the best result.

To over come this problem, we propose a multiple pyramids based image inpainting algorithm using gradient based image composition. Our main contributions are as follows: (1) build multiple pyramids of the input image with different starting scales; (2) search for candidate patches in different sub levels of the pyramid and run image inpainting method in each pyramid to produce different inpainted images; (3) combine the inpainted images by gradient-based image composition to produce the final inpainted image. Here, we first build multiple pyramids with different resolution of the input image in the coarsest levels of the pyramids, and then obtain an inpainted image in each of the finest levels of the pyramids using traditional pyramid-based approach. So by this way we get multiple inpainted images, one for each of the pyramids. Then we

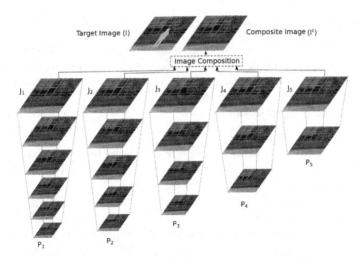

Fig. 1. Overview of the proposed algorithm. $P_1, P_2, \ldots, P_5$ are the pyramids with different resolution of the input image in the coarsest levels. $J_1, J_2, \ldots, J_5$ are the inpainted images obtained from the pyramids $P_1, P_2, \ldots, P_5$ respectively using traditional image inpainting algorithms. I^c is the final inpainted image produced by the image composition of $J_1, J_2, \ldots, J_5$.

combine these inpainted images by gradient-based image composition to produce a final inpainted image. In image composition, our assumption is that most of the inpainted images produced by the pyramids are quite good. However, some of them may have artifacts due to the dependency of inpainting on the resolution of the input image in the coarsest level. Our image composition method based on [23] successfully eliminates these artifacts in the final inpainted image. For image inpainting, we use sparsity-based method [20] in the coarsest level and exemplar-based method [2] in each sub-level of the pyramids. The reason behind the choice of two different algorithms is that the sparsity-based method is able to capture the structure information efficiently compared to the exemplar-based method. But for textural information the exemplar-based method gives better result compared to the sparsity-based methods. Figure 1 shows an overview of the proposed algorithm.

Rest of the paper is organized as follows. The main steps of the proposed method: multiple pyramid-based image inpainting and gradient-based image composition are presented in Sect. 2. In Sect. 3, experimental results and comparisons with some previous methods are explained. The concluding notes and further prospects of the proposed work are given in Sect. 4.

2 Proposed Inpainting Method

The proposed image inpainting method consists of two basic frameworks: multiple pyramid-based image inpainting and gradient-based image composition.

2.1 Multiple Pyramid-Based Inpainting

In this section we describe our proposed image inpainting method based on generating multiple pyramids of the input image. The method consists of several intermediate steps such as multiple pyramids building, searching for candidate patches and sub-level image inpainting. Each of these steps is described elaborately in the following subsections.

Multiple Pyramids Building: Here our goal is to build multiple pyramids for different starting scales of the input image and obtain an inpainted image for each of the pyramids. We choose the blur kernel B to be a Gaussian kernel with a given variance σ_B^2. The value s is an integer scalar factor (e.g., 4 or 5), by which the HR input image I_H is downsampled to the LR image I_L, which to be inpainted first and then upscaled gradually to obtain the HR inpainted image $\hat{I}_H$, i.e. if the input image I_H is of size $X \times Y$, the LR image at the coarsest level will have a size of $\frac{X}{s} \times \frac{Y}{s}$. The LR images at different levels of the pyramid is obtained by

$$I_{-n} = (I_H * B_n) \downarrow_{r^n} \tag{1}$$

where r is the pyramid cross-level scale factor. The LR image I_{-n} is the downsampled version of the original HR input image I_H with total rescale factor r^n.

So far we have discussed how to generate a pyramid of LR images from a HR input image. Now we want to generate K pyramids $P_1, P_2, \ldots, P_K$ from the HR image I_H with different rescale factors. For this, we define the scale factor r by

$$r_p = r_{p-1} + z \qquad \text{for} \quad p = 2, 3, \ldots, K \tag{2}$$

where z is the factor which controls the scale of the image in the coarsest level of the pyramids. The value of r_1 is set to 1.35 in our experiments. Typically, the parameter z takes the value 0.03. The pyramid P_1 is generated using the scale factor r_1, similarly the pyramid P_2 is generated using r_2 and so on.

Searching for Candidate Patches: Several searching algorithms [1,3,10] are proposed in literature using traditional pyramid based framework. These methods search the candidate patches in the same sub-level in which the image is inpainted. In natural images, local image structure, which can be captured by small patch, repeats across different scales of an image. So we can use the input image to be inpainted, with up-sampled or down-sampled images, for searching the candidate patches. Previously, these types of multi sub-level search algorithm were proposed for super-resolution [7,21,22]. They had used either one-step search algorithm or a pyramid of recursively scaled images to search the patches.

Similar to one-step approach, we construct a pair of scaled images with the original image for estimating the search region. The reason behind this motivation is that the most relevant patches similar to the target patch can be found

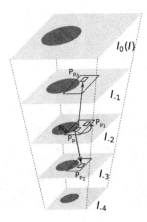

Fig. 2. Overview of the search algorithm. I_{-2} is the current level for image inpainting. For a target patch P_p, we search for the candidate patches in a neighborhood of P_p in I_{-1}, I_{-2} and I_{-3} and select the patches P_{p_3}, P_{p_1} and P_{p_2} respectively.

within the images with small rescaled factor. It is observed that the sufficient amount of good patches could be found by only one rescaling. Let $\mathcal{D}$ denotes an image downscaling operator, s.t. $\mathcal{D}(I) = (I) \downarrow_r$, where r is a suitably chosen small scale factor; let $\mathcal{U}$ denotes an image upscaling operator, s.t. $\mathcal{U}(I) = (I) \uparrow_r$. To inpaint an image I in any sub-level of a pyramid, the image I itself along with $\mathcal{D}(I)$ and $\mathcal{U}(I)$ can be used as sources for searching the candidate patches. However, for the coarsest level, since no downscale image is available, only upscale image is used as source; and on contrary, for the finest level, since no upscale image is available, only downscale image is used as source.

The method, namely, pyramid of recursively scaled images use all the sub-levels as the most relevant source for searching the candidate patches. To avoid the exhaustive search, since it is time consuming, several authors solved it by reducing the search region to a local window [12,13], directional search [6,11], search along user-specified curves [17]. Similar to local search window [12,13], we consider a neighborhood of the target patch in the form of a rectangular region.

In this work, the search region depends on the scale of the pyramid. If in the n-th sub-level the input image is I_{-n} of scale factor r^n, and the search radius is bounded by $\Omega = \min\{r^{-n} \times \kappa, \min(p/2, q/2)\}$ where $p \times q$ is the size of the image in the n-th sub-level, then the radius for one-step search algorithm i.e., for the images I_{-n-1} and I_{-n+1} are Ω/r and $r\Omega$ respectively. Other than this, if we consider Ω for all the three images, then the search range will increase for I_{-n-1} and decrease for I_{-n+1} with respect to the scale of the images. To fix the search range uniformly through out the scale of the images, we have applied varying size of search window with a particular scale factor. Figure 2 shows an overview of the proposed patch searching algorithm.

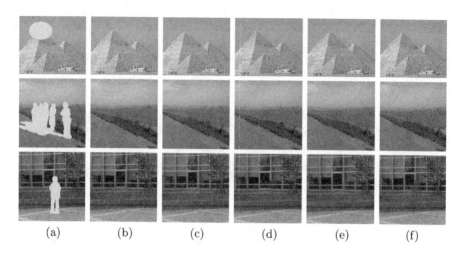

Fig. 3. (a) Target image. (b–f) Inpainted images obtained from 5 pyramids.

Sub-level Image Inpainting: This step proposes a combined approach for image inpainting algorithm applied on the multiple pyramids. Each of the pyramids follow this combined approach to get the inpainted images $J_i = \hat{I}(P_i)$ for $i = 1, 2, \ldots, K$ at the finest level of the pyramids. The updated image at each level of the pyramid is obtained by

$$I_{-n}(T) = \mathcal{U}(\hat{I}_{-n-1}(T)) \tag{3}$$

where $\hat{I}_{-n-1}$ is the LR inpainted image at level $n + 1$ and $I_{-n}(T)$ is the HR image obtained by upscaling (using the upscaling operator $\mathcal{U}$) the LR image $\hat{I}_{-n-1}$. Here T denotes the target region. The LR image at the coarsest level of the pyramid is inpainted using the sparsity-based approach [20].

In practice, we upscaled the LR inpainted image $\hat{I}_{-n-1}$ by Bicubic interpolation and copy the inpainted region (i.e. the inferred target area) of $\mathcal{U}(\hat{I}_{-n-1}(T))$ followed by replacing it to the target region of I_{-n}. In this way we obtain I_{-n} with known target region at the n-th sub-level but this known target region may not be as sharp as the source region of I_{-n} due to the interpolation. To solve this problem we now apply the exemplar-based image inpainting method [2] on I_{-n} considering the source region of I_{-n} as the search region for the candidate patches.

Thus we obtain several inpainted images, one for each of the pyramids, as shown in Fig. 3. The figure shows that artifacts appear in different pyramids such as Fig. 3(c) for the first example near the right structure, Fig. 3(d–f) for the second example in water and grass areas; and Fig. 3(d, f) for the third example in the structure area. It reveals that if we choose those pyramids with a particular starting scale for image inpainting the resulted image is visually unpleasant. This is the main drawback of traditional single pyramid based approach. But, here we also see that most of the inpainted images for a particular example are artifact free and this motivate us to combine them to obtain a better inpainted image.

2.2   Gradient-Based Image Composition

To obtain the final inpainted image, the immediate approaches are either the average or the median operator as given below:

$$\hat{I}^a(x,y) = \frac{1}{K} \sum_{i=1}^{K} J_i(x,y) \tag{4}$$

$$\hat{I}^m(x,y) = \Delta_{i=1}^{K} J_i(x,y) \tag{5}$$

where Δ is a median operator. The main advantage of these approaches is their simplicity with respect to both conceptually and implement wise. Instead of this, they have some drawbacks. The main drawback is the point operation where it only considers the current pixel, and it does not consider the neighboring pixels of the current pixel to update it. Neighborhood processing proves its superiority than point processing to obtain spatially coherent resulted image. Also, the average operator explicitly introduces blur effect in the resulted image, shown in Fig. 4.

To handle these problems, namely blur and spatial consistency of the final image, we introduce a gradient-based image composition for combining the intermediate inpainted images. Here we assume that at a particular position most of the images have similar gradient and some of them may vary due to the appearance of artifact. We want to remove this artifact and recover the texture quality in the final inpainted image. The proposed work is motivated by multiexposure composition [23].

The gradient direction will change in the inpainted images if some artifacts appear in the target region. To get artifact free inpainted image, we capture local inconsistencies based on the changes of gradient direction within a local window. At each pixel (x, y) of the i-th image, its gradient direction change with respect to the j-th image is computed as

$$D_{ij}(x,y) = \frac{\sum_{l=-\omega}^{\omega} |\theta_i(x+l, y+l) - \theta_j(x+l, y+l)|}{(2\omega + 1)^2} \tag{6}$$

where the size of the window is $(2\omega + 1) \times (2\omega + 1)$ and ω is set to 9 in our experiments. Note that, $D_{ij}(x,y) = D_{ji}(x,y)$ and $D_{ii} = 0$ for all i. Since we assume that local inconsistencies may appear in a small number (one or two) of images, a measure T_i for each image is computed to expose its consistency with respect to the others. The measure T_i can be defined as

$$T_i(x,y) = \sum_{j=1}^{K} \exp\left(\frac{-D_{ij}^2(x,y)}{2\sigma^2}\right) \tag{7}$$

where σ is standard deviation and set to .04 in the experiments. A large value of T implies a small gradient changes, that means the information is frequently occurred in the images. The final weight matrix is obtained by

$$W_i(x,y) = \frac{T_i(x,y)}{\sum_{i=1}^{K} T_i(x,y) + \delta} \tag{8}$$

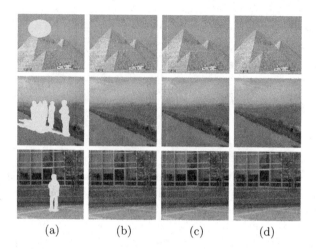

(a)   (b)   (c)   (d)

Fig. 4. (a) Target image. (b) Results obtained by averaging all inpainted images from Fig. 3(b–f). (c) Results due to median operator. (d) Results due to image composition.

where δ is a small value such as 10^{-10} to avoid singularity.

So the final inpainted image $\hat{I}^c$ may be expressed as

$$\hat{I}^c(x, y) = \sum_{i=1}^{K} W_i(x, y) J_i(x, y) \qquad (9)$$

For combining all the images seamlessly we apply the multiresolution scheme proposed in [14]. Figure 4 shows some result of image composition applied on 5 different inpainted images from Fig. 3 along with the images obtained by mean and median operators. However, the final inpainted image obtained from the image composition is visually pleasant and almost artifact free.

3 Experiments and Results

Here we set the parameters and evaluate the proposed method by qualitative analysis on object removal. For comparison, we take some of the previous state-of-the-art methods based on Xu's sparsity [20], Komodakis's p-BP [10][1], Darabi's image melding [3][2], and Liu's graph cuts [13]. The size of the patch is set to 9 in our experiments. The value of κ (control the patch search region) is set to 40. The number of pyramids K is set to 5. The sparsity-based method [20] and the proposed method are implemented in MATLAB environment. For other methods we have used the auothor's implementation code/results for our comparison. The three examples of Fig. 5 have taken 298, 413 and 613 s respectively to inpaint the target region by our proposed method.

---

[1] http://lafarren.com/image-completer/.

[2] http://www.ece.ucsb.edu/~psen/melding/.

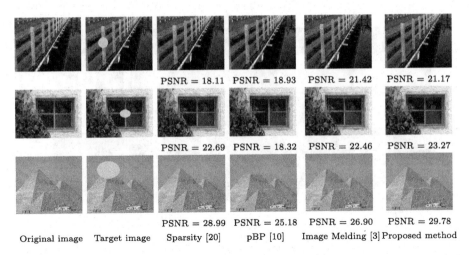

PSNR = 18.11   PSNR = 18.93   PSNR = 21.42   PSNR = 21.17

PSNR = 22.69   PSNR = 18.32   PSNR = 22.46   PSNR = 23.27

PSNR = 28.99   PSNR = 25.18   PSNR = 26.90   PSNR = 29.78

Original image   Target image   Sparsity [20]   pBP [10]   Image Melding [3] Proposed method

Fig. 5. Quantitative and qualitative comparison of different inpainting methods for blob removal.

In Fig. 5, we have shown some quantitative comparison for blob type target region. We have considered peak-signal-to-noise ratio (PSNR) as the quantitative measure, computed only over the inpainted region. The PSNR values, computed for individual color channels (R,G,B), are averaged and the average values are given below the corresponding inpainted images. The average PSNR values over all the images are 23.26, 20.81, 23.59, 24.74 respectively due to four said methods. So the quantitative comparison reveals that our method performs better than the other methods.

In Fig. 6, we consider large blob type target region for inpainting. The figure shows the target images and the inpainted images due to sparsity [20], p-BP [10], image melding [3] and the proposed method. The figure clearly shows that the proposed method produces better inpainted images compared to sparsity [20] in the 2nd example (2nd row, 2nd column), image melding in the first example (1st row, 4th column); and the method produces comparable results with p-BP [10]. In the other examples, our method produces either better or comparable results with respect to the images provided by the previous methods.

Figure 7 shows the comparisons of the proposed method with graph cuts [13], sparsity-based [20] and p-BP [10]. The figure shows that the proposed method is surely better than [10,20], and almost comparable with graph cuts [13]. However, in the first example, the texture clarity of [13] is slightly better than the proposed method.

Figure 8 shows comparison with multi-direction feature (MDF) based method [12] and sparsity-based [20]. Here in both examples our method successfully recover the structure information whereas other methods fail to recover it perfectly. For example, in the first case, the propagation of curve structure by our method is almost free of error. On the other hand, the previous methods produce similar results with wrong propagation of structure.

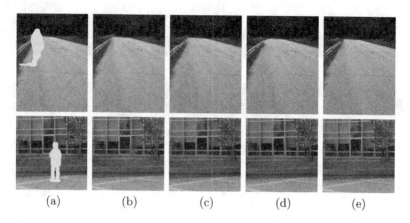

(a)   (b)   (c)   (d)   (e)

Fig. 6. (a) Target image. (b) Sparsity-based [20]. (c) p-BP [10]. (d) Image melding [3]. (e) Proposed method.

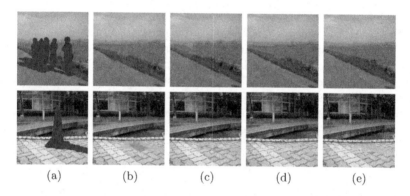

(a)   (b)   (c)   (d)   (e)

Fig. 7. (a) Target image. (b) Sparsity-based [20]. (c) p-BP [10]. (d) Graph cuts [13]. (e) Proposed method.

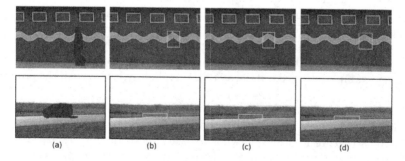

(a)   (b)   (c)   (d)

Fig. 8. (a) Target image. (b) Sparsity-based [20]. (c) MDF [12]. (d) Proposed method.

(a)   (b)   (c)   (d)   (e)

Fig. 9. Failure case. (a) Target image. (b) Sparsity-based [20]. (c) p-BP [10]. (d) Image melding [3]. (e) Proposed method.

Figure 9 shows an example where the proposed method along with competitive methods fail to recover the target region with proper pattern. However, even in this case, the proposed method produces relatively better inpainted image compared to the other approaches. Our result shows that, for random texture, a blurring effect may appear in the texture part of the target region.

4   Conclusion

In this paper we have proposed scale-invariant image inpainting method using gradient-based image composition. The proposed method try to solve the problem of traditional single pyramid based approaches in image inpainting. Technical contribution and experimental results clearly indicate that the proposed multiple pyramid based approach can produce visually satisfactory results compared to the other competitive methods. In future, we will try to incorporate a robust image feature in the proposed image inpainting for recovering more difficult examples of object removal.

References

1. Barnes, C., Shechtman, E., Finkelstein, A., Goldman, D.B.: Patch-Match: a randomized correspondence algorithm for structural image editing. ACM Trans. Graph. **28**(3), 1–11 (2009)
2. Criminisi, A., Pérez, P., Toyama, K.: Region filling and object removal by exemplar-based inpainting. IEEE Trans. Image Process. **13**(9), 1200–1212 (2004)
3. Darabi, S., Shechtman, E., Barnes, C., Goldman, D.B., Sen, P.: Image melding: combining inconsistent images using patch-based synthesis. ACM Trans. Graph. (TOG) **31**(4), 82:1–82:10 (2012)
4. Efros, A., Leung, T.: Texture synthesis by non-parametric sampling. In: Proceedings of the IEEE International Conference on Computer Vision, vol. 2, pp. 1033–1038 (1999)
5. Fadili, M.J., Starck, J.L., Murtagh, F.: Inpainting and zooming using sparse representations. Comput. J. **52**(1), 64–79 (2009)
6. Fang, C.-W., Lien, J.-J.J.: Rapid image completion system using multiresolution patch-based directional and nondirectional approaches. IEEE Trans. Image Process. **18**(12), 2769–2779 (2009)
7. Freedman, G., Fattal, R.: Image and video upscaling from local self-examples. ACM Trans. Graph. (TOG) **30**(2), 12 (2011)

8. Ghorai, M., Chanda, B.: An image inpainting algorithm using higher order singular value decomposition. In: 2014 22nd International Conference on Pattern Recognition (ICPR), pp. 2867–2872. IEEE (2014)

9. Ghorai, M., Chanda, B.: An image inpainting method using pLSA-based search space estimation. Mach. Vis. Appl. **26**(1), 69–87 (2015)

10. Komodakis, N., Tziritas, G.: Image completion using efficient belief propagation via priority scheduling and dynamic pruning. IEEE Trans. Image Process. **16**(11), 2649–2661 (2007)

11. Le Meur, O., Gautier, J., Guillemot, C.: Examplar-based inpainting based on local geometry. In: 2011 18th IEEE International Conference on Image Processing, pp. 3401–3404. IEEE (2011)

12. Li, Z., He, H., Tai, H.-M., Yin, Z., Chen, F.: Color-direction patch-sparsity-based image inpainting using multidirection features. IEEE Trans. Image Process. **24**(3), 1138–1152 (2015)

13. Liu, Y., Caselles, V.: Exemplar-based image inpainting using multiscale graph cuts. IEEE Trans. Image Process. **22**(5), 1699–1711 (2013)

14. Mertens, T., Kautz, J., Van Reeth, F.: Exposure fusion: a simple and practical alternative to high dynamic range photography. In: Computer Graphics Forum, vol. 28, pp. 161–171. Wiley Online Library (2009)

15. Qin, Y., Wang, F.: A curvature constraint exemplar-based image inpainting. In: International Conference on Image Processing and Signal Processing, pp. 263–267 (2010)

16. Shen, B., Hu, W., Zhang, Y., Zhang, Y.: Image inpainting via sparse representation. In: Proceedings of the IEEE International Conference on Acoustics, Speech and Signal Processing, pp. 697–700 (2009)

17. Sun, J., Yuan, L., Jia, J., Shum, H.: Image completion with structure propagation. In: Proceedings of the SIGGRAPH2005, pp. 861–868 (2005)

18. Wohlberg, B.: Inpainting by joint optimization of linear combinations of exemplars. IEEE Signal Process. Lett. **18**(1), 75–78 (2011)

19. Wu, J., Ruan, Q.: Object removal by cross isophotes exemplar-based inpainting. In: Proceedings of the 18th International Conference on Pattern Recognition, vol. 3, pp. 810–813 (2006)

20. Xu, Z., Sun, J.: Image inpainting by patch propagation using patch sparsity. IEEE Trans. Image Process. **19**(5), 1153–1165 (2010)

21. Yang, M.-C., Wang, C.-H., Hu, T.-Y., Wang, Y.-C.F.: Learning context-aware sparse representation for single image super-resolution. In: 2011 18th IEEE International Conference on Image Processing, pp. 1349–1352. IEEE (2011)

22. Zhang, K., Gao, X., Tao, D., Li, X.: Single image super-resolution with multi-scale similarity learning. IEEE Trans. Neural Netw. Learn. Syst. **24**(10), 1648–1659 (2013)

23. Zhang, W., Cham, W.-K.: Gradient-directed multiexposure composition. IEEE Trans. Image Process. **21**(4), 2318–2323 (2012)

Recursive Structure from Motion

M. Chebiyyam$^{(\boxtimes)}$, S. Chaudhury, and I.N. Kar

Department of Electrical Engeneering, Indian Institute of Technology Delhi,
New Delhi, India
manaswi94@gmail.com, {santanuc,ink}@ee.iitd.ac.in

Abstract. In this paper we present a technique that estimates the Structure from Motion (SFM) in a recursive fashion. Traditionally successful SFM algorithms take the set of images and estimate the scene geometry and camera positions either using incremental algorithms or the global algorithms and do the refinement process [2] to reduce the reprojection error. In this work it is assumed that we don't have complete image set at the start of the reconstruction process, unlike most of the traditional approaches present in the literature. It is assumed that the set of images come in at the regular intervals and we recursively perform the SFM on the incoming set of images and update the previously reconstructed structure with the structure estimated from the current set of images. The proposed system has been tested on two datasets which consist of 12 images and 60 images respectively and reconstructions obtained show the validity of our proposed technique.

Keywords: Structure from Motion · Similariy transformation · Recursive update

1 Introduction

Structure from Motion (SFM) is one of the well studied and established field among the computer vision research community. There are very good benchmark algorithms that came out in recent times which perform the reconstruction from unordered large scale image collections. Among these algorithms the one's that reconstruct in incremental fashion are [1,6] and in global fashion [4,7]. All these algorithms are very successful in providing reliable large scale 3D structures from unordered image collections. Some of the shortcomings in the existing algorithms that reconstruct in incremental fashion [1,6] are (1) their reconstruction is highly dependent on the initial pair that is chosen (2) sensitive to the degenerate configuration. Indeed if the baseline is small then it is not possible to reliably estimate the translations [8]. Since these methods rely on a well estimated structure for adding new cameras, degenerate geometries may cause them to fail. To avoid this authors in [1,6] removes configurations where the data can be well fitted to a homography. Incremental methods also have to perform the repeated bundle adjustments [2] to prevent the errors from accumulating in the system and as the structure grows in size this becomes a very costly operation to perform.

© Springer International Publishing AG 2017
S. Mukherjee et al. (Eds.): ICVGIP 2016, LNCS 10481, pp. 109–119, 2017.
https://doi.org/10.1007/978-3-319-68124-5_10

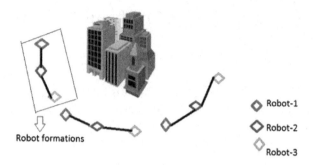

Fig. 1. A illustration of the robots capturing structure

Global methods [4,7] solve some of the problems present in the incremental approach like initial configuration and small baseline geometries however they pose the challenge of the reliably estimating the initial solution for the bundle adjustment to converge. This is because of the large dimensionality of the problem specified for refinement, bundle adjustment may not converge or take significant amount of time in doing so without good initial solution. Recently this problem has been addressed by rotational and translational averaging schemes proposed in [3,5].

The problem we take in this work is to recursively estimate the 3D structure from the sets of images captured by the multiple robots moving in a formation. An illustration of the proposed scheme using three robots is described in Fig. 1, although the proposed algorithm can be extended for any number of robots moving in a formation. In this formation relative distance between consecutive robots is maintained. Every time multi-robot formation captures the structure, corresponding image set can be sent to ground station. As the robot formation moves around capturing the structure in regular intervals it can be assumed that captured image sets are sequential extensions of structure. In the ground station the reconstruction process is started with initial set of images and then structure is recursively updated with new 3D points whenever new set of images are made available. The added advantage to this kind of formulation is that several small SFM problems are solved and then updated to produce the complete reconstruction, instead of solving one big problem which can be very hard to refine at times. Note that it is shown in [6] that for small dimensional problems bundle adjustment [2] that is used for refinement is linear in time.

The rest of the paper is organized as follows. Section 2 describes the related work to our setting and Sect. 3 describes the approach of our algorithm. Section 4 reports the results of our experiments on two data sets, and Sect. 5 concludes with a discussion and directions for future work.

2   Related Work

The earlier work in SFM has dealt with the problem of 3D reconstruction with the camera moving on a vehicle. Among them prominent ones are reported in

[9–12]. All of these works move around in an urban environment with calibrated camera mounted on top of a car to do the city-block scale reconstructions. While [10] uses the Kalman filtering [16] setting in the SFM framework to refine the camera parameters and 3D structure, [12] fuses the data from the GPS devices and SFM in the Kalman filtering setting to get the 3D reconstructions using calibrated camera. In [13] we found that authors have considered the similar scenario of deploying a robot with calibrated camera to estimate the 3D structure in projective space. Some of the work done under Simultaneous Localization and Mapping (SLAM) such as [14,15] also used calibrated camera as sensor to map the environment. To refine the map and camera localization in the environment many authors used Kalman filtering [14] and Particle filtering [15]. Although these authors show scalability of their approaches their representative capabilities of the environment are limited due to the high volume of the data that is coming in at every instant. Unlike the above mentioned works we assume uncalibrated camera for the present work. We use the EXIF image tags from the images to get the initial estimate of the focal length and refine them further as in [1].

There are other class of algorithms that uses factorization methods to compute structure and motion which are derived from [24]. In [24] it was shown that from a noise-free measurement matrix of point tracks the 3D locations of all tracked points and camera positions can be easily obtained from a factorization for an affine camera when the data are centered at the origin. This method is limited by the outliers, missing data and can only be applied for complete image set. In [25] authors proposed a sequential version of the factorization algorithm, which allows to operate on image set in incremental fashion. Recent work in [26] solved the problem of missing data, outliers in which authors update the factorization matrices that represent structure and motion every time a new image is available. This work has similar goal that of ours but presents a different approach in solving the problem.

3 System Overview

Our system has mainly two components first is to perform the SFM on current set of images and the second component is to update the previously reconstructed structure with the reconstruction from the current set of images. Both the components are described in detail below.

3.1 SFM on Current Image Set

In this work SFM on the current image set is done in incremental fashion as in [1,6]. The SFM process is initialized by doing SIFT matching [17] on pairs of images to create a image connectivity graph. Unlike in [1] we do not use the vocabulary tree approach [18] to generate the initial pairs of connected components and the query expansion [19] to generate the complete image connectivity graph for full geometric estimation. Instead we consider every image in the set with only the next two images as a candidate for pairwise matching as the formations capture structure in orderly fashion. An edge between the pair is formed only when the number of SIFT matches between the pair exceeds the threshold α as the first filter. In the later step only those edges in which estimation essential matrix succeeds, view angle between the cameras exceeds a threshold ($5°$) are retained. These retained candidate pairs under go full geometric estimation in our system.

In the next step Best First Search (BFS) is performed on the image connectivity graph to generate the skeletal set. BFS is performed based on the heuristic which is the linear function of number of the sift matches and the angle between the camera pairs with positive coefficients. Then the 3D points are triangulated and the camera pairs are merged incrementally based on the skeletal set obtained from the BFS algorithm. Refinement is not performed in any of the intermediate stages of the incremental process because of the small size of the estimation problem due to recursive nature of the system. Finally, the initial rotation and translation estimates and the 3D points estimated from the skeletal set are passed to bundle adjustment [2] and then outlier points (large reprojection error) are removed after the refinement.

3.2 Recursive Update

In the previous section it is shown that how to estimate the structure from the given image set. As stated in the introduction every SFM estimation is followed by the update step which updates previously reconstructed structure with the structure reconstructed from the current image set. We call this setting as recursive update of the structure. The update is performed by finding the common 3D points in two structures which correspond to the same world point and then by finding a similarity transformation using these 3D matched points which transforms the coordinate system of the current structure to match with the coordinate system of the previously reconstructed structure.

To find the common 3D points between two reconstructions that represent same world point we take the last image in the previous reconstruction and the first image in the current reconstruction and find the 3D points that are estimated from these images in their reconstructions. These sets are referred as X1 - 3D points estimated in the last image of the previous reconstruction and X2 - 3D points estimated in the first image of the current reconstruction. The SIFT descriptors corresponding to the image locations of these 3D points are taken from their respective images and the bi-directional matching of descriptors is performed on these two sets. All the descriptors that match should correspond to the same world point. The subset of the matched 3D points from X1 and X2 is referred as $X1_s$ and $X2_s$ respectively. The similarity transformation 'S' that we intend to find should satisfy the relation

$$X1_s = S * X2_s$$

This similarity transformation 'S' can be used to transform the coordinate system of current reconstruction to match with the previous reconstruction. If the transformation 'S' is derived directly by the least squares solution [20] then the transformation will assume more degrees of freedom than that of similarity transformation due to the errors in the matching process. In which case shape, angles may not be preserved after transformation. Infact it is found that direct least squares solution projects the structure in to the affine space, which do not preserve the angles.

This problem is solved by decoupling the transformation into degrees of freedom that it has and solving for them in non-linear least squares setting using Levenberg-Marquardt (LM) algorithm [21]. In general any similarity transformation can be written in the form

$$S = \begin{bmatrix} sR & t \\ 0 & 1 \end{bmatrix}$$

It has 7-dof (3-rotation, 3-translation and 1-scale). Rotation in angle-axis representation is parameterized by 3 parameters $[\phi_1 \ \phi_2 \ \phi_3]$ and translation is represented as $[t_1 \ t_2 \ t_3]$. Finally 'S' is represented in our non-linear least squares setting as a vector v

$$v = [\phi_1 \ \phi_2 \ \phi_3 \ t_1 \ t_2 \ t_3 \ s]$$

where s is the scale factor in similarity transformation. These 7-dof are solved using the LM algorithm [21] with random initialization to reduce the residual error

$$\epsilon = ||X1_s - S * X2_s||_2$$

Note that 'S' is formed from v while calculating the residual error 'ϵ' in LM algorithm. As we know that non-linear least squares is not robust to outliers (matching errors) we compensate for this by using the RANSAC algorithm [22] in combination with non-linear least squares. LM algorithm runs in every RANSAC trail to find best transformation with randomly chosen samples and then the number of inliers are calculated with that transformation. Although 3 matched points are enough to find the 7-dof in each trail, we found that allowing more number of points (5~10) in every trail reduced the number of trials required. RANSAC algorithm in this setting gives the transformation that satisfies maximum number of 3D matches from its trails. The coordinate system of current reconstruction is then transformed using the similarity transformation obtained from RANSAC step and all the 3D points from the current reconstruction are added to previous reconstruction. Complete recursive algorithm is summarized in Algorithm 1 and process of finding similarity transformation in every update is summarized in Algorithm 2.

Algorithm 1. Recurssive algorithm for Structure from Motion

initial reconstruction←SFM(initial image-set)
previous reconstruction←initial reconstruction
previous image-set←initial image-set
while incoming image-set **do**
    current image-set ← incoming image-set
    current reconstruction←SFM(current image-set)
    X1←3D points from last frame of previous reconstruction
    X2←3D points from first frame of current reconstruction
    F1←SIFT features correspond to X1 from last frame of previous reconstruction
    F2←SIFT features correspond to X2 from first frame of current reconstruction
    current reconstruction←Similarity transformation $(X1, X2, F1, F2,$current reconstruction)
    previous reconstruction← update(previous reconstruction, current reconstruction)
    previous image-set ← current image-set
end while

Algorithm 2. Algorithm for finding Similarity Transformation

procedure SIMILARITY TRANSFORMATION($X1, X2, F1, F2,$reconstruction)
    $(id1, id2)$←SIFT Matching(F1,F2)
    $X1_s$ ← X1(id1)
    $X2_s$ ← X2(id2)
    $\epsilon ← ||X1_s - S * X2_s||_{L2}$
    S_{int} ← [rand(3) rand(3) rand(1)] ▷ initial solution [rotation translation scaling]
    S ← RANSAC($X1_s, X2_s,$@LM(ϵ, s_{int}))
    reconstruction← transform coordinate system(S,reconstruction)
    return reconstruction
end procedure

4   Experimental Results

To simulate the proposed algorithm we have taken two datasets of different sizes House dataset and the Hall dataset each containing 12 and 60 images respectively. Each dataset is divided in to many disjoint image sets with few images in each image set. These image sets are given to the algorithm over time as in they come from the multi-robot formation. The proposed method was able to find the similarity transformation's over all the updates and do the complete reconstruction in both the cases. Most part of the implementation is written in the MATLAB except for bundle adjustment which is written in C++ using ceres solver package and integrated to system with a MATLAB wrapper. This is because MATLAB's implementation of the LM algorithm is very time consuming, so we used ceres solver for bundle adjustment which is very efficient. Some of the code provided in [23] is used for implementing the proposed algorithm. All the experiments were ran on a PC with an 2.5 GHz Intel Core i7 6500U processor and 8 GB RAM.

Fig. 2. Sample images from the House dataset

Fig. 3. Sample images from the Hall dataset

House dataset. House dataset consists of 12 images of a house taken in a sequential manner. The dataset is split in to 3 image sets of 4 images each as in image set-1 contains first four images of dataset and then image set-2 contains next four and so on respectively. As described in our model we start the SFM process with the first image set and then recursively update the structure using similarity transformation every time after a new image set is received. In each image set the threshold for number of SIFT matches between the pair 'α' is set to 30. Figure 2 shows sample images from the dataset. Partial reconstructions from each of the three image sets are shown in Fig. 4(a)–(c). Complete structure formed after all the updates is shown from three different views in Fig. 5(a)–(c). A total of 1910 3D points are present in the final model.

Table 1 specifies the time taken to compute the similarity transformation between successive reconstructions and the corresponding number of 3D point matches between them for each update step in both the datasets.

Hall dataset. Hall dataset consists of 60 images of a building taken in sequential manner. This dataset is divided into 10 image sets containing 6 images each. The division is done in the similar manner as prviously described for the House

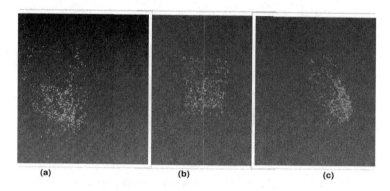

Fig. 4. Partial reconstructions of house from different image-sets

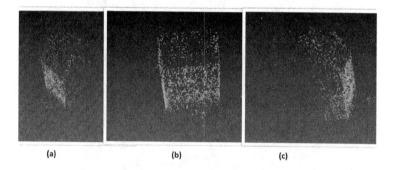

Fig. 5. Complete reconstruction of house from different views

Table 1. Table above specifies time taken in seconds to compute the similarity transformation in each update step and number of corresponding 3D point matches for each update step

Dataset		Update-1	Update-2	Update-3	Update-4	Update-5	Update-6	Update-7	Update-8	Update-9
House	Time	2.1	2.8	-	-	-	-	-	-	-
	3D-Matches	140	170							
Hall	Time	5.6	5.1	5.1	4.8	4.6	4.7	4.5	4.9	4.5
	3D-Matches	236	28	80	24	78	84	40	76	185

dataset. Figure 3 shows the sample images from this dataset. In each image set the threshold for number of SIFT matches between the pair 'α' is set to 30. A total of 5230 3D points are present in final model after updating initial reconstruction with 3D points estimated from all the image-sets. Figure 6 shows the time evolution of the structure in our algorithm, where Fig. 6(a) shows the state of the reconstruction after updating initial reconstruction two times with 6-images in each update. Figure 6(b) shows the state after 5-updates which is equivalent to structure seen from first 36 images of the dataset. Bottom two images Fig. 6(c) and (d) show the final reconstruction from two different views.

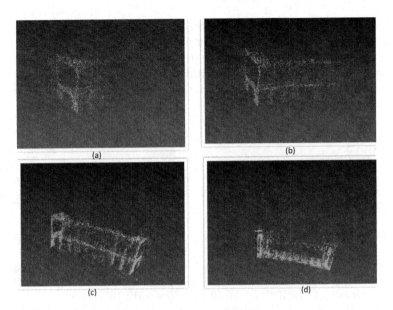

Fig. 6. Growth of structure over time

Table 2. Table above compares the mean reprojection error of the estimated 3d-points for both recursive and cecntralised algorithms.

Dataset		Recursive	Centralized
House	Mean reprojection error	0.766	1.17
Hall	Mean reprojection error	3.09	4.96

Comparisons. Structure estimated with the recursive algorithm described above is compared with the structure estimated with the centralized algorithm in which all the images are available from the start time. Centralized algorithm is same as doing SFM on each image set in the recursive algorithm described in previous section except that structure is estimated from all the images of the dataset in one go. Mean re-projection error metric is used to compare the structure in both the cases. Table 2 specifies the values in both the cases. As it can be noted that mean re-projection error in recursive algorithm is low compared to centralized algorithm for both the datasets. This is because of the fact that recursive algorithm solves several small SFM problems and fuses them to form final structure and for small dimensionality problem it is known that bundle adjustment is effective in finding the solution.

5   Conclusions and Future Work

In this work we have presented an algorithm where the structure is updated upon the arrival new image data. The model presented here can be easily parallelized in case of high incoming rate of image sets as doing SFM on each of these image sets can be done independently. Currently our model can be directly implemented on a multi-robot system moving in a formation for structure estimation. In future we intend to modify this algorithm so that it can take advantage of the formation information such as intra formation distances and formation dynamics in estimating the 3D structure.

References

1. Agarwal, S., Snavely, N., Simon, I., Seitz, S.M., Szeliski, R.: Building Rome in a day. In: International Conference on Computer Vision (ICCV), Kyoto, Japan (2009)
2. Agarwal, S., Snavely, N., Seitz, S.M., Szeliski, R.: Bundle adjustment in the large. In: Daniilidis, K., Maragos, P., Paragios, N. (eds.) ECCV 2010. LNCS, vol. 6312, pp. 29–42. Springer, Heidelberg (2010). doi:10.1007/978-3-642-15552-9_3
3. Wilson, K., Snavely, N.: Robust global translations with 1DSfM. In: Fleet, D., Pajdla, T., Schiele, B., Tuytelaars, T. (eds.) ECCV 2014. LNCS, vol. 8691, pp. 61–75. Springer, Cham (2014). doi:10.1007/978-3-319-10578-9_5
4. Crandall, D., Owens, A., Snavely, N., Huttenlocher, D.P.: Discrete-continuous optimization for large-scale structure from motion. In: IEEE Conference on Computer Vision and Pattern Recognition (CVPR) (2011)
5. Chatterjee, A., Govindu, V.M.: Efficient and robust large-scale rotation averaging. In: Proceedings of International Conference on Computer Vision (ICCV) (2013)
6. Wu, C.: Towards linear-time incremental structure from motion. In: Proceedings of the 2013 International Conference on 3D Vision (3DV 2013), pp. 127–134. IEEE Computer Society, Washington, D.C
7. Olsson, C., Enqvist, O.: Stable structure from motion for unordered image collections. In: Heyden, A., Kahl, F. (eds.) SCIA 2011. LNCS, vol. 6688, pp. 524–535. Springer, Heidelberg (2011). doi:10.1007/978-3-642-21227-7_49
8. Enqvist, O., Kahl, F., Olsson, C.: Non-sequential structure from motion. IEEE International Conference on Computer Vision Workshops (ICCV Workshops), pp. 264–271 (2011)
9. Mordohai, P., Frahm, J.M., Akbarzadeh, A., Clipp, B., Engels, C., Gallup, D., Merrell, P., Salmi, C., Sinha, S., Talton, B., Wang, L., Yang, Q., Stewnius, H., Towles, H., Welch, G., Yang, R., Pollefeys, M., Nistr, D.: Real-time video-based reconstruction of urban environments. In: 3D-ARCH 2007: 3D Virtual Reconstruction and Visualization of Complex Architectures, Zurich, Switzerland, July 2007
10. Clipp, B., Welch, G., Frahm, J.-M., Pollefeys, M.: Structure from motion via a two-stage pipeline of extended Kalman filters. In: Proceedings of the British Machine Vision Conference 2007 (BMVC 2007), British Machine Vision Association, BMVA (2007)
11. Pollefeys, M., Nistr, D., Frahm, J.-M., Akbarzadeh, A., Mordohai, P., Clipp, B., Engels, C., Gallup, D., Kim, S.J., Merrell, P., Salmi, C., Sinha, S., Talton, B., Wang, L., Yang, Q., Stewnius, H., Yang, R., Welch, G., Towles, H.: Detailed real-time urban 3D reconstruction from video. Int. J. Comput. Vis. **78**(2–3), 143–167 (2008)
12. Clipp, B., Raguram, R., Frahm, J.-M., Welch, G., Pollefeys, M.: A mobile 3D city reconstruction system. In: IEEE VR workshop on Cityscapes, March 2008

13. Beardsley, P.A., Zisserman, A., Murray, D.W.: Sequential updating of projective and affine structure from motion. Int. J. Comput. Vis. **23**(3), 235–259 (1997)

14. Bleser, G., Becker, M., Stricker, D.: Real-time vision-based tracking and reconstruction. J. Real-Time Image Proc. **2**(2–3), 161–175 (2007)

15. Eade, E., Drummond, T.: Scalable monocular SLAM. In: Proceedings of the 2006 IEEE Computer Society Conference on Computer Vision and Pattern Recognition, (CVPR 2006), vol. 1, pp. 469–476. IEEE Computer Society, Washington, D.C. (2006)

16. Welch, G., Bishop, G.: An introduction to the Kalman filter. In: Tutorial of SIGGRAPH 2001, pp. 1–81 (2001)

17. Lowe, D.G.: Distinctive image features from scale-invariant keypoints. Int. J. Comput. Vis. **60**(2), 91–110 (2004)

18. Nister, D., Stewenius, H.: Scalable recognition with a vocabulary tree. In: Proceedings of the 2006 IEEE Computer Society Conference on Computer Vision and Pattern Recognition (CVPR 2006), vol. 2, pp. 2161–2168. IEEE Computer Society, Washington, D.C. (2006)

19. Chum, O., Philbin, J., Sivic, J., Isard, M., Zisserman, A.: Total recall: automatic query expansion with a generative feature model for object retrieval. In: Proceedings of the 11th International Conference on Computer Vision, Rio de Janeiro, Brazil (2007)

20. Charnes, A., Frome, E.L., Yu, P.L.: The equivalence of generalized least squares and maximum likelihood estimates in the exponential family. J. Am. Stat. Assoc. **71**(353), 169–171 (1976)

21. Levenberg, K.: A method for the solution of certain non-linear problems in least squares. Q. Appl. Math. **2**, 164–168 (1944)

22. Fischler, M.A., Bolles, R.C.: A paradigm for model fitting with applications to image analysis and automated cartography. Commun. ACM **24**(6), 381–395 (1981). doi:10.1145/358669.358692

23. Xiao, J.: SFMedu. http://vision.princeton.edu/courses/SFMedu/

24. Tomasi, C., Kanade, T.: Shape and motion from image streams under orthography: a factorization method. Int. J. Comput. Vis. **9**(2), 13–154 (1992)

25. Morita, T., Kanade, T.: A sequential factorization method for recovering shape and motion from image streams. Pattern Anal. Mach. Intell. **19**(8), 858–867 (1997)

26. Kennedy, R., Balzano, L., Wright, S.J., Taylor, C.J.: Online algorithms for factorization-based structure from motion. Comput. Vis. Image Underst. (2016). http://dblp.uni-trier.de/rec/bib/journals/corr/KennedyBWT13

A Hybrid Deep Architecture for Face Recognition in Real-Life Scenario

A. Sanyal[1], U. Bhattacharya[2(✉)], and S.K. Parui[2]

[1] Department of CSE, Indian Institute of Technology, Kanpur, India
amartya18x@gmail.com
[2] CVPR Unit, Indian Statistical Institute, Kolkata, India
{ujjwal,swapan}@isical.ac.in

Abstract. This article describes our recent study of a real-life face recognition problem using a hybrid architecture consisting of a very deep convolution neural network (CNN) and a support vector machine (SVM). The novel aspects of this study include (i) implementation of a really deep CNN architecture consisting of 11 layers to study the effect of increasing depth on recognition performance by a subsequent SVM, and (ii) verification of the recognition performance of this hybrid classifier trained by samples of a certain standard size on test face images of smaller sizes reminiscent to various real-life scenarios. Results of the present study show that the features computed at various shallow levels of a deep architecture have identical or at least comparable performances and are more robust than the deepest feature computed at the inner most sub-sampling layer. We have also studied a simple strategy of recognizing face images of very small sizes using this hybrid architecture trained by standard size face images and the recognition performance is reported. We obtained simulation results using the cropped images of the standard extended Yale Face Database which show an interesting characteristic of the proposed architecture with respect to face images captured in a very low intensity lighting condition.

Keywords: Convolutional neural network · Support vector machine · Face recognition

1 Introduction

The success story of face recognition research is quite encouraging among various other applications of image analysis techniques. It has, in the recent past, found a wide range of commercial applications due to its viable role in the law enforcing scenarios. However, there is a limit to its trail of success because several such applications require a few stricter conditions such as recognition of face images acquired from an outdoor environment affected by severely non-uniform lighting conditions or images captured at different angles and of very small sizes etc. In reality, available face recognition technologies cannot perform efficiently in various near extreme but not so rare conditions. Useful comprehensive surveys of

© Springer International Publishing AG 2017
S. Mukherjee et al. (Eds.): ICVGIP 2016, LNCS 10481, pp. 120–132, 2017.
https://doi.org/10.1007/978-3-319-68124-5_11

up-to-date face recognition research can be found in [14, 20, 27, 32]. The research studies discussed in these surveys show that the state-of-the-art technologies of face recognition are capable of providing high recognition rates even when a large number of classes are involved but usually as long as the test images are captured in some controlled environment. On the other hand, when image quality suffers due to uncontrolled lighting, arbitrary changes in facial expressions, or reduction of size of the image, such recognition rates fall drastically. Some of the major problems which are faced by the current face recognition research have been discussed in [7] and the same has motivated us in undertaking the present study. In the present article, we have focussed on two such real-life issues – small size of input images and poor illumination conditions.

Face recognition techniques may be broadly divided into two categories one of which is feature-based in which explicit features utilizing face knowledge [4, 29] are computed. In the other category, face recognition is viewed as a general object recognition problem [4] and the pixel values of a face image are directly used for recognition purpose without computing specific features. In the second category of approaches, face information is exploited implicitly through training of the underlying classifiers. The proposed approach belongs to the latter category and it employs a hybrid architecture consisting of a convolutional neural network and support vector machines to recognize the input face image on the basis of its pixel values. A deep CNN architecture is trained here to extract features from an input face image and an SVM is trained for recognition using these features.

An earlier study [13] showed that CNN architectures are efficient to learn invariant features for object recognition purposes although they are not equally efficient for classification tasks whereas SVMs are efficient classifiers provided they are fed with good features representing the underlying objects. In an object recognition task, the features were computed by a CNN to train an SVM and obtained superior classification performance compared to each of the two underlying individual classifiers. The significant performance improvement by this hybrid architecture was established using a standard object image dataset. A 6-layer CNN architecture was used in [13], and the values computed at the last convolution layer were used to train an SVM with Gaussian kernel.

The purpose of our present study is two-fold. One is to use a really deep convolution neural network architecture to study the comparative performance of the features (when these are fed to an SVM) obtained at its various convolution layers of increasing depths, i.e., to get an answer to the question: does a deeper convolution layer of a CNN architecture provide more efficient features? The other goal of this study is to find an answer to a second question of whether such a hybrid architecture, trained on image samples of a certain standard size, can recognize a face from its smaller size or a poorly illuminated image obtained in a real-life scenario. The answer to the first question is NO and that to the second question is YES. A brief literature survey and the details of our study including its simulation results on the publicly available cropped Yale B face database [18] are presented below.

2   Brief Survey of Existing Face Recognition Research

Research on automatic face recognition started as early as in 1960s [3]. Later, in 1971 [9], a small set of features was proposed for computer identification of human faces. However, even in recent years, after half a century since the first study on human face recognition was reported, the human skill of identifying thousands of people has encouraged many researchers to focus on more efficient approaches to automatic face recognition. The majority of the real life applications of person identification and verification demand more robust, scalable and computationally efficient methods suitable for complex viewing and environmental conditions. Over the years various genres of algorithms have been used and a few of these are mentioned below.

2.1   Handcrafted Feature Based Approaches

In a feature based recognition approach, important local facial features such as nose, eyes, lips and their geometric relationship are explored to identify the input facial image based on certain statistical similarity measures. First in [15], Kanade proposed 16 such facial features which include a few ratios of areas, distances and angles and used a simple Euclidian distance based similarity metric to recognize facial images. Brunelli and Poggio [4] developed a database of face images to compare a similar feature based face recognition approach against a template matching strategy. They obtained 100% accuracy by template matching method while the feature based method provided 90% accuracy on their database of face images. Among more sophisticated feature based face recognition methods, there exist approaches based on deformable templates [5, 24, 31], Hough transform [21], symmetry operator [23], filtering and morphological operations [10] etc. These feature based methods usually involve a set of rules restricting the search subspace with geometrical constraints. Cox et al. [6] used a 30-dimensional feature vector and obtained 95% recognition accuracy on a database of 685 face images. In another approach by Wiskott et al. [30], faces were represented by labeled graphs based on Gabor wavelet transform.

In a number of studies, faces were recognized from their profile images. Kaufman and Breeding [16] used such a recognition approach and reported 90% accuracy. Harmon et al. [11] used a 17-dimensional feature vector to represent a face and computed these feature components as averages of three different poses and considered a fourth pose for testing purpose. In [19], scale-space filtering was used for face recognition from profile image.

A major advantage of feature based methods is that the features can be made invariant with respect to size, orientation or lighting condition of the input image. Also, they can provide compact representation of a face image suitable for its fast matching. However, determining a set of discriminating features is a crucial issue and inefficiency in this task may lead to poor recognition results. The alternative to such a strategy is the use of a description of the input face based on the entire image. This is usually computationally intensive and is based on either statistical or machine learning tools.

2.2   Statistical Methods

A basic statistical approach to the present recognition problem can be implemented by generating an intensity matrix for each sample image in the available database (collection) and the query image can be identified by computing its correlation with each sample image in the dataset. In this approach the query image is classified as the one belonging to the set that provides the highest correlation with the input query image. Such an approach can provide good results in controlled environmental circumstances such as uniform illumination, scale and pose. But it is computationally very expensive and it suffers from the usual drawbacks of correlational methods such as sensitivity to face size, its orientation, pose and illumination [12]. However, more sophisticated statistical methods have been studied which work at lower dimensional spaces.

Sirovich and Kirby [26] first used principal components analysis (PCA) in the study of face images and it was shown that any face image can be represented as projections along the eigenpicture coordinate space. In a later study [28], it was shown that these projections could be used as features along with some classifier to perform face recognition. Thus, the concept of eigenfaces was developed and these correspond to the eigenvectors associated with the dominant eigenvalues of the face covariance matrix. Though the eigenface strategy was fairly robust to illumination variations, its performance degrades with scale changes.

Since the Eigenface method uses PCA for dimensionality reduction, it yields projection directions that maximize the total scatter across all face images and thus it retains various unwanted variations. On the other hand, Fisher's Linear Discriminant has been applied in different areas of computer vision including face recognition. However, dimensionality reduction can be performed using linear projection preserving linear separability. This helps in achieving insensitivity to lighting conditions. Belhumeur et al. [1] used Fisher's Discriminant Analysis based class specific linear methods for dimensionality reduction and simple classifiers in the reduced feature space, to achieve better recognition rates than with the Eigenface method.

2.3   Machine Learning Based Methods

Different tools of the machine learning paradigm like multilayer perceptron (MLP), convolutional neural network (CNN), support vector machine (SVM) and several others have been studied in the literature on face recognition.

Lawrence et al. [17] presented a hybrid neural network combining local image sampling, a self-organizing map (SOM) neural network, and a convolutional neural network for human face recognition. Recognition results obtained using this approach were presented using a database of 400 face images of 40 individuals.

Rowley et al. [25] presented a retinally connected neural network-based face detection method. It operates over small windows on raw pixel images and uses multiple networks to improve the performance. Pontil and Verri [22] used SVMs to recognize faces directly from their pixel images without implementing a feature extraction module. In [8], a CNN architecture based approach was proposed for face detection without using any preprocessing operation or any hand-crafted features. It acts like a pipeline of simple convolution and subsampling modules that use the raw input image as a whole.

Huang and LeCun [13] presented an object recognition system consisting of a CNN architecture and a Gaussian-kernel SVM. The support vector machine is trained from the features learned by the convolutional network. The authors simulated this hybrid system on a large generic object recognition task with six categories consisting of samples of each object category under various poses, illuminations, and backgrounds. The simulation results show that this hybrid classifier system improves the performance of each individual classifier.

3   Proposed Architecture

Design of the proposed architecture encompasses two major models of machine learning- Convolutional Neural Network (CNN) and Support Vector Machine (SVM). Combination of these two algorithms have been successfully used in the past by several other researchers. However, here we have applied it in a slightly different manner and in some cases the results that we have obtained are quite interesting. We test the output of different intermediate layers of the CNN as input features for SVM to observe the trend of classification accuracies. Logistic regression is used for training of CNN. The CNN network was implemented using the Theano [2], which is a Python framework optimizing evaluation of mathematical expressions with multi-dimensional arrays and taking care of various other issues towards fast execution of computationally complex algorithms.

Convolutional neural network architectures are dependant on the size of the input image. One of the distinguishing features about CNN is that it deals with the raw input image with minimal (here none) preprocessing. In some sense, the convolutional layers try to extract the spatial features available in the image. Intuitively, it makes sense that the amount of feature extraction cannot exceed the amount of features present in the image. Taking a hint from the famous LeNet architecture, each of the convolutional filter layers in our architecture is followed by a downsampling layer that reduces the image size (here, half of the input size) on both dimensions. The strategy for this downsampling in our implementation is maxpooling.

3.1   192 × 168 Yalefaceb Cropped Images

In the present study, we used the cropped Yale B face image database [18] consisting of 192 × 168 image samples. Here, a CNN architecture consisting of five Convolution-cum-Downsampling layers is used. The kernel sizes for various convolution operations and the respective numbers of feature maps considered are shown in Table 1. At each layer, the downsampling operation used 2 × 2 windows.

Table 1. Convolution-cum-downsampling layers

Layer no.	Kernel		Feature maps	Image	
	Width	Height		Width	Height
1	5	5	20	168	192
2	5	5	50	82	94
3	4	4	120	39	45
4	5	4	250	18	21
5	2	2	600	7	9

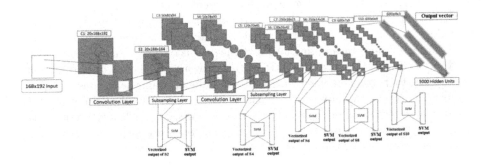

Fig. 1. Architecture of the proposed hybrid deep classifier system.

The above Convolution-cum-Downsampling layers are followed by a fully connected multilayer perceptron network cosisting of 5000 neurons at its hiddden layer. This part receives an input feature vector of size 7200. The output layer is a fully connected logistic regression layer. This entire architecture of the convolutional neural network is trained for 3500 iterations using batch backpropagation algorithm with a batch size of 50 training image samples.

Once the network is trained to a certain optimum level (determined with the help of a validation set of samples), the batch gradient descent is stopped. The output at each convolution-cum-downsampling layer is used to train a distinct SVM classifier with RBF kernel. Thus, five SVM classifiers are also trained in addition to the logistic regression classifier discussed above. A schematic representation of the architecture of the classifier system discussed here is shown in Fig. 1. The input feature vector size (N) of each such SVM is shown below.

$$N = f * (i_w - k_w + 1) * (i_h - k_h + 1)/4, \tag{1}$$

where f = number of feature maps, i_w = image width, i_h = image height, k_w = kernel width, k_h = kernel height.

Table 2. Convolution-cum-downsampling layers

Layer no.	Kernel		Feature maps	Image	
	Width	Height		Width	Height
1	5	4	20	24	21
2	5	4	50	10	9

3.2   24 × 21 Yalefaceb Cropped Reduced Images

For the purpose of the said goal of the present study, we resized each sample image of the database to the size as small as 24 × 21 and used the corresponding training samples to train a smaller CNN architecture consisting of two convolution-cum-downsampling layers. Some details of these two layers are given in Table 2. As usual, the above part of the network is followed by a fully connected logistic regression classifier. In this experimentation, the number of inputs to this fully connected part is 450 and the hidden layer size is 300. Training of this smaller architecture is done as before. Also, two distinct SVMs with non-linear kernel are trained using the outputs of the two convolution-cum-downsampling layers as in the case of the larger architecture.

4   Experimental Results and Discussions

The number of image samples of yaleB standard face database used in the present study is 2442. We do not consider any larger sample database due to the limitation in the available computing resources. These samples are divided into training, validation and test sets consisting of 1500, 342 and 600 samples respectively. Training samples are used to train both the CNN and all the SVMs. The validation samples are used to determine the stopping point of backpropagation training preventing overlearning of the network. Results discussed below are obtained on the test samples. Samples of the test set do not play any role in the training process and these are considered to be "unseen" to the trained network. All of these three sample sets are nearly uniform with respect to the type of images contained in them. Each of them contains images of every output class and also images of very bad, neutral and very good illumination conditions.

In the initial attempt, we obtained recognition performance of the larger CNN architecture only excluding the SVMs and the corresponding accuracy is 98.5% on the test samples. A few test samples correctly identified by the trained larger CNN architecture are shown in Fig. 2.

Though the recognition performance of the CNN network alone is quite impressive, this is further improved by an SVM trained using the values at the hidden nodes of the fully connected part of the network corresponding to the same set of training samples and this improved accuracy figure is 99.33% for the test samples. Another SVM trained using the 7200 (600 × 4 × 3) values

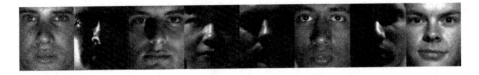

Fig. 2. Some image samples correctly classified by the CNN

at the final convolution-cum-subsampling layer of the larger CNN provided a similar accuracy of 99.33%. Four image samples were misclassified out of 600 test samples in each of these two latter cases.

However, when we trained the SVM on the output of the first, second, third convolution-cum-downsampling layers, the error further reduced to only three misclassifications thus giving a recognition rate of 99.50%.

The next problem we consider pertains to classification of face images of very small size. In real life, similarly small size images are very much prevalent mainly among images captured by CCTV cameras or in an image of a crowd where an individual face occupies a very small area. Such a small size that we consider in the present study is only 24×21 pixels. Here, we study two different approaches to recognition of such small images.

– Enlarging the small size images using bi-cubic interpolation and feeding them to the already trained CNN network for feature extraction which is fed to an SVM. A few samples of enlarged images are shown in Fig. 3.
– Training a smaller CNN architecture using reduced size training samples for feature extraction and then performing recognition with the extracted features fed to an SVM.

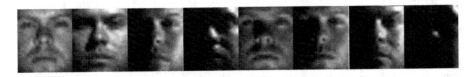

Fig. 3. Samples of enlarged images computed from respective small size images

4.1   Enlarged Sample Images

The recognition performance of the larger CNN architecture alone described in Sect. 3.1 on the enlarged images is only 42.5% on the test set. However, when the outputs of the second convolution-cum-downsampling layer is used as features to the corresponding SVM, the recognition accuracy on test samples shoots up to 97.83% and only 13 test samples are misclassified. The experiment is repeated with outputs at 3rd, 4th and 5th convolution-cum-downsampling layers and the recognition performances of respective SVMs are noted. When features generated by the 3rd layer are fed to the corresponding SVM, it provides 98.17% accuracy, misclassifying only 11 test samples. However, the accuracy provided by the SVM corresponding to the output of the 4th layer of the CNN architecture drops to 95.67%. The accuracy further decreases for the features generated by the last convolution-cum-subsampling layer and the corresponding accuracy is 88.5%. In this case, the number of misclassified samples is 69.

4.2 Original Small Images

The recognition performance of the smaller CNN architecture alone on the 24×21 test image samples is 87.83% misclassifying 73 out of 600 test samples. When the SVM corresponding to the feature generated by the second or last convolution-cum-downsampling layer is used, the recognition rate improves to 94.17% misclassifying 35 out of 600 test images. The recognition rate further increases, though marginally, when the output of the hidden nodes of the fully connected part of the network is used as the input feature vector to an SVM and the improved accuracy value is 94.50%, where 32 samples are misclassified.

The 192 × 168 face image samples which were misclassified when only CNN was used can clearly be divided into two sets. One set can be identified by human observers while the other set cannot be identified by human observers (due to the extremely poor illumination conditions). However, an interesting observation is that samples belonging to the first set are completely identified by the CNN as its first or second choice. Thus, the CNN identified all the humanly identifiable images, if not as the first choice, then as the second. The images that cannot be identified even as the second choice are too dark to be recognized even by a human. Figure 4 shows some of the image samples belonging to either validation set or test set which are recognized by the CNN not as the first choice but as the second choice. As can be seen in Fig. 5 the differences in resolution and illumination condition of the original images (Fig. 5a) used to train the larger network and the enlarged images (Fig. 5b) to be recognized by this larger architecture are significant. In a real world scenario, the facebank is expected to have good resolution images in proper illumination conditions. However, when images of a crowd are captured by CCTV cameras, or by telescopic cameras from a long distance, it is not uncommon that the size of the target face in the whole image is very small in size and/or in a poor illumination condition. Results of our study shows that the proposed deep hybrid architecture performs quite efficiently in similar scenarios. Further analysis of the recognition performances of the CNN alone and the same of different SVMs revealed that the set of faces

Fig. 4. Images not identified as the first choice but identified as the second choice

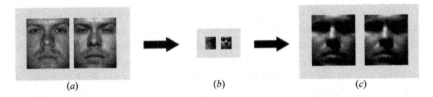

(a)   (b)   (c)

Fig. 5. (a) Good quality easy-to-recognize face images. (b) Very small sized face images that are difficult to recognize. (c) Enlarged versions of small images shown in (b).

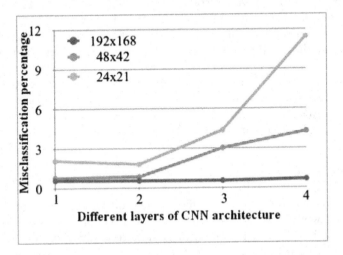

Fig. 6. Plot of misclassification percentage versus features taken from different layers of the CNN network. Marks 1, 2, 3, 4 along the horizontal axis denote respectively S6, S8, S10 and hidden layer of the architecture shown in Fig. 1. Graphs of different colors correspond to different sizes of face image. (Color figure online)

misclassified by the CNN alone and the set of faces misclassified by any one of the SVMs are disjoint. Moreover, it was interesting to note that the images misclassified by any one of the SVMs cannot be termed as bad quality images. On the contrary, all the humanely unidentifiable images due to extremely poor illumination condition could be properly classified by the SVMs. Thus, it can be concluded that under poor illumination condition it is better to employ an SVM trained with features extracted by the CNN to recognize human faces. If one observes, the error rate vs the index of layer whose output was used to train the SVM in case of the resized images (Fig. 6), we can see that the error decreases to a minimum in the output of the third layer and then rises again rapidly. This rapid rise can possibly be explained by the fact that the maximum amount of features was already extracted from the image after layer numbered three. This is because these images are resized images. They have been interpolated from smaller images. This increase in size did not add any new feature to the image. Hence, when the output of layer three was convolved and downsampled again, it did not provide any new useful information, rather it operated on these "good" features that were obtained and produced features of lesser quality. This is an empirical proof that it is not always true that the last layer of the CNN produces the best features. In fact, as we have seen before the last layer doesn't produce the best feature for the previous example even when the network is very deep. The position of this "best-feature" layer depends on the amount of information contained in the original input image which is dependant on its resolution and so does the rate with which the error increases after this layer.

To verify the result, the same strategy was tested with resized 42×48 images. This must contain slightly more information than the resized 24×21 images. It can be seen that a similar minimum is observed here. However, in this case the deviation from the minimum in the later layers is lesser than observed in the case of 24×21 images.

The method also performs considerably better on the resized images than training separate networks for various sized images. It can be seen as an indication that a single network can operate on images of varying sizes, which would otherwise have required more than one size-dependent networks to be trained.

5   Conclusions

The present paper provides a very efficient method for facial recognition based on images of low visual-quality, specially images of very small size and low illumination. Its applicability lies in, among many, face recognition from crowd images, CCTV facial identification, facial identification in spaces with low illumination. This does not require the neural network to be trained too robustly as the SVM handles the error margins. This can provide considerable benefit in online training systems if it is applied suitably. The application of CNN also produces a very high classification speed if parallel processing can be employed. It also shows that one need not train separate networks for various sizes of images, as we know that CNN architecture is dependent on the size of the input image. Hence, a standard network can be trained with the training data and the data at the user-end can be resized to this standard size. This has given better results as shown above in comparison to the other option.

References

1. Belhumeur, P.N., Hespanha, J.P., Kriegman, D.J.: Eigenfaces vs. fisherfaces: recognition using class specific linear projection. IEEE Trans. Pattern Anal. Mach. Intell. **19**, 711–720 (1997)
2. Bergstra, J., et al.: Theano: deep learning on GPUs with python. In: Big Learn Workshop, NIPS 2011 (2011)
3. Bledsoe, W.W., Chan, H.: Man-machine facial recognition. Technical report PRI 22, Panoramic Res. Inc., Palo Alto, CA (1966)
4. Brunelli, R., Poggio, T.: Face recognition: feature versus templates. IEEE Trans. Pattern Anal. Mach. Intell. **15**, 1042–1052 (1993)

5. Colombo, C., Bimbo, A.D., Magistris, S.D.: Human-computer interaction based on eye movement tracking. In: Proceedings of Computer Architectures for Machine Perception (CAMP 1995), pp. 258–263 (1995)

6. Cox, I.J., Ghosn, J., Yianilos, P.N.: Feature based face recognition using mixture-distance. In: Proceedings of IEEE Conference on Computer Vision and Pattern Recognition (CVPR 1996), pp. 209–216 (1996)

7. Ding, X., Fang, C.: Discussions on some problems in face recognition. In: Li, S.Z., Lai, J., Tan, T., Feng, G., Wang, Y. (eds.) SINOBIOMETRICS 2004. LNCS, vol. 3338, pp. 47–56. Springer, Heidelberg (2004). doi:10.1007/978-3-540-30548-4_7

8. Garcia, C., Delakis, M.: Convolutional face finder: a neural architecture for fast and robust face detection. IEEE Trans. Pattern Anal. Mach. Intell. **26**, 1408–1423 (2004)

9. Goldstein, R.J., Harmon, L.D., Lesk, A.B.: Identification of human faces. Proc. IEEE **59**, 748–760 (1971)

10. Graf, H.P., Chen, T., Petajan, E., Cosatto, E.: Locating faces and facial parts. In: International Workshop on Automatic Face- and Gesture-Recognition, pp. 41–46 (1995)

11. Harmon, L., Khan, M., Lasch, R., Ramig, P.: Machine identification of human faces. Pattern Recogn. **13**, 97–110 (1981)

12. Heseltine, T., Pears, N., Austin, J.: Evaluation of image preprocessing techniques for eigenface based face recognition. In: Proceedings of SPIE, vol. 4875, pp. 677–685 (2002)

13. Huang, F.J., LeCun, Y.: Large-scale learning with SVM and convolutional nets for generic object categorization. In: Proceedings of IEEE Computer Society Conference on Computer Vision and Pattern Recognition (CVPR 2006), vol. 1, pp. 284–291 (2006)

14. Jafri, R., Arabnia, H.R.: A survey of face recognition techniques. Inf. Process. Syst. **5**, 41–68 (2009)

15. Kanade, T.: Picture processing system by computer complex and recognition of human faces. Kyoto University, Japan, Ph.D. thesis (1973)

16. Kaufman, G.J., Breeding, K.J.: Automatic recognition of human faces from profile silhouettes. IEEE Trans. Syst. Man Cybern. **6**, 113–120 (1976)

17. Lawrence, S., et al.: Face recognition: a convolutional neural-network approach. IEEE Trans. Neural Netw. **8**(1), 98–113 (1997)

18. Lee, K., Ho, J., Kriegman, D.: Acquiring linear subspaces for face recognition under variable lighting. IEEE Trans. Pattern Anal. Mach. Intell. **27**, 684–698 (2005)

19. Liposščak, Z., Lončarič, S.: A scale-space approach to face recognition from profiles. In: Proceedings of the International Conference on Computer Analysis of Images and Patterns, pp. 243–250 (1999)

20. Messer, K., et al.: Face authentication test on the BANCA database. In: Proceedings of the International Conference on Pattern Recognition, vol. 4, pp. 523–532 (2004)

21. Nixon, M.: Eye spacing measurement for facial recognition. Proc. SPIE **0575**, 279–285 (1985)

22. Pontil, M., Verri, A.: Support vector machines for 3-D object recognition. IEEE Trans. Pattern Anal. Mach. Intell. **20**, 637–646 (1998)

23. Reisfeld, D.: Generalized symmetry transforms : attentional mechanisms and face recognition. Tel-Aviv University, Ph.D. thesis (1994)

24. Roeder, N., Li, X.: Experiments in analyzing the accuracy of facial feature detection. In: Vision Interface 1995, pp. 8–16 (1995)

25. Rowley, H., Baluja, S., Kanade, T.: Neural network based face detection. IEEE Trans. Pattern Anal. Mach. Intell. **20**, 23–38 (1998)
26. Sirovich, L., Kirby, M.: Low-dimensional procedure for the characterization of human faces. J. Opt. Soc. Am. A: Opt. Imaging Sci. Vis. **4**, 519–524 (1987)
27. Tan, X., Chen, S., Zhou, Z., Zhang, F.: Face recognition from a single image per person: a survey. Pattern Recogn. **39**, 1725–1745 (2006)
28. Turk, M., Pentland, A.: Eigenfaces for recognition. J. Cogn. Neurosci. **3**, 71–86 (1991)
29. Valentin, D., et al.: Connectionist models of face processing: a survey. Pattern Recogn. **27**, 1209–1230 (1994)
30. Wiskott, L., Fellous, J.-M., Krüger, N., von der Malsburg, C.: Face recognition by elastic bunch graph matching. IEEE Trans. Pattern Anal. Mach. Intell **19**, 775–779 (1997)
31. Yuille, A.L., Hallinan, P.W., Cohen, D.S.: Feature extraction from faces using deformable templates. Int. J. Comput. Vis. **8**(2), 99–111 (1992)
32. Zhao, W., Chellappa, R., Rosenfeld, A., Phillips, P.J.: Face recognition: a literature survey. ACM Comput. Surv. **35**(4), 399–458 (2003)

Brain Tumor Segmentation from Multimodal MR Images Using Rough Sets

Rupsa Saha[1](✉), Ashish Phophalia[2], and Suman K. Mitra[1]

[1] Dhirubhai Ambani Institute of Information and Communication Technology,
Gandhinagar 382007, Gujarat, India
{rupsa_saha,suman_mitra}@daiict.ac.in
[2] Indian Institute of Information Technology,
Vadodara, Gandhinagar 382028, Gujarat, India
ashish_p@iiitvadodara.ac.in

Abstract. Automatic segmentation of brain tumors from Magnetic Resonance images is a challenging task due to the wide variation in intensity, size, location of tumors in images. Defining a precise boundary for a tumor is essential for diagnosis and treatment of patients. Rough set theory, an extension of classical set theory, deals with the vagueness of data by determining the boundary region of a set. The aim of this work is to explore the possibility and effectiveness of using a rough set model to represent the tumor regions in MR images accurately, with Quadtree partitioning and simple K-means as precursors to indicate and limit the possible relevant regions. The advantage of using rough sets lie in its ability to represent the impreciseness of set boundaries, which is one of the major challenges faced in tumor segmentation. Experiments are carried out on the BRATS 2013 and 2015 databases and results are comparable to those reported by recent works.

Keywords: Brain tumor · Magnetic resonance imaging · Rough sets

1 Introduction

Glioma is a general term used to refer to brain tumors which arise from the glial cells. Gliomas vary with respect to location, cell characteristics, severity and responsiveness to treatment. The World Health Organization defines a grading system for tumors, where Grade I is the least severe and having the best prognosis, and grade IV is the most severe with worst prognosis of the disease. High-grade gliomas are the ones which are most aggressive in their spread, affording patients an average survival rate of only about two years after discovery and treatment consisting of surgery followed by radiotherapy [1]. Low-grade gliomas offer a much better chance of survival and a longer span of life expectancy. In order to offer patients the best possible chance of recovery, diagnosis of gliomas is thus a time-critical problem.

Brain tumor segmentation is carried out for a wide variety of lesion (area of abnormality in tissue) images. A major challenge in automatic segmentation is

© Springer International Publishing AG 2017
S. Mukherjee et al. (Eds.): ICVGIP 2016, LNCS 10481, pp. 133–144, 2017.
https://doi.org/10.1007/978-3-319-68124-5_12

the fact that lesions are identified by the difference in their intensity profile with relation to the surrounding normal tissue. This often makes their identification a relative rather than an absolute process, and there are major variations even in case of manual segmentation by experts. Tumor boundaries become ambiguous if the intensity variation is smooth, or if there are artifacts present in the imaging. Artifacts in MRI imaging arise from patient motion (due to breathing, blood flow, heart beat), equipment motion, etc [2]. Multiple modes or types of MR Imaging are available, namely: T1, T2, T1-contrast, FLAIR (Fluid Attenuated Inversion Recovery) etc., each of which provide different anatomical and functional information, which are combined to draw meaningful conclusions about the tumor. Both the tumor and Cerebrospinal fluid (CSF) appear dark in T1 and bright in T2. In terms of image capture, FLAIR is the same as T2, with the added property of reduced CSF brightness. T1-contrast imaging is especially useful in identifying and enhancing active soft tissue lesions by increasing the visual contrast in the image [3].

Intensity normalization [4], registration, skull-stripping [5] are employed as preprocessing steps in MRI. Image intensity and texture are two of the most common features used for segmentation. Positional information is also used in some. Certain algorithms use a combination of these features along with various statistics obtained from them as added features. Early techniques use local or global thresholding [6], region growing [7], morphological edge detection [8], snack methods [9] etc.(Refer to [10] for detailed survey). Threshold-based methods compare ROI intensity with pre-determined intensity thresholds for segmentation. Thresholds can be determined either from prior knowledge or from various image statistics. Region-based methods use the similarity of pixels with their neighbors to combine them and form similar regions. Out of these similar regions, some would be the unhealthy tissue, which can be determined from previous knowledge about the appearance of such tissue. For region growing methods, the initial seed for starting the algorithm is of utmost importance.

Algorithms are based on classification or clustering methods such as Fuzzy C-Means (FCM) [11], Markov Random Fields or Conditional Random Fields, Support Vector Machines [12], Artificial Neural Networks [11], etc., have been developed. Neighborhood, shape or locality constraints can be added to make a more context-aware decision. Support Vector Machine based algorithms have also been widely used in brain tumor segmentation. Good training data, specially from multiple modes of same case, allow the algorithms to learn the expected tumor features and segment accordingly [12]. Atlas-based algorithms [13] use brain atlases constructed by creating a collection of averaged images of a large number of subjects. This allows for use of existing knowledge of normal brain structures in order to segment out the abnormal portions. However, inter-personal variance of the structures can lead to poor performance of these methods.

According to Hirano and Tsumoto [14], rough sets are a good base for tumor segmentation techniques since usage of rough approximations can model the differences between the expected and the observed shape and/or structure of the region of interest. The outer and inner approximations in a rough set can be thought of as the approximations of a region of interest in an image in terms of granules. By using rough sets, one can attempt to represent inconsistency between the existing knowledge of the ROI and the region obtained from the image itself. The authors propose that if there are N types of prior knowledge available about the image. Each of these available knowledge can be used to further refine the rough result obtained by the previous knowledge. Roy and Maji [15] have proposed a post-processing technique for brain tumor segmentation using Rough-Fuzzy clustering and unsupervised feature selection. In their approach, they have used Multiresolution wavelet analysis to extract scale-space feature vectors. The assumption here is that different tissue classes have different texture classes, and all pixels belonging to one class will have similar vectors. Clustering is also carried out using Rough-Fuzzy C-Means method (abbreviated to rRCM). It combines the concept of membership of fuzzy sets and the concept of lower and upper approximations from the theory of rough sets.

The manuscript is organized as follows: Sect. 2 describe the fundamentals of Rough Set theory. Section 3 explains proposed methodology in depth followed by Results over various measures in Sect. 4. Section 5 concludes the manuscript.

2   Rough Set Preliminaries

Conventional sets specify an object can either clearly belonging or clearly not belonging to a set X. Rough sets, first introduced by Pawlak in 1982 [16], is an approximation of sets, which is required where lack of exact knowledge prevent such absolute labeling of an object with respect to X. Rough sets look to define what constitutes the boundary of the set. If the boundary is empty, then the set is considered to be crisp. If boundary is not empty, it indicates that the set could not be defined precisely, hence it is rough.

The *lower approximation* of a set X with respect to indiscernibility relation $\mathbb{R}$ is defined as the set of all objects, which can be classified as X with certainty. This is the union of all equivalence classes that form a proper subset of X. For all elements x belonging to universe $\mathbb{U}$, this is denoted by: $\underline{\mathbb{R}}X = \bigcup_{x \in \mathbb{U}} \{\mathbb{R}(x) :$ $\mathbb{R}(x) \subseteq X\}$.

The *upper approximation* of the set X with respect to $\mathbb{R}$ is defined as the set of all objects, which can possibly be classified as X. This formed by all those equivalence classes that have non-empty intersection with X, and is expressed as: $\overline{\mathbb{R}}X = \bigcup_{x \in \mathbb{U}} \{\mathbb{R}(x) : \mathbb{R}(x) \cap X \neq \phi\}$.

The *boundary region* of set X can be defined as the set of all objects that cannot be precisely classified as either X or not-X. This is given by the set difference of $\overline{\mathbb{R}}X$ and $\underline{\mathbb{R}}X$, that is, all the elements in the upper approximation that are not present in the lower approximation, i.e. BND(X) : $\overline{\mathbb{R}}X - \underline{\mathbb{R}}X$.

In order to use rough set approximation on images, each image has to be broken up into a collection of granules. The simplest method to do this is to consider the image as the universe $\mathbb{U}$ consisting of pixels. $\mathbb{U}$ is then divided into a number

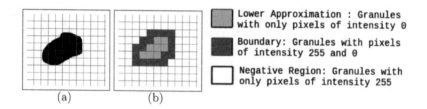

Fig. 1. (a) Original image with grids (b) Showing identified granules

of non-overlapping (or overlapping) blocks, each having multiple pixels. Each such block is considered a granule G. Shown in Fig. 1 is a simple interpretation of segmentation of region of interest using rough sets. In this example, the rough set rules (used to decide which region a granule lies in) are defined on the basis of the number of pixels with intensity 0 in each granule. A granule with all pixels of 0 intensity is said to belong to the Lower Approximation. A granule with some, but not all, black pixels, are part of the Boundary of the set. Any other granule is not part of the set. The rules are mentioned in the Fig. 1 with color coding for easy visualization.

3   Methodolgy

Identification of tumor region and various substructures require information from the different modes to be combined. This section describes first the general architecture, followed by the specifics for identifying different tumor substructures.

Granulation: One way of achieving variable, non-overlapping partitioning of the image space is to use quad-tree decomposition. The image is first divided into four parts (hence the name "Quad" tree). The 256×256 image is initially divided into 16384 2×2 blocks before quad-tree partitioning. These 2×2 blocks are taken as the smallest possible part to be reached via partitioning. Taking 2×2 blocks gives more neighborhood information than is possible from using just one pixel. For partitioning, the correlation vector v_i for each block b_i is calculated. Each vector has 8 values, $v_{ij}, j = 1 \, to \, 8$, v_{ij} is the correlation between the block b_i and its jth neighboring block b_{ij}. The final result of calculating the correlation arrays is a 16384×8 matrix of correlation vectors.

The pairwise difference between the correlation vectors of blocks in a granule are calculated. If the discrepancy between the minimum and maximum of these pairwise differences is large, then the granule is partitioned further. This threshold is used to control the granularity that is required to achieve. A higher threshold will allow more dissimilar components to belong to the same granule. In the present discussion, Euclidean distance is used to measure similarity, with greater distance between two vectors implying less similarity between them. Figure 2 shows the varying granularity achieved by varying the partitioning threshold. Thus after all partitioning is complete, a larger granule size means a larger area of comparatively low variation (i.e. a homogeneous area).

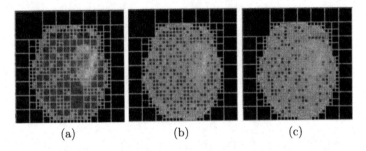

Fig. 2. Size and Number of granules vary as the partitioning threshold takes values (a) 1.75, (b) 1.25, (c) 0.75

Finer granules ensure that the area inside a granule is strictly homogeneous, but it also means a large number of granules will have to be processed. Coarser granules have less homogeneity and are less in number. The amount of granularity has to strike a balance between the accuracy (of homogeneity inside a granule) and the amount of computation involved. Since quad-tree partitioning is performed on a square matrix, all the resultant granules, while unequal, are square matrices too.

After granulation, the next task involves identifying which granules belong to the tumor region (our region of interest). Typically, the region of interest is a small portion of the entire image. For expert judgment, the intensity of the region is the primary indication as to whether or not it is the region of interest, as discussed earlier. Designing a rough set rule based on intensity is difficult since the brightness and contrast of all images are not constant. Hence, it is problematic to assign a single threshold between tumor and non-tumor intensities which works equally well across all cases. The rule has to be obtained from the information afforded by a single case itself.

K Means Clustering: In order to do this, we use simple K-means clustering to infer a crude estimate of the intensity values that are there in the tumor region. We have three classes for clustering: tumor, possibly tumor and not tumor. Each class is initialized with a granule that we are reasonably sure of representing said class. In T2, T1-contrast and FLAIR modes of MRI, the regions of interest (and certain other regions as well) are characterized by high intensity. Calculating the image histogram, the tumor class is initialized by a granule, all of whose pixels are above the 90th percentile in the histogram. The possibly tumor class is initialized by a granule more than half but not all of whose pixels are above the 90th percentile. The granules that are found to belong to these two classes are a smaller subset of all the available granules, and contain the regions of interest.

Rough Sets: From each of the classes obtained from K-Means, we get the mean and standard deviation of intensity ($mean_t$ and std_t for class 1(tumor), $mean_m$ and std_m for class 2(maybe tumor)). Out of the 300 images provided as part of the BRATS database, granules generated by 100 randomly selected images were used to craft the rules which we use to distinguish between Upper and Lower

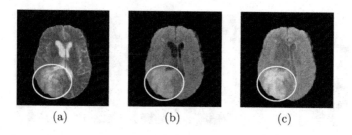

(a)   (b)   (c)

Fig. 3. (a) T2, (b) FLAIR, (c) T2 and FLAIR combined

Approximation of rough sets. The Granules with all pixels above $mean_t - f*std_t$ are said to be in the Lower Approximation (i.e. surely of ROI). All the granules of Lower Approximation, plus those granules whose mean intensity is above $mean_m - f*std_m$ is said to be in the Upper Approximation of the ROI. The multiplying parameter f is adjusted according to the percentile of the image intensities that the two means lie at. If there is a small difference between the two, f is kept small, since a smaller range of intensities need to accounted for. If, however, the distance between $mean_t$ and $mean_m$ is large, a larger value of f is chosen to better span the intermediate range.

For identifying the **whole tumor region**, the FLAIR and T2 mode is used. In order to incorporate the information from both modes, a combined image is produced, having 30% contribution from T2 and 70% from FLAIR. This helps to maintain the hyper-intensity of the tumor region, and at the same time suppress the intensity of other irrelevant areas.

Calculating rough sets, as described previously, we obtain the regions where the tumor is located. However, due to various imaging differences (as discussed earlier), there may still be spurious regions detected. If multiple components have similar size and high intensity, then it is probable that they are multiple sites of tumor growth. However, if such multiple sites are highly symmetrical about the central axis, then it likely that it is normal brain structures, like the brain stem or ventricles, since tumors are usually at random locations with uncontrolled growth. Also, spurious bright bands are sometimes present at the edge of the brain image. The following formula, devised experimentally, tries to incorporate these factors as (Fig. 3):

$$w = size_c/size_l + 1/(intensity_c - intensity_l) - 0.02 * pixels_{center} - 0.02 * pixels_{edge}$$

where

$size_c$ = number of pixels in the component considered
$size_l$ = number of pixels in the largest connected component
$intensity_c$ = mean intensities of the component considered
$intensity_l$ = mean intensities of the largest connected component
$pixels_{center}$ = pixels of the component very close to the center,
i.e. are possibly part of the brain-stem and not tumor regions
$pixels_{edge}$ = pixels of the component on the edge of the brain image

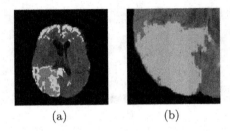

(a)   (b)

Fig. 4. (a) Results of rough set calculation: Lower Approximation (pink) and Boundary (yellow) (b) tumor Region shown in green. For colours please refer to the pdf. (Color figure online)

Hence it rewards similarity of size and intensity, while penalizing the areas where stray brightness is usually noticed (i.e. at the center and at the edges). Finally, the components with high score (>0.75, decided by experiments) are retained. Results are shown in Fig. 4.

The **enhancing tumor region** is the area of active tumor growth with fresh lesions. Since this region has good blood flow, hence usage of a contrasting medium enhances the region in the T1-contrast mode. It lies within the area acquired in the previous step.

For this ROI, the initialization of K-mean centroids and subsequent rough set classification is done as discussed previously. Results are shown in Fig. 5. The sites of dead tissue which previously had tumors, also known as necrotic tissue regions, are usually located inside of adjacent to the enhancing tumor region obtained previously. Other tissue occurring near the active tumor region are termed as the non-enhancing core tissues. These three regions (non-enhancing, enhancing and necrotic) are together termed as the **gross tumor core**. Process of initialization and rough set calculation is done on the T2 image in a manner similar to the above and the results are shown in Fig. 6.

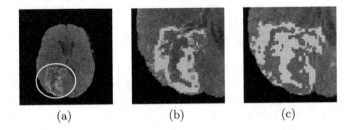

(a)   (b)   (c)

Fig. 5. (a) T1-Contrast with tumor area marked (b) Enhancing tumor region: Lower Approximation (pink) and Boundary (yellow) (c) Enhancing tumor region visualized in red over whole tumor region. For colours please refer to the pdf. (Color figure online)

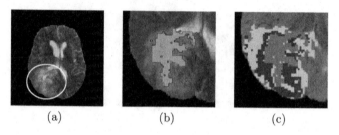

(a)   (b)   (c)

Fig. 6. (a) T2 with tumor region marked, (b) Gross tumor region: lower approximation (pink) and Boundary (yellow) (c) The necrotic and non-enhancing regions in ochre visualized over previously obtained tissue substructures. For colours please refer to the pdf. (Color figure online)

4   Results and Discussion

The algorithm is tested on the BRATS database [17,18] which provides a collection of High Grade Gliomas (HGG), and Low Grade Gliomas(LGG) as training data, along with the ground truth segmentations. The database contains fully anonymized images from the Cancer Imaging Archive. The performance measures used here are Dice Coefficient, Positive Predictive Value and Sensitivity. The **Dice Coefficient** is a similarity measure between two sets A and B, and is given by

$$DC = \frac{2 \mid A \cap B \mid}{\mid A \mid + \mid B \mid}$$

Positive Predictive Value is a popular measure used for diagnostic tests that gives the probability of a positive prediction being correct (according to the ground truth), with respect to all positive predictions made by a system. A higher value can be said to correspond to a higher accuracy of the system. It is given by

$$PPV = \frac{no.\ of\ true\ positives}{no.\ of\ true\ positives + no.\ of\ false\ positives}$$
$$= \frac{no.\ of\ true\ positives}{no.\ of\ positive\ calls}$$

Sensitivity is another measure widely used and is also referred to as the hit rate. It gives the probability of a positive case being identified properly by a system. It is the probability of a positive prediction, given that the case is true as per the ground truth. It is given by

$$Sensitivity = \frac{no.\ of\ true\ positives}{no.\ of\ true\ positives + no.\ of\ false\ negatives}$$

The Dice Coefficient, Positive Predictive Values (PPV) and Sensitivity obtained from segmenting the images as compared to the ground truth provided are given in Table 1. As of 2015, the best results reported in the MICCAI-BRATS are in the range of 73 (Hoogi)(for 100 cases) to 88.4 (Bakas)(all cases)

Table 1. Results of evaluation on BRATS 2013 and 2015 training databases. Performance measures are given as *Mean ∓ StandardDeviation* and *Median ∓ MedianAbsoluteDeviation* for each scoring method.

Regions		Dice score	PPV	Sensitivity
Whole tumor	Mean	81.62 ∓ 11.68	80.75 ∓ 4.16	86.97 ∓ 3.58
	Median	84.42 ∓ 8.76	88.13 ∓ 15.2	93.43 ∓ 7.16
Gross core	Mean	70.58 ∓ 12.1	82.66 ∓ 16.52	66.21 ∓ 19.57
	Median	73.11 ∓ 9.1	92.6 ∓ 19.86	63.41 ∓ 19.23
Enhancing	Mean	71.65 ∓ 17.18	82.1 ∓ 19.62	80.61 ∓ 15.92
	Median	69.66 ∓ 16.10	92.18 ∓ 15.41	78.82 ∓ 16.46

mean Dice Coefficient value for the complete tumor region and between 60.6 (Vaidhya)(24 cases) to 82 (Agn)(30 cases) for the gross tumor core region. For the enhancing core region, the average Dice scores lie between 50.9 (Vaidhya) and 75 (Pereira)(all cases) [19]. In the proceedings of the MICCAI Brats 2014 [20], the average Dice Score for the 1st subtask (identifying the whole tumor region), varies between 0.79 (Davy) to 0.87 (Kleesiek and Urban). For the gross tumor core segmentation sub-task, reported average Dice Score has varied from 0.66 (Reza) to 0.79 (Kwon).

Direct comparison between results is difficult since various methods have been tested on different number of cases (and different cases) from the databases, and hence the details of these reported results are also not being included in this work. The algorithm performs at par with the reported methods on the entire dataset. Usage of a combination of K-Means and rough sets help to concentrate the search for the ROI in a much smaller set of possible areas than the whole image.

The following portion shows some of the atypical cases seen during experimentation, which highlight the challenges faced by the algorithm. All the images have four sub-images. The first sub-image shows the mode from which the segmentation has been carried out, and the second shows the truth image for that slice. Third shows the corresponding region as defined by the sub-task and final sub-image shows the obtained region for that particular sub-task. Comparing the last two sub-images will give the reader an idea of the differences (or similarities) between the expected and obtained results.

In Fig. 7, the Dice Score obtained for the whole tumor region is 0.95. Figure 8 shows a case where the brain stem also gets included in the tumor region, since they are very close together and forms one connected component which reduces the Dice score to 0.59. In Fig. 9, there is a region of brightness (within the whole tumor region previously determined) which does not correspond well to the given ground truth, leading to a low Dice score of 0.59. Figure 10 shows a case where the enhancing tumor region is close to the expected region as given in the ground truth, with Dice score 0.89.

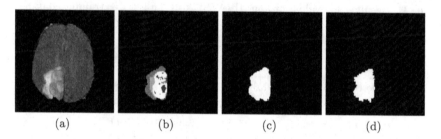

Fig. 7. (a) Flair combined with T2 (b) Ground truth supplied (c) Area to be obtained for whole tumor region (d) Area obtained by algorithm (Dice Score: 0.95)

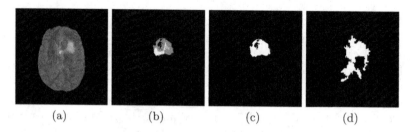

Fig. 8. (a) Flair combined with T2 (b) Ground truth supplied (c) Area to be obtained for whole tumor region (d) Area obtained by algorithm (Dice Score: 0.59)

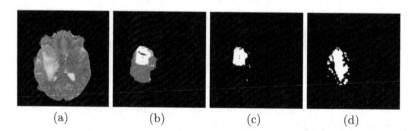

Fig. 9. (a) Negative T1 combined with T2 (b) Ground truth supplied (c) Area to be obtained for gross tumor region (d) Area obtained by algorithm (Dice Score: 0.59)

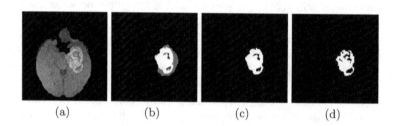

Fig. 10. (a) Flair combined with T2 (b) Ground truth supplied (c) Area to be obtained for enhancing tumor region (d) Area obtained by algorithm (Dice Score: 0.89)

5   Conclusion and Future Scope

In this paper, a Rough Set based approach is presented for Tumor segmentation. The proposed method utilizes the uncertainty handling capabilities of Rough set using approximation spaces. For identification of precise tumor boundaries, K-Means is used as an initial seed algorithm. The novelty of the method lies in the fusion of various modality to exact tumor information available in T2 and Flair images. Although, the present method is its nascent stage with few open parameter. However, result are quite encouraging and the method is competitive enough with state-of-the-art method.

References

1. Khosla, D.: Concurrent therapy to enhance radiotherapeutic outcomes in glioblastoma. Ann. Transl. Med. **4**(3) (2016)
2. Krupa, K., Bekiesińska-Figatowska, M.: Artifacts in magnetic resonance imaging. Pol. J. Radiol. **80**, 93 (2015)
3. Schild, H.H.: MRI Made Easy. Berlex Laboratories, Whippany (1999)
4. Vovk, U., Pernuš, F., Likar, B.: A review of methods for correction of intensity inhomogeneity in MRI. IEEE Trans. Med. Imaging **26**(3), 405–421 (2007)
5. Christine Fennema-Notestine, I., Ozyurt, B., Clark, C.P., Morris, S., Bischoff-Grethe, A., Bondi, M.W., Jernigan, T.L., Fischl, B., Segonne, F., Shattuck, D.W., et al.: Quantitative evaluation of automated skull-stripping methods applied to contemporary and legacy images: effects of diagnosis, bias correction, and slice location. Hum. Brain Mapp. **27**(2), 99–113 (2006)
6. Stadlbauer, A., Moser, E., Gruber, S., Buslei, R., Nimsky, C., Fahlbusch, R., Ganslandt, O.: Improved delineation of brain tumors: an automated method for segmentation based on pathologic changes of 1 H-MRSI metabolites in gliomas. Neuroimage **23**(2), 454–461 (2004)
7. Kaus, M.R., Warfield, S.K., Nabavi, A., Black, P.M., Jolesz, F.A., Kikinis, R.: Automated segmentation of MR images of brain tumors. Radiology **218**(2), 586–591 (2001)
8. Gibbs, P., Buckley, D.L., Blackband, S.J., Horsman, A.: Tumour volume determination from mr images by morphological segmentation. Phys. Med. Biol. **41**(11), 2437 (1996)
9. Nakhmani, A., Kikinis, R., Tannenbaum, A.: MRI brain tumor segmentation and necrosis detection using adaptive sobolev snakes. In: SPIE Medical Imaging, p. 903442. International Society for Optics and Photonics (2014)
10. Gordillo, N., Montseny, E., Sobrevilla, P.: State of the art survey on MRI brain tumor segmentation. Magn. Reson. Imaging **31**(8), 1426–1438 (2013)
11. Hall, L.O., Bensaid, A.M., Clarke, L.P., Velthuizen, R.P., Silbiger, M.S., Bezdek, J.C.: A comparison of neural network, fuzzy clustering techniques in segmenting magnetic resonance images of the brain. IEEE Transactions on Neural Networks **3**(5), 672–682 (1992)
12. Zhou, J., Chan, K.L., Chong, V.F.H., Krishnan, S.M.: Extraction of brain tumor from MR images using one-class support vector machine. In: 27th Annual International Conference of the Engineering in Medicine and Biology Society. IEEE-EMBS 2005, pp. 6411–6414. IEEE (2006)

13. Cabezas, M., Oliver, A., Lladó, X., Freixenet, J., Cuadra, M.B.: A review of atlas-based segmentation for magnetic resonance brain images. Comput. Methods Prog. Biomed. **104**(3), e158–e177 (2011)
14. Hirano, S., Tsumoto, S.: Segmentation of medical images based on approximations in rough set theory. In: Alpigini, J.J., Peters, J.F., Skowron, A., Zhong, N. (eds.) RSCTC 2002. LNCS, vol. 2475, pp. 554–563. Springer, Heidelberg (2002). doi:10.1007/3-540-45813-1_73
15. Maji, P., Roy, S.: Rough-fuzzy clustering and unsupervised feature selection for wavelet based MR image segmentation. PLoS ONE **10**(4), e0123677 (2015)
16. Pawlak, Z.: Rough sets. Int. J. Parallel Program. **11**, 341–356 (1982)
17. Menze, B., et al.: The multimodal brain tumor image segmentation benchmark (BRATS). IEEE Trans. Med. Imaging, 33 (2014)
18. Kistler, M., Bonaretti, S., Pfahrer, M., Niklaus, R., Büchler, P.: The virtual skeleton database: an open access repository for biomedical research and collaboration. J. Med. Internet Res. **15**(11), e245 (2013)
19. Menze, B.H., et al.: The multimodal brain tumor image segmentation benchmark (BRATS). IEEE Trans. Med. Imaging **34**(10), 1993–2024 (2015)
20. MICCAI. MICCAI Brain Tumor Image Segmentation Challenge-BRATS, Boston, Massachusetts, September 2014

A Text Recognition Augmented Deep Learning Approach for Logo Identification

Moushumi Medhi[1](✉), Shubham Sinha[2], and Rajiv Ranjan Sahay[3]

[1] Computational Vision Lab, Department of Computer Science and Engineering,
Indian Institute of Technology Kharagpur,
Kharagpur 721302, West Bengal, India
medhi.moushumi@gmail.com
[2] Department of Computer Science and Technology,
Indian Institute of Engineering Science and Technology,
Shibpur 711103, West Bengal, India
shubham_sinha@hotmail.com
[3] Department of Electrical Engineering,
Indian Institute of Technology Kharagpur,
Kharagpur 721302, West Bengal, India
rajiv@ee.iitkgp.ernet.in

Abstract. Logo/brand name detection and recognition in unstructured and highly unpredictable natural images has always been a challenging problem. We notice that in most natural images logos are accompanied with associated text. Therefore, we address the problem of logo recognition by first detecting and isolating text of varying color, font size and orientation in the input image using affine invariant maximally stable extremal regions (MSERs). Using an off-the-shelf OCR, we identify the text associated with the logo image. Then an effective grouping technique is employed to combine the remaining stable regions based on spatial proximity of MSERs. Deep learning has the advantage that optimal features can be learned automatically from image pixel data. This motivates us to feed the clustered logo candidate image regions to a pre-trained deep convolutional neural network (DCNN) to generate a set of complex features which are further input to a multiclass support vector machine (SVM) for classification. We tested our proposed logo recognition system on 32 logo classes, and a non-logo class obtained by combining FlickrLogos-32 and MICC logo databases, amounting to a total of 23582 training and testing images. Our method yields robust recognition performance, outperforming state-of-the-art techniques achieving 97.8% precision, 95.7% recall and 95.7% average accuracy on the combined MICC and FlickrLogos-32 datasets and a precision of 98.6%, recall of 97.9% and average accuracy of 99.6% on only the FlickrLogos-32 dataset.

Keywords: Logo detection · Logo recognition · DCNN · MSER

© Springer International Publishing AG 2017
S. Mukherjee et al. (Eds.): ICVGIP 2016, LNCS 10481, pp. 145–156, 2017.
https://doi.org/10.1007/978-3-319-68124-5_13

1   Introduction

Logo detection is a pattern recognition application which is very useful in advertising, enterprise identification, indoor localization in malls, analyzing business and administrative documents, corporate website access, and related applications. However, it still continues to pose challenges because of the extensively varying types, classes and patterns of logos. The detection problem is further exacerbated when dealing with unstructured scenes replete with huge sources of variation and inherent complexities. To address this challenging problem, we propose to combine maximally stable extremal region (MSER) based text detection and recognition with logo/brand image recognition using convolutional neural networks (CNN). Prior segmentation of text regions in natural images containing logos has a two-fold advantage in our proposed logo detection method. Apart from remarkably reducing the computational overhead in subsequent logo detection stages by progressively removing regions less likely to contain logo, it also facilitates the additional task of optical character recognition (OCR) which recognizes the text associated with the logo image. This is useful in cases where logo detection mechanism fails and thereby augments the accuracy of the overall logo recognition system. We evaluate the proposed logo classification algorithm on 32 logo classes obtained by combining Flickr-32 and MICC logo datasets. We out-perform several state-of-the-art methods to obtain 97.83% precision, 95.74% recall and 95.74% average accuracy by using a pre-trained CNN-SVM logo image classifier. By augmenting the logo image classifier with OCR performed on the detected text regions we are able to boost the average accuracy to 97.17%.

In Sect. 2 we provide an overview of the relevant literature. In Sect. 3, we describe the proposed methodology. Section 4 presents the results of the experiments performed and also provides a brief comparison with state-of-the-art techniques. We identify directions for future work and conclude in Sect. 5.

2   Previous Work

Alaei et al. [1] proposed a fine-to-coarse logo detection scheme for document images. The algorithm [2] employed homography matching for intra-class pair of logo images using SIFT descriptors and RANSAC algorithm. Romberg et al. [3] proposed a method for indexing the relative spatial layout of SIFT features and derived a quantized representation of the logo regions based on the analysis of the local features and basic spatial structures such as edges and triangles. A three stage TV logo recognition algorithm was proposed by [4] which used HOG features of candidate logos. Sahbi et al. [5] recognized logos by matching logo features minimizing an energy function. A new concept called logo density was presented in [6] to develop an individualized matching strategy for query and a logo. Hassanzadeh et al. [7] used a logo decision classifier after merging fragmented parts of logo and then considered centroid coordinate and intersection of each logo's bounding box. A large-scale logo image database (LOGO-Net) was introduced in [8] where region-based convolutional networks (RCNN) were used for logo detection and brand recognition. [9] utilized fast-RCNN for logo detection with and without localization of logos within images of Flickr-32 dataset using Alexnet [10] model. Gonçalo et al. [11] used selective search algorithm and two CNN models for logo detection. In selective search algorithm, similar segments were merged in a hierarchical manner [12]. In contrast to [8, 9, 11] our proposed work employed MSER features to find regions with stable local binarization over a range of thresholds while combining DCNN and SVM for logo classification.

3   Proposed Methodology

Our work proposes a novel, robust logo brand detection, localization and classification algorithm using MSER [13] and deep learning [14]. The proposed algorithm is depicted in the block diagram shown in Fig. 1.

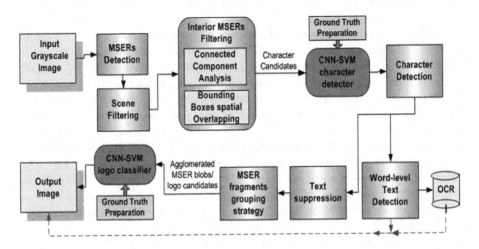

Fig. 1. Block diagram of the proposed algorithm.

3.1   Detection of MSERs

The input RGB color image is pre-processed by converting it into a grayscale image, and then re-sized to a form beneficial for detection of stable regions, preserving the original aspect ratio. MSERs are exploited for detection of co-variant regions with stable intensity profile and region size ranging from 10 pixels to 60% of the size of the original input image. As can be seen from Fig. 2(b), both fine and large structures are detected in the initial step to ensure detection of regions-of-interest (ROIs) with no missing foreground objects. Then background is subtracted based on the proportions of MSER pixels to that of their convex envelopes, rectangular enclosures and other geometrical properties as shown in Fig. 2(c). Shape parameters such as solidity, extent, eccentricity, Euler number, etc. were used to get the filtered MSER pixels.

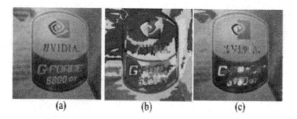

(a)   (b)   (c)

Fig. 2. MSERs detection and filtering: (a) Original image. (b) Detected MSERs. (c) MSER filtered image using shape parameters.

3.2   Text Region Proposals

This section corresponds to the "interior MSER filtering" block of the block diagram shown in Fig. 1. An MSER in the filtered image shown in Fig. 2(c) are then bounded by minimum bounding rectangles (MBR) of their respective convex hulls for representation and detection as shown in Figs. 3(a), (b), (c), (d) and (e). All the other MSERs are similarly enclosed by their respective MBRs as shown in Fig. 3(f). Jaccard Indices [15] are computed to obtain similarity measures among the MBRs in order to filter out the inner MBRs or partially overlapping MBRs. A minimum threshold value of 0.05 of Jaccard index is set to eliminate or merge MSERs with higher coefficient values of their bounding boxes. An undirected graph model is created where each node represents an MBR hypothesis and the Jaccard similarity coefficients are considered as the weights of the edges connecting the two end nodes as shown in Fig. 3(h). Connected component analysis is carried out on the nodes of the graph based on the weights of the connecting edges. Nodes are assigned to the same connected component if there is a path between the nodes. There are a total of 197 minimum perimeter bounding boxes in Fig. 3(f), which is reduced to 30 boxes as shown in Fig. 3(g), through formation of clusters of 30 components as shown in Fig. 3(h).

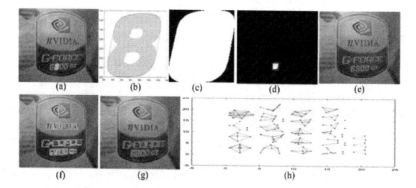

(a)   (b)   (c)   (d)   (e)

(f)   (g)   (h)

Fig. 3. (a) Detected MSER. (b) Pixels of the detected MSER enclosed by its convex envelope. (c) Binary convex hull image with pixels within the hull set to 1. (d) Bounding box of the binary convex hull image. (e) Bounding box for the MSER in the original image. (f) MBRs of all the filtered MSERs. (g) Elimination of inner MBRs and merging of partially overlapping MBRs. (h) Graph of the connected components of MSER regions in Fig. 3(f).

3.3   Text Detection

The text region proposals, as shown in Fig. 4(a), are obtained using procedures described in Sects. 3.1 and 3.2. Each of the generated text regions proposals are given as input to a pre-trained DCNN model to extract features for character detection which are subsequently fed to a binary SVM. This method of detecting text was motivated from the work done in [16] where a two convolutional layered network was employed to extract a 96 dimension feature vector of the detected MSERs in the text image. The feature vector was given as input to an SVM for text detection in [16]. We however have used a pre-trained Alexnet [10] CNN which has a 23 layered architecture. We extract a feature vector of dimension 4096 from the 19th layer which was given as input to an SVM to generate a text confidence score for every text region proposal. Figure 4(b) shows the detected characters. The bounding boxes around each of the characters detected are expanded on all their four sides by an equal, small amount to form a chain of arbitrarily oriented, partially overlapping bounding boxes, as shown in Fig. 4(c), which are later merged to form text lines or words as shown in Fig. 4(d).

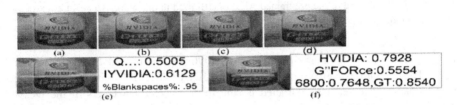

Fig. 4. Stages of text detection. (a) Character proposals. (b) Detected characters. (c) Chain of overlapping characters. (d) Word level detection. (e) OCR text recognition on full image. (f) OCR text recognition on our detected text regions.

The OCR function in Matlab R2016a has been used to obtain the recognition confidences of the detected text words as shown in Figs. 4(e) and (f). As can be seen from the OCR word recognition scores, the performance of OCR is enhanced by feeding probable text image patches rather than the original image as a whole. Note that Fig. 4(e) has many wrongly classified regions with high word confidence scores.

3.4   Logo Detection and Classification

The detected text blocks are subsequently suppressed and the remaining neighboring non-text MSERs were agglomerated based on connected component analysis to form logo region proposals which are input to the logo classifier.

Feature Extraction

We have used a pre-trained Alexnet CNN [10] model for feature extraction from the logo region proposals. The architecture of the CNN model used in our work is shown in Fig. 5(a). It consists of five convolutional layers, three max pooling and three fully connected layers. Since it is not feasible to train an entire DCNN from scratch with a small logo database, transfer learning was performed by using the Alexnet [10] model

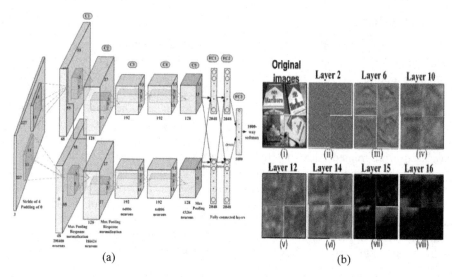

(a)   (b)

Fig. 5. (a) Architecture of the pre-trained Alexnet [10] used in our work. (b) Features extracted by several hidden layers of our pre-trained CNN from sample input logo images.

in Caffe framework. Features of dimension 4096 were extracted from hidden 19th layer. The activations were computed on an NVIDIA K620 GPU with mini-batch size of 32 images. The features extracted by the respective hidden layers of the DCNN model are shown in Fig. 5(b).

Figure 5(b) shows the activations of neurons in different layers of the pre-trained CNN model on application of different samples of logo images of the same class as shown in Fig. 5(a) (i). Figures 5(b) (ii) and (iii) depict the generic features such as edges and blobs of the objects captured by the initial layers of the CNN model. The activations of the third convolutional layer exaggerate the distinct visual characteristics of the image as shown in Fig. 5(b) (iv). The fourth convolutional layer feature map has learned the filters to produce higher level feature map as shown in Fig. 5(b) (v). In Fig. 5(b) (vi), the fifth convolutional layer combines and processes the primitive features of previous layer to generate yet more complex features. The output of the fifth convolutional layer is thresholded using a Rectified Linear Unit (RELU) [22] activation function as shown in Fig. 5(b) (vii). In Fig. 5(b) (viii), max pooling is performed on the output of the 15th layer with a stride of 2 and pooling of 3 × 3 regions.

Logo Classification

We use an SVM classifier to classify logos into one of the 32 different classes of trademarks used. The set of feature vectors, each of length 4096 extracted by the pre-trained CNN of Fig. 5(a), are forwarded to an assembly of 32 binary SVMs for the purpose of training it using a fast stochastic gradient descent solver and adopting one-against-all technique.

4 Experiments and Discussions

4.1 Dataset

For detection of text, Chars74k dataset [17] has been used for training purpose which consists of 74000 natural, handwritten, and synthesized English character images. For realistic evaluation on logo detection, localization and classification, the proposed system has been tested on a subset of the challenging MICC-Logos [5] and FlickrLogos-32 (FlickrLogos) [3] natural image databases. A large collection of diverse textural, natural background and centered foreground single object images in addition to synthetically generated and augmented images are taken as negative examples during training for both text and logo detection. MICC-Logo dataset is composed of 720 real world images, categorized into 13 logo classes with images per class varying from 15 to 87. FlickrLogos-32 dataset contains 32 logo brands bearing 7 logo brands identical to that of MICC dataset. Out of the total 38 distinct classes obtained by the combination of FlickrLogos-32 and MICC datasets, we report results for 32 classes. The originally 32 class logo image dataset used by us is then moderately augmented via random shift, rotation and introduction of manual occlusion.

4.2 Preprocessing Training/Testing Dataset

Almost 95% of the character images of the Chars74k character database is pre-processed to tightly fit into a rectangular contour, so as to best resemble the generated character region proposals. The rest 5% of the character images displays adverse effects on outline fitting and hence were excluded from the pre-processing task. Few instances of the prepared text character images from Chars74k database are presented in Fig. 6(a). Figure 6(b) shows some of the representative training logo images, consisting of both graphics logo and mixed text-graphics logos some of which retains certain amount of background or foreground noise, or are partially or slightly occluded, blurred, disoriented and typically consist of disproportionate fragments. The text element embedded in the graphics part of the logo is not treated the same as regular text but as part of the whole logo picture. Ground truths of the entire collection were manually created using Matlab Training Image Labeller Application while ensuring to shun too loose bounding boxes during dataset preparation.

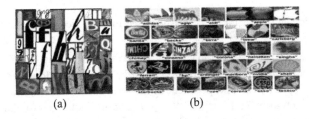

(a)   (b)

Fig. 6. Sample training dataset. (a) Pre-processed Chars74k [17] image dataset. (b) Sample images of preprocessed training logo images of different classes (Flickr + MICC) with wide intra class variations in appearances, chrominance and luminance levels as well as changes introduced due to rotations, transformations and occlusions.

Selectively pre-processing a text dataset as large as 74000 images and manually annotating the regions of interest (ROI) of an entire logo database is a time consuming process. The images were rescaled to a fixed size of 227 × 227 for use with the pre-trained Alexnet [10] model.

Out of the total 38 distinct logo classes, we tested the validity of our method on 32 different classes considering 40% of the samples per class. The size of the augmented and preprocessed training logo dataset is 14148 images consisting of 1774 logo and 12374 non-logo images. Testing data size for logo classification is 9434 images consisting of 1184 logo and 8250 non-logo images. Despite unavailability of a large public logo image dataset, the proposed system yields good generalization results for logo classification.

4.3   Performance Evaluation

The learning curves of the SVM classifier used for logo image recognition are shown in Fig. 7(a). We used radial basis function (RBF) kernel in the SVM trained for logo classification. As can be seen from Fig. 7(a), cross validation error increases and the classifier suffers from overfitting as training sample size exceeds 16.5 k images which amounts to 70% of the total data. Hence the training size of the classifier was limited to 60% of the total data available. Receiver operating characteristic (ROC) curves for each of the 32 binary classifiers corresponding to the 32 logo classes are plotted in Fig. 7(b). The accuracy of the classification algorithm is evident from these ROC curves in Fig. 7(b), which nearly follow the vertical axis for most part.

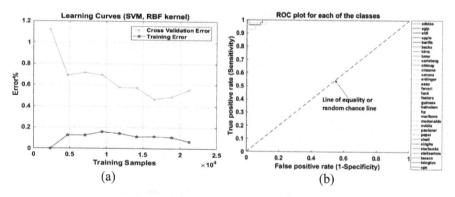

Fig. 7.   (a) Learning Curves for SVM classifier used for logo recognition. (b) ROC curve.

Our logo classification technique yields an average accuracy of 95.74% without taking into account the task of text identification in the image. However, many of the logo test images appear with text pertinent to the logo brand name in near proximity to each other in the input natural images. We were thereby motivated to address the logo recognition problem with text identification in the image so as to enhance the accuracy of logo recognition in cases of failure of the proposed CNN + SVM logo classifier or errors in generation of appropriate logo candidate regions. This resulted in an increased overall average accuracy of 97.17% as evident from the plots shown in Fig. 8. We show the improvement in accuracies for each of the 32 logo classes in our database with text recognition in the input images using OCR augmenting the performance of the proposed CNN + SVM logo image classifier.

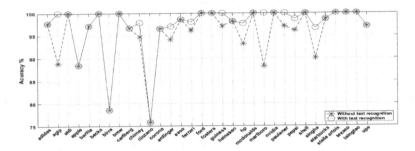

Fig. 8. Accuracy plot of the proposed logo detection algorithm.

In Fig. 9, we illustrate some intermediate and final outputs of our proposed algorithm using three different cases: natural image containing only logo without text (left), with arbitrary text (middle), and with text pertinent to the logo class present in the image (right). The detection of text characters is followed up by word level text formation for word recognition and identification as shown in Fig. 9(a) using an off-the-shelf OCR as described in Sect. 3.3. No text is detected in the left image or in the logo region of the middle image as the logo is considered as a whole picture with one or more parts and the embedded text is effectively cut off from the set of text proposals. False text detections with zero or very low OCR recognition scores, as shown in the middle image in Fig. 9(a), can be removed in subsequent steps. The detected text regions are subtracted in the succeeding intermediate steps and the graphical ROIs are agglomerated using connected component analysis to form the logo candidates as shown in Fig. 9(b) as discussed in Sect. 3.4. In the final output image shown in Fig. 9(c), the logo detected is classified into one of the 32 classes of our dataset containing Flickr and MICC logo classes, as discussed in Sect. 3.4.

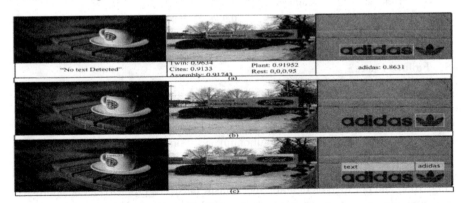

Fig. 9. Assessment of the proposed method using three different types of logo images. (a) Word formation and subsequent OCR application. (b) Logo candidate generation. (c) Final output images.

4.4   Comparison with State-of-the-Art Algorithms

A number of significant works in logo detection have used the FlickrLogos-32 dataset. We have listed their performance in Table 1. Romberg et al. [3] achieved a precision rate of 98% and a recall rate of 61% using SIFT features detected in the logo images. Revaud et al. [18] used a bag-of-words (BoW) model to achieve a high precision value greater than 98% but with low recall of 73%. Romberg and Lienhart [19], extended the BoW by aggregating local features with spatial neighbourhood features into bundles to get the highest precision of 99%, though at a moderate recall value of 83%. Iandola et al. [9] acquired precision rates of 73.3% and 73.5% using fast-RCNN for single (entire image) and multiple region proposal schemes, respectively, without performing classification. The recall metric was not reported. Oliveira et al. [11] achieved precision and recall values of 93% and 89%, respectively using caffenet CNN model. The authors of [11] reported precision and recall values of 95.5% and 91%, respectively using another deep CNN model. Our method achieves state-of-the-art performance with precision of 97.8%, recall of 95.7%, F-score of 96.7% and accuracy of 95.7% on the combined MICC and FlickrLogos-32 datasets. Alone on the FlickrLogos-32 dataset, 98.6% precision, 97.9% recall and 99.6% accuracy is achieved. An F-score of 98.2% is obtained on the FlickrLogos-32 dataset which outperforms all other methods as shown in Table 1.

Table 1. Comparison with state-of-the-art on FlickrLogos-32 dataset.

Method	Year	Precision	Recall	F-Measure
Romberg et al. [3]	2011	0.982	0.610	0.752
Revaud et al. [18]	2012	≥ 0.980	0.726	0.834
Romberg et al. [19]	2013	0.999	0.832	0.908
Farajzadeh [20]	2015	0.931	0.857	0.892
Iandola et al. [9] - AlexNet	2015	0.735	Not reported	Not reported
Liu et al. [21]	2016	0.962	0.864	0.910
Oliveira et al. [11] - Caffenet	2016	0.928	0.891	0.909
Proposed method (only FlickrLogos-32)	–	**0.986**	**0.979**	**0.982**

4.5   Failure Cases

We observed that the proposed algorithm fails when the input image is blurred, contains non-overlapping textures in very close proximity to logos and text logos. However, our logo image classifier is well trained on blurred and poor quality images and yields high accuracy even on low resolution images. Sometimes our algorithm fails due to limitations of MSER detector with blurred images. Figure 10 shows a logo image wherein text lines (noise), placed too close to the logo, form part of the logo as shown in Fig. 10(e) and our logo recognition mechanism fails. The problem can be addressed by incorporating more training data with increased noise levels. However detected text ("PAULANER") can be identified by the OCR. For purely text logo images such as "FEDEX", "GOOGLE", etc., our algorithm fails irrevocably, suppressing them as text

Fig. 10. A failure case of the proposed algorithm. (a) Character proposals. (b) Detected characters. (c) Detected text region. (d) Residual non-text regions after suppression of detected characters. (e) Logo region proposals formed after expansion and agglomeration of non-text regions. (f) Output image.

at intermediate stages and hence such logos would be detected as regular text rather than as logo brand names. Hence, we have not considered such purely text-based logos in our database.

5   Conclusion and Future Work

This paper has demonstrated a computationally feasible and fairly accurate, size and orientation invariant algorithm that detects and classifies logos in complex, natural background. The presence of any text in the image had also been detected, followed by its recognition to ameliorate the problem of incorrect logo image identification. The detected text related to the logo serves as a backup in cases of failure of identification of images of logos. Certain extensions of this work worthy of future consideration include redressing the failure cases and optimization of CNN architecture. The speed and scalability of the method also needs to be improved to address real world applications.

References

1. Alaei, A., Delalandre, M., Girard, N.: Logo detection using painting based representation and probability features. In: ICDAR, pp. 1235–1239 (2013)
2. Boia, R., Florea, C., Florea, L., Dogaru, R.: Logo localization and recognition in natural images using homographic class graphs. Mach. Vis. Appl. **27**(2), 287–301 (2016)
3. Romberg, S., Pueyo, L.G., Lienhart, R., Zwol, R.V.: Scalable logo recognition in real-world images. In: Proceedings of the 1st ACM International Conference on Multimedia Retrieval, pp. 965–968 (2011)
4. Chen, W., Lan, S., Xu, P.: Multiple feature fusion via hierarchical matching for TV logo recognition. In: Proceedings of the 8th International Congress on Image and Signal Processing, IEEE (2015)
5. Sahbi, H., Ballan, L., Serra, G., Bimbo, A.: Context-dependent logo matching and recognition. IEEE Trans. Image Process. **22**(3), 1018–1031 (2013). IEEE
6. Zhang, Y., Zhang, S., Liang, W., Guo, Q.: Individualized matching based on logo density for scalable logo recognition. In: ICASSP, pp. 4324–4328 (2014)

7. Hassanzadeh, S., Pourghassem, H.: Fast logo detection based on morphological features in document images. In: Proceedings of the 7th International Colloquium on Signal Processing and its Applications, pp. 283–286 (2011)

8. Hoi, S.C.H., Wu, X., Liu, H., Wu, Y., Wang, H., Xue, H., Wu, Q.: LOGO-net: largescale deep logo detection and brand recognition with deep region-based convolutional networks. arXiv:1511.02462 (2015)

9. Iandola, F.N., Shen, A., Gao, P., Keutzer, K.: DeepLogo: hitting logo recognition with the deep neural network hammer. arXiv:1510.02131 (2015)

10. Krizhevsky, A., Sutskever, I., Hinton, J.E.: Imagenet classification with deep convolutional neural networks. Adv. Neural Inf. Process. Syst. 1097–1105 (2012)

11. Oliveira, G., Frazão, X., Pimentel, A., Ribeiro. B.: Automatic graphic logo detection via fast region-based convolutional networks. arXiv:1604.06083 (2016)

12. Uijlings, J.R.R., Van De Sande, K.E.A., Gevers, T., Smeulders, A.W.M.: Selective search for object recognition. Intl. J. Comput. Vis. **104**(2), 154–171 (2013). Springer

13. Matas, J., Chum, O., Urban, M., Pajdla, T.: Robust wide baseline stereo from maximally stable extremal regions. Image Vis. Comput. **22**(10), 761–767 (2002)

14. Zeiler, M.D., Fergus, R.: Visualizing and understanding convolutional networks. In: Fleet, D., Pajdla, T., Schiele, B., Tuytelaars, T. (eds.) ECCV 2014. LNCS, vol. 8689, pp. 818–833. Springer, Cham (2014). doi:10.1007/978-3-319-10590-1_53

15. Hancock, J.M.: Jaccard distance (Jaccard Index, Jaccard Similarity Coefficient). Dictionary Bioinform. Comput. Biol (2004)

16. Huang, W., Qiao, Y., Tang, X.: Robust scene text detection with convolution neural network induced MSER trees. In: Fleet, D., Pajdla, T., Schiele, B., Tuytelaars, T. (eds.) ECCV 2014. LNCS, vol. 8692, pp. 497–511. Springer, Cham (2014). doi:10.1007/978-3-319-10593-2_33

17. de Campos, T.E., Babu, B.R., Varma, M.: Character recognition in natural images. In: Proceedings of the 4th International Conference on Computer Vision Theory and Applications, pp. 273–280 (2009)

18. Revaud, J., Douze, M., Schmid, C.: Correlation-based burstiness for logo retrieval. In: Proceedings of the 20th ACM International Conference on Multimedia, pp. 965–968 (2012)

19. Romberg, S., Lienhart, R.: Bundle min-hashing for logo recognition. In: Proceedings of the 3rd ACM Conf. on International Conference on Multimedia Accessed, pp. 113–120 (2013)

20. Farajzadeh, N.: Exemplar-based logo and trademark recognition. Mach. Vis. Appl. **26**(6), 791–805 (2015)

21. Liu, Y., Wang, J., Li, Z., Li, H.: Efficient logo recognition by local feature groups. Multimedia Syst. 1–9 (2016)

22. Nair, V., Hinton, G.: Rectified linear units improve restricted boltzmann machines. In: ICML (2010)

High Frame Rate Real-Time Scene Change Detection System

Sanjay Singh[1(✉)], Ravi Saini[1], Sumeet Saurav[1], Pramod Tanwar[1],
Kota S. Raju[1], Anil K. Saini[1], Santanu Chaudhury[1], and Idaku Ishii[2]

[1] CSIR-Central Electronics Engineering Research Institute (CSIR-CEERI),
Academy of Scientific and Innovative Research (AcSIR),
Pilani 333031, Rajasthan, India
sanjay@ceeri.res.in
[2] Robotics Laboratory, Hiroshima University, Hiroshima 739-8527, Japan

Abstract. Scene change detection, one of the fundamental and most important problem of computer vision, plays a very important role in the realization of a complete industrial vision system as well as automated video surveillance system - for automatic scene analysis, monitoring, and generation of alerts based on relevant changes in a video stream. Therefore, in addition to being accurate and robust, a successful scene change detection system must also be of very high frame rate in order to detect scene changes which goes off within a glimpse of the eye and often goes unnoticeable by the conventional frame rate cameras. Keeping the high frame rate processing as main focus, a very high frame rate real-time scene change detection system is developed by leveraging VLSI design to achieve high performance. This is accomplished by proposing, designing, and implementing an area-efficient scene change detection VLSI architecture on FPGA-based IDP Express platform. The developed prototype of complete real-time scene change detection system is capable of processing 2000 frames per second for 512×512 video resolution and is tested for live incoming video streams from high speed camera. The proposed and implemented system architecture is adaptable and scalable for different video resolutions and frame rates.

Keywords: High speed scene change detection · VLSI architecture · FPGA implementation · Automated video surveillance system

1 Introduction

The long-term monitoring of high-speed phenomena using high frame rate cameras requires a large amount of storage space and high communication bandwidth over a network. Real-time high frame rate scene change detection allows more efficient hard disk storage by only archiving video frames where actual change in a scene has occurred and also reduces the communication and further processing overheads in a remote video surveillance scenario by selecting the frames of relevant scene changes. However, the most of the existing implementations of scene change detection algorithms are done for conventional video camera (25 fps to 30 fps), and, therefore, these are not capable of automatically detecting the high speed scene change phenomena.

© Springer International Publishing AG 2017
S. Mukherjee et al. (Eds.): ICVGIP 2016, LNCS 10481, pp. 157–167, 2017.
https://doi.org/10.1007/978-3-319-68124-5_14

In this work, we have addressed this problem by developing a real-time very high frame rate system for automatic scene change detection in live incoming video streams from high frame cameras. The high performance computing was achieved by leveraging VLSI design based approach. A dedicated VLSI architecture has been proposed and designed for computationally efficient clustering based scene change detection scheme [1]. The designed architecture is coded in VHDL, simulated using ModelSim, and synthesized using Xilinx ISE 10.1 design tool chain. The architecture has been integrated with real-time video interfaces. The complete final design has been implemented on FPGA-based IDP Express platform. The implemented scene change detection system is capable of processing 2000 frames per second for 512×512 video resolution in live incoming video streams from high frame rate camera. It has been tested for different real-world scenarios for scene change detection and the system shows good results.

The rest of the paper is organized as follows: in the next section, we present a literature review of existing scene change detection schemes. A brief of clustering based scene change detection scheme is presented in section three. The details of complete high frame rate scene change detection system and associated VLSI architecture are presented in section four. The synthesis results and scene change detection results are presented in section five and six, respectively. Finally, we conclude this paper with a short summary.

2 Literature Review

The importance of scene change detection for designing industrial vision systems and automated video surveillance systems can be gauged from the availability of a large number of robust and complex algorithms and their implementations that have been developed to-date, and the even larger number of articles that have been published on this topic so far. The simplest change detection approach is the frame differencing method in which change in video scene can be detected by finding the difference of the pixels between two adjacent frames. If the difference is higher than a threshold, the pixel is identified as change pixel otherwise background pixel. The threshold is chosen empirically. Different methods and criteria for choosing the threshold have been surveyed and their comparative results have been reported in the literature [2–4]. The simplicity of frame differencing based approaches comes at the cost of change detection quality. For a chosen threshold, simple differencing based approaches are unlikely to outperform the more advanced algorithms proposed for real-world surveillance applications. A comprehensive description and comparative analysis of these methods has been presented by Radke et al. [5].

The practical real-world video surveillance applications demand a continuous updating of the background frame to incorporate any permanent scene change i.e. if a pixel has remained stationary for a sufficient number of frames, it must be copied into the background frame such as, for example, light intensity changes in day time must be a part of the background. For this purpose, several researchers [6–8] have described adaptive background subtraction techniques for change detection. They have used single Gaussian Density Function to model the background. These algorithms succeed in learning and refining the single background model. They are capable of handling illumination changes in a scene and are well suited for stationary background scenarios.

Due to pseudo-stationary nature of the background in real-world scenes, assuming that background is perfectly stationary for surveillance applications is a serious flaw. For example, in a real-world video scene, there may be swaying branches of trees, moving tree leaves in windows of rooms, moving clouds, the ripples of water on a lake, or moving fan in the room. These are small repetitive changes (typically not important) and so should be incorporated into background. The single background model based approaches mentioned above are incapable of correctly modeling such pseudo-stationary backgrounds. Stauffer and Grimson [9] recognized that these kinds of pseudo-stationary backgrounds are inherently multi-model and hence they developed the technique of an Adaptive Background Mixture Models, which models each pixel by a mixture of Gaussians. However, maintaining these mixtures for every pixel is an enormous computational burden and results in low frame rates when compared to previous approaches. Butler et al. [10] proposed a new approach, similar to that of Stauffer and Grimson [9], but with a reduced computational complexity. The processing, in this approach, is performed on YC_rC_b video data format, but it still requires many computations and needs large amounts of memory for storing background models. In order to address this problem of reducing the computational complexity, Chutani and Chaudhury [1] proposed a block-based clustering scheme with a very low complexity for change detection. On one hand this scheme is robust enough for handling pseudo-stationary nature of background, and on the other it significantly lowers the computational complexity and is well suited for designing standalone systems for real-time applications. For this reason we have selected the clustering based change detection scheme for designing the real-time standalone high frame rate change detection system which features real-time high frame rate processing and is capable of discarding irrelevant changes using adaptive background models.

3   Clustering Based Change Detection Algorithm

In this section, we briefly describe the clustering based change detection technique and for a more detailed description refer to [1]. Clustering based change detection uses a block-based similarity computation scheme. At the heart of this scheme is a very low complexity method for maintaining some limited but important information about the history of each pixel. To start with, each incoming video frame is partitioned into 4×4 pixel blocks. Each 4×4 pixel block is modeled by a group of four clusters where each cluster consists of a block centroid and a frame number which updated the cluster most recently. Optionally, for each block there may be a change flag field. The group of four clusters is necessary to correctly model the pseudo-stationary background, as a single cluster is incapable of modeling multiple modes that can be present in pseudo-stationary backgrounds. The group size is selected as four because it has been reported by Chutani and Chaudhury [1] that four clusters per group yield a good balance between accuracy and computational complexity. The basic computational scheme is shown in Fig. 1. The sequence of steps for change detection using

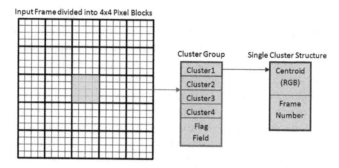

Fig. 1. Clustering-based change detection scheme.

clustering-based scheme is Block Centroid Computation, Cluster Group Initialization, Cluster Matching, Cluster Update, Cluster Replace, and Classifications.

The above mentioned clustering-based change detection scheme has been implemented by us in C/C++ programming language. For running the code, a Dell Precision T3400 workstation (with Windows XP operating system, quad-core Intel® Core™2 Duo Processor with 2.93 GHz Operating Frequency, and 4 GB RAM) was used. The Open Computer Vision (OpenCV) libraries have been used in the code for reading video streams (either stored or coming from camera) and displaying change detection results.

4   High Frame Rate Scene Change Detection System

In order to achieve high frame rate real-time change detection processing, as required in many industrial and surveillance applications for recording high speed phenomena, we have developed a complete prototype system for high frame rate real-time scene change detection. The system has been developed by designing a dedicated VLSI architecture for high performance computing of clustering-based scene change detection scheme and implementing it on FPGA-based IDP Express Platform [11]. The high frame rate camera has been connected to the IDP Express Platform for capturing of live video streams.

A simplified conceptual block diagram of the proposed and developed FPGA-based high frame rate real-time scene change detection system is shown in Fig. 2 to illustrate the data flow within the system. The main components of a complete high frame rate scene change detection system are high frame rate *Camera* and *IDP Express Platform*. The image data captured by high frame rate *Camera* is transferred to the *IDP Express Platform*. The three main components of *IDP Express Platform* are: *Serial to Parallel Conversion*, *Virtex-5(XC5VLX50T) Xilinx FPGA*, and *Spartan-3 (XC3S5000) Xilinx FPGA*. The serial data received from high frame rate *Camera* is converted to parallel data by *Serial to Parallel Conversion* module. *Virtex-5(XC5VLX50T) Xilinx FPGA* is used for implementations of high speed video data interface and PCI bus interface. *Spartan-3 (XC3S5000) Xilinx FPGA* is used for implementations of high frame rate scene change detection VLSI architecture and interface FIFOs. *Data Format*

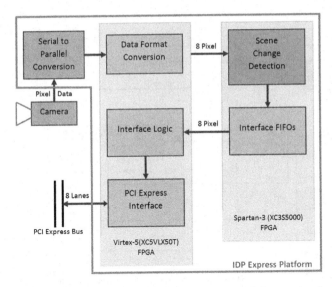

Fig. 2. Dataflow diagram of the developed high frame rate real-time scene change detection system.

Conversion module implemented on *Virtex-5(XC5VLX50T) Xilinx FPGA* provides eight pixels in parallel. The *Scene Change Detection* module, implemented on *Spartan-3 (XC3S5000) Xilinx FPGA*, receives these eight pixels, stores them, and processes. The scene change detected data is given back to *Interface Logic* module implemented on *Virtex-5(XC5VLX50T) Xilinx FPGA*. Finally the data is transferred to *PCI Express Bus* of the system through *PCI Express Interface* module. Video timing signals (Pixel Clock, Hsync, Vsync, and Blank) are used for synchronization among different modules of the complete system.

The detailed proposed VLSI architecture of Scene Change Detection module is shown in Fig. 3. Pixel Data arrives from the Data Format Conversion module (implemented on Virtex-5(XC5VLX50T) Xilinx FPGA) row by row. As scene change detection scheme is based on the processing of 4 × 4 image blocks, therefore, streaming video processing cannot be used for clustering based scene change detection scheme. For this reason, the four rows of image data are buffered in input memory (INPUT MEM) before processing begins. The output from INPUT MEM is four pixel data coming out in parallel. BLCENT COMPUTATION UNIT computes the average centroid for 4 × 4 image block by taking pixel data from the input memory (four clock cycles are required for reading 16 pixels from the input memory buffer). This computation is done by adding 16 pixel values of current block and then dividing the sum by 16. The read address, write address, and write enable signals for input memory are generated by the corresponding INPUT-MEM RADD-WRADD WEN module.

The change computation enable (CCEN) signal is generated by CHANGE COMPUTATION ENABLE UNIT. This signal is used as the enable signal in different modules of the designed scene change detection architecture as shown in Fig. 3.

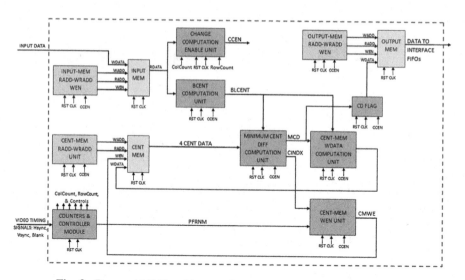

Fig. 3. Proposed VLSI architecture for scene change detection algorithm.

As mentioned in algorithm section, clustering-based scheme stores associated centroid information for each 4 × 4 image block. It, therefore, requires the assignment of a unique identity (or address) to each block. This is done by using row and column counters generated by *COUNTERS & CONTROLLER MODULE*. This unit takes the video timing signals (Hsync, Vsync, Blank, CLK, RST) from camera interface module and generates the different counter values (RowCount, ColCount, PFRNM) and control signals (Controls) required for the proper functioning of the complete system.

For storing pixel related information in the clustering-based algorithm, a centroid memory (*CENT MEM*) is used. Each centroid memory location contains four Centroid values (corresponding to four clusters) which contain the background color and intensity related information. The read address and write address signals for *CENT-MEM* are generated by the corresponding *CENT-MEM RADD-WRADD UNIT*.

During initialization phase, control signals are generated in such a way that the four clusters are initialized. For all subsequent frames, the generated control signals enable the change detection process. After initialization, the matching cluster is searched within the cluster group of four clusters. For this purpose, first difference between cluster Centroid value (*CENT DATA*) and incoming current block Centroid value (*BLCENT*) is computed for all four clusters by reading the cluster Centroid values (*4 CENT DATA*) from *CENT MEM* corresponding to current 4 × 4 image block and taking absolute sum of differences with current block Centroid value (*BLCENT*). From the four difference values, minimum Centroid difference value is selected. This complete task is carried out by the *MINIMUM CENT DIFF COMPUTATION UNIT*. It outputs *MCD* (minimum centroid difference value) and *CINDX* (Centroid Index). *CINDX* gives the cluster number corresponding to *MCD* (minimum centroid difference value).

The *MCD* and *BLCENT* values are used by *CENT-MEM WDATA COMPUTATION UNIT* to compute the write data for Centroid Memory (*CENT MEM*). *MCD* is compared with a user defined threshold. For *MCD* less than or equal to the threshold (i.e. matching cluster is found), the write data for *CENT MEM* is the average value of current block Centroid value (*BLCENT*) and matching cluster Centroid value (matching cluster number is given be *CINDX*). For *MCD* greater than threshold (i.e. no matching cluster is found), the write data for *CENT MEM* is current block Centroid value (*BLCENT*) and in this case the cluster number for which value is replaced is determined by *CENT-MEM WEN UNIT* which generates the write enable signal for *CENT MEM*.

The *CINDX* value is used by *CENT-MEM WEN UNIT* for generating the write enable signals for *CENT MEM*. The write enable signals help for selecting the cluster for which the centroid value is to be updated or replaced.

The change detection flag generation module (*CD FLAG*) takes *MCD* as input and compares it with a user defined threshold. A 1-bit Flag signal is generated which is low if difference is less than the threshold (i.e. current block matches with background model and therefore, no change is detected) and high if the difference is greater than the threshold (i.e. current block is change detected block). This change information data of 4 × 4 pixel block is written to the output memory (*OUTPUT MEM*) and corresponding addresses for this memory are generated by *OUTPUT-MEM RADD-WRADD WEN* module. The processed output data is stored in output memory (*OUTPUT MEM*) for synchronization purpose before sending it to *Interface FIFOs* implemented on *Spartan-3 (XC3S5000) Xilinx FPGA*. This is because the output data of *Scene Change Detection* architecture is for 4 × 4 pixel block while the data sent to *Interface Logic* (implemented on *Virtex-5(XC5VLX50T) Xilinx FPGA*) is row by row. Finally, the scene change detected data is read from this output buffer memory (*OUTPUT MEM*) and sent to *PCI Express Bus* through *Interface Logic* module and *PCI Express Interface* module (implemented on *Virtex-5(XC5VLX50T) Xilinx FPGA*).

All design modules (mentioned above) of proposed VLSI architecture for clustering based change detection scheme have been coded in VHDL, simulated using ModelSim, and synthesized using Xilinx ISE 10.1 tool chain. Frame rate achieved through the VLSI/hardware implementation is far higher than that obtained for software implementation on a workstation.

5 Synthesis Results

All the modules of the proposed VLSI architecture for clustering based change detection scheme were coded in VHDL and simulated using ModelSim. A top level design module was created which invoked all the designed modules of scene change detection architecture. A User Constraint File (UCF) was created to map the input/output ports of the design on actual pins of the FPGA. This top level design was synthesized using Xilinx ISE 10.1 tool chain. The resulting configuration file was loaded into Spartan-3 FPGA on IDP Express platform. Thus a complete prototype system for real-time high frame rate automatic scene change detection system was developed and is shown in Fig. 4. The FPGA resource utilization results for post-place and route are shown in Table 1.

Fig. 4. Complete setup of high frame rate real-time scene change detection system.

Table 1. FPGA resource utilization by complete high frame rate real-time scene change detection system.

Resources	Resources utilized	Available resources	Percentage of utilization
Slice registers	1012	66560	1.52%
Slice LUTs	1242	66560	1.87%
Occupied slices	1265	32280	3.92%
BRAMs	72	104	69.23%
Memory (Kb)	1296	1872	69.23%
IOs	193	633	30.49%

Performance of the proposed, designed, and implemented system is compared with some recently published scene change detection implementations. The performance comparison is shown in Table 2. Kristensen et al. [12] and Jiang et al. [13] have presented the design of a digital surveillance system running in real-time on an embedded platform. The change detection/segmentation unit of the circuit proposed by these researchers is able to run at 83 MHz on Virtex-IIPro (xc2pro30-5ff1152) FPGA. The change detection/segmentation architectures presented by Genovese et al. [14] and Genovese and Napoli [15] were designed for OpenCV GMM algorithm and were implemented on Virtex5 (xc5vlx50-2ff1153) FPGA. The scene change/motion segmentation circuit proposed by Genovese and Napoli in [16] has been implemented on both Virtex6 (xc6vlx75t-3ff784) and Virtex5 (xc5vlx50-2ff1153) FPGAs and is an improved version of the work presented by them in [14, 15]. Singh et al. [17] have implemented change detection architecture on Virtex5 (xc5fx130t-2ff1738) FPGA platform. The architecture proposed and implemented in this paper for scene change detection scheme outperforms existing implementations in terms of processing speed. An apple to apple comparison of FPGA resource utilization with existing literature

Table 2. Performance comparison with existing scene change detection implementations.

Target FPGA device	Implementation	Video resolution	Frame rate (fps)
IDP Express Platform Spartan3 (xc3s5000-4fg900)	Our implemented prototype system	512 × 512	2000
Virtex5 (xc5fx130t-2ff1738)	[17]	720 × 576	178
Virtex5 (xc5vlx50-2ff1153)	[16]	720 × 576	315
	[15]	720 × 576	121
	[14]	720 × 576	113
Virtex-IIPro (xc2pro30-5ff1152)	[12, 13]	720 × 576	200

does not make proper sense as the scene change detection algorithms used, number of background models considered, and the video formats and sizes considered in the existing implementations are different than in our implementation. For this reason, one to one FPGA resource utilization comparisons are not tabulated in this paper.

The system architecture for high frame rate real-time scene change detection, proposed, designed, and implemented in this paper is adaptable and scalable for different video sizes and frame rates.

6 Scene Change Detection Results

For robust and real-time testing of the implemented system, the system was run for real-world scenarios. Different real-world scenarios are broadly classified into two categories i.e. static background situations and pseudo-stationary background situations. Figure 5 shows examples of real-world situations of static background scenarios captured by the camera. In all the cases of Fig. 5, the background is static and the moving objects are present in the scene. Scene changes detected by our implementation in different frames are shown just below the respective images. It can be clearly seen that only moving objects have been detected by the implemented scene change detection system.

Fig. 5. Moving objects in video scene and corresponding change detected outputs for static background scenarios.

Scenarios of pseudo-stationary background with moving foreground objects are considered in Fig. 6. Despite movements of leaves of trees in the background, only moving objects in the foreground are detected by the implemented scene change

Fig. 6. Moving objects in video scene and corresponding change detected outputs for pseudo-stationary background scenarios.

detection system. Results of the tests show that the system is robust enough to detect only the relevant scene changes in a live video scene and eliminates the continuous unwanted movements in the background itself.

If a change threshold is not crossed in a video frame, the frame is rejected at this stage and if a change threshold is crossed in a video frame, the frame is selected for further processing. This filtering of frames of interest reduces the communication and processing overheads of an automated video surveillance system for remote video surveillance scenarios.

The quantitative analysis of the scene change detection quality of proposed hardware implementation is done against the software implementation of the clustering-based scene change detection algorithm by using video streams of different real-world scenarios and computing the mean square error (MSE). The computed MSE for every frame of all the test videos is zero and it confirms that the proposed hardware (VLSI) implementation produces the same scene change detection results as the software implementation of the clustering based scene change detection scheme but at much higher frame rates than software implementation of clustering based scene change detection algorithm [1].

7   Conclusions

In this paper, we have presented the design and implementation of a high frame rate real-time prototype system for scene change detection. To address the issue of high performance requirements, a dedicated VLSI architecture has been proposed, designed, and integrated with video interfaces. The complete system has been prototyped on FPGA-based IDP Express board. The developed system prototype was tested for live incoming video streams from high frame rate camera and it robustly and automatically detects scene changes in real-time at 2000 fps for 512×512 resolution video streams. The implemented system can be effectively used as a standalone system for high frame rate industrial and surveillance applications (for detection of high-speed phenomena).

Acknowledgments. Sanjay Singh is thankful to Prof. Raj Singh, Chief Scientist and Group Leader, IC Design Group, CSIR-CEERI, Pilani and Dr. A.S. Mandal, Chief Scientist, CSIR-CEERI, Pilani for their constant support and motivation. The financial support of Ministry of Electronics & Information Technology (MeitY), Govt. of India is gratefully acknowledged.

References

1. Chutani, E.R., Chaudhury, S.: Video trans-coding in smart camera for ubiquitous multimedia environment. In: Proceedings: International Symposium on Ubiquitous Multimedia Computing, pp. 185–189 (2008)
2. Rosin, P.L.: Thresholding for change detection. In: Proceedings: Sixth International Conference on Computer Vision, pp. 274–279 (1998)
3. Rosin, P.L., Ioannidis, E.: Evaluation of global image thresholding for change detection. Pattern Recogn. Lett. **24**(14), 2345–2356 (2003)
4. Smits, P.C., Annoni, A.: Toward specification-driven change detection. IEEE Trans. Geosci. Remote Sens. **38**(3), 1484–1488 (2000)
5. Radke, R.J., Andra, S., Kofahi, O.A., Roysam, B.: Image change detection algorithms: a systematic survey. IEEE Trans. Image Process. **14**(3), 294–307 (2005)
6. Cavallaro, A., Ebrahimi, T.: Video object extraction based on adaptive background and statistical change detection. In: Proceedings: SPIE Visual Communications and Image Processing, pp. 465–475 (2001)
7. Huwer, S., Niemann, H.: Adaptive change detection for real-time surveillance applications. In: Proceedings: Third IEEE International Workshop on Visual Surveillance, pp. 37–46 (2000)
8. Kanade, T., Collins, R.T., Lipton, A.J., Burt, P., Wixson, L.: Advances in cooperative multi-sensor video surveillance. In: Proceedings: DARPA Image Understanding Workshop, pp. 3–24 (1998)
9. Stauffer, C., Grimson, W.E.L.: Learning patterns of activity using real-time tracking. IEEE Trans. Pattern Anal. Mach. Intell. **22**(8), 747–757 (2000)
10. Butler, D.E., Bove, V.M., Sridharan, S.: Real-time adaptive foreground/background segmentation. EURASIP J. Appl. Signal Process. **2005**, 2292–2304 (2005)
11. IDP Express Platform. http://www.photonics.com/Product.aspx?PRID=46288
12. Kristensen, F., Hedberg, H., Jiang, H., Nilsson, P., Öwall, V.: An embedded real-time surveillance system: implementation and evaluation. J. Signal Process. Syst. **52**(1), 75–94 (2008)
13. Jiang, H., Ardö, H., Öwall, V.: A hardware architecture for real-time video segmentation utilizing memory reduction techniques. IEEE Trans. Circuits Syst. Video Technol. **19**(2), 226–236 (2009)
14. Genovese, M., Napoli, E., Petra, N.: OpenCV compatible real time processor for background foreground identification. In: Proceedings: International Conference on Microelectronics, pp 467–470 (2010)
15. Genovese, M., Napoli, E.: FPGA-based architecture for real time segmentation and denoising of HD video. J. Real Time Image Process. **8**(4), 389–401 (2013)
16. Genovese, M., Napoli, E.: ASIC and FPGA implementation of the Gaussian mixture model algorithm for real-time segmentation of high definition video. IEEE Trans. Very Large Scale Integr. **22**(3), 537–547 (2014)
17. Singh, S., Shekhar, C., Vohra, A.: FPGA-based real-time motion detection for automated video surveillance systems. Electronics **5**(1), 1–18 (2016). MDPI. Article No. 10

Painting Classification Using a Pre-trained Convolutional Neural Network

Sugata Banerji[1][(✉)] and Atreyee Sinha[2]

[1] Lake Forest College, 555 North Sheridan Road, Lake Forest, IL 60045, USA
banerji@lakeforest.edu
[2] Edgewood College, 1000 Edgewood College Drive, Madison, WI 53719, USA
asinha@edgewood.edu

Abstract. The problem of classifying images into different predefined categories is an important high-level vision problem. In recent years, convolutional neural networks (CNNs) have been the most popular tool for image classification tasks. CNNs are multi-layered neural networks that can handle complex classification tasks if trained properly. However, training a CNN requires a huge number of labeled images that are not always available for all problem domains. A CNN pre-trained on a different image dataset may not be effective for classification across domains. In this paper, we explore the use of pre-trained CNN not as a classification tool but as a feature extraction tool for painting classification. We run an extensive array of experiments to identify the layers that work best with the problems of artist and style classification, and also discuss several novel representation and classification techniques using these features.

Keywords: CNN · Painting classification · Feature extraction · Image classification · SVM · Deep learning

1 Introduction

Image classification is one of the most important Computer Vision problems being addressed by researchers around the world today. Classification is the task of labelling images with different predefined category labels. These category labels may be based on some low-level features such as color, texture or shape, but most often, they are based on more high-level features such as semantic description, activity or artistic style. In the past few years, convolutional neural networks (CNNs) have been popular among vision researchers for a variety of classification tasks. The initial use of CNNs was made possible by the availability of large labelled image datasets such as ImageNet and Places and the large improvement in object and scene classification results obtained thereafter [7]. Later, researchers have adapted the network for different tasks by modifying the architecture or tweaking the network parameters [4]. Convolutional neural networks typically contain multiple convolution and pooling layers followed by a few

© Springer International Publishing AG 2017
S. Mukherjee et al. (Eds.): ICVGIP 2016, LNCS 10481, pp. 168–179, 2017.
https://doi.org/10.1007/978-3-319-68124-5_15

fully connected layers and a soft-max classifier. It has been demonstrated in [12] that using the output from the last fully connected layer pre-trained CNNs [13] with linear classifiers such as support vector machines (SVMs), yields better classification performance. In [10], the authors use max and average pooling on the penultimate layer before the fully connected layers for retrieval of similar images.

Painting classification is an emerging research area in computer vision, which is gaining increasing attention in the recent years [11]. It has many potential applications in museums, industries, painting theft investigation, forgery detection, art education, etc. From the computer vision point of view, conventional features cannot capture the key aspects of computational painting categorization. A comparative evaluation of different conventional features by [6] for artist and style classification clearly suggests the need for more powerful visual features specific to painting categorization tasks. This is our primary motivation in selecting this problem for our current work.

In this paper, we propose a novel approach to using the outputs of these intermediate layer features for classification and retrieval of paintings from the large Painting-91 [6] dataset. This is inspired by the works of [9,17,18]. Using CNNs pretrained on ImageNet [7] we consider the response maps computed at several different layers before the fully connected layers and compare their performance. We demonstrate that these features are more effective for the retrieval task and also the artist and style classification tasks. We also provide an in-depth visualization and discussion on the suitability and effectiveness of the different layer features for a painting dataset. The intuition behind the proposed approach is that in initial layers of the CNN, the encoded information is more low-level

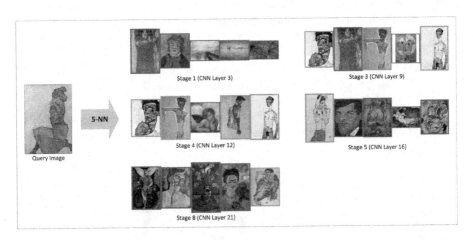

Fig. 1. Images retrieved using the query on the left and raw CNN features from intermediate layers of a pre-trained CNN. Note that the early layers results contain similarities in low-level features such as color (red) while the latter layer results contain similar subjects (person). Green borders indicate painting by the same artist as the query and red borders indicate those by a different artist. (Color figure online)

and spatially localized, and as we move up the layers, the information becomes more and more semantic. In the fully connected layers the information is fully semantic and free from stylistic details or spatial fluctuations. Figure 1 shows the different nearest neighbors to a query image for features extracted from different layers of the pre-trained CNN.

The rest of this paper is organized as follows. Section 2 describes the proposed method of feature extraction, representation and classification in detail. Section 3 describes our experiments and discusses our results. Section 4 summarizes our findings and lists future areas for extending this work.

2   Proposed Method

The proposed method uses a pre-trained CNN for extracting features at various stages and compares their performance for both artist classification and style classification problems. We use several different methods for image representation using these features and compare the classification results from three different classifiers. These steps are discussed in detail in Subsects. 2.1, 2.2 and 2.3.

2.1   Feature Extraction

We use the OverFeat image features extractor [13] for feature extraction. Over-Feat is based on a convolutional network similar to [7] trained on the 1000-category ImageNet dataset [3]. OverFeat also includes a classifier but we do not use this classifier as it classifies into one of the ImageNet categories. The 'fast' network of OverFeat uses input images of size 231×231 and has 21 layers before the final softmax output stage divided into 8 stages. The first six of these stages consist of convolution and pooling layers and the last two stages are fully connected layers. OverFeat can be used to extract the output from any of these layers and use them as features for representation. In the proposed method we extract features following each of the first six stages as well as the layers in between the stages, and use them with our own classifiers. This is shown in Fig. 2.

It has been shown that the features from each of the intermediate layers consist of detectors for high-level features [10] and each of these detectors generates

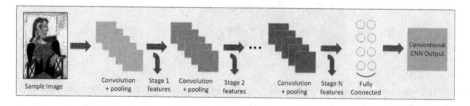

Fig. 2. The proposed image representation uses features from intermediate layers of a pre-trained CNN. These features are used for retrieval and classification. The process is described in detail in Sect. 2

a response map that is a low-resolution version of the image. Even simple average or max pooling on these response maps can yield state-of-the-art retrieval results [10] for object and scene retrieval tasks. However, the max and average pooling strategies remove finer details and smaller objects which may be essential for painting classification. In this work we use these features to form a vocabulary of visual patterns.

2.2   Quantization and Histogram Formation

The features from the various layers of the CNN are of the form $n \times a \times a$ where each $a \times a$ response map is a low resolution representation of the input image. Each of these maps are responses from detectors of different patterns. We break up this $n \times a \times a$ feature into $a \times a$ vectors of length n by running 'skewers' through all the response maps. This process is explained graphically in Fig. 3. After extracting these feature vectors from all training images, we use the K-means algorithm to cluster them into a vocabulary of visual patters. Finally, we represent each training and test image as a histogram of these visual patterns. We experimented with several vocabularies of sizes ranging from 100 to 10,000 and found the best vocabulary size depends CNN layer being used. The best classification results for each layer were attained for vocabulary sizes 1000 or greater, and the performance peaked for layer 11 features and a vocabulary size of 8000.

To better understand the characteristics of the features extracted from each stage and to test the effectiveness of these features for the artist and style classification tasks, we also represent the raw-CNN features from each image as a single-dimensional vector in a separate set of experiments and put these directly to the classifier.

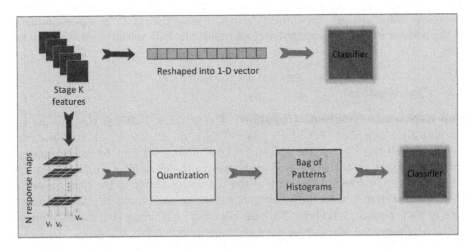

Fig. 3. The features from the intermediate layers of the CNN are used to form a vocabulary of visual patterns and each image is represented by a histogram of these patterns. For comparison, the raw features from the CNN are also fed to the classifier directly. More details are given in Sect. 2

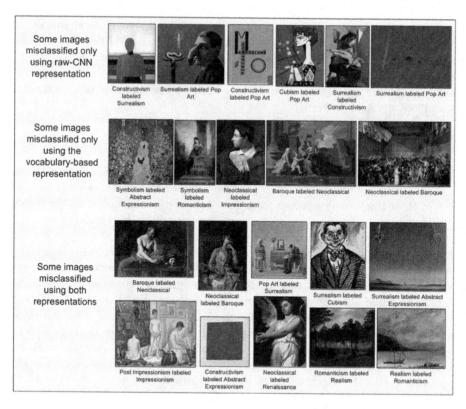

Fig. 4. Results from the style classification task. The top row shows some images misclassified by the raw-CNN representation, but correctly classified using the vocabulary-based method. The middle row shows some images incorrectly classified by the vocabulary-based method, but correctly classified using the raw-CNN representation. At the bottom, we show images that are misclassified by both the methods to the same class.

2.3   Classification

The K-Nearest Neighbor Classifier. The simplest classifier that we use is the K-nearest neighbor (KNN) classifier. This is an unsupervised classification technique. All the images are ranked by their distance from the query image, and the closest k matches are used to determine the class label for the query. If k is 1, then we just assign the class of the nearest neighbor to the query image. If k is greater than 1, then the query image is categorized by taking the majority vote of its k nearest neighbors. For this classifier, a training step is not needed as the neighbors are taken from a set of images whose class is known.

The EFM-KNN Classifier. Principal component analysis, or PCA, which is the optimal feature extraction method in the sense of the mean-square-error, derives the most expressive features for signal and image representation [5].

However, they are not the optimum features for classification. Fisher's Linear Discriminant (FLD), a popular method in pattern recognition, first applies PCA for dimensionality reduction and then discriminant analysis for feature extraction.

The FLD method, however, often leads to overfitting when implemented in an inappropriate PCA space. To improve the generalization performance of the FLD method, a proper balance between two criteria should be maintained: the energy criterion for adequate image representation and the magnitude criterion for eliminating the small-valued trailing eigenvalues of the within-class scatter matrix. The Enhanced Fisher Model (EFM) improves the generalization capability of the FLD method by decomposing the FLD procedure into a simultaneous diagonalization of the within-class and between-class scatter matrices [8]. The simultaneous diagonalization demonstrates that during whitening the eigenvalues of the within-class scatter matrix appear in the denominator. As shown by [8], the small eigenvalues tend to encode noise, and they cause the whitening step to fit for misleading variations, leading to poor generalization performance. To enhance performance, the EFM method preserves a proper balance between the need that the selected eigenvalues account for most of the spectral energy of the raw data (for representational adequacy), and the requirement that the eigenvalues of the within-class scatter matrix (in the reduced PCA space) are not too small (for better generalization performance).

After dimensionality reduction and feature extraction by EFM, we use the KNN classifier on the reduced feature vector for the final classification. The EFM feature extraction process followed by nearest neighbor classification has been shown to perform well with a large number of classes [2,14].

The Linear SVM Classifier. The Support Vector Machine (SVM) minimizes the risk functional in terms of both the empirical risk and the confidence interval [15]. SVM is very popular and has been applied extensively for pattern classification, regression, and density estimation since it displays a good generalization performance. We use the one-vs-all method to train an SVM for each class.

The SVM implementation used for our experiments is the one that is distributed with the VlFeat package [16]. The parameters of the support vector machine are tuned empirically using only the training data, and the parameters that yield the best average precision on the training data are used for classification of the test data. We use a Hellinger kernel (Bhattacharyya's coefficient) classifier for most of our experiments but instead of computing kernel values we explicitly compute the feature map, so that the classifier remains linear in the new feature space. This can be achieved by taking the square root of the feature values and normalizing the resulting vector to unit Euclidean norm [1].

3   Experiments

We run two sets of experiments, one with the raw one-dimensional CNN vector obtained from each layer, and the other with the vocabulary-based bag-of-visual patterns histograms. We use both the representations with all three classifiers to see their effectiveness in the painting categorization problem. Furthermore, we apply this complete methodology to two tasks - artist classification and style classification. The dataset used for our work is the Painting-91 dataset which is described in the following subsection.

3.1 Dataset

We evaluate our representation and classification techniques on the challenging Painting-91 dataset [6]. The dataset consists of paintings from 91 different artists, containing 4266 fine art painting images. These images have been collected from the Internet and feature an extensive artwork collection from different eras, with 13 distinct styles, namely: Abstract Expressionism, Baroque, Constructivism, Cubism, Impressionism, Neoclassical, Pop Art, Post Impressionism, Realism, Renaissance, Romanticism, Surrealism and Symbolism. The number of images per artist vary ranging from 31 (Frida Kahlo) to 56 (Sandro Botticelli). The average images of the 91 artist categories are shown in Fig. 5.

For the task of style classification, we use 2388 images since ambiguous images and works of artists whose body of work spans multiple styles are not used for this task. Since each style class contains paintings of different artists, the training and classification is not easy. For both artist classification and style classification tasks, we use 25 images from each class for training the classifiers, and the rest for testing. The training and test splits are provided by [6] along with the dataset. In retrieval tasks, all images other than the query image itself are used as the retrieval set.

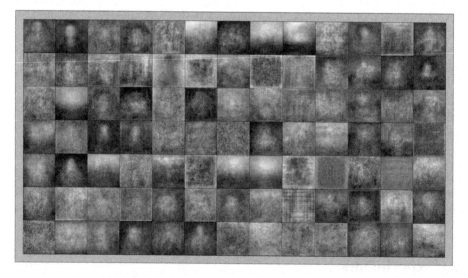

Fig. 5. The average images from the 91 artist categories of the Painting-91 dataset. It can be seen that most of the artists have a distinct visual style, not only in terms of technique but in terms of composition as well.

3.2 Results

The classification experiments show that the CNN features from the intermediate layers (layers 9–17) outperform the features from both the lower and higher layers. In particular, the highest classification accuracy that we get for the artist classification task is 45% which is about 1% more than the highest yield from a single visual cue reported by [6]. We get this result with the layer 12 raw CNN features and the SVM classifier. We get comparable results with the raw features and KNN and EFM-KNN classifiers as well. For artist classification, the EFM-KNN classifier performs more consistently well as compared to the SVM classifier. All these features perform better than the stage 8 (final CNN output) layer that is obtained after the fully connected layers. These results are shown in Table 1.

In the style classification task, the raw CNN features from layers 9–16 again outperform the final layer features from the CNN. In particular, the highest classification accuracy that we get here is 64.5% which is obtained with the SVM classifier and stage 4 raw features. It should be noted that this classification accuracy is nearly an 8% improvement over the highest classification result from a single visual cue reported by [6] and over 2% above the combined performance of 62.2% reported in the same work. The detailed results on this task are compiled in Table 2. The confusion matrix for this result is shown in Fig. 8.

Figure 4 shows some examples of misclassification. First we show images that were misclassified using the raw representation but labeled correctly using the vocabulary-based method. Next we show images that were mislabeled by the vocabulary-based method but classified correctly using the raw CNN representation. Finally, we show some examples that were assigned the same wrong label by both methods. The class-wise classification results obtained by using an SVM classifier with the raw CNN and the proposed vocabulary-based representation are compared in Fig. 6. It can be seen from the figure that the raw CNN performs better for styles like the Baroque, Neoclassical, Realism and Symbolism styles where the overall subject is unambiguously evident from the painting. The

Table 1. Comparison of artist classification performance (%) between the best-performing CNN Layers on the Painting-91 dataset

CNN features used	KNN	EFM-KNN	SVM
Layer 9 raw	35.6	41.9	44.3
Layer 12 raw	38.9	42.8	**45.0**
Layer 16 raw	42.4	43.0	41.0
Layer 21 raw	31.6	41.7	31.6
Layer 10 vocabulary-based	35.1	33.7	38.7
Layer 11 vocabulary-based	36.0	34.4	39.0
Layer 14 vocabulary-based	38.5	35.7	38.6

Table 2. Comparison of style classification performance (%) between the best-performing CNN Layers on the Painting-91 dataset

CNN features used	KNN	EFM-KNN	SVM
Layer 9 raw	48.2	44.9	60.6
Layer 12 raw	53.1	42.5	**64.5**
Layer 16 raw	54.3	41.9	51.2
Layer 21 raw	48.9	38.8	48.3
Layer 9 vocabulary-based	52.9	39.1	56.7
Layer 11 vocabulary-based	54.3	40.1	60.4
Layer 14 vocabulary-based	42.7	34.7	59.5

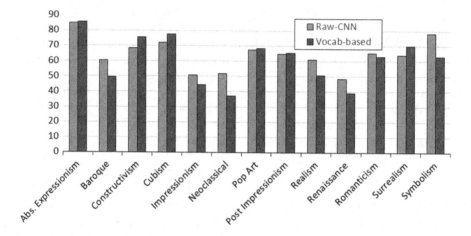

Fig. 6. A Comparison of the class-wise classification performance between the best raw-CNN feature and the best vocabulary-based feature. Both the features use an SVM classifier.

part-based representation wins in categories such as Constructivism, Cubism and Surrealism where there is focus on smaller elements within the picture for classification.

A surprising result observed from the two sets of experiments is that the raw CNN features outperformed the vocabulary-based representation for many of the classes. This is more evident in case of the artist classification problem and less evident in case of the style classification task. Another observation that goes against intuition is that in most of the KNN experiments, the performance was best when the value of K was 1. In other words, the nearest neighbor has the correct class label most of the time. Both of these apparent anomalies can be explained by the fact that many paintings have duplicates or near-duplicates in the dataset. If a query image has a duplicate in the dataset, it always turns up at rank 1 and has the correct label in both style and artist classification problems. Also, since the paintings by the same artist have a similar spatial composition

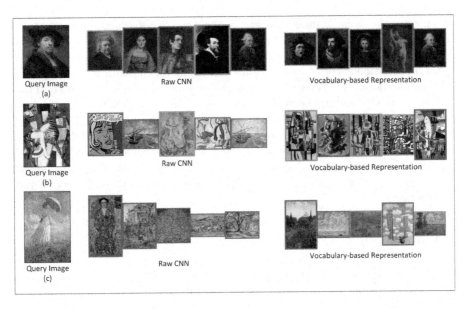

Fig. 7. Top five retrieval set comparisons between raw CNN features and vocabulary-based representation for the same stage outputs for three sample query images. Query (a) shows results using stage 3 features, query (b) shows results using stage 4 features and query (c) shows results using stage 5 features. In case of queries (a) and (b), green borders on results signify images in the same style category as the query. In case of query (c), green borders signify paintings by the same artist as the query. (Color figure online)

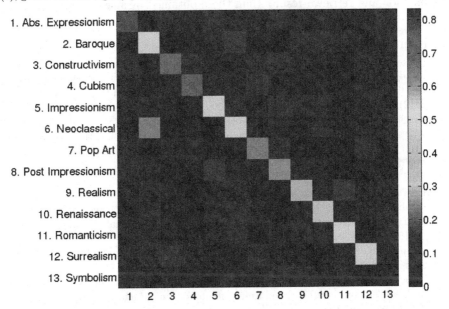

Fig. 8. The confusion matrix for style classification using stage 4 CNN features and SVM classifier. The rows show the real style categories and the columns show the assigned style categories.

as seen from the average images in Fig. 5, the raw CNN features perform much better than the vocabulary-based representation in that task.

Retrieval results are shown in Figs. 1 and 7. In particular, Fig. 1 shows the type of information encoded by different CNN layers for the same image. Figure 7 shows three examples of retrieval using features from the stages 3, 4 and 5 of the CNN respectively. As can be seen, in all cases, the raw CNN features retrieve images that have subjects that are semantically more close to the subject of the query image, while the proposed vocabulary-based representation fetches images that have similar stylistic elements. In the first two samples, the green and red borders around retrieval results indicate correct and incorrect style class labels, respectively. In the third example, the correct and incorrect labels refer to artist classification.

4   Conclusions

We have proposed a novel vocabulary-based image representation based on features extracted from intermediate layers of a pre-trained CNN, and combined this representation with three different classifiers to perform two classification tasks on a large image dataset. Our proposed representation performs better than raw CNN features at retrieval tasks when retrieving works with similar stylistic elements is desired.

In future, we would like to extend this work by fusing the information encoded by the different layers, either at feature level or at decision level, to obtain better classification and retrieval results than those obtained by single layers.

References

1. Arandjelović, R., Zisserman, A.: Three things everyone should know to improve object retrieval. In: IEEE Conference on Computer Vision and Pattern Recognition (2012)
2. Banerji, S., Sinha, A., Liu, C.: New image descriptors based on color, texture, shape, and wavelets for object and scene image classification. Neurocomputing **117**, 173–185 (2013). http://www.sciencedirect.com/science/article/pii/S0925231213001987
3. Deng, J., Dong, W., Socher, R., Li, L.J., Li, K., Fei-Fei, L.: ImageNet: a large-scale hierarchical image database. In: CVPR 2009 (2009)
4. Donahue, J., Jia, Y., Vinyals, O., Hoffman, J., Zhang, N., Tzeng, E., Darrell, T.: Decaf: a deep convolutional activation feature for generic visual recognition. CoRR abs/1310.1531 (2013). http://arxiv.org/abs/1310.1531
5. Fukunaga, K.: Introduction to Statistical Pattern Recognition, 2nd edn. Academic Press, Cambridge (1990)
6. Khan, F.S., Beigpour, S., de Weijer, J.V., Felsberg, M.: Painting-91: a large scale database for computational painting categorization. Mach. Vis. Appl. (MVAP) **25**(6), 1385–1397 (2014). http://cat.uab.es/joost/painting91
7. Krizhevsky, A., Sutskever, I., Hinton, G.E.: ImageNet classification with deep convolutional neural networks. In: NIPS, pp. 1106–1114 (2012)

8. Liu, C., Wechsler, H.: Robust coding schemes for indexing and retrieval from large face databases. IEEE Trans. Image Process. **9**(1), 132–137 (2000)

9. Long, J., Shelhamer, E., Darrell, T.: Fully convolutional networks for semantic segmentation. In: CVPR, November 2015, (to appear)

10. Mousavian, A., Kosecka, J.: Deep convolutional features for image based retrieval and scene categorization. CoRR abs/1509.06033 (2015). http://arxiv.org/abs/1509.06033

11. Puthenputhussery, A., Liu, Q., Liu, C.: Color multi-fusion fisher vector feature for fine art painting categorization and influence analysis. In: 2016 IEEE Winter Conference on Applications of Computer Vision (WACV), pp. 1–9, March 2016

12. Razavian, A.S., Azizpour, H., Sullivan, J., Carlsson, S.: CNN features off-the-shelf: an astounding baseline for recognition. CoRR abs/1403.6382 (2014). http://arxiv.org/abs/1403.6382

13. Sermanet, P., Eigen, D., Zhang, X., Mathieu, M., Fergus, R., LeCun, Y.: OverFeat: integrated recognition, localization and detection using convolutional networks. CoRR abs/1312.6229 (2013). http://arxiv.org/abs/1312.6229

14. Sinha, A., Banerji, S., Liu, C.: Novel color Gabor-LBP-PHOG (GLP) descriptors for object and scene image classification. In: ICVGIP, p. 58 (2012)

15. Vapnik, Y.: The Nature of Statistical Learning Theory. Springer, Heidelberg (1995). doi:10.1007/978-1-4757-3264-1

16. Vedaldi, A., Fulkerson, B.: VLFeat: an open and portable library of computer vision algorithms (2008)

17. Zeiler, M.D., Fergus, R.: Visualizing and understanding convolutional networks. In: Fleet, D., Pajdla, T., Schiele, B., Tuytelaars, T. (eds.) ECCV 2014. LNCS, vol. 8689, pp. 818–833. Springer, Cham (2014). doi:10.1007/978-3-319-10590-1_53

18. Zhou, B., Khosla, A., Lapedriza, À., Oliva, A., Torralba, A.: Object detectors emerge in deep scene CNNs. CoRR abs/1412.6856 (2014). http://arxiv.org/abs/1412.6856

Eigen Domain Transformation for Soft-Margin Multiple Feature-Kernel Learning for Surveillance Face Recognition

Samik Banerjee[(✉)] and Sukhendu Das

CSE, IIT Madras, Chennai, India
samik@cse.iitm.ac.in, sdas@iitm.ac.in

Abstract. Face Recognition (FR) is the most accepted method of biometric authentication due to its inherent passive nature. This has attracted a lot of researchers over past few decades to achieve an moderately high accuracy under controlled environments. In order to achieve such an accuracy for FR under surveillance scenario has been proved to be a major hurdle in this area of research, mainly due to the difference in resolution, contrast, illumination and camera parameters of the training and the testing samples. In this paper, we propose a novel technique to find the optimal feature-kernel combination by SML_MFKC (Soft-margin Learning for Multi-Feature-Kernel Combination) to solve the problem of FR in surveillance, followed by an Eigen Domain Transformation (EDT) to bridge the gap between the distributions of the gallery and the probe samples. Rigorous experimentation has been performed on three real-world surveillance face datasets : FR_SURV [24], SCface [17] and ChokePoint [35]. Results have been shown using Rank-1 Recognition rates, ROC and CMC measures. Our proposed method outperforms all other recent state-of-the-art techniques by a considerable margin. Experimentations also show that the recent state-of-the-art Deep Learning techniques also fail to perform appreciably compared to our proposed method for the afore-mentioned datasets.

Keywords: Kernel selection · Surveillance · Multiple kernel learning · Domain adaptation · RKHS · Hallucination

1 Introduction

The classical problem of Face Recognition (FR) has a clear advantage of being natural and passive over other biometric techniques requiring co-operative subjects. Researchers have found several efficient algorithms to deal with FR under controlled environment. Face images obtained by an outdoor panoramic surveillance camera, are often confronted with severe degradations (e.g., low-resolution, blur, low-contrast, interlacing and noise). This significantly deteriorates the performance of face recognition systems used for binding "security with surveillance" applications. The images taken under a well controlled environment are

© Springer International Publishing AG 2017
S. Mukherjee et al. (Eds.): ICVGIP 2016, LNCS 10481, pp. 180–191, 2017.
https://doi.org/10.1007/978-3-319-68124-5_16

used for training the system, which are captured in an indoor setup (laboratory, controlled environment), whereas the images used for testing are captured when a subject comes under a surveillance scene. Most classifiers fails to perform to an appreciable level when both the resolution and contrast of face templates used for recognition differ a lot from the training set. Under surveillance scenario, a face recognition system is trained to recognize a face in an unconstrained environment passively. Degradation in the quality of the faces captured by surveillance cameras is quite evident owing to low-resolution and camera-blur. Abrupt variations in illumination of the faces not only degrades the accuracy for recognition but occasionally reduces the performance of face detection, an essential step of face recognition. To deal with such issues involved in FR under surveillance conditions, a novel method of combining feature-kernel pairing with Domain Adaptation (DA) has been proposed in this paper.

In this paper, the *Chehra* face tracker [4] is used to find a tightly cropped face image for all the face samples from both gallery and probe. DA formulated using eigen-domain transformation (EDT) has been designed to bridge the gap between the distribution of the features obtained from the gallery and the probe samples. A Multiple kernel Learning (MKL) based learning method, termed SML_MFKC [7], is then used to obtain an optimal feature-kernel combinations for FR under surveillance. The novelty of the method proposed in this paper is to find optimal pairing of feature and kernel to provide best performance with EDT based transfer learning for FR. Results of performance analysis on three real-world surveillance datasets (SCFace [17], FR_SURV [24], ChokePoint [35]) exhibit the superiority of our proposed method of combining the feature selection process by SML_MFKC with EDT in Reproducing Kernel Hilbert Space (RKHS) [12].

2   Discussion on Related Work

The problem of automatic face recognition includes the key step of face detection. The most widely used face detection algorithm proposed by Viola et al. [32], is based on an efficient classifier build using the ADABOOST learning algorithm, which selects a subset of critical visual features from a very large set of potential features. Our proposed technique includes the face detection technique based on the set of 49 fiducial landmark points detected by the Chehra [4] face detector.

A large scale implementation of support vector machine (SVM) for large number of kernels, known as sequential minimal optimization (SMO), was proposed by Bach et al. [5]. MKL based on sparse representation-based classification (SRC) proposed in [27], represents the non-linearities in the high-dimensional feature space based on kernel alignment criteria. Conic combinations of kernel matrices for classification proposed in [18] lead to a convex quadratically constrained quadratic problem (QCQP). Sonnenburg et al. [28] generalized the formulation to a larger class of problem.

The work proposed in [29] performs domain adaptation based on the calculation of weights of the instances in the source domain. Yang et al. [37] proposed a method to effectively retrain a pre-trained SVM for target domain data, based on the calculated weights of the instances in the source domain. Duan et al. [11] proposed a domain adaptive machine (DAM), which learns a robust decision function for labeling the instances in the target domain, by leveraging a set of base classifiers learned on multiple source domains. Transfer component analysis (TCA), proposed in [20], minimizes the disparity of distribution by comparing the difference in the means between two domains and preserving the local geometry of the underlying manifold. Subspaces are calculated based on eigen-vectors [13] of two domains, such that the basis vectors of the transformed source and target domains are aligned. Wang et al. [34] considered the manifold of each domain and estimated a latent space, where the manifolds of both the domains are similar to each other. A new method of unsupervised DA was proposed by Samanta et al. [25] using the properties of the of the sub-spaces spanning the source and target domains, when projected along a path in the Grassmannian manifold.

Surveillance cameras produce images at very low resolution to cope with the high transmission speed and optimality of the storage data, which also contain noise and distortions (defocus, blur, low contrast), due to their uncontrolled environmental conditions during capture. A matching algorithm based on transformation learning through an iterative majorization algorithm, in the kernel space, was proposed by Biswas et al. [10], known as multi-dimensional scaling (MDS). Ren et al. [23] proposed the Coupled Kernel Embedding approach, where they map the low and high resolution face images to different kernel spaces and then transform them to a subspace for recognition. Rudrani et al. in [24] proposed an approach with the combination of partial restoration (using super-resolution) of probe samples and degradation of gallery samples. An outdoor surveillance dataset, FR_SURV, was also proposed in [24], for evaluating their approach. A Dynamic Bayesian Network (DBN) based unconstrained face recognition under surveillance scenario has been proposed by An et al. [2] to integrate the information from all the three cameras in the ChokePoint [35] dataset. The work proposed in [8] aims to bridge the gap of resolution and contrast using super-resolution and contrast stretching on the probe samples and degrading the gallery samples. A DA technique based on EDT was proposed to make the distributions of gallery (as source) features identical to that of probe (as target) samples. Banerjee et al. in [6,7] proposed two methods (S_BDA and MKL_EDT respectively) to combine feature and kernel using the MKL framework.

In the following sections, we first briefly present a few technical background details, followed by our proposed framework and experimental results, before concluding the paper.

3   Proposed Method

The stages of the overall proposed framework for FR, as shown in Fig. 1, is briefly discussed below:

3.1   Face Detection

The Face detection stage is based on the 49 fiducial points obtained from the Chehra [4] face detector, to obtain a tightly cropped facial region.

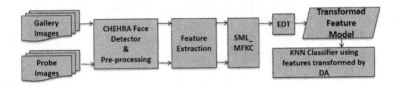

Fig. 1. Overall proposed framework of SML-MKFC with EDT.

3.2   Pre-processing

Pre-processing of both the gallery and probe samples are required to bridge the gap between the face images obtained from the gallery and probe samples. The stages of pre-processing are the same as described in [8]. The empirical values of the parameters in the pre-processing algorithms (see [8] for details) are: the Gaussian blur kernel, σ, for degradation of the gallery; and γ used for contrast enhancement of the probes, are given in Table 1, for the three datasets used for performance analysis. An example showing the degraded gallery and enhanced probe for each dataset is shown in Fig. 2.

Table 1. Values of σ for gallery degradation and γ for the contrast-stretching in probe enhancement. For details see [8].

Datasets	σ	γ
FR_SURV [24]	1.75	1.75
SCFace [17]	1.70	1.50
ChokePoint [35]	1.20	1.25

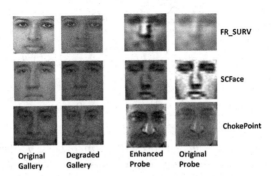

Fig. 2. Example shots from the three datasets (one sample each), showing the degraded gallery and the enhanced probe images on the cropped faces provided by Chehra [4].

3.3   Feature Extraction

The feature extraction process in the proposed method is based on the set of features extracted from the degraded gallery and the enhanced probe face images. The set of features used in the methods proposed includes Local Binary Pattern (LBP) [1], Eigen Faces [31], Fisher Faces [9], Gabor faces [19], Weber Faces [33], Bag of Words (BOW) [14], Vector of Linearly Aggregated Descriptors encoding based on Scale Invariant Feature Transform (VLAD-SIFT) [3], Fisher Vector encoding based on SIFT (FV-SIFT) [22].

3.4   Soft-Margin Learning for Multiple Feature-Kernel Combinations (SML-MFKC)

The process of selecting the best performing kernel function and its parameters in an SVM during training, generally consists of a cross-validation procedure. MKL techniques have been used to cope with this, where instead of selecting a specific kernel function, multiple kernels are learned using a weighted combination along with its corresponding parameters. The proposed technique (S_EDT) takes into consideration both the kernel and feature to be selected from a single framework. Given a training set $(x_i, y_i), \forall i = 1, ..., N$, of N instances, each consisting of an image $x_i \in X$ and a class label $y_i \in 1, ..., C$, and given a set of F image features $V_m : X \to R^{d_m}, \forall m = 1, ..., F$, where d_m denotes the dimensionality of the m-th feature, the problem of learning a classification function $y : X \to 1, ..., C$ from the features and training set is called the feature combination problem [15].

Since we associate image features with kernel functions (k_m), kernel-selection translates naturally into a feature-selection problem, as proposed by Banerjee et al. [7]. The objective of SML-MFKC is to jointly optimize over a linear combination of kernels, $k^*(x, y) = \sum_{m=1}^{F} \beta_m k_m(x, y)$, $\beta_m \in \mathcal{R}$, $\boldsymbol{\beta} \in \mathcal{R}^F$ and the parameters, $\boldsymbol{\alpha} \in \mathcal{R}^N$ and $b \in \mathcal{R}$ of an SVM. The objective function which determines the optimal combination of the feature and the kernel for the method, is given by the following proposed (novel) soft-margin cost function:

$$\text{sup argmin}_{\beta^q \in \mathcal{R}^F} \frac{1}{2} \sum_{m=1}^{F} \beta_m^q \boldsymbol{\alpha}^T V_m^q \boldsymbol{\alpha}$$

$$+ C \sum_{i=1}^{N} L(y_i, b + \sum_{m=1}^{F} \beta_m^q \boldsymbol{\alpha}^T V_m^q \boldsymbol{\alpha}) \tag{1}$$

$$\text{s.t} \sum_{m=1}^{F} \beta_m^q = 1, \beta_m^q \geq 0, \forall m, q = 1, ...P.$$

where, $L(y, t) = max(0, 1 - y_t)$ denotes the *Hinge Loss*, P denotes the total number of kernels used for learning, V_m^q denotes the m-th feature for the q-th kernel function, and $\beta_m^q \in \mathcal{R}$ denotes the weight coefficient for the m-th feature and the q-th kernel combination.

Table 2. Different kernels used in SML-MFKC and their formula.

Types of kernel functions	Formula
Linear	$k(x,y) = x^T y + c$
Polynomial	$k(x,y) = (\alpha x^T y + c)^d$
Gaussian	$k(x,y) = exp\left(-\frac{\|x-y\|^2}{2\sigma^2}\right)$
RBF	$k(x,y) = exp\left(-\frac{\|x-y\|}{2\sigma^2}\right)$
Chi-square	$k(x,y) = 1 - \Sigma_{i=1}^n \frac{(x_i-y_i)^2}{\frac{1}{2}(x_i+y_i)}$
RBF + Chi-square	$k(x,y) = 1 - \Sigma_{i=1}^n \frac{(x_i-y_i)^2}{\frac{1}{2}(x_i+y_i)} + exp\left(-\frac{\|x-y\|}{2\sigma^2}\right)$

Block-wise coordinate-descent based approach has been used to solve the problem of minimization given in Eq. 1 (see [15], for proof of convexity), as proposed by Xu et al. [36], to obtain the local mimima, β^q. For each of the q-th kernel, among the P kernels, the best selected feature, $\tilde{V}_q$ is based on the supremum over the set, β^q. The optimal feature-kernel combinations $< M^i, Q^i >$, $\forall i \in \{1, ..., P\}$ is thus obtained, where $M^i \in \{\tilde{V}_1, ..., \tilde{V}_F\}$ and Q^i is an element (k_m) from the set of P kernels (see Table 2). Each of these features, M^i, are projected in RKHS using Q^i to obtain a new feature representation to be used in EDT.

3.5 Eigen Domain Transformation (EDT)

The distribution of data can be estimated using the covariance matrix or eigen-vectors. The distributions of the two datasets are approximately similar to each other, if the eigen-vectors of two datasets are same. Hence, in this paper we aim to transform the source domain in such a way that the eigen-vectors of the transformed source domain is same as that of the target domain. We extend this idea of transformation of source domain in Reproducing Kernel Hilbert Space (RKHS) [12] to handle non-linear transformation of data, when necessary. Hence we use the EDT proposed by Banerjee et al. [8], to transform the source domain data into the target domain in RKHS. The number of test samples used as targets for EDT is given in Table 3.

Table 3. Number of probe samples (per subject) used for EDT.

Dataset	No. of probe samples for EDT
FR_SURV [24]	5 per subject, from 20 random subjects
SCFace [17]	3 per subject, from 30 random subjects
ChokePoint [35]	6 per subject, from 5 males and 2 females per profile

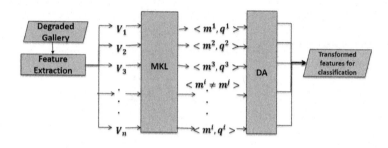

Fig. 3. The training phase.

The Training Phase. In this phase of our proposed framework as shown in Fig. 3, we have a set of feature V and a set of kernels K pairings.

$$V = \{LBP, EigenFaces, FisherFaces, Gaborfaces, WeberFaces, \qquad (2)$$
$$VLAD - SIFT, FV - SIFT, BOW\}$$

where each $V_i \in V$ is the feature extracted from a face image; and

$$K = \{Linear, Polynomial, Gaussian, RBF, Chi-square, RBF+Chi-square\} \qquad (3)$$

where each $K_i \in K$ is a kernel function for the projection in the RKHS, $\mathcal{H}_i$.

The combination of V_a and K_b is passed into the SML_MFKC module to obtain the set of optimized pairs of $\{M_j, Q_j\}$ using the feature-selection method described in Sect. 3.4. The optimal feature-kernel combinations $< M^i, Q^i >$, $\forall i \in \{1, ..., P\}$ is thus obtained, where $M^i \in \{\tilde{V}_1, ..., \tilde{V}_F\}$ and Q^i is an element (k_m) from the set of P kernels. Based on the best feature-kernel pairs obtained, the feature vector is projected into a higher dimensional space of RKHS. The training in EDT is performed to obtain the final model parameters along with the feature-kernel pairs. The number of probe samples used as targets for DA is mentioned in the Table 3. Majority voting strategy is used to obtain the final class-id.

Classification. Once we obtain the Gram matrices $\hat{K}_{\tilde{S}\tilde{S}}$ and $\hat{K}_{\tilde{S}T}$, we can calculate the overall Gram matrix

$$\hat{K} = \begin{bmatrix} \hat{K}_{\tilde{S}\tilde{S}} & \hat{K}_{\tilde{S}T} \\ \hat{K}_{\tilde{S}T}^T & K_{TT} \end{bmatrix} \qquad (4)$$

where, S and T are the source and target domains respectively. We can now calculate the Euclidean distance between any two instances (i and j) in RKHS, which is given by:

$$dist(i, j) = \hat{K}(i, i) + \hat{K}(j, j) - 2 \times \hat{K}(i, j) \qquad (5)$$

Hence, we can now use this distance matrix for classifying test samples using KNN-classifier. The unsupervised method of DA, enhances the performance of FR algorithm on surveillance conditions.

4 Details of Surveillance Face Databases Used

For the experimentation purpose we have used three real-world surveillance face datasets, FR_SURV [24], SCFace [17] and ChokePoint [35]. In all the three real-world datasets the gallery samples are taken in laboratory conditions, while for probes SCFace [17] and ChokePoint [35] are shot indoor and FR_SURV [24] is shot outdoor.

5 Experimental Results

Three real-world datasets; *SCface* [17], *FR_SURV* [24], and *ChokePoint* [35] are considered for rigorous experimentation. The proposed method (S_EDT) are compared with several other recent state-of-the-art methods and the results are reported in Table 4 using Rank-1 Recognition Rate.

Banerjee et al. in [8] proposed EDA1, where DA technique is based on EDT, following the projection of the data into RKHS, which is termed as KDA1. Biswas et al. in [10] proposed a technique termed as multi-dimensional scaling (MDS), where both the gallery and the probe samples are projected into a common subspace to aid classification. Rudrani et al. [24] (COMP_DEG) proposed that the gap between distributions of the gallery and the probe samples can be bridged, when both are projected into a lower dimensional subspace based on the principal components of the holistic feature extracted from each face. The authors also revealed results on the dataset, FR_SURV [24], which acts as the source for this dataset. Two DA based techniques used for cross-domain object classification was proposed by Gopalan et al. [16] and Kliep [29]. MKL based

Table 4. Rank-1 Recognition Rate for different methods of FR. Results in bold, exhibit the best performance.

Sl.	Algorithm	SCface [17]	FR_SURV [24]	ChokePoint [35]
1	EDA1 [8]	47.65	7.82	54.21
2	COMP_DEG [24]	4.32	43.14	62.59
3	MDS [10]	42.26	12.06	52.13
4	KDA1 [8]	35.04	38.24	56.25
5	Gopalan [16]	2.06	2.06	58.62
6	Kliep [29]	37.51	28.79	63.28
7	Deep Face [21]	41.25	29.35	62.15
8	Naive	77.45	48.23	69.51
9	BaseMKL	53.36	36.54	66.12
10	S_BDA [7]	79.86	56.44	85.59
11	MKL_EDT [6]	78.31	55.23	84.62
12	S_EDT	**82.3**	**60.38**	**87.19**

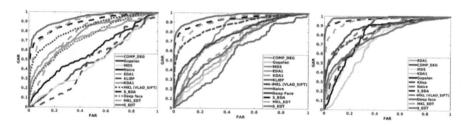

Fig. 4. ROC plots for performance analysis of different methods, using FR_SURV [24] (left), SCFace [17] (center) and ChokePoint [35] (right) datasets.

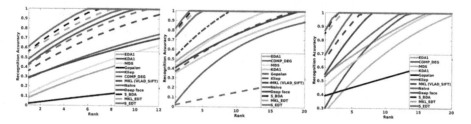

Fig. 5. CMC plots for performance analysis of different methods, using FR_SURV [24] (left), SCFace [17] (center) and ChokePoint [35] (right) datasets.

technique for only multiple-kernel selection based on VLAD_SIFT is also experimented for comparison. Recent techniques proposed by Banerjee et al. in [7] (S_BDA) and [6] (MKL_EDT) involve methods for multiple feature-kernel combinations. Deep Face [21] is a state-of-the-art deep learning technique for FR. Our proposed method (S_EDT) has outperformed (our results are given in bold, in Table 4) all the other competing methods by a considerable margin.

ROC (for identification) and CMC (for verification) curves, given in Figs. 4 and 5, also show the superior performance of our method, for the three datasets under experimentation, where GAR and FAR indicates the Genuine and False Acceptance Rates, respectively. The red curves, in each of these plots depict the performance of our proposed method, which perform considerably better than the other competing methods. On an average, the second and third best performance are given by S_BDA [7] and MKL_EDT [6], which shows that selecting feature-kernel combination with DA in RKHS helps to boost the performance of FR under surveillance scenario, since these helps in better adaptation of the source domain to the target domain.

The recent trends in Convolutional Neural Network (CNN) models in the area of Computer Vision shows improved performances for several FR techniques. We compare our method with a few state-of-the-art Deep Learning techniques and the results (using Rank-1 Recognition Rate) has been reported in Table 5. These results also reveal the superiority (results in bold) of our method over the recent CNN models for other FR tasks. This justifies our claim that the CNN-based techniques fail to adapt efficiently to the variations in appearance of the gallery and probe samples, compared to our proposed technique, since the training set available has limited amount of data.

Table 5. Rank-1 Recognition Rate for different methods Deep Learning based FR methods. Results in bold, exhibit the best performance.

Sl.	Algorithm	# CNN Layers	FR_SURV [24]	SCface [17]	ChokePoint [35]
1	FV Faces + AlexNet [8]	8	12.64	35.24	61.59
2	DeepFace [21]	19	29.35	41.25	62.15
3	DeepID-2,2+,3 [30]	60	34.94	32.92	66.86
4	FaceNet + Alignment [26]	22	36.53	48.21	71.65
5	VGG Face Descriptor + DeepFace [21]	19	32.57	46.25	69.86
6	S_EDT [7]	–	**60.38**	**82.3**	**87.19**

The Tables 4 and 5 show that the FR_SURV dataset has the least accuracy leaving a further scope of improvement in this field. The gallery samples in FR_SURV are all taken in Indoor laboratory conditions and the probe samples are taken in Outdoor conditions which results in the vast variance between the distributions of the gallery and probe samples. The ChokePoint dataset is the easiest to handle among the three, since there is no gap in the resolution of the gallery and the probe samples. The SCface and the ChokePoint datasets are two indoor surveillance datasets. Experiments are done in both identification and verification mode. There is still scope of improvement to find a more effective transformation such that the distribution of the features of the gallery and the probe become similar. The other two datasets have both the gallery and the probe taken in Indoor scenario. The effectiveness of the non-linear transformations in KDA1 [8] motivates us to concentrate on the DA in RKHS. The Naive combination results shows the effectiveness of the MKL based methods, which fares pretty well in all the three datasets. The Naive combination is the complete Framework without the DA module, incorporating the MKL process. Combining DA with multiple feature-kernel combination learning boosts our proposed method (S_EDT) to outperform all other methods by a considerable margin.

6 Conclusion

In this paper, we have discussed an efficient method to tackle the hurdles of FR under surveillance scenario. The proposed S_EDT handles the problem of low-contrast and low-resolution with appreciable success. The proposed method efficiently finds an optimal combination of the feature and kernel using SML_MFKC [7] along with EDT [8] to bridge the gap between the distributions of the gallery and the probe samples, to boost the accuracy of the FR under surveillance. The three metrics used to compare the performance of our proposed method with the recent state-of-the-art techniques, show a great deal of superiority of our method than the other techniques, using three real-world surveillance face datasets. Our method also outperforms the recent state-of-the-art techniques of Deep Learning for FR, in surveillance conditions.

References

1. Ahonen, T., Hadid, A., Pietikainen, M.: Face description with local binary patterns: application to face recognition. IEEE T-PAMI **28**(12), 2037–2041 (2006)
2. An, L., Kafai, M., Bhanu, B.: Dynamic bayesian network for unconstrained face recognition in surveillance camera networks. IEEE JESCTS **3**(2), 155–164 (2013)
3. Arandjelovic, R., Zisserman, A.: All about VLAD. In: IEEE CVPR, pp. 1578–1585 (2013)
4. Asthana, A., Zafeiriou, S., Cheng, S., Pantic, M.: Incremental face alignment in the wild. In: CVPR (2014)
5. Bach, F.R., Lanckriet, G.R., Jordan, M.I.: Multiple kernel learning, conic duality, and the SMO algorithm. In: ICML, p. 6. ACM (2004)
6. Banerjee, S., Das, S.: Kernel selection using multiple kernel learning and domain adaptation in reproducing kernel hilbert space, for face recognition under surveillance scenario. arXiv preprint arXiv:1610.00660 (2016)
7. Banerjee, S., Das, S.: Soft-margin learning for multiple feature-kernel combinations with domain adaptation, for recognition in surveillance face dataset. In: IEEE Biometrics Workshop, CVPRW, pp. 169–174 (2016)
8. Banerjee, S., Samanta, S., Das, S.: Face recognition in surveillance conditions with bag-of-words, using unsupervised domain adaptation. In: ICVGIP. ACM (2014)
9. Belhumeur, P.N., Hespanha, J.P., Kriegman, D.J.: Eigenfaces vs fisherfaces: recognition using class specific linear projection. IEEE T-PAMI **19**(7), 711–720 (1997)
10. Biswas, S., Bowyer, K.W., Flynn, P.J.: Multidimensional scaling for matching low-resolution face images. IEEE T-PAMI **34**(10), 2019–2030 (2012)
11. Duan, L., Xu, D., Tsang, I.W.: Domain adaptation from multiple sources: a domain-dependent regularization approach. IEEE T-NNLS **23**(3), 504–518 (2012)
12. Dym, H.: J Contractive Matrix Functions, Reproducing Kernel Hilbert Spaces and Interpolation, vol. 71. American Mathematical Soc., Providence (1989)
13. Fernando, B., Habrard, A., Sebban, M., Tuytelaars, T.: Unsupervised visual domain adaptation using subspace alignment. In: IEEE ICCV (2013)
14. Filliat, D.: A visual bag of words method for interactive qualitative localization and mapping. In: IEEE ICRA (2007)
15. Gehler, P., Nowozin, S.: On feature combination for multiclass object classification. In: IEEE ICCV, IEEE (2009)
16. Gopalan, R., Li, R., Chellappa, R.: Domain adaptation for object recognition: an unsupervised approach. In IEEE ICCV, pp. 999–1006 (2011)
17. Grgic, M., Delac, K., Grgic, S.: Scface-surveillance cameras face database. Multimedia Tools Appl. **51**(3), 863–879 (2011)
18. Lanckriet, G.R., De Bie, T., Cristianini, N., Jordan, M.I., Noble, W.S.: A statistical framework for genomic data fusion. Bioinformatics **20**(16), 2626–2635 (2004)
19. Liu, C., Wechsler, H.: Gabor feature based classification using the enhanced fisher linear discriminant model for face recognition. IEEE TIP **11**(4), 467–476 (2002)

20. Pan, S.J., Tsang, I.W., Kwok, J.T., Yang, Q.: Domain adaptation via transfer component analysis. IEEE T-NN **22**(2), 199–210 (2011)
21. Parkhi, O.M., Vedaldi, A., Zisserman, A.: Deep face recognition. BMVC **1**(3), 6 (2015)
22. Perronnin, F., Sánchez, J., Mensink, T.: Improving the fisher kernel for large-scale image classification. In: Daniilidis, K., Maragos, P., Paragios, N. (eds.) ECCV 2010. LNCS, vol. 6314, pp. 143–156. Springer, Heidelberg (2010). doi:10.1007/978-3-642-15561-1_11
23. Ren, C.-X., Dai, D.-Q., Yan, H.: Coupled kernel embedding for low-resolution face image recognition. IEEE TIP **21**(8), 3770–3783 (2012)
24. Rudrani, S., Das, S.: Face recognition on low quality surveillance images, by compensating degradation. In: Kamel, M., Campilho, A. (eds.) ICIAR 2011. LNCS, vol. 6754, pp. 212–221. Springer, Heidelberg (2011). doi:10.1007/978-3-642-21596-4_22
25. Samanta, S., Das, S.: Unsupervised domain adaptation using eigenanalysis in kernel space for categorisation tasks. IET Image Process. **9**(11), 925–930 (2015)
26. Schroff, F., Kalenichenko, D., Philbin, J.: Facenet: a unified embedding for face recognition and clustering. In: Proceedings of the IEEE Conference on Computer Vision and Pattern Recognition, pp. 815–823 (2015)
27. Shrivastava, A., Patel, V.M., Chellappa, R.: Multiple kernel learning for sparse representation-based classification. IEEE TIP **23**(7), 3013–3024 (2014)
28. Sonnenburg, S., Rätsch, G., Schäfer, C., Schölkopf, B.: Large scale multiple kernel learning. JMLR **7**, 1531 (2006)
29. Sugiyama, M., Nakajima, S., Kashima, H., von Bünau, P., Kawanabe, M.: Direct importance estimation with model selection and its application to covariate shift adaptation. In: NIPS, pp. 1962–1965 (2007)
30. Sun, Y., Wang, X., Tang, X.: Deep learning face representation from predicting 10,000 classes. In: IEEE CVPR, pp. 1891–1898 (2014)
31. Turk, M., Pentland, A.: Eigenfaces for recognition. J. Cogn. Neurosci. **3**(1), 71–86 (1991)
32. Viola, P., Jones, M.J.: Robust real-time face detection. IJCV **57**(2), 137–154 (2004)
33. Wang, B., Li, W., Yang, W., Liao, Q.: Illumination normalization based on weber's law with application to face recognition. IEEE SPL **18**(8), 462–465 (2011)
34. Wang, C., Mahadevan, S.: Heterogeneous domain adaptation using manifold alignment. In: IJCAI, vol. 22, p. 1541 (2011)
35. Wong, Y., Chen, S., Mau, S., Sanderson, C., Lovell, B.C.: Patch-based probabilistic image quality assessment for face selection and improved video-based face recognition. In: IEEE Biometrics Workshop, CVPRW (June 2011)
36. Xu, X., Tsang, I.W., Xu, D.: Soft margin multiple kernel learning. IEEE T-NNLS **24**(5), 749–761 (2013)
37. Yang, J., Yan, R., Hauptmann, A.: Cross-domain video detection using adaptive svms. In: ICM. ACM (2007)

A Beta Distribution Based Novel Scheme for Detection of Changes in Crowd Motion

Soumyajit Pal[1][✉], Sounak Mondal[1], Sanjoy Kumar Saha[1],
and Bhabatosh Chanda[2]

[1] Department of Computer Science and Engineering, Jadavpur University,
Kolkata, India
soumyajit.pal221b@gmail.com, sounakmondal2012@gmail.com,
sks_ju@yahoo.co.in
[2] Electronics and Communication Sciences Unit, Indian Statistical Institute,
Kolkata, India
chanda@isical.ac.in

Abstract. An automated system for crowd behaviour analysis has gained significance in the context of surveillance and public management. Detecting the changes in the crowd behaviour demarcates one activity or event from another. Thus, change detection is a fundamental step that enables the subsequent characterisation of the activities and analysis of the transition from one state to another. Proposed work deals with high density crowd. Global motion is an important cue for studying the behaviour of such crowd. In this work, crowd motion is modelled using beta distribution. Change in the distribution parameter is an indicator for change in crowd motion pattern. Proposed methodology has been tested with number of synthetic and natural video sequences and the performance is satisfactory.

Keywords: Crowd behaviour analysis · Crowd motion analysis · Change in crowd behaviour · Beta distribution

1 Introduction

Automated surveillance and analysis of social gathering has been an interesting problem in the field of computer vision. Traditional surveillance requires a considerable amount of manpower and usually requires circumspect vigilance of the personnel. To relieve these demanding problems using technology will be a great help to various organizations which require top notch surveillance at all time. Hence there has been a considerable amount of work in the field of crowd analysis in recent times as surveyed in [15]. In recent times, crowd analysis has been applied in designing the public spaces such as railway stations,airports, shopping malls. This plays a vital role in managing huge crowds in certain places. Another interesting application is surveillance where anomalies in crowd behaviour is of interest. Here, any change in crowd behaviour can be pinpointed as an anomaly.

S. Mukherjee et al. (Eds.): ICVGIP 2016, LNCS 10481, pp. 192–203, 2017.
https://doi.org/10.1007/978-3-319-68124-5_17

Crowd behaviour analysis usually encompasses three broad sections namely, *feature extraction, crowd modelling* and *event detection*. Crowd analysis has various purposes and each of these many purposes demand analysis of different properties and features of the crowd. Hence, feature extraction is done based on the target application. Tracking methodologies based on human body model [12,16] have been extensively used. Particle filter technique, also known as CONDENSATION [4] is very popular for tracking. Tracking methodologies basically trace the trajectory of certain objects of interest, although tracking multiple objects is challenging.

Since crowd behaviour is recurrent and there is usually a predictable underlying pattern, analysis of crowd dynamics can be done by constructing crowd models. This is particularly helpful in identifying crowd events. Zhan et al. [14] proposed a crowd model implemented by two probability density function models that can be used to find a major path of the crowd. Andrade et al. [1] explained crowd behaviour through HMM motion models with the goal of detecting anomalies in crowd pattern. Other methods use social force models applied to pedestrian dynamics as suggested in the work of Helbing and Molnar [3]. Event detection in crowd analysis has a lot of importance in the field of crowd analysis. An unsupervised method of anomaly detection based on spatial-temporal motion features has been done by Xie et al. [13]. Fradi et al. [2] has proposed a histogram based modelling of crowd density and motion to detect changes in crowd dynamics. Analysis of crowd flux has been used by Nam [8] for the same purpose. Mehran et al. [6] used social force model to model crowd behaviour and consequently detect abnormal behaviour in crowds.

Survey of past work indicates crowd behaviour analysis is an active area of research and still in nascent stage. Efforts are normally directed to cater a specific application. In this work, we try to model the global motion pattern of dense crowd and thereafter to detect any change in the pattern. The paper is organized as follows. Section 2 elaborates the methodology. Feature point extraction, motion pattern modelling and its analysis are discussed. Section 3 presents the experimental results and concluding remarks are put in Sect. 4.

2   Proposed Methodology

In this work, we focus on analysing the motion pattern of high density human crowd. Lots of scenarios exist where people in large numbers move. Rallies, mass gatherings, entry and exit points of the public places like the railway stations etc. are such examples. Certain stimuli may give rise to change in the motion pattern demanding attention. In this work, global motion pattern characterises the crowd behaviour and our goal is to detect the change in the motion pattern.

The overall flowchart of the proposed methodology is depicted in Fig. 1. It consists of two major steps namely, *feature point extraction* and *motion modelling*. Feature extraction module is responsible for detecting the feature points. Subsequently motion is modeled based on the spatial distribution of feature points. We have adopted a statistical approach for modelling that can support

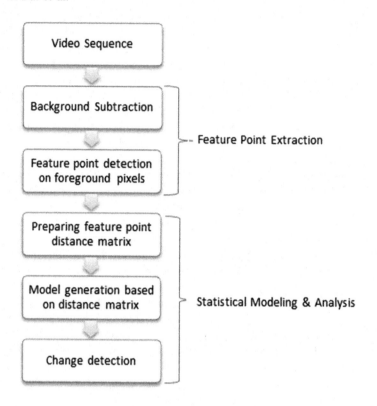

Fig. 1. Overall flowchart of the proposed methodology

near real time analysis of crowds. It does not require the tracking of feature points and unlike the machine learning based approaches it does not require any training.

2.1   Feature Point Extraction

In order to analyze the behaviour of a crowd in general, the foremost task is to break down the crowd into meaningful components. Depending on the requirement a component may be an individual or number of individuals in a close spatial proximity. Ideally, we focus on individuals in a crowd and thereafter generate a model based on spatial distribution of the individuals. Hence in our work a component stands for an individual. Unlike the cases for crowd density estimation or counting people, there is no requirement of precise identification.

To extract the feature points, foreground is first extracted and thereafter points of interest are extracted from the foreground. Considering mixture of Gaussians, a background model is generated for the video [5]. Foreground is then extracted by subtracting the background. The foreground is further refined using morphological opening and linking. To extract the feature points we focus on the corner points as they correspond to sharp change in gradient which is relatively easier to detect and track. We have followed Shi Tomasi Corner Detection [11] technique. For a video capturing the top view of the dense crowd, detected corner points mostly correspond to contours of the heads. There may exist additional corner points which correspond to other parts of the body. As we try to approximate an individual by one feature point, a post-processing is applied to merge the corner points in the close vicinity. In our experiment, points in a window of size $w \times w$ are merged and their average is taken as the feature point. There may be cases of merging or splitting of individuals. As we try to model the motion pattern globally, such approximation does not bear much impact and hence selection of w is not too critical.

2.2   Statistical Modelling and Change Detection

Each feature point is treated as a crowd element. We intend to find out the motion pattern by studying the spatial distribution of the elements. Proximity of the nearest neighbour of the elements and their variation are the reflection of the nature of the motion. We try to fit Beta distribution on the distances of the nearest neighbour in each frame of the video sequence. Subsequently, the analysis of motion behaviour is done based on the distribution parameters.

Preparing Distance Matrix: To determine the distance of the nearest neighbor of an element, a pie-shaped region centered at the element itself is considered. It is shown in Fig. 2. C denotes the element and radius R stands for the assumed maximum distance between the crowd elements. In an application, it can be chosen based on the crowd density and generally expected motion behaviour. We refer to such region as field of vision for the element. To find out out the nearest neighbor, the central angle θ_v is initially aligned with the global direction of motion, which is taken as an input parameter. If there is no element present in the current field of vision then only the search for neighbor continues in the wider field of vision obtained by changing the angle by $\pm \delta_\theta$. The element at the minimum distance in the field of vision is taken as the nearest neighbor. It stands for the closest element along the direction with minimum deviation from the global direction of the motion. For each feature point, the search for the nearest neighbor is carried out. Figure 3 illustrates a graph of nearest neighbors, where blue arrow represents the selected nearest neighbour, and red arrow shows

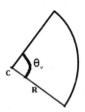

Fig. 2. A crowd element and the projected pie-shaped region to find the nearest neighbour

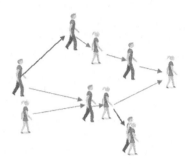

Fig. 3. An illustration depicting the nearest neighbour of crowd elements (Color figure online)

the neighbour out of the field of vision. Finally, a distance matrix Y containing the distance of the nearest neighbor of every crowd element is formed for each frame. In our work, we have considered Euclidean distance.

Fitting Beta Distribution: Distribution of the distances of the neighbors in the crowd reflects the state of its global motion behaviour. The distribution will also change along with the deviation in the motion pattern. We intend to extract a model based on the probability of having crowd elements at various distances so that motion pattern can easily be analysed using the model parameters. In reality, very often the crowd at the exit/entry of a public place or in a rally are generally unidirectional and maintains certain inter-individual distance. Such distance is not large, particularly for a non-sparse crowd. Unless there is a sudden event this separation among two individuals is maintained. So, the inter individual distance is normally bounded in a small limit. This behavioural feature motivates us to consider Beta distribution.

Beta distribution is a family of continuous probability distributions defined on the interval $(0, 1)$ parameterized by two positive shape parameters, denoted by α and β, that appear as exponents of the random variable and control the shape of the distribution. In a frame, each element of Y denotes the distance of nearest element of a unique crowd element in the direction of the general motion. Every element in set Y is considered as the random variable which needs to be bounded within $(0, 1)$ and a continuous probability distribution has to be estimated for Y. The normalization process is as follows.

- Let $x_{min} = \min(Y)$ and $x_{max} = \max(Y)$
- Let $X' = \{x_i - x_{min} \| x_i \in Y \& x_i \neq x_{min}\}$. This is to ensure that X' does not include 0 as we are considering a domain of $(0,1)$. Also let $\mu_{X'} = mean(X')$ and $\sigma^2_{X'} = variance(X')$
- Let $K = \max(x_{max}, 0.5/\mu_{X'}, 0.5/\sigma_{X'})$
- Data set $X = \{x'/K \| x' \in X'\}$.

K is chosen in a way so that the relation between $mean(X')$ and $\sigma_{X'}$ as demanded by Beta distribution is preserved. With X, we try to estimate the continuous probability distribution.

Based on X a normalized histogram of distance is formed. It can be taken as a probability distribution. But it is of discrete nature. We need to extract the underlying continuous probability distribution function. Kernel Density Estimation (KDE) with Gaussian kernels is used for this purpose that estimates the probability distribution function from a finite number of data points by using Gaussian kernel function. The bandwidth of the kernel is selected according to D.W. Scott's guideline [10]. This continuous distribution is then fitted into Beta distribution. The probability density function can be defined as follows.

$$P(x; \alpha, \beta) = \frac{(1-x)^{\beta-1}x^{\alpha-1}}{B(\alpha, \beta)} = \frac{\Gamma(\alpha+\beta)}{\Gamma(\alpha)\Gamma(\beta)}(1-x)^{\beta-1}x^{\alpha-1} \tag{1}$$

where $B(\alpha, \beta)$ is the beta function, a normalization constant to ensure that the total probability integrates to 1 and $\Gamma(X)$ is the gamma function. We fit the probability distribution function we acquired from Gaussian KDE to a Beta distribution by using iterative log-likelihood function as Maximum Likelihood Estimator and consequently the parameters α, β of the fitted distribution [9] are obtained.

Change Detection: In Beta distribution, the expected value (μ) represents the estimate of the distribution, which ideally remains invariant for a specific model extracted from the data of quasi-static nature. μ can be computed as follows.

$$\mu = E[X] = \int_0^1 xP(x; \alpha, \beta)dx = \int_0^1 x\frac{(1-x)^{\beta-1}x^{\alpha-1}}{B(\alpha, \beta)} = \frac{\alpha}{\alpha+\beta} \tag{2}$$

It is expected that μ will change when there is a change in motion behaviour. In a natural video, it is unlikely to have abrupt transition in the behaviour. So comparing the distribution of consecutive frames may lead to miss in detection. Keeping all these in mind we compare the μ of current frame with accumulated history of recent past.

In order to detect whether a change is initiated or not at i-th frame, we rely on the μ calculated in the previous $2S$ frames. Let μ_j denote the mean calculated from the j-th frame. We define

$$\mu_{pr} = \frac{1}{S}\sum_{j=i-2S+1}^{i-S}\mu_j, \qquad \mu_{cr} = \frac{1}{S}\sum_{j=i-S+1}^{i}\mu_j$$

where i is the current frame number. A change is detected if motion change detection criteria, $|\mu_{pr} - \mu_{cr}| > th_c$, is satisfied, where

$$th_c = \chi\sqrt{\frac{1}{S}\sum_{j=i-2S+1}^{i-S}(\mu_j - \mu_{pr})^2}$$

χ is a heuristic value which depends on how much deviation from the model parameters is considered to be a significant event. Naturally, we need the first 2S frames to get the first instances of μ_{pr} and μ_{cr} after which we can start detection of abnormality. For our experiments, the value of χ lying in the range $[2, 3]$ gives us satisfactory results. Once a change is detected, it is assumed that no transition occurs in following S frames. It enhances the immunity against the generation of false alarm.

3   Experimental Results

3.1   Validation of Model

We have worked with four video sequences of which one is synthetic and the other three as described in Table 1, are actual video data collected from various sources. Sequences depict non-sparse human crowd, generally in organized motion and there are changes in behaviour. The video is captured at 30 frames per second. The synthetic data is used for conceptualizing the model where the feature points follow a regular motion in horizontal direction and changes in the motion pattern is also incorporated in it. Once the model has been framed with this sequence it is tested with the other actual sequences.

Table 1. Description of data

Sequence name	Description	Number of frames
Sequence A	A clip of the Dandee march taken from the movie "Gandhi"	460
Sequence B	A footage of a Metal concert depicting the "Mosh" event	910
Sequence C	A clip showing rioting mobs, taken from the movie "Gandhi"	500

To form the model, the parameters are set as follows. To merge the feature points ω is taken as 7. To find out the nearest neighbor of a crowd element, R and θ determine the search region. A moderate value of R is good enough for a dense crowd and we have taken as 100 pixels. θ varies from $\pm 90°$ at a step $\pm \delta_\theta$ and δ_θ is taken as $10°$. Window size, S in change detection is same as frames per second (30 in our case) and the value of χ is taken as 2. In the figures depicting the experimental results, the term "dynamic mean" refers to the parameter mean (μ) calculated from the Beta distribution parameters α and β which have been extracted from the crowd behaviour in the current frame, and "rolling mean" refers to the aforementioned parameter μ_{cr}.

Sequence A shows two rallies merging to form a unified procession. In doing so, there are multiple changes in crowd motion as seen in Fig. 4. The initial coalescence of two rallies forces a change in direction and in density of crowd elements in the central region of the frame. Sequence B is from a Metal concert where an event called "Mosh" is depicted. Moshing or slamdancing is a style of dance where participants push or slam into each other, typically done in a large group as shown. Sequence C is a clip of two processions in opposite directions.

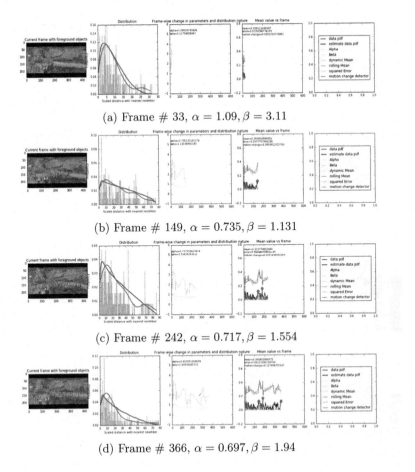

(a) Frame # 33, $\alpha = 1.09, \beta = 3.11$

(b) Frame # 149, $\alpha = 0.735, \beta = 1.131$

(c) Frame # 242, $\alpha = 0.717, \beta = 1.554$

(d) Frame # 366, $\alpha = 0.697, \beta = 1.94$

Fig. 4. Beta distribution model: Sequence A

Towards the middle of the video a some subjects break out of formation and participate in a chaotic altercation which results in a sharp change in the motion pattern.

Initial stages show high rates of inflection (Fig. 4(a)) in distribution parameters due to constant change in feature distribution (as the rally is still in motion), but this change is not considered according to our model. As the crowd progresses, number of feature points increases, so does the number of elements in close proximity. The distribution is shifted to lower α, β and μ as a result, which leads to a change in motion pattern (Fig. 4(b)). Second inflection is caused by a sudden lowering of crowd density in one of the flanks which breaks the motion pattern (Fig. 4(c)). After this, the data exhibits an almost monotonous model, with one inflection due to progress of the procession (Fig. 4(d)).

As is evident from the plots above, our proposed model is able to detect all the changes in motion behaviour of the crowd. Also, the distance model fits a Beta distribution, as hypothesized by our framework.

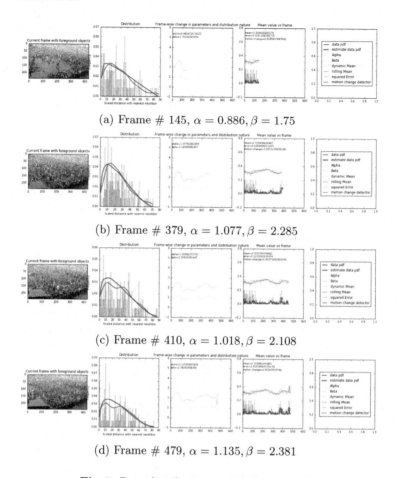

(a) Frame # 145, $\alpha = 0.886, \beta = 1.75$

(b) Frame # 379, $\alpha = 1.077, \beta = 2.285$

(c) Frame # 410, $\alpha = 1.018, \beta = 2.108$

(d) Frame # 479, $\alpha = 1.135, \beta = 2.381$

Fig. 5. Beta distribution model: Sequence B

The Mosh event is preceded by several frames of an almost static crowd with a very sparsely crowded area in the middle. The model based on closest neighbour distance fits a Beta distribution almost perfectly during this phase (Fig. 5(a)). After the initial aberrations when the model is being computed, the distribution has negligible changes during the static period. As shown in Fig. 5(b), there is sudden rise in α, β values when the Mosh starts. As a sudden wave of subjects come closer, the μ value decreases, resulting in an inflection categorized as a change in motion pattern by our detector algorithm. Figure 5(c) shows a stabilization of the crowd behavior which continues for a long period. There is another change detected in Fig. 5(d) due to reorganization of the crowd to create several empty pockets.

This dataset depicts an almost static crowd with only a burst of activity in the middle. However, the model generated from this data is also able to show the changes in crowd motion as proposed in our work.

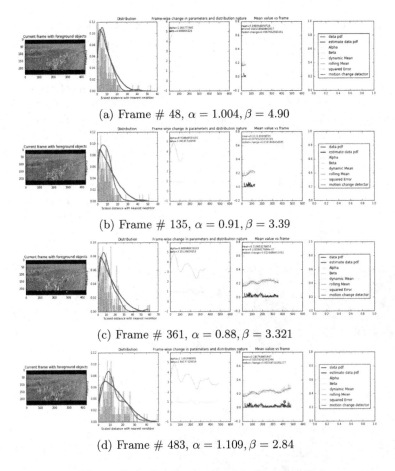

(a) Frame # 48, $\alpha = 1.004, \beta = 4.90$

(b) Frame # 135, $\alpha = 0.91, \beta = 3.39$

(c) Frame # 361, $\alpha = 0.88, \beta = 3.321$

(d) Frame # 483, $\alpha = 1.109, \beta = 2.84$

Fig. 6. Beta distribution model: Sequence C

For an organized procession with no fray element, the inter-personal distance distribution corresponds almost perfectly to a Beta distribution, as is evident from Fig. 6(a). Subsequently, with the introduction of lateral movement, the model is changed with gradual fall in distribution parameters (Fig. 6(b) and (c)). However, since the change in the behaviour of the crowd is extremely gradual, it does not trigger a detection very early. The distance distribution stabilizes over a period of time which can be seen in the flatness of the plot of μ. As the crowd disperses into a chaotic pattern, a change is detected (Fig. 6(d)) where the μ oscillates from the established model mean. Since the dispersed crowd remains distributed chaotically, no more change is detected.

3.2 Comparison with Social Force Model

Aside from the self-curated dense crowd data-sets ideal for our purpose, we have employed our method on a public data set of anomalous crowds released by University of Minnesota [7] and compared its performance with the method using social force model proposed by Mehran et al. [6] We have used several video sequences, three of which are shown in Fig. 7. Each row corresponds to a sequence. First column shows a representative frame of normal behaviour and the that of abnormal one is shown in second column. At the top of third column, ground-truth information is visually reflected where green colour denotes the progression of normal behaviour and red signifies abnormal sub-sequence. Our goal is to detect the transition in behaviour. In this context, comparison of performance (in terms of false positive and true positive) between the social force model based system and the proposed system is shown. It is observed that both the systems detect the actual transition correctly. The crowd in the video sequences is non-dense and that affects the proposed system. Even then, false positive is less in case of proposed system. Moreover, proper training is important for social force model based system and proposed model is free from that.

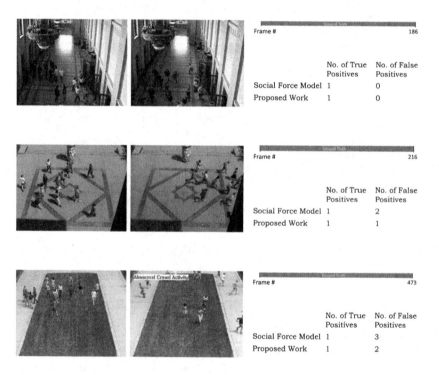

Fig. 7. Comparative results for three sample video sequences. (Color figure online)

4   Conclusion

In this work, we have presented a simple but novel methodology to model the global motion pattern of a dense crowd and to detect the change in the same. The distances of the nearest neighbour crowd components are fitted in a Beta distribution which is used to model the global motion. Based on the change in the distribution parameters, deviation in the crowd motion behaviour is identified. The methodology does not require tracking of feature points and is free from any prior training. Our method can also mark within a short range of frames where the anomaly starts. It can be optimized in future to make it viable for real time application. Experimental results indicates the effectiveness of the proposed methodology.

References

1. Andrade, E.L., Blunsden, S., Fisher, R.B.: Modelling crowd scenes for event detection. In: 18th International Conference on Pattern Recognition (ICPR 2006), vol. 1, pp. 175–178. IEEE (2006)
2. Fradi, H., Dugelay, J.L.: Spatial and temporal variations of feature tracks for crowd behavior analysis. J. Multimodal User Interfaces **10**, 1–11 (2015)
3. Helbing, D., Molnar, P.: Social force model for pedestrian dynamics. Phys. Rev. E **51**(5), 4282 (1995)
4. Isard, M., Blake, A.: A mixed-state condensation tracker with automatic model-switching. In: Sixth International Conference on Computer Vision, pp. 107–112. IEEE (1998)
5. Lee, D.S.: Effective Gaussian mixture learning for video background subtraction. IEEE Trans. Pattern Anal. Mach. Intell. **27**(5), 827–832 (2005)
6. Mehran, R., Oyama, A., Shah, M.: Abnormal crowd behavior detection using social force model. In: IEEE Conference on Computer Vision and Pattern Recognition, CVPR 2009, pp. 935–942. IEEE (2009)
7. University of Minnesota, D.o.C.S., Engineering: Unusual Crowd Activity Dataset. http://mha.cs.umn.edu/movies/crowdactivity-all.avi
8. Nam, Y.: Crowd flux analysis and abnormal event detection in unstructured and structured scenes. Multimedia Tools Appl. **72**(3), 3001–3029 (2014)
9. Owen, C.E.B.: Parameter estimation for the beta distribution (2008)
10. Scott, D.W.: Multivariate Density Estimation: Theory, Practice, and Visualization. Wiley, Hoboken (2015)
11. Shi, J., Tomasi, C.: Good features to track. In: 1994 IEEE Computer Society Conference on Computer Vision and Pattern Recognition, Proceedings CVPR 1994, pp. 593–600. IEEE (1994)
12. Wu, B., Nevatia, R.: Tracking of multiple, partially occluded humans based on static body part detection. In: 2006 IEEE Computer Society Conference on Computer Vision and Pattern Recognition (CVPR 2006), vol. 1, pp. 951–958. IEEE (2006)
13. Xie, S., Guan, Y.: Motion instability based unsupervised online abnormal behaviors detection. Multimedia Tools Appl. **75**, 1–22 (2015)
14. Zhan, B., Remagnino, P., Velastin, S.: Visual analysis of crowded pedestrain scenes. In: XLIII Congresso Annuale AICA, pp. 549–555 (2005)
15. Zhan, B., Monekosso, D.N., Remagnino, P., Velastin, S.A., Xu, L.Q.: Crowd analysis: a survey. Mach. Vis. Appl. **19**(5–6), 345–357 (2008)
16. Zhao, T., Nevatia, R.: Tracking multiple humans in complex situations. IEEE Trans. Pattern Anal. Mach. Intell. **26**(9), 1208–1221 (2004)

Reconstruction of Sparse-View Tomography via Banded Matrices

T. Prasad[1]([✉]), P.U. Praveen Kumar[1]([✉]), C.S. Sastry[1], and P.V. Jampana[2]

[1] Department of Mathematics, Indian Institute of Technology Hyderabad,
Hyderabad, Telangana, India
{ma13p1004,csastry}@iith.ac.in, praveen577302@gmail.com
[2] Department of Chemical Engineering, Indian Institute of Technology Hyderabad,
Hyderabad, Telangana, India
pjampana@iith.ac.in

Abstract. Computed Tomography (CT) is one of the significant research areas in medical image analysis. One of the main aspects of CT that researchers remain focused, is on reducing the dosage as X-rays are generally harmful to human bodies. In order to reduce radiation dosage, compressed sensing (CS) based methodologies appear to be promising. The basic premise is that medical images have inherent sparsity in some transformation domain. As a result, CS provides the possibility of recovering a high quality image from fewer projection data. In general, the sensing matrix in CT is generated from Radon projections by appropriately sampling the radial and angular parameters. In our work, by restricting the number of such parameters, we generate an under-determined linear system involving projection (Radon) data and a sparse sensing matrix, bringing thereby the problem into CS framework.

Among various recent solvers, the Split-Bregman iterative scheme has of late become popular due to its suitability for solving a wide variety of optimization problems. Intending to exploit the underlying structure of sensing matrix, the present work analyzes its properties and finds a banded structure for an associated intermediate matrix. Using this observation, we simplify the Split-Bregman solver, proposing thereby a CT-specific solver of low complexity. We also provide the efficacy of proposed method empirically.

Keywords: Compressed sensing · Split-Bregman · Computed tomography · Least squares

1 Introduction

Image reconstruction in Computed Tomography (CT) is a mathematical process [7] that generates images from X-ray projection data acquired at many different angles around the patient. Image reconstruction has a significant impact

© Springer International Publishing AG 2017
S. Mukherjee et al. (Eds.): ICVGIP 2016, LNCS 10481, pp. 204–215, 2017.
https://doi.org/10.1007/978-3-319-68124-5_18

on image quality and therefore on radiation dose [4]. For a given radiation dose it is desirable to reconstruct images with the lowest possible noise without loosing image accuracy and spatial resolution.

Two categories of methods, namely analytical and iterative, exist for CT image reconstruction. The commonly used analytical method is conventional filtered back-projection (FBP) reconstruction algorithm [9,10]. Despite its popularity, the FBP suffers from systematic geometric distortion and streak artifacts when the measured projection data are not sufficient like in sparse-view CT. When dealing with insufficient data, the iterative class of methods works well [1]. Iterative reconstruction [11] has recently received much attention in CT because it has many advantages, such as minimizing image artifacts, compared to conventional FBP techniques.

In recent years, the reconstruction methods [6] based on optimization have become popular due to their ability in reducing number of X-ray projection samples while maintaining good reconstruction fidelity. The basic premise behind these methods is akin to Compressed Sensing (CS) in exploiting natural sparsity present in CT images. Among optimization methods [5], the Split-Bregman iterative (SBI) technique has of late become very popular as it is extremely efficient. The SBI method is known to fast solve the problem of sparse recovery when the underlying sensing matrices have special structure [8]. In [2], a novel algorithm, called Linearized Split-Bregman (LSB) method, has been proposed to efficiently solve the sparse-view CT. The LSB approximately solves the intermediate linear system with dense matrix. The present work, however, is an attempt to design a data driven frame (or a basis) for replacing the intermediate dense matrix with a banded matrix, proposing therefrom a simplified Split-Bregman method for sparse-view tomography.

The remaining section of the paper is organized as follows: Sect. 2 presents the basics of CT and Split Bregman method. In Sect. 3, we discuss the motivation for present work and proposed method. The experimental results are presented in Sect. 4 and finally the conclusions and future work are detailed in Sect. 5.

2   Basics of CT

Let f refer to the density of cross-section to be recovered. The line integral of f along $\alpha \cos \theta + \beta \sin \theta = t$, called the Radon transform, is as follows:

$$g(t, \theta) = \int_{-\infty}^{+\infty} f(\alpha, \beta) \delta(\alpha \cos \theta + \beta \sin \theta - t) d\alpha d\beta, \tag{1}$$

where δ is the dirac delta function. The projection data $g(t, \theta)$, called the sinogram, is a function t and θ. Two types of data acquisition geometries are shown in Fig. 1.

In discrete CT, however, the underlying image ($x \in \mathbb{R}^n$) can be obtained by solving the system of equations $y = Ax$, where $y \in \mathbb{R}^m$ is a vector consisting of

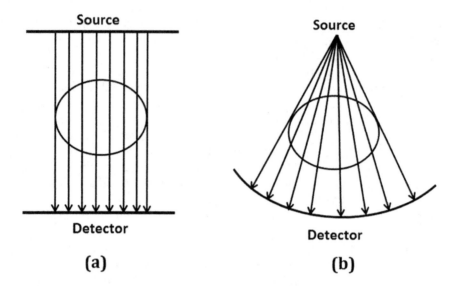

Fig. 1. Data acquisition in (a) Parallel-Beam and (b) Fan-Beam geometries

projection samples. The matrix $A \in \mathbb{R}^{m \times n}$ consists of the coefficients $a_{i,j}$:

$$a_{ij} = \begin{cases} w_{i,j}, & \text{if } i^{th} \text{ ray hits } j^{th} \text{ pixel} \\ 0, & \text{otherwise,} \end{cases} \tag{2}$$

which characterize the contribution ("length" or "weight") of each ray in each pixel in its travel, which is depicted in Fig. 2. By setting $w_{i,j}$ to 1, one generates a binary sensing matrix which approximates the original sensing matrix and simplifies reconstruction process. Besides, the binary sensing matrix enables one to use sparse storage techniques and reduces the memory requirements. The rows of the projection matrix A refer to different pairs of angular (θ) and radial (t) parameters. In sparse-view tomography, with rays corresponding to a limited set of parameters, the system $y = Ax$ becomes under-determined. In view of sparse structure of CT images, the area of Compressed Sensing appears to be promising for image reconstruction in sparse-view CT.

2.1   Compressed Sensing and Split Bregman Method

The generalized and constrained optimization problem

$$\min_{x} J(x) \quad \text{subject to} \quad Ax = y \tag{3}$$

can be converted as an unconstrained problem by using the method of Lagrange multipliers as follows:

$$\min_{x} J(x) + \frac{\lambda}{2} \|Ax - y\|^2. \tag{4}$$

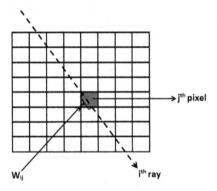

Fig. 2. Ray passing through object. Length of the ith ray in j^{th} pixel is $w_{i,j}$

In Compressed Sensing, the penalty function $J(x)$ is taken as $\|x\|_0$, which in turn is replaced by $\|x\|_1$. Under certain sparsity constraints [3], it is shown that the optimization problem

$$\min_x \|x\|_1 \quad \text{subject to} \quad Ax = y. \tag{5}$$

recovers the sparsest solution (that is, the solution with many zero components) of $y = Ax$. In general, when x *per se* is not sparse, one identifies a suitable transformation D such that Dx is sparse. In the sense of analysis-sparsity prior [8], such x may be recovered from

$$\min_x \|Dx\|_1 \quad \text{subject to} \quad Ax = y. \tag{6}$$

The objective function in (6) is neither smooth nor separable. The Split-Bregman method, however, reposes [8] the above optimization problem in the following way:

$$\min_x \|d\|_1 \quad \text{subject to} \quad Ax = y; \, d = Dx. \tag{7}$$

which involves separable and nonsmooth objective function. The unconstrained version of the above optimization problem may be considered as follows [8]:

$$\min_{x,d} \|d\|_1 + \frac{\lambda}{2}\|Ax - y\|_2^2, \quad \text{subject to} \quad Dx = d. \tag{8}$$

The solution to the above problem may be obtained through the following iterative steps [2]:

$$(x^{k+1}, d^{k+1}) = \arg\min_{x,d} \|d\|_1 + \frac{\lambda}{2}\|Ax - y\|_2^2 + \frac{\mu}{2}\|d - Dx - s^k\|_2^2$$
$$s^{k+1} = s^k - Dx^{k+1} - d^{k+1}, \tag{9}$$

which are explained in more detail as follows:

Algorithm 1. Split Bregman Algorithm [5]

1: Given initial points $x^0 = 0$, $d^0 = 0$, $s^0 = 0$, $0 < \epsilon \ll 1$ and $K \in \mathbb{Z}^+$. Set k = 0.
2: Update d :

$$d^{k+1} = arg \min_d \|d\|_1 + \frac{\mu}{2}\|d^{k+1} - Dx - s^k\|_2^2$$

3: Update x :

$$x^{k+1} = arg \min_x \frac{\lambda}{2}\|Ax - y\|_2^2 + \frac{\mu}{2}\|d^{k+1} - Dx - s^k\|_2^2$$

  stop if $r_k = \|x^{k+1} - x\|_2 < \epsilon$ or $k+1 > K$. Otherwise go to next step.
4: Update s :

$$s^{k+1} = s^k - Dx^{k+1} - d^{k+1}.$$

5: Set $k := k + 1$, return to step 2.

In actual simulations, the above Algorithm is implemented via the following steps:

$$d^{k+1} = \max\left(h^k - \frac{1}{\mu}, 0\right)\left(\frac{Dx^k + s^k}{h^k}\right)$$

$$(\lambda A^T A + \mu D^T D)x^{k+1} = \lambda A^T y + \mu D^T(d^{k+1} - s^k) \tag{10}$$

$$s^{k+1} = s^k + Dx^{k+1} - d^{k+1}.$$

3   Motivation for Present Work and Proposed Method

The matrix $\lambda A^T A + \mu D^T D$ is in general dense and hence solving the second equation of (10) for x^{k+1} is computationally more involved. For instance, the reconstruction of an image of size $n \times n$ involves n^2 as column size for $\lambda A^T A + \mu D^T D$. Consequently, the efficient implementation of second equation in (10) is of significance. In order to deal with this problem, the work embedded in [2] incorporates an iterative and approximate procedure by considering gradient operator as sparsifying transform. Motivated by the need for better way of handling the large scale system involving dense matrix as in (10), the present work banks on D and chooses it in such a way that the matrix $\lambda A^T A + \mu D^T D$ becomes banded. Consequently, the second equation in (10) can be solved with very less effort and low cost.

  Given the projection matrix A, as an example, we choose D in such a way that $\lambda A^T A + \mu D^T D$ becomes a diagonal matrix. In other words, for a given pair of parameters (μ, λ), the off-diagonal entries of $\mu D^T D$ are chosen as those of $\lambda A^T A$ but with reverse sign. The diagonal entries of $\mu D^T D$ are chosen keeping in mind the requirement of $D^T D$ being strictly positive definite. In particular, from the sensing matrix A, the matrix $\tilde{D} = [\tilde{d}_{ij}]$ with

$$\tilde{d}_{ij} = \begin{cases} -\frac{\lambda}{\mu}a_i^T a_j & \forall i \neq j \\ \frac{\lambda}{\mu}\sum_{l=1}^n a_i^T a_l & \text{when } i = j \end{cases} \tag{11}$$

appears to result in D possessing desired properties, where $\tilde{D} = D^T D$. Due to enforced diagonal structure on $\lambda A^T A + \mu D^T D$, the second equation in (10) can be solved easily.

In view of invertibility of D, the steps in (10) get simplified as detailed below:

$$\hat{d}^{k+1} = \max\left(h^k - \frac{1}{\mu}, 0\right)\left(\frac{x^k + \hat{s}^k}{h^k}\right)$$

$$(\lambda A^T A + \mu D^T D)x^{k+1} = \lambda A^T y + \mu D^T D(\hat{d}^{k+1} - \hat{s}^k) \qquad (12)$$

$$\hat{s}^{k+1} = \hat{s}^k + x^{k+1} - \hat{d}^{k+1}.$$

In (12), the notations used are: $d^k = D\hat{d}^k$ and $s^k = D\hat{s}^k$. From (12), it is clear that there is no need for D to be generated explicitly. Further, the first and third equations in (12) become free from matrix multiplication, reducing thereby the computational complexity. Figure 3 represents the structures of $\lambda A^T A + \mu \nabla^T \nabla$ and $\lambda A^T A + \mu D^T D$ with data driven basis D.

Remark: It is worth a mention here that the data driven basis D that we have chosen may not be a good option as a sparsifying transform. Nevertheless, this work is an attempt towards simplifying the process of Split-Bregman procedure via the careful choice of data driven D. We envisage that the data driven D which results in a tri-diagonal or penta-diagonal structure for $\lambda A^T A + \mu D^T D$ may be a good candidate for being a sparsifying basis.

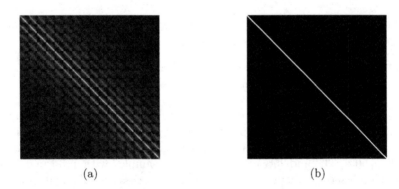

(a)   (b)

Fig. 3. Structure of (a). $\lambda A^T A + \mu \nabla^T \nabla$ and (b) $\lambda A^T A + \mu D^T D$, where D is a data driven basis and A is binary projection matrix.

4   Experimental Results

In generating Radon projection matrix as defined in (2), we have considered the following radial and angular sampling.

Radial Sampling:

$$t_m = \delta_r(p - (n/2)), \qquad (13)$$

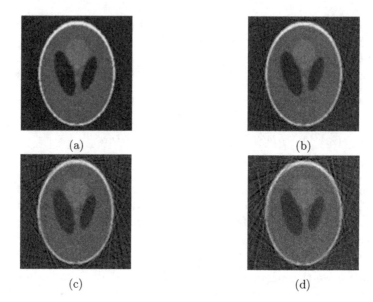

(a)   (b)

(c)   (d)

Fig. 4. Reconstruction of Shepp-Logan image using simplified Split Bregman with measurement matrix of 4 different sizes: (a) 16384×16384 (b) 8192×16384 (with 50% of projection samples) (c) 5462×16384 (with nearly 33% of projection samples) (d) 4096×16984 (with 25% of projection samples).

where $p = \{0, 1, \cdots, n-1\}$, δ_r is the length of detector and n is tied to the size of image (that is, $n \times n$) to be reconstructed.

Angular Sampling:

$$\theta_l = \frac{q + 0.5}{n}\pi, \tag{14}$$

where $q = \{0, 1, \cdots, n-1\}$. Subsequently, we have generated y, the Radon measurements in vector form, corresponding to these parameters. We have implemented the steps in (12) for measurement vectors of 4 different sizes (that is, with 100%, 50%, 33% and 25% of measurements) sampled with uniform distribution from a full set of measurements. The sizes of the associated sensing matrices are 16384×16384, 8192×16384, 5462×16384 and 4096×16384 respectively. For experimental purpose we took three different test images viz. Shepp-Logan, MRI-1 and MRI-2. The performance of CT image reconstruction obtained through the simplified Split-Bregman method is shown in Figs. 4, 5 and 6. We have also reconstructed the image using standard least squares method shown in Figs. 7, 8 and 9 to visually observe the reconstruction quality. The algorithms have been numerically implemented in the MatLab environment on a machine having 32 GB RAM and Intel Xeon processor with speed of 2.20 GHz.

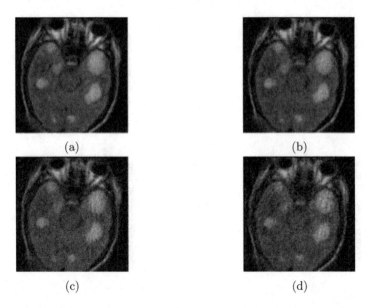

(a)   (b)

(c)   (d)

Fig. 5. Reconstruction of MRI - 1 image using simplified Split Bregman with measurement matrix of 4 different sizes: (a) 16384 × 16384 (b) 8192 × 16384 (with 50% of projection samples) (c) 5462 × 16384 (with nearly 33% of projection samples) (d) 4096 × 16984 (with 25% of projection samples).

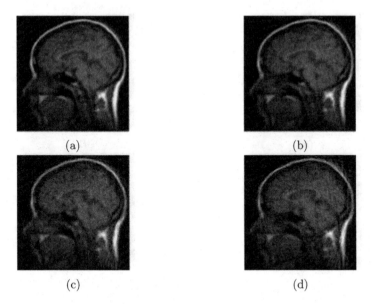

(a)   (b)

(c)   (d)

Fig. 6. Reconstruction of MRI - 2 image using simplified Split Bregman with measurement matrix of 4 different sizes: (a) 16384 × 16384 (b) 8192 × 16384 (with 50% of projection samples) (c) 5462 × 16384 (with nearly 33% of projection samples) (d) 4096 × 16984 (with 25% of projection samples).

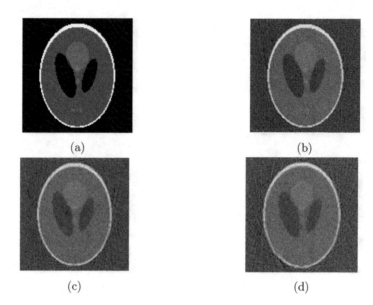

Fig. 7. Reconstruction of Shepp-Logan image using Least Squares with measurement matrix of 4 different sizes: (a) 16384×16384 (b) 8192×16384 (with 50% of projection samples) (c) 5462×16384 (with nearly 33% of projection samples) (d) 4096×16984 (with 25% of projection samples).

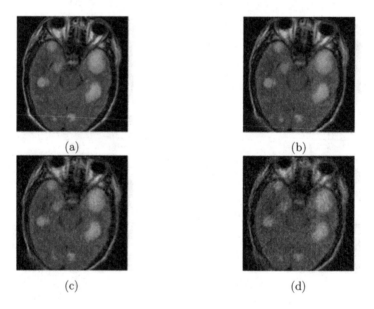

Fig. 8. Reconstruction of MRI - 1 image using Least Squares with measurement matrix of 4 different sizes: (a) 16384×16384 (b) 8192×16384 (with 50% of projection samples) (c) 5462×16384 (with nearly 33% of projection samples) (d) 4096×16984 (with 25% of projection samples).

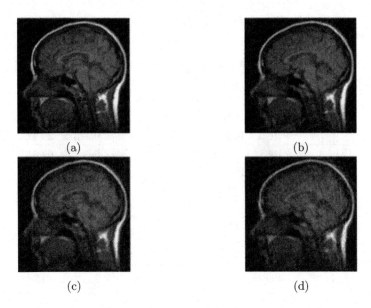

Fig. 9. Reconstruction of MRI - 2 image using Least Squares with measurement matrix of 4 different sizes: (a) 16384×16384 (b) 8192×16384 (with 50% of projection samples) (c) 5462×16384 (with nearly 33% of projection samples) (d) 4096×16984 (with 25% of projection samples).

Table 1. Performances of image reconstruction obtained using the proposed simplified Split Bregman with different sets of measurements.

Images	Dim. of binary sensing matrix	MSE	PSNR
Shepp-Logan	16384×16384	5.1e−3	22.95
	8192×16384	7.1e−3	21.52
	5462×16384	9.0e−3	20.46
	4096×16384	11.6e−3	19.36
MRI - 1	16384×16384	1.9e−3	26.09
	8192×16384	2.8e−3	24.54
	5462×16384	3.8e−3	23.24
	4096×16384	4.8e−3	22.20
MRI - 2	16384×16384	1.2e−3	29.12
	8192×16384	2.3e−3	26.32
	5462×16384	3.6e−3	24.41
	4096×16384	4.9e−3	23.11

In order to evaluate quantitatively the accuracy of reconstruction results, we have computed Mean Squared Error (MSE)

$$MSE = \frac{\sum_{i=1}^{m} \sum_{j=1}^{n} (x_{i,j} - \widehat{x}_{i,j})^2}{m \times n}, \tag{15}$$

Table 2. Performances of image reconstruction obtained using the Least Squares with different sets of measurements.

Images	Dim. of binary sensing matrix	MSE	PSNR
Shepp-Logan	16384×16384	3.3e−20	194.83
	8192×16384	3.9e−3	24.14
	5462×16384	6.4e−3	21.96
	4096×16384	9.0e−3	20.47
MRI - 1	16384×16384	4.5e−7	62.41
	8192×16384	1.6e−3	26.93
	5462×16384	2.8e−3	24.48
	4096×16384	4.3e−3	22.67
MRI - 2	16384×16384	9.3e−20	190.30
	8192×16384	1.0e−3	29.88
	5462×16384	2.6e−3	25.93
	4096×16384	4.2e−3	23.78

Table 3. Error estimation by varying λ and μ in the simplified Split Bregman method for three different test images which are considered for simulation

Shepp-Logan			MRI - 1			MRI - 2		
λ	μ	Error	λ	μ	Error	λ	μ	Error
1	0.06	17.98	1	0.06	9.96	1	0.06	12.33
35	0.5	9.11	35	0.5	5.69	35	0.5	4.58
50	0.06	8.98	50	0.06	5.65	50	0.06	4.47

and Peak Signal to Noise Ratio (PSNR)

$$PSNR = 10 * \log_{10} \frac{[\max_i |x_i|]^2}{MSE}. \tag{16}$$

In (15), $x_{i,j}$ is the pixel value of ground truth image and $\hat{x}_{i,j}$ is the pixel value of reconstructed image. Tables 1 and 2 respectively reports the MSE and PSNR values of simplified Split Bregman method, and least squares method. From Tables 1 and 2 it is observed that the MSE values are small for simplified Split Bregman method and PSNR values are approximately equal to least squares for the reconstruction based on simplified Split Bregman method in undersampled cases. Through simulations, we have observed that the choice of $\lambda = 50$ and $\mu = 0.06$ appears to provide the reconstruction of visually good quality. Table 3 reports reconstruction errors for different choices of λ and μ.

5   Conclusion and Future Work

In this paper, we have simplified the Split-Bregman solver for reconstructing the CT images from a reduced set of projection samples. The basic philosophy in the proposed method is to generate a banded structure for an intermediate matrix via a suitable choice of data driven basis, reducing thereby the overall complexity of reconstruction process. It is to be emphasized here that the preliminary results based on "not so good choice of data-driven D" indicate that a proper choice of D can potentially provide reconstruction of better quality while simplifying the matrix structure. Our future efforts shall attempt to answer the question of choosing D properly for accurate and simplified reconstruction procedure.

Acknowledgments. One of the authors (CSS) is thankful to CSIR (No. 25(219)/13/ EMR-II), Govt. of India, for its support.

References

1. Beister, M., Kolditz, D., Kalender, W.A.: Iterative reconstruction methods in X-ray CT. Phys. Med. **28**(2), 94–108 (2012)
2. Chen, C., Xu, G.: A new linearized split Bregman iterative algorithm for image reconstruction in sparse view X-ray computed tomography. Comput. Math. Appl. **71**(8), 1537–1559 (2016)
3. Elad, M.: Sparse and Redundant Representations: From Theory to Applications in Signal and Image Processing. Springer, Heidelberg (2010)
4. Frush, D.P., Donnelly, L.F., Rosen, N.S.: Computed tomography and radiation risks: what pediatric health care providers should know. Pediatrics **112**(4), 951–957 (2003)
5. Goldstein, T., Osher, S.: The split Bregman method for L1-regularized problems. SIAM J. Imaging Sci. **2**(2), 323–343 (2009)
6. Jorgensen, J.S., Hansen, P.C., Schmidt, S.: Sparse image reconstruction in computed tomography. Technical University of Denmark, Kongens Lyngby: PHD-2013; No. 293 (2013)
7. Kuchment, P.: The Radon transform and medical imaging, vol. 85. SIAM (2014)
8. Jian-Feng, C., Osher, S., Shen, Z.: Split Bregman methods and frame based image restoration. SIAM J. Multiscale Model. Simul. **8**(2), 337–369 (2009)
9. Jan, J.: Medical Image Processing, Reconstruction and Restoration: Concepts and Methods, CRC Press (2005)
10. Pan, X.C., Sidky, E.Y., Vannier, M.: Why do commercial CT scanners still employ traditional, filtered back-projection for image reconstruction? Inverse Prob. **25**(12), 1230009 (2009)
11. Zhang, H., Huang, J., Ma, J., Bian, Z., Feng, Q., Lu, H., Liang, Z., Chen, W.: Iterative reconstruction for X-Ray computed tomography using prior-image induced nonlocal regularization. IEEE Trans. Biomed. Eng. **61**(9), 2367–2378 (2014)

DAR

SPODS: A Dataset of Color-Official Documents and Detection of Logo, Stamp, and Signature

Amit Vijay Nandedkar$^{(\boxtimes)}$, Jayanta Mukherjee, and Shamik Sural

Department of Computer Science and Engineering,
Indian Institute of Technology, Kharagpur, India
amitnandedkar@sit.iitkgp.ernet.in,
{jay,shamik}@cse.iitkgp.ernet.in

Abstract. Office automation is an active area of research. It involves archival and retrieval of official documents. For developing a system for this purpose, it is necessary to have an extensive benchmark dataset consisting various types of official documents. However, it is hard to make available real world official documents as they are mostly confidential. In the absence of such benchmark datasets, it is difficult to evaluate newly developed algorithms. Hence, efforts have been made to build dataset consisting of different categories of documents that resemble real world official documents. In this work, we present a dataset called as scanned pseudo-official data-set (SPODS) which is created by us and made available online. Official documents are usually distinguished by presence of logo, stamp, signature, date, etc. The paper also presents a new approach for the detection of logo, stamp, and signature using spectral filtering and part based features. A comparative study on performances of the proposed method and existing algorithms on the SPODS dataset demonstrates the effectiveness of the proposed technique.

Keywords: Document analysis · Graphics recognition · Document understanding

1 Introduction

Enormous paper documents are still used in offices and organizations. In recent times, these volumes of paper documents are scanned and proliferated across offices. Innovative techniques are essential for the development of automated systems to store and retrieve document images. Document Image Retrieval (DIR) is an emerging area of research, though it is observed that there is a lack of availability of benchmark dataset in this area. However, a similar research area of Content Based Image Retrieval (CBIR) [13,19] in the field of image processing is well established with benchmark datasets [1].

There exist different kinds of official documents depending on the modes of communication and transactions, such as letters, memos, notices, circulars, orders, tenders, contracts, etc. These documents are characterized by visual attributes (e.g., logos, stamps, and signatures) and textual attributes, such as

© Springer International Publishing AG 2017
S. Mukherjee et al. (Eds.): ICVGIP 2016, LNCS 10481, pp. 219–230, 2017.
https://doi.org/10.1007/978-3-319-68124-5_19

document date, reference number, etc. A logo indicates a unique identity of document source to an observer, and a stamp provides its legitimacy. A signature is used as an evidence for document authentication. Hence, logo, stamp, and signature are important visual attributes present in document images, and can be used for their proper indexing and retrieval. Document image retrieval based on logo, stamp, signature, etc. is an interesting research area [9,11,12,17,18,20,24]. It is difficult to make the real world office documents available in public domain as they are confidential. There is a need to create a benchmark dataset with ground truth that resembles the real world office documents. A standard dataset can help the research community to test and compare algorithms.

In the past a number of efforts are reported in the literature, which consider retrieval and recognition of signature, logo, etc. [9,11,12,18,20,24]. Mostly, these techniques considered document image retrieval based on signature or logo in isolation. Notably, the dataset, Tobacco-800 [2], is the only black and white publicly available document dataset, used in [11,12,18,24] for developing logo and signature based document retrieval systems. In recent times, most of the official documents are available in color. The StaVer dataset reported in [15] consists of 400 color document images and it is used for detection of stamp and logo [4,7,15,16]. However, most documents in the StaVer dataset are without signature. That is why they are less suitable for testing signature based retrieval of documents. This paper presents a new color document image dataset called *Scanned pseudo-official data-set (SPODS)* for detection of logo, stamp, signature and retrieval of documents. This work also presents a unified approach for the detection of logo, stamp, and signature from scanned document images.

The SPODS dataset contains document images representing office work. These documents are characterized and distinguished by the presence of logo, stamp, signature. Groundtruth of this dataset is also made available by annotating the regions of logo, stamp, signature, and text in the documents. To our knowledge, this is a unique document image dataset, which provides the ground truth for signature at pixel level to represent the strokes in signature. The black and white Tobacco-800 dataset provides ground truth for signature in forms of minimum area bounding isothetic rectangles. Hence, the new dataset could be used in testing algorithms targeting retrieval, segmentation and identification of logo, stamp, signature, etc.

This paper describes the characteristics of SPODS dataset, how it is created and the scope of its research applicability. The dataset consists of 1088 color document images containing logos, stamps, signatures and printed text as representative of regular official communication. As real world official records are confidential, we have mimicked creation of different varieties and used them in generating fictitious official documents. Every document image is supplemented with detailed ground truth for logo, stamp, signature, and text regions which are generated manually. The dataset is also supported with a metadata containing records indicating the unique identification number for document, logo, stamp, signature, document type, and the mentioned document date. It provides multiple instances of each unique visual attribute for measuring performance of retrieval.

This work also proposes a new approach to detect logo, stamp, and signature using spectral filtering and the part based features. The proposed method utilizes the fact that the graphical regions such as stamps and logos have distinctive spectral characteristics, and is used to detect logo and stamp in a color document. The method identifies the signature region present in the document image using the part based features.

Section 2 provides the details of SPODS dataset and discusses its research applicability. In Sect. 3, we present a method based on *Spectral Filtering and Part-based Features (SFPF)* for logo, stamp, and signature detection. Experimental results are presented in Sect. 4.

2   SPODS Dataset

The SPODS dataset resembles the real world official documents with stamps, logos, signatures, etc. Typical examples of these document images are shown in Fig. 1. Figure 2 shows representative samples of logo, stamp, and signature present in the dataset. It may be noted that while preparing the dataset, presence of any handwritten contents is not considered except signatures. The SPODS dataset can be used to develop a system for archival and retrieval of official documents. It consists of 32 logos, 32 stamps, 32 signatures, and 12 document types. Overall there are 1088 document images in the SPODS dataset.

Fig. 1. Examples of document images of the SPODS dataset.

The workflow for generating the dataset is depicted in Fig. 3. The textual contents are composed following different formats and layouts in official communication such as relating to order, memo, letter, etc. Table 1 summarizes different categories of documents based on textual context of documents. We have formed 34 different pseudo text matters. Each textual matter is replicated in 32 different documents with slight variations in textual contents with different logos. The logos are completely synthetic with various shapes and colors. Some of the documents are kept without logos. To match real world scenario both graphical and textual stamps are used. There are 10 graphical and 22 textual stamps of varying sizes. Furthermore, the textual contents are represented using different

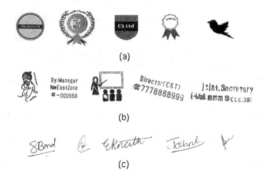

Fig. 2. Examples of (a) logo (b) stamp and (c) signature of the SPODS dataset.

Fig. 3. Workflow of document image dataset creation.

Table 1. Document types present in SPODS dataset

Doc. type	Description	No. of documents
1	Order	64
2	Table	96
3	Circular	224
4	Notice	96
5	Letter (copy to many correspondence)	128
6	Letter (one to one correspondence)	288
7	Invitation for tender pre-qualification	32
8	Call for bid	32
9	Contract	32
10	Tender	32
11	Employment advertisement	32
12	Memo	32
Total No. of documents		1088

font styles and sizes. The documents consist of regular textual contents, tabular representation of textual contents, stamps, logos, signatures, etc. The details of different font styles and sizes used in composing them are presented in Table 2. Table 3 shows different dates mentioned in documents with the number of documents containing these dates. Different date formats are used to represent dates in SPODS dataset.

Table 2. Font styles and sizes used in SPODS dataset

Font styles used	Font sizes used
Times New Roman	10, 11, 11.5, 12, 14
Calibri	
Trebuchet MS	
Bookman Old Style	
Arial	
Comic Sans MS	
Century Gothic	
Courier New	
Batang	
Arabic TypeSetting	
Helvetica	

Table 3. Different dates mentioned in SPODS dataset

Dates mentioned in documents (dd/mm/yy)	No. of documents
4/1/15, 20/1/15	38
1/1/15, 2/1/15, 5/1/15, 10/1/15, 28/1/15	29
3/1/15, 6/1/15, 7/1/15, 8/1/15, 9/1/15, 11/1/15, 13/1/15, 16/1/15, 17/1/15, 18/1/15, 19/1/15, 21/1/15, 23/1/15, 24/1/15, 25/1/15, 26/1/15, 27/1/15, 31/1/15	30
12/1/15, 14/1/15, 15/1/15, 22/1/15, 29/1/15, 1/2/15, 2/2/15	31
30/1/15	44
No date (Document images without date)	32

A total of 1088 documents are created using Microsoft Office® 2010. These color documents are printed using RICOH®-Aficio MP C3001 on commonly used A4 size white papers. The printed documents are manually stamped and signed by volunteers. All documents are scanned using HP® Scanjet N9120 scanner. Nowadays, the use of such sophisticated scanners is normal practice in various offices and organizations. The SPODS dataset is made available in 300 dpi resolution. The ground truth images are generated for all 1088 images in the dataset. The ground truth depicts segments of logo, stamp, signature, and text in a document. The SPODS dataset is made publicly available[1].

---

[1] The dataset is available at http://www.facweb.iitkgp.ernet.in/~jay/spods/.

2.1   Ground Truths and Scope of SPODS Dataset

There are two types of ground truths, namely, GT1 and GT2. In GT1, for each document image present in the dataset, we have manually created binarized ground truth images depicting logo, stamp, signature, and text. This ground truth is useful for measuring the performance of detection using measures such as precision and recall. The ground truth GT2 created in an OpenDocument Spreadsheet (ods) file format. It consists of details regarding logo, stamp, signature and document date, if they are present in the image. It also provides the information about document type as given in Table 1. For every document image present in the dataset, there is a corresponding record in the ground truth GT2. The ground truth GT2 is provided for computation of performance of retrieval. Figure 4 shows an example of metadata contents in GT2.

Image No	Logo ID	Signature ID	Date	Document_Typ	Stamp ID
1	1	17	0	2	1
2	2	28	0	2	1
3	3	18	0	2	1
4	4	19	0	2	1
5	5	29	0	2	1

Fig. 4. Example of meta data contents in GT2.

It may be noted that if any attribute value in GT2 is 0, it indicates the absence of that attribute in the document image. For example, in Fig. 4, the first document contains logo with logo $ID = 1$, signature with signature $ID = 17$, document date: absent and stamp with stamp $ID = 1$. Corresponding to these unique IDs, the respective signature, logo, stamp images are mentioned along with GT2. Hence, the SPODS dataset is suitable for testing and verification of document retrieval systems using the visual attributes and textual attributes.

3   Detection of Logo, Stamp, and Signature Using Spectral Filtering and Part Based Features

In the past, Zhu and Doermann [23] proposed an automatic logo detection method using a boosting strategy across multiple image scales. It considers a priori knowledge of possible logo positions in document images. A logo detection method with an assumption that logos normally have a background and are isolated, is reported in [21]. These methods are meant for black and white document images.

A few techniques [4,8,15] are proposed using color, geometric features for stamp detection. Dey et al. [8] proposed a color stamp detection technique from document image in HSV color space. It targets document images containing printed text and stamp imprints. In [15], Micenkova and van Beusekom presented a method for stamp detection using color and geometrical features. The method is limited to non-black colored stamps of any shape and form. Ahmed et al. [4] proposed a technique for detection of stamp using geometric features and key point descriptors. This technique needs training to detect black and white, and colored stamps. It reported low recall and precision, and acknowledged its inability to handle severely overlapped stamps. In [7], a logo and stamp detection technique is presented using outlier detection in feature space along with logo specific geometric features. The techniques reported in [4,7,15] targeted the StaVer color document dataset [15], in which the majority of documents are without signature.

Zhu et al. [24] presented a technique using multi-scale saliency map for detecting signature in document images. In [14], Mandal et al. proposed the use of conditional random field for segmentation of signatures from document images. Signature detection is addressed in [3] considering the part based SURF features [5] and a majority voting mechanism for classification. The performance of [3,14] was reported on a subset of 105 document images from black and white Tobacco-800 dataset [2].

This work proposes a new approach using *spectral filtering and the part based features* (SFPF) to detect logo, stamp, and signature.

The computation is performed in three stages:

- suppression of text contents by frequency selective filtering,
- identification and separation of graphical and textual regions, and
- logo, stamp, signature detection.

The proposed method uses the fact that the graphical regions such as stamps and logos have distinctive spectral characteristics, and is used to detect logo and stamp in a color document. It characterizes the signature regions present in the document image using the part based features. SURF is a part based technique as it represents an image as a set of key points associated with their respective local descriptors. This work is an extension of our previously reported technique [16], which assumes the absence of signature in document images for the detection of logo and stamp. The details are discussed in the following sections.

3.1 Frequency Selective Filtering

The overall objective of frequency selective filtering [16] is to suppress textual contents present in the input document. It helps to retain logo, stamp, signature, and suppresses the text. The high pass filtered image Y is created using the gray scale image G of the input color document image D. The magnitude of pixels in Y is proportional to the frequency characteristics of input document image D. With reference to Y, the frequency selective operation [16] retains pixels in the area of relatively lower spatial frequencies along with the preservation of chromatic information in the region of graphical objects into the filtered output image F'_L.

(a)   (b)   (c)

Fig. 5. (a) Input document, (b) text image, and (c) graphics image. (Color figure online)

3.2 Post Processing

In the post-processing step, separation of candidate graphical and text regions is carried out using the filtered image F'_L. First, the filtered image is median filtered and then Gaussian blurring operation is performed. The median and Gaussian filtering together assist to suppress noise because of textual residuals. Next, the color quantization and mean-shift segmentation [6] operations are performed to obtain segmented image Z.

In the segmented image Z, the region with the largest area is considered as a background. The remaining regions are considered as foreground candidates for graphical regions. These candidate regions are processed to remove textual residuals using geometrical constraints on areas, heights and widths of bounding boxes. The refined set of foreground regions is used to create binary mask M representing their positions. The mask M is utilized for the extraction of graphical regions from the document image D. The extracted graphical image is called $D_{\text{GRAPHICAL}}$. In a similar way, the textual image D_{TEXTUAL} is generated by using the complement of binary mask M of foreground regions.

Figure 5(b) and (c) present the text-graphics separated images for the document image shown in Fig. 5(a). It is also observed that color signature (e.g., signature signed using blue ink pen) may appear in the graphical output image as shown in Fig. 5(c) and black signature (e.g., signature signed using black ink pen) may appear in the text output image. The detection of logo, stamp, and signature is discussed in the subsequent section.

3.3 Localization of Candidate Regions

To detect logo, knowledge of probable logo-position in the document dataset is used. A k-means clustering algorithm [10] is applied to cluster the centroid and spread of logos from the ground truths in normalized space. The normalization is performed with respect to height of the document. In our experiment, we empirically choose the value of k as 10 for the SPODS dataset. Number of

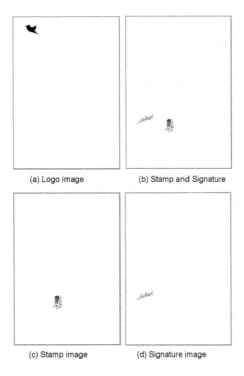

(a) Logo image   (b) Stamp and Signature

(c) Stamp image   (d) Signature image

Fig. 6. Example of logo, stamp, and signature detection.

foreground pixels are computed within a window surrounding each centroid of a cluster in the graphical image $D_{\text{GRAPHICAL}}$ (e.g., Fig. 5(c)). A candidate logo with number of foreground pixels greater than a threshold value is declared as a logo. Figure 6(a) illustrates an example of logo detected image, and Fig. 6(b) depicts an example of the remaining (stamp and signature) image after the detection of logo from the graphics image (refer to Fig. 5(c)).

In the next step, separation of the stamp and signature is performed. To do this, we use the part based signature detection mechanism using SURF and majority voting scheme. The SURF descriptors with total 64 dimensions are computed at each detected key point in the input document image using the fast Hessian technique [5]. The SURF descriptors are extracted from the grayscale version (G) of the input image (e.g., Fig. 6(b)). The training phase consists of extracting SURF features from labeled training data, and bagging them into signature and non-signature feature sets. These two feature sets are used during testing to find the closest class-label (stamp or signature) using Euclidean distance. The binary image of G is dilated to merge nearby connected components. This operation reduces the number of connected components to be classified. Now, for each connected component present in the dilated image, the part based features are taken from the respective region in G and used in voting. If majority of the part based features vote for signature class, the corresponding region is declared as a signature region. Otherwise, signature is not present in the graphical image $D_{\text{GRAPHICAL}}$. The rest of the non-signature regions of $D_{\text{GRAPHICAL}}$ are considered to be of stamp regions. Figure 6(c) and (d) depict detection of stamp and signature, respectively. A similar signature detection technique is applied for the textual D_{TEXTUAL} image to verify the presence of any black signature. Here, the smaller regions identified after run length smearing operation [22] are neglected from the detected signature image to suppress noise.

4   Experimental Results

In our experiments, to evaluate the performance of detection of logo, stamp and signature, we consider the techniques reported in [3, 4, 16]. The performance comparison in terms of precision, recall, and F-score metrics of the detection methods for the new SPODS dataset is presented in Table 4. We have implemented the techniques for detection of stamp [4] and signature [3], and verified their results on datasets reported in [4], and [3], respectively.

For the technique detecting stamps in [4], we have used a training set consisting of 10 documents from the SPODS dataset and performance results are reported on the remaining 1078 document images. The performance of technique [16] to detect logo and stamp is also reported in Table 4. As the technique [16] does not consider the presence of signature in document, its precision for stamp detection is low.

To train the classifier using majority voting scheme, we have used a signature dataset separately obtained by volunteers. These samples are not taken from the SPODS dataset. These are used to evaluate the performances of the technique reported in [3] and for the proposed SFPF. This training set consists of 110 different signatures. For non-signature training set, we have used a few document images from StaVer [15] dataset containing logos, stamps, text, etc. The results of this experiment show that the performance of the proposed approach to detect logo, stamp, and signature is satisfactory. The signature detection is reported at pixel level depicting strokes in the signature. Hence, the signature detection is reported with more precision in locating them.

Table 4. Performance evaluation on SPODS dataset

Technique	Detected region	Recall	Precision	F-score
ORB based method [4] to detect stamp	Stamp	0.64	0.66	0.67
Method [3] to detect signature	Signature	0.84	0.82	0.85
Method [16] to detect (logo, stamp)	Logo	0.98	0.99	0.99
	Stamp	0.91	0.69	0.76
Proposed SFPF method to detect (logo, stamp, signature)	Logo	0.98	0.99	**0.99**
	Stamp	0.90	0.89	**0.87**
	Signature	0.86	0.93	**0.90**

5   Conclusion

In this paper, we present a new document image dataset SPODS and the SFPF technique for detection of logo, stamp, and signature. The dataset consists of documents, which mimic the real world official documents. The SPODS dataset is useful for evaluation of retrieval of document images using logo, stamp, signature based queries as well as textual attribute based queries such as document date, etc. The dataset is provided with proper pixel-level ground truth images for logo, stamp, signature, and text contents for evaluating performance of detection and classification. To our knowledge, till date this is the only document image dataset, which provides the ground truth for signature at pixel level to represent the strokes in signature. Also, the ground truth data useful for measuring retrieval performance is provided. It would help for standardizing the evaluation and comparison of different methods proposed for document image retrieval.

The proposed SFPF technique provides a unified framework for detection of logo, stamp, and signature present in document images. It uses spectral filtering and part based features. The performance of SFPF technique to detect logo, stamp, and signature is found to be satisfactory in terms of precision, recall, and F-score.

Acknowledgments. This work is partially sponsored by the Ministry of Communications & Information Technology, Govt. of India; Ref.: MCIT 11(19)/2010-HCC (TDIL) dt. 28-12-2010.

References

1. CBIR benchmark databases. http://savvash.blogspot.in/2008/12/benchmark-data bases-for-cbir.html. Accessed 11 Jan 2016
2. Tobacco 800 dataset. http://www.umiacs.umd.edu/~zhugy/tobacco800.html. Accessed 7 Dec 2015
3. Ahmed, S., Malik, M.I., Liwicki, M., Dengel, A.: Signature segmentation from document images. In: International Conference on Frontiers in Handwriting Recognition (ICFHR), pp. 425–429. IEEE (2012)
4. Ahmed, S., Shafait, F., Liwicki, M., Dengel, A.: A generic method for stamp segmentation using part-based features. In: Proceedings of the 12th International Conference on Document Analysis and Recognition (ICDAR), pp. 708–712. IEEE (2013)
5. Bay, H., Ess, A., Tuytelaars, T., Van Gool, L.: Speeded-up robust features (surf). Comput. Vis. Image Underst. **110**(3), 346–359 (2008)
6. Comaniciu, D., Meer, P.: Mean shift: a robust approach toward feature space analysis. IEEE Trans. Pattern Anal. Mach. Intell. **24**(5), 603–619 (2002)
7. Dey, S., Mukherjee, J., Sural, S.: Logo and stamp detection from document images by finding outliers. In: Proceedings of the 5th National Conference on Computer Vision, Pattern Recognition, Image Processing and Graphics (NCVPRIPG). IEEE (2015)
8. Dey, S., Mukherjee, J., Sural, S., Bhowmick, P.: Colored rubber stamp removal from document images. In: Maji, P., Ghosh, A., Murty, M.N., Ghosh, K., Pal, S.K. (eds.) PReMI 2013. LNCS, vol. 8251, pp. 545–550. Springer, Heidelberg (2013). doi:10.1007/978-3-642-45062-4_75

9. Doermann, D., Tombre, K., et al.: Handbook of Document Image Processing and Recognition. Springer, London (2014)
10. Duda, R.O., Hart, P.E., Stork, D.G.: Pattern Classification. Wiley, Hoboken (2012)
11. Jain, R., Doermann, D.: Logo retrieval in document images. In: Proceedings of the 10th IAPR International Workshop on Document Analysis Systems, pp. 135–139. IEEE (2012)
12. Le, V.P., Nayef, N., Visani, M., Ogier, J.M., De Tran, C.: Document retrieval based on logo spotting using key-point matching. In: Proceedings of the 22nd International Conference on Pattern Recognition (ICPR), pp. 3056–3061. IEEE (2014)
13. Liu, L., Yu, M., Shao, L.: Multiview alignment hashing for efficient image search. IEEE Trans. Image Process. **24**(3), 956–966 (2015)
14. Mandal, R., Roy, P.P., Pal, U.: Signature segmentation from machine printed documents using conditional random field. In: Proceedings of the 11th International Conference on Document Analysis and Recognition (ICDAR), pp. 1170–1174. IEEE (2011)
15. Micenková, B., van Beusekom, J.: Stamp detection in color document images. In: Proceedings of the 11th International Conference on Document Analysis and Recognition (ICDAR), pp. 1125–1129. IEEE (2011)
16. Nandedkar, A.V., Mukhopadhyay, J., Sural, S.: Text-graphics separation to detect logo and stamp from color document images: a spectral approach. In: Proceedings of the 13th International Conference on Document Analysis and Recognition (ICDAR), pp. 571–575. IEEE (2015)
17. Roy, P.P., Pal, U., Lladós, J.: Document seal detection using GHT and character proximity graphs. Pattern Recogn. **44**(6), 1282–1295 (2011)
18. Rusiñol, M., Lladós, J.: Efficient logo retrieval through hashing shape context descriptors. In: Proceedings of the 9th IAPR International Workshop on Document Analysis Systems, pp. 215–222. ACM (2010)
19. Smeulders, A.W., Worring, M., Santini, S., Gupta, A., Jain, R.: Content-based image retrieval at the end of the early years. IEEE Trans. Pattern Anal. Mach. Intell. **22**(12), 1349–1380 (2000)
20. Srihari, S.N., Shetty, S., Chen, S., Srinivasan, H., Huang, C., Agam, G., Frieder, O.: Document image retrieval using signatures as queries. In: Proceedings of the 2nd International Conference on Document Image Analysis for Libraries (DIAL), pp. 198–203. IEEE (2006)
21. Wang, H., Chen, Y.: Logo detection in document images based on boundary extension of feature rectangles. In: Proceedings of the 10th International Conference on Document Analysis and Recognition (ICDAR), pp. 1335–1339. IEEE (2009)
22. Wong, K.Y., Casey, R.G., Wahl, F.M.: Document analysis system. IBM J. Res. Dev. **26**(6), 647–656 (1982)
23. Zhu, G., Doermann, D.: Automatic document logo detection. In: Proceedings of the 9th International Conference on Document Analysis and Recognition (ICDAR), vol. 2, pp. 864–868. IEEE (2007)
24. Zhu, G., Zheng, Y., Doermann, D., Jaeger, S.: Signature detection and matching for document image retrieval. IEEE Trans. Pattern Anal. Mach. Intell. **31**(11), 2015–2031 (2009)

Text and Non-text Separation in Scanned Color-Official Documents

Amit Vijay Nandedkar$^{(\boxtimes)}$, Jayanta Mukherjee, and Shamik Sural

Department of Computer Science and Engineering, Indian Institute of Technology, Kharagpur, Kharagpur, India
amitnandedkar@sit.iitkgp.ernet.in, {jay,shamik}@cse.iitkgp.ernet.in

Abstract. Official documents consist of text and non-textual elements such as logo, stamp, and signature. Separation of these elements from a scanned document plays a significant role in document image retrieval, recognition, and verification. This paper presents a novel scheme to separate text and non-text elements of official documents using part-based features. In this work, we exploit the fact that intensity distributions of text and non-text elements in HSV color space are of distinctive nature. A new approach to compute part-based features using S and V channels is proposed. The classification of text and non-text components is performed based on majority voting scheme and K-approximate nearest neighbors. The knowledge base acquired during training is indexed using kD-tree indexing scheme. Subsequently, the method is extended for detection of logo, stamp, and signature. Experimental results show the effectiveness of the proposed approach.

Keywords: Text/non-text separation · Graphics recognition · Document recognition · Color document image

1 Introduction

Paper documents are integral parts of official correspondence and records. In developing countries like India, still official documents are printed, stamped, and personally signed in offices. Digitization of these documents is must for storage and proliferation. A large number of paper documents are scanned for this purpose. Once the document is scanned, retrieving information from it is a challenging task. Therefore, advanced techniques are necessary for the development of automated systems for storage, maintenance and retrieval of images of such documents. *Document Image Retrieval* (DIR) is an active area of research in document image processing. In this work, we consider processing of such documents to accomplish this task.

Official document image may contain several visual attributes such as logos, stamps, signatures, printed and handwritten textual contents. Some of these attributes, e.g., logos, stamps, signatures, indicate the legitimacy and identity of the document source to a reader. Hence, detection of logo, stamp, and signature

© Springer International Publishing AG 2017
S. Mukherjee et al. (Eds.): ICVGIP 2016, LNCS 10481, pp. 231–242, 2017.
https://doi.org/10.1007/978-3-319-68124-5_20

is an important task, needed for document verification, indexing, and retrieval. In the past, a number of works have been reported on retrieval of document images using logo, stamp, signature, etc. [8, 12, 13, 20, 21, 25].

A useful approach for DIR is to apply *Optical Character Recognition* (OCR) algorithms to convert the scanned document images to text data. The textual contents are used in text-based document indexing and retrieval. Text and non-text separation is a necessary step before application of OCR [14]. In recent times, speed and precision of OCR techniques have improved. Moreover, sophisticated scanners are available providing high quality scanned images. It helps in enhancing overall accuracy of OCR algorithms. The text/non-text separation technique should be capable of handling different layout and spatial organization of document contents such as text, signatures, logos, stamps. Some of the approaches are discussed below.

In [22], a run length smoothing technique is proposed for localizing text and image regions. Fletcher and Kasturi [10] proposed Hough transform based grouping of connected components into a logical character string for identifying graphics. Jain and Zhong [11] presented a page segmentation method using texture features and neural network based classification. Qiao et al. [19] proposed a Gabor filter and geometrical property based text extraction from document images containing text, natural scene, artificial pictures, and figures. Chen et al. [6] presented a text line segmentation on scanned images of historical manuscript using color and texture. In [2], the authors presented a method using part-based features for extraction of text touching graphic components in a data set of architectural floor plans and geographical maps.

In the past, there are a few approaches reported for detection and identification of logos and stamps. Zhu and Doermann [24] presented an automatic logo detection method using a boosting strategy across multiple image scales. It considers a priori knowledge of possible logo positions in document images. In [23], the authors presented a logo detection method with an assumption that logos normally have a background, and are isolated by white spaces. These methods handle black and white document images.

For detection of stamp, a few techniques used color, and geometric features. Dey et al. [7] introduced a method to detect color stamp from a document image in HSV color space. It targets document images containing printed text and stamp imprints. In [16], Micenková and van Beusekom presented a method for stamp detection using color clustering and geometrical features. The method is limited to colored stamps of any shapes and forms. Ahmed et al. [4] proposed a stamp detection technique based on geometric features and binary keypoint descriptors that needs training to detect stamps both in black and white, and colored forms. It reported low recall and precision. Nandedkar et al. [18] proposed a spectral approach for text-graphics separation to detect logo and stamp from office documents. The methods reported in [4, 16, 18] targeted the StaVer color document dataset [16], in which the majority of documents are without signature.

A few works have been reported in the literature on signature detection. Zhu et al. [25] presented a technique using multi-scale saliency map for detecting signature in document images. In [15], Mandal et al. proposed the use of a conditional random field for segmentation of signatures from document images. Signature detection is addressed in [3] considering the part-based features and a majority voting mechanism for classification. The performance of [15], and [3] is reported on a subset of 105 document images from black and white Tobacco-800 dataset [1].

The local part-based features are found to be useful in the field of document image processing [2–4]. The part-based features represent an image as a set of key points and their respective robust local descriptors. In this paper, we present a novel approach for the text/non-text separation using proposed part-based features. We further perform the detection of logo, stamp, and signature in non-textual segments. The technique is intended to remove redundant textual contents to simplify non-text (e.g., logo, stamp, signature) based DIR. The separated textual contents can further be processed to support standard text based document retrieval. This work proposes a novel part-based feature descriptor by considering the intensity properties of text/non-text regions in S and V channels of HSV color space. We have applied the well known *Speeded-Up Robust Features* (SURF) [5] descriptor as a tool to analyze characteristics of S and V channels, and proposed a new part-based descriptor for characterizing components of official documents.

The text/non-text separation technique is tested on a dataset of scanned pseudo-official document images (SPODS)[1] prepared by us. This data set is prepared by scanning printed documents with pseudo-official contents mimicking different types of official communication and transactions. These printed documents are manually stamped and signed by volunteers before scanning. Due to confidentiality of real-world official documents, we have used the SPODS data set containing these pseudo-official documents. The SPODS dataset consists of 1088 scanned documents containing logos, stamps, signatures, and printed text. These documents are scanned using HP® Scanjet N9120 scanner. The dataset contains ground truths for the logo, stamp, signature, and text regions. It takes care of variation in font size, style as well as changes in logos, stamps, textual contents, etc. We have also tested our technique on a few original official documents. In the subsequent section, the proposed method for text/non-text separation, and detection of logo, stamp, and signature are discussed. Section 3 presents the performance analysis and Sect. 4 concludes the paper.

2   Part-Based Features for Text/Non-text Separation

The computation is performed in two stages as follows:

(1) Classification and separation of each of the connected components present in a document image into text and non-text elements using proposed part-based features, and
(2) Detection of logo, stamp, and signature from the separated non-textual regions.

---

[1] The dataset is available at http://www.facweb.iitkgp.ernet.in/~jay/spods/.

2.1   Text/Non-text Separation Using Part-Based Feature

The objective of this operation is to compute distinct part-based descriptors, which are useful to identify and separate textual and non-textual contents of a color document image I. The HSV color space is close to the human vision system. We observed that it is effective to use S and V channels of HSV color space for computation of distinct part-based features from color document image. To the best of our knowledge, this is the first effort to compute part-based features using S and V channels of input color document image. The operation of color quantization is performed on the input image I to produce an output image C. The color quantization process reduces the number of colors to 64 (Fig. 1(b)). Next, the image C is converted to HSV color space, and let it be denoted as R. Let G be the gray scale image of I. G is computed as per *National Television System Committee* (NTSC) standard for luminance. The Hessian key points [5] are identified within the gray image G. SURF [5] uses blob detection for identifying key points. In the next step, for the set of detected Hessian keypoints $KEY = \{P_1, P_2, \ldots, P_N\}$, we compute SURF descriptors using S and V channels at the coordinates corresponding to each of Hessian keypoints present in the set KEY.

In case of an official document image, it is observed that in S channel, mostly the graphical objects are highlighted, and the most of textual contents and background are suppressed (refer to Fig. 1(c)), whereas the V channel contains the structural details of the elements present in document image (refer to Fig. 1(d)). If the graphical objects are achromatic in nature, then only structural details are present in V channel and in S channel corresponding region has less information. The part-based descriptors computed using S channel within the region of achromatic texts do not have significant variation in intensity distribution around the key points, whereas the descriptors computed at the same key points using V channel have variation in intensity distribution around the key points. In case of the graphical regions depending on chromaticity, we may have information in both S and V channels. Hence, the S and V channels give different regional properties surrounding key points. Information may be present in either one or

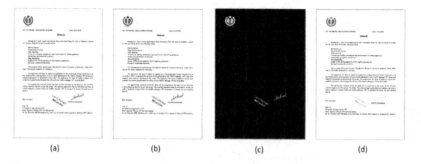

(a)   (b)   (c)   (d)

Fig. 1. (a) Input document (b) color-quantization output (c) S-channel image and (d) V-channel image. (Color figure online)

Table 1. Text and non-text statistics for total 136,195 key points

Group	No. of samples (N)	Set			S-channel	Set			V-channel
Text	126679	A	Mean		5.0	E	Mean		205.4
			SD		6.6		SD		26.7
		B	Mean		26.2	F	Mean		89.6
			SD		15.4		SD		20.8
Non-text	9516	C	Mean		68.2	G	Mean		219.5
			SD		50.6		SD		51.9
		D	Mean		88.0	H	Mean		43.2
			SD		27.7		SD		35.9

Note: (i) A, C, E, and G indicate set of average intensity values around key points, (ii) B, D, F, and H indicate set of standard deviations of intensity values around key points.

both channels (S and V) depending on chromaticity of the objects. As V channel contains most of the structural details present in the document, the color information is not always required for text/non-text separation. The method is designed to deal with achromatic non-text objects as well.

In this work, we exploit these facts for text/non-text separation. Table 1 represents an analysis of intensity distribution within the neighborhood of detected Hessian key points for text and non-text regions. This analysis is performed for the S and V channels of image separately. It shows statistics of their values (called intensity here) for regions around 126679 and 9516 key points detected in text and non-text regions, respectively. These keypoints are detected from 10 different representative document images. The neighborhood size ($20\,s \times 20\,s$) is determined by the scale s at which the respective Hessian key point [5] is detected. Here, s represents the value in scale space relevant to the detected Hessian key point.

From Table 1, it can be concluded that in S channel, the textual regions have low average intensity and the standard deviation is also less compared to non-textual regions. Also, it is observed that the textual areas show significant intensity variations in V channel. The statistical significance test (Student's t-test) is performed using Matlab® on the observed facts. The outcome of Student's t-test is given in Table 2 by comparing different sets of data. The observations are also summarized in Table 2.

These facts are considered for text/non-text separation by computing the keypoint descriptors using S and V channels. Hence, a combination of two types of descriptors computed using S and V channels is more discriminative to classify the textual and non-textual regions. Now, the descriptors computed using S and V channels are concatenated to provide new distinct part-based features (refer to Fig. 2) as: $D_i = [D_{S_i} \| D_{V_i}]_{1 \times 128}$, where D_{S_i} and D_{V_i} are 64 dimensional SURF descriptors at key point P_i $(1 \leq i \leq N)$ computed using S and V channels, respectively, in HSV color space of image C. Here, N indicates the number of the

Table 2. Student's t-test for verification of observed facts

Assumption	Set 1	Set 2	Hypothesis result (h)	P-value	Degree of freedom (df)	Confidence interval (ci)		Observation
						Lower bound	Upper bound	
Equal mean and variance	A	C	1	0	136193	-63.5	-62.9	Ob1
	B	F	1	0	253356	-63.5	-63.2	Ob2
	A	E	1	0	253356	-200.5	-200.2	Ob3
Equal mean, but not equal variance	A	C	1	0	9539	-64.2	-62.2	Ob1
	B	F	1	0	233985	-63.5	-63.2	Ob2
	A	E	1	0	142247	-200.5	-200.2	Ob3

Note: The significance level of ($\alpha = 0.05$) is used for Student's t-test. Here, $h = 1$ indicates hypothesis is rejected (i.e. $p < \alpha$) and negative value of confidence interval indicates the set 2 is having higher mean value.
Ob1: Textual regions in S-channel have low average intensity compared to non-textual regions in S-channel.
Ob2: Textual regions in S-channel have low standard deviation of intensity compared to standard deviation of intensity of textual regions in V-channel.
Ob3: Textual regions in S-channel have low average intensity compared to average intensity of textual regions in V-channel.

key points, and '$\parallel$' denotes concatenation operation. Now, the part-based features D_i are bagged for each connected component CC_j present in the document image separately. The bagging operation provides a set of proposed part-based features corresponding to the key points present inside the bounding box of connected component CC_j. Here, $j \leq M$, and M indicates the number of connected components present in the document image I. If the coordinates of detected key points are within the bounding box of CC_j, their respective modified part-based features D_i are bagged together for classification using majority voting scheme.

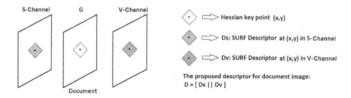

Fig. 2. Computation of proposed part-based descriptor for color document image. (Color figure online)

Figure 3 shows the block diagram of the proposed text/non-text separation process used for classification of each of the connected components present in the document image I. Here, the training set consists of a set of text and non-text samples. Their respective modified part-based features are computed and retained as an acquired knowledge base. Here, the Fast Library for Approximate Nearest Neighbors (FLANN) [17] is used. The features present in the knowledge base are indexed using the kD-tree indexing scheme available in FLANN. The bagged part-based features of connected component CC_j are used for the classification of CC_j. For each part-based feature, the class labels of three nearest neighbors present in the knowledge base are identified using FLANN. Finally, the technique counts the number of votes for text and non-text class. The class

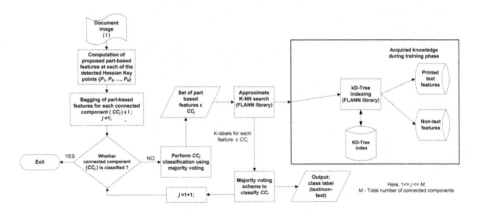

Fig. 3. Block diagram of proposed process of text/non-text separation.

label with the maximum voting number is assigned to the respective connected component CC_j. Hence, the regions declared as textual areas are used for formation of the textual output image by extracting respective regions from the document image I. The extracted textual image is called $D_{TEXTUAL}$. In a similar way, the non-textual $D_{NON\_TEXTUAL}$ image is generated. Figures 4(b) and (c) present the text/non-text separated images of a document image (refer to Fig. 4(a)).

To show the effectiveness of proposed part-based features, in Table 3, we have compared the performance of text/non-text separation using SURF and proposed part-based features. It is observed that the performance of proposed part-based descriptor is better compared to SURF, and is found to retain most of the non-textual elements. Hence, the proposed descriptor D_i is suitable for separation of text/non-text elements from document images. In the subsequent section, the details of detection of logo, stamp, and signature are discussed.

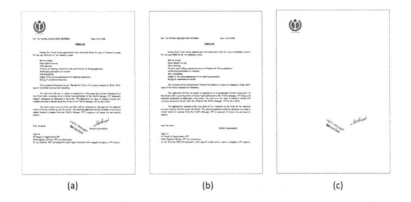

Fig. 4. An example of (a) input document (b) text image and (c) non-text image.

Table 3. Performance comparison using SURF and proposed part-based features on SPODS dataset

Method	Detected region	Recall	Precision	F-score
Method 1 (using SURF features)	Text	0.997	0.979	0.988
	Non-text	0.923	0.993	0.955
Method 2 (using proposed part-based features)	Text	0.992	0.993	0.995
	Non-text	0.995	0.971	0.981

2.2 Detection of Candidate Regions Depicting Logo, Stamp, and Signature

For detection of logos, we have considered knowledge of probable positions of logos in the document dataset as mentioned in [18]. A k-means clustering algorithm [9] is used to cluster the centroid and spread of logos from the ground truths in a normalized coordinate space. The normalization is performed by the height of the document. In our experiment, we empirically kept the number of clusters 10. The number of foreground pixels is computed in the surrounding of each probable logo position within a window in the non-textual output image (refer to Fig. 4(c)). A candidate logo with the number of foreground pixels greater than a threshold value is declared as a logo. Figure 5(a) presents an example of logo detected image, and Fig. 5(b) depicts the remaining (stamp and signature) non-text image (refer to Fig. 4(c)). In the next step, the stamp and signature are separated. Here, we use the part-based SURF features and majority voting scheme using FLANN. The part-based SURF features of 64 dimensions are computed at each detected Hessian key point in the input image. We extract the part-based features from G, the grayscale version of the input image (e.g., Fig. 5(b)). During the training phase, we use labeled training data representing

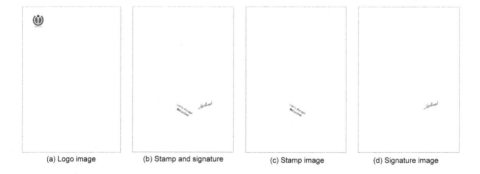

(a) Logo image   (b) Stamp and signature   (c) Stamp image   (d) Signature image

Fig. 5. An example of logo, stamp, and signature detection.

signature and non-signature feature sets. Each of the connected components are classified using majority voting scheme with three approximate nearest neighbors. If majority of the features vote for signature class, the corresponding region is declared as a signature region. Otherwise, the signature is not present in the non-text output. Figures 5(c) and (d) illustrate the detected stamp image and signature image, respectively, after applying the signature detection process.

3   Experimental Results and Discussion

Performance measures such as precision, recall, and F-score are used to evaluate detection of the logo, stamp, and signature in the SPODS dataset. They are presented in Table 4. In these experiments, to compare the performance of text/non-text separation, and detection of logo, stamp and signature, we consider the techniques reported in [3,4,18]. For stamp detection [4], we have used a training set of 10 documents from the SPODS dataset and performance results are reported on the remaining 1078 document images. The performance of the SFTGS [18] technique for text, non-text, logo and stamp detection is also presented here. As the SFTGS algorithm does not assume the presence of a signature in the document, its precision for stamp detection is low.

In case of signature detection, a separate training set of 110 different signatures is created. The instances of the signatures present in the training set

Table 4. Performance evaluation on SPODS dataset

Method	Detected region	Recall	Precision	F-score
ORB based method [4] to detect stamp	Stamp	0.64	0.66	0.67
Method [3] to detect signature	Signature	0.84	0.82	0.85
SFTGS [18] to detect (text, non-text, logo, and stamp)	Text	0.97	0.98	0.96
	Non-text	0.96	0.94	0.94
	Logo	0.98	0.99	0.99
	Stamp	0.91	0.69	0.76
Proposed method to detect (text, non-text, logo, stamp, and signature)	Text	0.99	0.99	**0.99**
	Non-text	0.99	0.97	**0.98**
	Logo	0.98	0.99	**0.99**
	Stamp	0.95	0.91	**0.92**
	Signature	0.92	0.84	**0.89**

are not present in any of the SPODS dataset document images. These 110 signatures are taken from a completely different group of volunteers. For other elements of documents, we have used images of logos, stamps, text from StaVer [16] dataset for creating training sets. These sets are used to train the signature detection method [3] and the proposed method. The training sets are different from SPODS dataset to verify the generalization capability of the proposed technique. The results of this experiment show that performance of the proposed approach to separate text/non-text and to detect stamp, and signature is superior to other techniques. Performance of signature detection is reported at a precise pixel-level as the ground truths of signatures are available as a set of pixels depicting strokes in the signature.

Figures 6 and 7 present typical examples of text and non-text separation of some real office documents using the proposed approach. It is noted that the proposed technique is also able to separate the non-targeted graphical elements such as photo (refer to Fig. 6). However, graphics styled chromatic text may appear in the non-textual output image as noise. It may affect the performance of text/non-text separation and any subsequent process depending on text/non-text separation. Figure 7(a) shows the document image containing achromatic

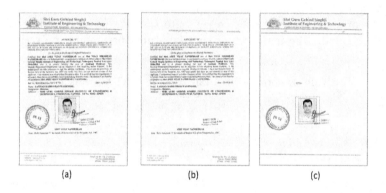

(a)   (b)   (c)

Fig. 6. (a) Office document (1) (b) text image and (c) non-text image.

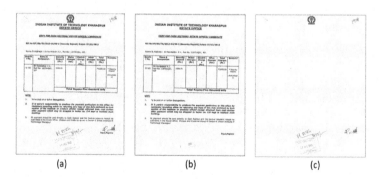

(a)   (b)   (c)

Fig. 7. (a) Office document (2) (b) text image and (c) non-text image. (Color figure online)

logo, signature, and color stamp, and Fig. 7(c) depicts the separation of such non-textual elements. The part-based features are not always suitable for the separation of severely overlapped text and non-text regions as classification is on the basis of connected components.

4 Conclusion

In this paper, we present a novel method for text/non-text separation and detection of the logo, stamp, and signature. The proposed technique is based on newly proposed part-based features computed using S and V channels of HSV color space. From the separated non-text elements, it detects logo, stamp, and signature regions. The knowledge base acquired during training phase is indexed using KD-tree indexing scheme, and is found suitable for text/non-text separation. Experimental results show a satisfactory performance of the proposed technique on a large dataset. The text/non-text separation operation can simplify the document image retrieval using either text based or visual attributes based document retrieval.

Acknowledgments. This work is partially sponsored by the Ministry of Communications & Information Technology, Govt. of India; Ref.: MCIT 11(19)/2010-HCC (TDIL) dt. 28-12-2010.

References

1. Tobacoo 800 dataset. http://www.umiacs.umd.edu/~zhugy/tobacco800.html. Accessed 7 Dec 2015
2. Ahmed, S., Liwicki, M., Dengel, A.: Extraction of text touching graphics using SURF. In: 10th IAPR International Workshop on Document Analysis Systems (DAS), pp. 349–353. IEEE (2012)
3. Ahmed, S., Malik, M.I., Liwicki, M., Dengel, A.: Signature segmentation from document images. In: International Conference on Frontiers in Handwriting Recognition (ICFHR), pp. 425–429. IEEE (2012)
4. Ahmed, S., Shafait, F., Liwicki, M., Dengel, A.: A generic method for stamp segmentation using part-based features. In: 12th International Conference on Document Analysis and Recognition (ICDAR), pp. 708–712. IEEE (2013)
5. Bay, H., Ess, A., Tuytelaars, T., Van Gool, L.: Speeded-up robust features (SURF). Comput. Vis. Image Underst. **110**(3), 346–359 (2008)
6. Chen, K., Wei, H., Liwicki, M., Hennebert, J., Ingold, R.: Robust text line segmentation for historical manuscript images using color and texture. In: 22nd International Conference on Pattern Recognition (ICPR), pp. 2978–2983. IEEE (2014)
7. Dey, S., Mukherjee, J., Sural, S., Bhowmick, P.: Colored rubber stamp removal from document images. In: Maji, P., Ghosh, A., Murty, M.N., Ghosh, K., Pal, S.K. (eds.) PReMI 2013. LNCS, vol. 8251, pp. 545–550. Springer, Heidelberg (2013). doi:10.1007/978-3-642-45062-4_75
8. Doermann, D., Tombre, K., et al.: Handbook of Document Image Processing and Recognition. Springer, London (2014). doi:10.1007/978-0-85729-859-1
9. Duda, R.O., Hart, P.E., Stork, D.G.: Pattern Classification. Wiley, Hoboken (2012)

10. Fletcher, L.A., Kasturi, R.: A robust algorithm for text string separation from mixed text/graphics images. IEEE Trans. Pattern Anal. Mach. Intell. **10**(6), 910–918 (1988)

11. Jain, A.K., Zhong, Y.: Page segmentation using texture analysis. Pattern Recogn. **29**(5), 743–770 (1996)

12. Jain, R., Doermann, D.: Logo retrieval in document images. In: 10th IAPR International Workshop on Document Analysis Systems, pp. 135–139. IEEE (2012)

13. Le, V.P., Nayef, N., Visani, M., Ogier, J.M., De Tran, C.: Document retrieval based on logo spotting using key-point matching. In: 22nd International Conference on Pattern Recognition (ICPR), pp. 3056–3061. IEEE (2014)

14. Maderlechner, G., Suda, P., Brückner, T.: Classification of document by form and content. Pattern Recogn. Lett. **18**, 1225–1231 (1997)

15. Mandal, R., Roy, P.P., Pal, U.: Signature segmentation from machine printed documents using conditional random field. In: International Conference on Document Analysis and Recognition (ICDAR), pp. 1170–1174. IEEE (2011)

16. Micenková, B., van Beusekom, J.: Stamp detection in color document images. In: International Conference on Document Analysis and Recognition (ICDAR), pp. 1125–1129. IEEE (2011)

17. Muja, M., Lowe, D.G.: Fast approximate nearest neighbors with automatic algorithm configuration. Int. Conf. Comput. Vis. Theory Appl. (VISAPP) **2**, 331–340 (2009)

18. Nandedkar, A.V., Mukhopadhyay, J., Sural, S.: Text-graphics separation to detect logo and stamp from color document images: a spectral approach. In: 13th International Conference on Document Analysis and Recognition (ICDAR), pp. 571–575. IEEE (2015)

19. Qiao, Y.L., Li, M., Lu, Z.M., Sun, S.H.: Gabor filter based text extraction from digital document images. In: International Conference on Intelligent Information Hiding and Multimedia Signal Processing, (IIH-MSP), pp. 297–300. IEEE (2006)

20. Roy, P.P., Pal, U., Lladós, J.: Document seal detection using ght and character proximity graphs. Pattern Recogn. **44**(6), 1282–1295 (2011)

21. Rusiñol, M., Lladós, J.: Efficient logo retrieval through hashing shape context descriptors. In: Proceedings of the 9th IAPR International Workshop on Document Analysis Systems, pp. 215–222. ACM (2010)

22. Wahl, F.M., Wong, K.Y., Casey, R.G.: Block segmentation and text extraction in mixed text/image documents. Comput. Graph. Image Process. **20**(4), 375–390 (1982)

23. Wang, H., Chen, Y.: Logo detection in document images based on boundary extension of feature rectangles. In: 10th International Conference on Document Analysis and Recognition (ICDAR), pp. 1335–1339. IEEE (2009)

24. Zhu, G., Doermann, D.: Automatic document logo detection. In: 9th International Conference on Document Analysis and Recognition (ICDAR), vol. 2, pp. 864–868. IEEE (2007)

25. Zhu, G., Zheng, Y., Doermann, D., Jaeger, S.: Signature detection and matching for document image retrieval. IEEE Trans. Pattern Anal. Mach. Intell. **31**(11), 2015–2031 (2009)

Multi-font Telugu Text Recognition Using Hidden Markov Models and Akshara Bi-grams

Koteswara Rao Devarapalli[1,2]($\boxtimes$) and Atul Negi[2]

[1] Department of Computer Science and Engineering,
Mahatma Gandhi Institute of Technology, Hyderabad 500075, India
`dkrao@mgit.ac.in`
[2] School of Computer and Information Sciences, University of Hyderabad,
Gachibowli, Hyderabad 500046, India

Abstract. Recent advances in the information technology made possible to introduce many Unicode Telugu fonts for the documentation needs of present society. But the recognition of documents printed in a variety of fonts poses new challenges in building Telugu OCR systems. In this paper, we demonstrate multi-font Telugu printed word recognition using implicit segmentation approach that provides segmentation as a by-product of recognition. Our word recognition approach relies on Hidden Markov Models and *akshara* bi-gram language model to recognize word images in terms of *aksharas* (characters). The training set of word images is prepared from document images of popular books and the synthetic document images generated using 8 different Unicode fonts. The testing involves matching the feature vector sequence against sequence of *akshara* HMMs based on bi-grams. The CER and WER of this system are 21% and 37% respectively. The performance of our system is very encouraging.

Keywords: Akshara · Bi-gram · DCT · HMM · Telugu OCR · Word recognition

1 Introduction

With advances in information technology, many Telugu fonts are introduced for the documentation needs of present society. Recently developed Unicode fonts for Telugu text editing has made the documentation amazing. A wide variety of font types are in daily use for the documentation needs of print, electronic media, and different organizations. Although there are some contributions made to recognize multi-font Telugu printed text [4,11,13], they target for the recognition of text printed in a few commonly used fonts and those methods can not be directly used for the recognition of text printed in a wide variety of fonts. Hence, the conversion of document images of multi-font Telugu printed text to machine readable form needs suitable novel methods and the necessity of Telugu OCR system to recognize printed text with variations in font has arisen. In addition

© Springer International Publishing AG 2017
S. Mukherjee et al. (Eds.): ICVGIP 2016, LNCS 10481, pp. 243–254, 2017.
https://doi.org/10.1007/978-3-319-68124-5_21

to the complexity of Telugu script, printed text with font variations has become a big challenge to the Telugu OCR systems. The Telugu OCR systems need to be robust enough to recognize arbitrary collection of printed documents with font variations and degradations. In achieving that there are the limitations such as lack of enough examples with natural variations and lack of documentation available about the possible font variations [4]. In Fig. 1, we show an example of multi-font Telugu printed text.

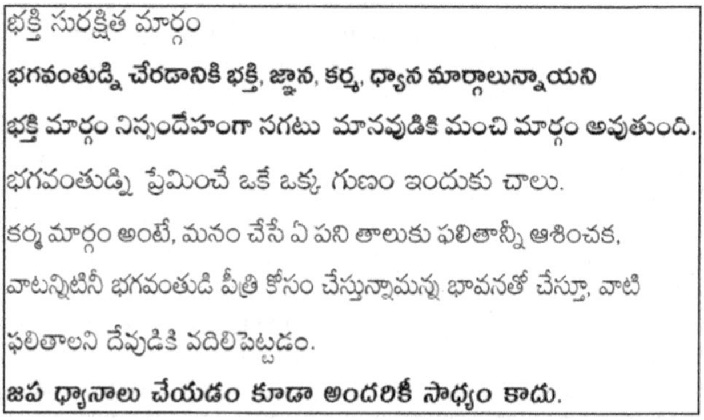

Fig. 1. Example of multi-font Telugu printed text. The lines are shown from the top to bottom in eight unicode fonts called Mandali, Ramabhadra, Ramaraja, Peddana, Mallanna, Tenali Ramakrishna, Suranna, and Timmana, respectively.

Telugu language is mainly spoken in two south Indian states: Andhra Pradesh and Telangana. Telugu has its own beautiful script, which is written from left-to-right and the text is composed of *aksharas* (characters). An *akshara* is a basic unit of writing that is made up of glyphs. The Telugu orthography has glyphs for vowels, vowel modifiers, consonants, and consonant modifiers. The basic *akshara* set consists of 16 vowels and 36 consonants, though the script is written from left-to-right, vowel modifiers are placed above the consonants and consonant modifiers are written at the below-left, below, and below-right sides of consonants. According to Unicode, the whole *akshara* set comprises of *aksharas* of the form: C^*V^*, where C is a consonant or consonant modifier, and V is a vowel or vowel modifier. In Unicode representation, codes from 0C01 to 0C39, 0C3E to 0C56, and 0C66 to 0C6F are given for Telugu basic *aksharas*, vowel modifiers and numerals respectively. A special character halant (0C4D) is used to define Unicode representation for a consonant modifier. The development of Telugu OCR system involves *akshara* recognition, which is challenging due to large number of like-shaped *aksharas*.

Many of the previous contributions are made for building Telugu OCR based on connected component approach [5,9] and very few of them used language models for recognition. One of the first work appeared in [13] for the recognition of multi-font Telugu characters printed in three popular fonts such as

Harshapriya, Godavari, and Hemalatha in three font sizes. They used connected component approach for segmenting the basic symbols and identified 386 classes of basic symbols that form Telugu basic and compound characters. Based on the type of font used, vowel as well as consonant modifiers may be separated from or connected to a base character that defines the number of basic symbols. They extracted direction features and employed nearest neighbor classifier scheme for recognition.

Another work presented in [11], they explored multi-font Telugu character recognition using histogram of oriented gradients (HOG) features extracted on samples of 359 character classes printed in 15 fonts and SVM classifier is trained. The work presented in [4], they described how to recognize robustly seven major Indic scripts despite font variations and large degradations. They used profile features to represent a word image as a feature sequence and bidirectional long-short term memory (BLSTM) recurrent neural network scheme is used for classification. This neural network scheme allows words to be presented as a sequence of unsegmented features in order to overcome the character segmentation issues in Indian Languages. In [1], they demonstrated omni-font English and Arabic character recognition systems using HMMs. In the literature, many contributions appeared for building character recognition systems based on HMMs in [2,3,8,12].

In our work, we model *akshara* shapes for building Telugu OCR system. Though it has similarity with Hindi OCR based on HMMs. Here, we use 180 *akshara* models to establish the recognition system for Telugu script, whereas Hindi OCR in [8] reported recognition performance based on 50 character models. Our system encompasses the extraction of DCT features to model left-to-right continuous density *akshara* HMMs for representing *akshara* shapes. DCT feature extraction method aims to represent each *akshara* shape as frequency coefficients. The main objective of applying HMMs is to attempt implicit segmentation for Telugu word image recognition that does not need prior segmentation of words into *aksharas* and achieve the segmentation by recognition. The word recognition consists of matching feature vector sequence against sequence of akshara HMMs based on *akshara* bi-gram language model in a maximum likelihood manner.

The paper is organized as follows: we discuss the Hidden Markov Model method in Sect. 2. Language models computation is described in Sect. 3. In Sect. 4, the proposed approach is given. We describe the training of *akshara* HMMs and testing of Telugu words in Sect. 5. Our experiments are described in Sect. 6. Finally, the conclusions are made in Sect. 7.

2   Hidden Markov Models

A Hidden Markov Model is a doubly stochastic process [10]. The Hidden Markov Models are successfully applied for modeling sequence data. Speech recognition is a well known application of HMMs. Similar to speech signal as well as hand-written script, and other real world patterns such as Telugu printed word images written from left-to-right composed of *aksharas* can be modeled as the sequence data that pass through a sequence of states. The states are hidden whereas observation at each point along the word image implies the state. For representing each akshara, we use a 8-state left-right continuous density HMM that has been shown in Fig. 2 with first and last states are empty in order to allow the connectivity between *akshara* models for specifying words. The probability of generating observation is determined by Gaussian mixture components. The state is described by the mean, variance vectors and mixture component weights and it is represented by the frame of an akshara. The system variables such as the frame width, and number of states per *akshara* model are 8-pixels, and 8-states respectively. All these variables are chosen empirically and experimental details are given in Sect. 6.

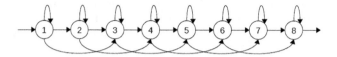

Fig. 2. Structure of *akshara* HMM.

3 Language Models

Language models have widely employed in speech and handwritten recognition applications. The intent of a language model is to predict the sequence of patterns occurring in test data from the frequency of its occurrence in training data. The characters and words are very common patterns in the OCR applications. Further, an n-gram is a sequence of n patterns and the n-gram language model can be used to predict each pattern in the sequence given its n − 1 predecessors. Particularly, the bi-gram is a sequence of two patterns, whereas tri-gram is a sequence of three patterns. Both bi-gram and tri-gram language models have widely applied for building character recognition applications in the literature. There are few previous contributions that applied language models for Telugu character recognition. Our work includes the use of *akshara* bi-gram language model to predict the next *akshara* in a sequence of two *aksharas* given its predecessor. The probability of an *akshara* sequence, $P(\hat{A})$ can be approximated as a product of conditional probabilities [15] and is given as follows:

$$\hat{P}(a_1, a_2, \ldots, a_m) \simeq \prod_{i=1}^{m} \hat{P}(a_i | a_{i-n+1}, \ldots, a_{i-1}) for \ n \geq 1 \qquad (1)$$

$$\text{where } \hat{P}(a_i | a_{i-n+1}, \ldots, a_{i-1}) = \frac{C(a_{i-n+1}, \ldots, a_i)}{C(a_{i-n+1}, \ldots, a_{i-1})}$$

where C(.) is the count of a given *akshara* sequence in the context. Particularly, the probabilities in an n-gram model can be estimated by counting *akshara* sequences in the ground truth as given in Eq. 1.

4   Proposed Approach

Despite HMMs suitability to model sequential data with variations such hand written text and speech. Our novel approach to recognize multi-font Telugu printed text uses two morphological operations: thinning [6] and re-thickening. Actually the idea of thinning *akshara* patterns of word images then re-thickening to standard thickness is aimed to increase robustness in view of font variation. We use sliding window [2,3] method to obtain frames from Telugu word images. For each frame, we extract a DCT feature vector. The feature vectors are used to model one left-to-right continuous density *akshara* HMM per one *akshara* class [8,12]. We model 180 very frequently occurred *akshara* shapes for Telugu OCR. The Telugu word recognition uses implicit segmentation that involves matching feature vector sequence of testing word image against sequence of *akshara* HMMs based on *akshara* bi-gram language model in a maximum likelihood manner.

4.1   Preprocessing

The main role of preprocessing is to convert the input Telugu document images into data of desirable form in such a way that it can be readily used for extracting useful features. Different preprocessing tasks such as noise removal, binarization, line segmentation, and word segmentation are used in this work. First, we use 3×3 median filter for the removal of commonly occurred kind of noise called salt-and-pepper noise. The binarization is performed using Otsu's method to convert Gray scale document images into binary images. The horizontal projection profiles (HPPs) and vertical projection profiles (VPPs) of binary document images are used to segment lines and words respectively. We also exploit two morphological operations: thinning and re-thickening of Telugu word images to bring them into standard form despite font variation.

4.2   Thinning

We intend to perform thinning operation on Telugu word images for reducing *akshara* patterns as much as possible without changing their general shape. Thinning reduces an image while keeping its topological and geometric properties unchanged. Actually thinning involves either deleting or retaining a foreground pixel based on the configuration of pixels in its local neighborhood. We perform thinning operation based on standard algorithms for converting Telugu word images with font variations into standard form [6,14]. The outcome of thinning is a skeleton which is a collection of thin arcs and curves. In our work, thinning reduces each *akshara* pattern of the given word into a skeleton through deleting layers of pixels on its boundary.

4.3   Re-thickening

The re-thickening operation consists of changing the width of strokes of *aksharas* uniformly despite font variations. That is, it involves increasing the width of

Fig. 3. Structuring element used for dilation operation.

strokes of a pattern using dilation operation. Dilation is the basic operation to add pixels on the boundary of a given image. Since thinning operation causes an image to loss successive layers of pixels on its boundary, the image can regain pixels on its boundary to standard thickness through re-thickening. We use the standard structuring element shown in Fig. 3 to perform dilation in order to uniformly increase *akshara* stroke width in such a way that the *akshara* has standard thickness. The sample multi-font Telugu printed word images and their equivalents after performing the morphological operations: thinning and re-thickening are shown in Fig. 4.

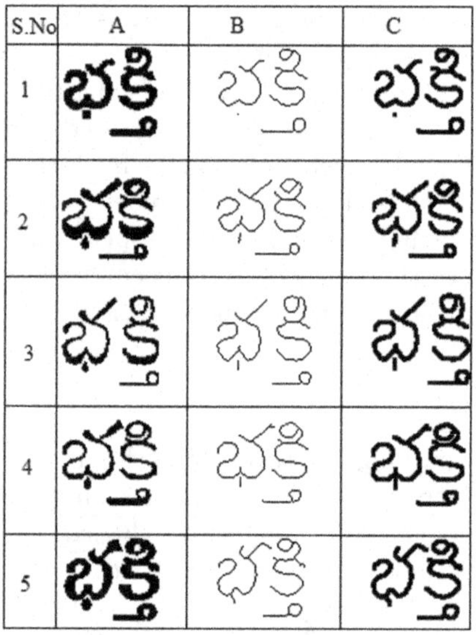

Fig. 4. Examples of multi-font word images, their thinned and re-thickened equivalents are given in A, B and C columns respectively.

4.4 Feature Extraction

We intend to use discrete cosine transform (DCT) to extract significant information from Telugu word images in order to represent *akshara* shapes. The DCT is a real-valued discrete sinusoidal unitary transform. It is a widely used mathematical tool for converting an image from the spatial domain to frequency domain through projecting onto a set of basis functions. Thus the DCT allows us to extract elementary frequency components as features from an image without changing its information content.

$$Dpq = \alpha_p \alpha_q \sum_{k=0}^{M-1} \sum_{l=0}^{N-1} I_{kl} \cos \frac{\pi(2k+1)p}{2M} \cos \frac{\pi(2l+1)q}{2N} \qquad (2)$$

$$\text{where } \alpha_p = \sqrt{1/M} \ if \ p = 0, \ \sqrt{2/M} \ if \ p \neq 0$$

$$\alpha_q = \sqrt{1/N} \ if \ q = 0, \ \sqrt{2/N} \ if \ q \neq 0$$

where I and D are the frame of an *akshara* and its DCT transform respectively. During feature extraction, we use sliding widow along word images in writing order to obtain frames. In Fig. 5(a), all operations performed toward extraction of frames are shown. The width and height of our sliding window is 8 and 80 pixels respectively with no overlapping between windows. So the feature vector is of 640-dimensional. For each frame, we perform DCT transform and then map the resultant matrix into a 1-D feature vector. We make use of feature vectors extracted from training set for modeling *akshara* HMMs, while feature vectors obtained from test set are matched against sequence of *akshara* HMMs based on bi-grams to recognize *aksharas* and words.

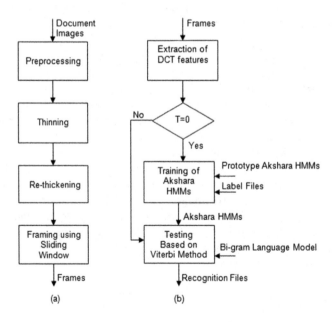

Fig. 5. The structure of multi-font Telugu printed word recognition system: (a) framing, (b) training and testing.

5   Training and Testing Processes

The HMM tool kit (HTK) development environment is used for training of *akshara* HMMs and to test Telugu word images [15]. The training is performed using the HERest tool of HTK that is based on Baum-Welch algorithm. Whereas the HVite tool, which is based on Viterbi algorithm, is used for testing. Both the processes are shown in Fig. 5 and the control variable T is used to choose between them.

5.1   Training Process

The training process involves various tasks such as prototype *akshara* HMM specification, initialization of *akshara* HMMs, parameter estimation and model refinement. The input to the training process are feature vectors extracted from training set, prototype *akshara* HMMs and label files. During training, once the feature vectors extracted from training set are ready, we use HCompV tool to compute global variance. Then, the states of prototype model are set in such a way that mean is initialized to vector of zeros, while the variance is set to global variance. Thus all required initial models are defined based on the prototype *akshara* HMM. Finally we employ embedded training approach for parameter estimation that involves simultaneous estimation of mean, variance, and Gaussian component mixture weights of all states of all *akshara* models appeared in the training set. The model refinement consists of modifying the models and then re-estimating their parameters.

5.2   Testing Process

The whole objective of the system can be fulfilled through testing process. The testing process involves recognition of words and *aksharas* through matching feature vector sequences against *akshara* HMMs. The standard Viterbi decoder is used to match feature vector sequence against *akshara* HMMs, whereas the HVite decoder can be used for matching feature vector sequence against sequence of *akshara* HMMs (word). The HVite decoder is based on both Viterbi and token passing algorithm [15]. During testing, the decoder needs feature vectors extracted on testing set of word images, trained *akshara* HMMs, and bi-gram language model. The testing process consists of matching the feature vector sequence against sequence of akshara HMMs based on bi-gram language model in order to find the maximum likelihood *akshara* HMM sequence that describes the recognized word in the system.

6   Experiments

Our training and testing data are 7000 word images segmented from 35 document images of books printed in 4 widely used Telugu fonts. Data also includes 900 word images segmented from synthetic document images generated in 8 Unicode

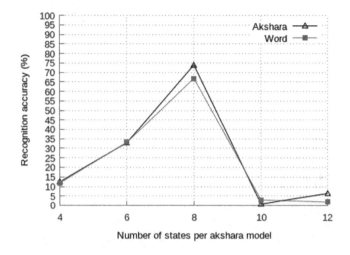

Fig. 6. *Akshara* and word recognition percent accuracies as the functions of states.

fonts. In our experiment, we extract DCT features from 4950 Telugu word images to train 180 *akshara* models. Whereas the *akshara* bi-grams are computed for 180 *aksharas* on the text corpus of 10,000 words that are most frequently used in the Telugu language. We use 850 word images to validate our approach, whereas the test set of 700 word images is employed to establish the performance.

Validation of the approach is performed to evaluate how our recognition system is meeting the requirements and to fix system parameters such as sliding window width and number of states per model. The standard metric called *percent accuracy* is used to demonstrate how the system recognition capability varies with number of states per model. In order to fix the number of states per *akshara* model, we define *akshara* models with a different number of states such as 4, 6, 8, 10 and 12. Then, the models are trained using feature vectors extracted from fixed width frames of 8-pixels and both the *akshara* as well as word recognition capabilities are evaluated. We empirically observe good recognition capability with *akshara* models of 8-states and frame width of 8-pixels. The percent accuracy curves of *akshara* and word recognition results are shown in Fig. 6. Moreover, the character error rate (CER), and word error rate (WER) metrics are used for representing cost to the user of a given recognition system [7] in the literature, so we intend to report the system performance using the CER, and WER. The CER is defined as follows:

$$CER = \frac{D + I + S}{T} \tag{3}$$

where D, I, S, and T denote deletion, insertion, substitution errors and T represents the total number of characters in the ground truth respectively. For each word of the test set of 700 word images, feature vector sequence computed is matched against sequence of *akshara* HMMs based on bi-gram language model

Table 1. Telugu *akshara* and word error rates

Type of preprocessing	CER	WER
Without preprocessing	35	50
After thinning	35	56
After thinning and re-thickening	21	37

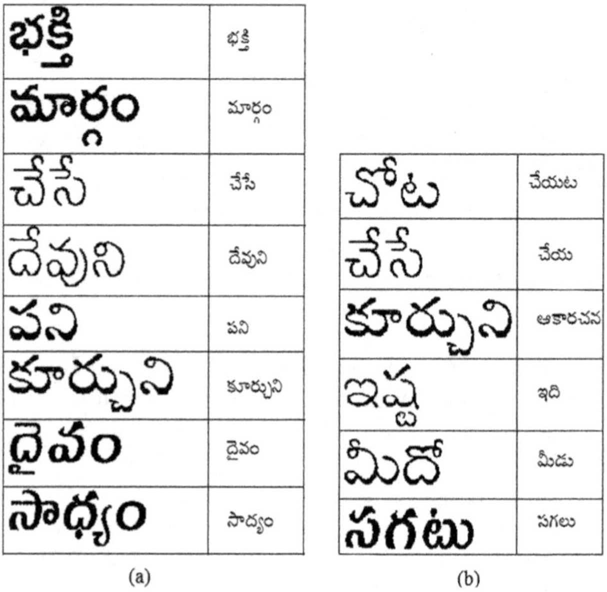

(a)   (b)

Fig. 7. Example multi-font Telugu printed word images: (a) successfully recognized words with their equivalent text, (b) word images recognized with some *akshara* errors.

to find the maximum likelihood sequence (word). Finally the error rates are estimated. The CER and WER of our system are given in Table 1. The error rates are compared to demonstrate the significance of thinning and re-thickening. The merit of using bi-gram language model is that it does not need to specify the sequences of *akshara* HMMs (words). This system does not use lexicon either during recognition or at post-processing level. The lexicon along with bi-grams can be useful to reduce the error rates [8] further. In Fig. 7(a), a sample of successfully recognized multi-font Telugu word images are shown along with their equivalent text. Thus the given Telugu words are recognized through implicit segmentation based on HMMs. This approach makes use of bi-gram language model and does not need prior segmentation of words into *aksharas* before recognition. We also show example word images that are recognized with some *akshara* errors in Fig. 7(b).

7 Conclusion

We proposed a novel approach for multi-font Telugu printed word recognition using Hidden Markov Models. In addition to the HMMs suitability to model sequential data with variations, this approach further uses the thinning and re-thickening operations to obtain *aksharas* of standard stroke width in view of font variation and extracts DCT features through sliding window for modeling the shape of *aksharas* using HMMs. The merit of implicit segmentation for Telugu word recognition is to achieve segmentation by recognition. The presented system does not rely on lexicon, but we intend to use lexicon to reduce errors. Our future work includes applying this approach for recognition of line images based on tri-grams and using a combination of classification approaches for improving the performance.

References

1. Bazzi, I., Schwartz, R., Makhoul, J.: An omnifont open-vocabulary OCR system for English and Arabic. IEEE Trans. Pattern Anal. Mach. Intell. **21**(6), 495–504 (1999)
2. Elms, A., Procter, S., Illingworth, J.: The advantage of using an HMM-based approach for faxed word recognition. Int. J. Doc. Anal. Recogn. **1**(1), 18–36 (1998)
3. Khorsheed, M.S.: Offline recognition of omnifont Arabic text using the HMM toolkit (HTK). Pattern Recogn. Lett. **28**(12), 1563–1571 (2007)
4. Krishnan, P., Sankaran, N., Singh, A.K., Jawahar, C.V.: Towards a robust OCR system for Indic scripts. In: 2014 11th IAPR International Workshop on Document Analysis Systems (DAS), pp. 141–145, April 2014
5. Kumar, P.P., Bhagvati, C., Negi, A., Agarwal, A., Deekshatulu, B.L.: Towards improving the accuracy of Telugu OCR systems. In: ICDAR, pp. 910–914. IEEE Computer Society (2011)
6. Lam, L., Lee, S.-W., Suen, C.: Thinning methodologies-a comprehensive survey. IEEE Trans. Pattern Anal. Mach. Intell. **14**(9), 869–885 (1992)
7. Natarajan, P., Lu, Z., Schwartz, R., Bazzi, I., Makhoul, J.: Multilingual machine printed OCR. Int. J. Pattern Recogn. Artif. Intell. **15**(01), 43–63 (2001)
8. Natarajan, P., MacRostie, E., Decerbo, M.: The BBN byblos Hindi OCR system. In: Govindaraju, V., Setlur, S. (eds.) Guide to OCR for Indic Scripts. Advances in pattern recognition, pp. 173–180. Springer, London (2010). doi:10.1007/978-1-84800-330-9_9
9. Negi, A., Bhagvati, C., Krishna, B.: An OCR system for Telugu. In: ICDAR, pp. 1110–1114. IEEE Computer Society (2001)
10. Rabiner, L.: A tutorial on hidden Markov models and selected applications in speech recognition. Proc. IEEE **77**(2), 257–286 (1989)
11. Rasagna, V., Jinesh, K.J., Jawahar, C.V.: On multifont character classification in Telugu. In: Singh, C., Singh Lehal, G., Sengupta, J., Sharma, D.V., Goyal, V. (eds.) ICISIL 2011. CCIS, vol. 139, pp. 86–91. Springer, Heidelberg (2011). doi:10.1007/978-3-642-19403-0_14
12. Roy, P., Roy, S., Pal, U.: Multi-oriented text recognition in graphical documents using HMM. In: 2014 11th IAPR International Workshop on Document Analysis Systems (DAS), pp. 136–140, April 2014

13. Vasantha Lakshmi, C., Patvardhan, C.: A multi-font OCR system for printed Telugu text. In: 2002 Proceedings of Language Engineering Conference, pp. 7–17, December 2002
14. Wu, Y., Shivakumara, P., Wei, W., Lu, T., Pal, U.: A new ring radius transform-based thinning method for multi-oriented video characters. IJDAR **18**(2), 137–151 (2015)
15. Young, S., Evermann, G., Gales, M., Hain, T., Kershaw, D., Liu, X.A., Moore, G., Odell, J., Ollason, D., Povey, D., Valtchev, V., Woodland, P.: The HTK Book (for HTK Version 3.4). Cambridge University Engineering Department (2006)

Anveshak - A Groundtruth Generation Tool for Foreground Regions of Document Images

Soumyadeep Dey[✉], Jayanta Mukherjee, Shamik Sural,
and Amit Vijay Nandedkar

Department of Computer Science and Engineering,
Indian Institute of Technology Kharagpur, Kharagpur 721302, India
soumyadeepdey@cse.iitkgp.ernet.in, amitnandedkar@sit.iitkgp.ernet.in

Abstract. We propose a graphical user interface based groundtruth generation tool in this paper. Here, annotation of an input document image is done based on the foreground pixels. Foreground pixels are grouped together with user interaction to form labeling units. These units are then labeled by the user with the user defined labels. The output produced by the tool is an image with an XML file containing its metadata information. This annotated data can be further used in different applications of document image analysis.

1 Introduction

Document digitization has attracted attention for several years. Conversion of a document image into electronic format requires several types of document image analysis. Typical document image analysis includes different types of segmentation, optical character recognition (OCR), etc. Numerous algorithms have been proposed to achieve these objectives. The performance of these algorithms can be measured with the help of groundtruth. The data with groundtruth is of immense importance in document image analysis. It is required for training, machine learning based algorithms, and it is also used for evaluation of various algorithms. The generation of groundtruth is a manual and time consuming process. Hence, the groundtruth generation tool should be user friendly, reliable, effective, and capable of generating data in a convenient manner.

Several systems for groundtruth generation have been reported in the literature for producing benchmark datasets to evaluate competitive algorithms. Pink Panther [21] is one such groundtruth generator, and is mainly used for evaluation of layout analysis. PerfectDoc [19] is a groundtruth generation system for document images, based on layout structures. Various layout based groundtruth generation tools are present in the literature [9,15,20]. These groundtruth generators [7,9,19], only support rectangular regions for annotation. Hence, they fail to generate groundtruth for documents with complex layout.

A recent groundtruth generator $GEDI$ [5], supports annotation by generating a polygonal region. However, it is observed that the tool is quite inefficient for images of larger size (600 dpi). PixLabeler [13] is an example of pixel level

S. Mukherjee et al. (Eds.): ICVGIP 2016, LNCS 10481, pp. 255–264, 2017.
https://doi.org/10.1007/978-3-319-68124-5_22

groundtruth generator. Similar tools are also reported in [11, 14, 18]. Pixel level annotation gives more general measure for annotation, but it involves more time for completing the annotation task.

In this paper, we propose a tool to annotate a document image at pixel level. The main objective of the tool is to efficiently annotate data using less amount of time. Towards this, we have provided a semi-automatic interactive platform to annotate document images efficiently. Since our main goal is to annotate foreground pixels, we segment foreground pixels from its background with user assistance. Next, we group foreground pixels such that neighboring pixels of similar types get connected. Finally, annotation of each such group of pixels is performed with a predefined set of labels.

The system is called Anveshak and its functionality is described in Sect. 2. Implementation details are discussed in Sect. 3. Section 4 provides the details of groundtruth generation with Anveshak. Finally, we conclude in Sect. 5.

2 Functionality

The work-flow of the Anveshak system is shown in Fig. 1. Some semi-automated modules are implemented to speed up the annotation process.

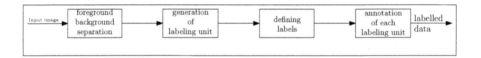

Fig. 1. Work flow of Anveshak system

2.1 Foreground Background Separation

We are mainly concerned with the annotation of foreground pixels of a document image. A module is integrated with Anveshak to efficiently segment foreground pixels from its background. This task can be performed with three types of thresholding techniques, first, *GUI* based thresholding, second, a *GUI* based adaptive thresholding technique [1], and third, the *Otsu's* thresholding technique [12]. Here, a user can segment foreground from its background efficiently, using either of these three thresholding techniques. An example of foreground background separation module using *GUI* based thresholding is shown in Fig. 2.

2.2 Generation of Labeling Units

Anveshak has a unique technique to predefine labeling units. Labeling units are generated using *GUI* based morphological operations. Morphological operations included in Anveshak are, *erosion*, *dilation*, *closing*, *opening*, *gap-filling*, and *smoothing*.

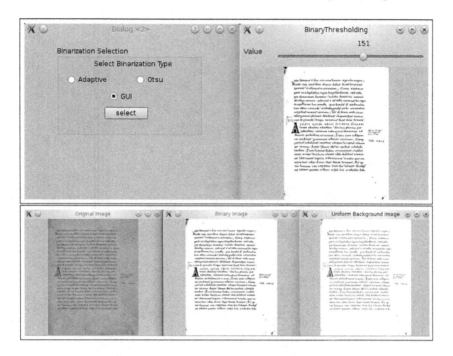

Fig. 2. Foreground background separation module.

A labeling unit is a collection of foreground pixels, grouped together using a suitable morphological operator. Pixels are grouped together by choosing either of these morphological operations - *erosion, dilation, closing,* and *opening* [8]. The user can select an ideal element size and element type, in order to group pixels. A user can also accumulate pixels to form a group by a smoothing operation [17], where choosing of run length parameter is an interactive process. Foreground pixels can also be grouped together using gap filling operation [4], where selection of the parameter, gap size in horizontal and vertical directions, is a user driven process. An instance of Anveshak for generating labeling units is shown in Fig. 3.

After grouping the pixels, contours of each group is obtained using the method described in [16]. Each contour is then approximated to a polygon by applying Douglas-Peucker algorithm [6]. The polygons thus computed are the basic units for annotation in Anveshak. An example of a collection of labeling units is shown in Fig. 4, where each labeling unit is represented using a unique colors.

2.3   Defining Labels

There are some predefined labels in Anveshak. The tool provides an option to add and delete labels, as shown in Fig. 5. After defining all the labels, a user can annotate the labeling units of the input document with the defined labels.

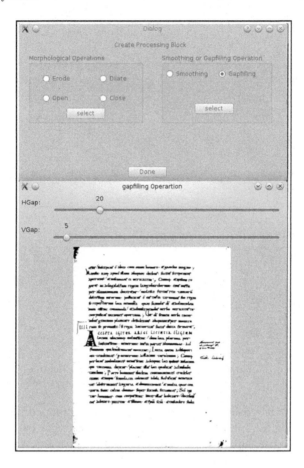

Fig. 3. Module of Anveshak for generating labeling unit with gap filling operation

A unique index number and a color is assigned to each label, which are used in the later stages of annotation.

2.4   Annotation of Labeling Units

Overall annotation process can be summarized using a flow chart given in Fig. 6. Annotation of labeling units is performed in two ways as shown in Fig. 7. A user can label unlabeled units one by one with the predefined labels. In this case, an unlabeled unit is displayed in a window and the user is prompted for a label for the displayed unit. This process continues until each of the units is labeled, or the user chooses to label the units by selecting a region of interest (*ROI*).

Another method of labeling units is to select a region of interest. In this module, a user can select an *ROI*, which can be annotated with the defined labels. At first, all units are determined which are completely present within the selected *ROI*. After selection of an *ROI*, units present within the *ROI* can be

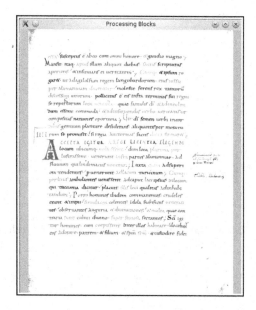

Fig. 4. Labeling units generated by Anveshak with user intervention (Color figure online)

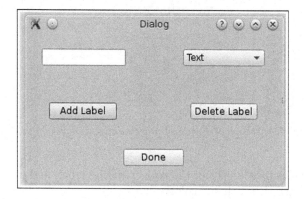

Fig. 5. An instance of Anveshak to set labels

labeled using three different modes (Fig. 8). A user can annotate all units within the *ROI* with one label, and update all units with the selected label. Another way of annotation is by labeling all units belonging to the selected *ROI* with a particular type. Lastly, a user can annotate each unit belonging to the selected *ROI* individually with a label. Pixels belonging to a particular labeling unit are updated with the unique index corresponding to the label of *ROI*, and color of those pixels is updated with the color of that label. Belongingness of a pixel to a particular labeling unit is computed through point-polygon test. At each stage of the annotation process, the updated color image is displayed, where labeled

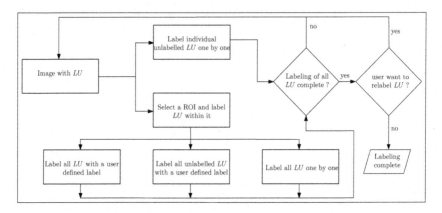

Fig. 6. Work flow of the annotation unit of Anveshak

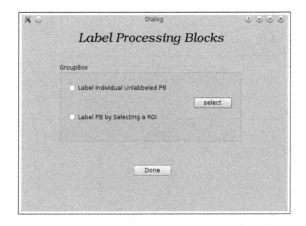

Fig. 7. Instance of Anveshak for choosing annotation mode

pixels are displayed with color of the corresponding label, and unlabeled pixels are displayed with their original color value.

The process of annotation continues until all labeling units are marked. After completion of annotation, the user is asked, whether he/she wants to update any label, or finalize the labels. After finalizing the labels, output labeled image and its corresponding XML file are generated. An example of different stages of labeling is shown in Fig. 9.

3   Implementation Details

Anveshak is implemented in $C + +$, using cross-platform application framework Qt for graphical user interface and with customized modules developed using OpenCV [1]. Annotation of an image is achieved through the user interface and after completion, a single image in *.png* format is generated. Each pixel

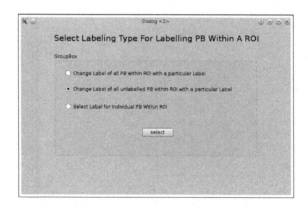

Fig. 8. Options prompted for choosing labeling mode for a *ROI*.

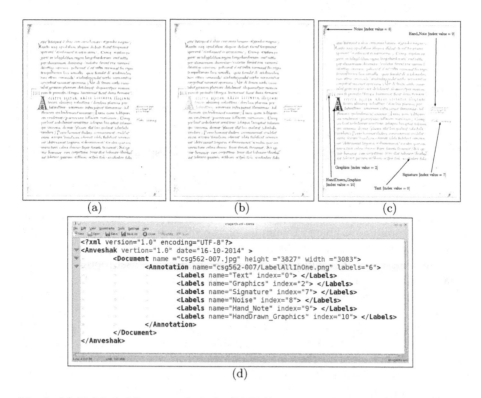

(a)   (b)   (c)

```
<?xml version="1.0" encoding="UTF-8"?>
<Anveshak version="1.0" date="16-10-2014" >
    <Document name ="csg562-007.jpg" height ="3827" width ="3083">
        <Annotation name="csg562-007/LabelAllInOne.png" labels="6">
            <Labels name="Text" index="0"> </Labels>
            <Labels name="Graphics" index="2"> </Labels>
            <Labels name="Signature" index="7"> </Labels>
            <Labels name="Noise" index="8"> </Labels>
            <Labels name="Hand_Note" index="9"> </Labels>
            <Labels name="HandDrawn_Graphics" index="10"> </Labels>
        </Annotation>
    </Document>
</Anveshak>
```

(d)

Fig. 9. (a) Unlabeled foreground pixels; (b) Half annotated foreground pixels; (c) Full annotated foreground pixels with a unique color per label; (d) *XML* output after annotation of Fig. 9(a) (Color figure online)

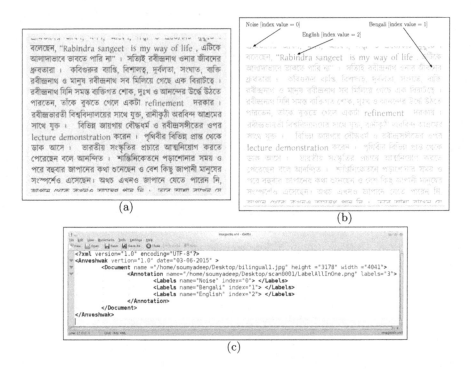

Fig. 10. (a) An input bilingual image (b) Annotated image for Fig. 10(a) with a unique color per label; (c) *XML* output after annotation of Fig. 10(a) (Color figure online)

of the output image is represented with an index corresponding to a particular annotation.

The metadata of the concerned image is stored in an *XML* file, which also includes the information of the source image along with the annotated image. In the *XML* file, an index corresponds to the unique pixel value for a particular label in the annotated image. Examples of two different annotated images and their corresponding *XML* files are respectively shown in Figs. 9(c), (d) and 10(a), (b). Anveshak is tested to annotate 344 images from the dataset reported in [10]. It has been observed by the annotator that, the labeling can be performed in a much easier and faster way than it could be performed with PixLabeler [13] or *GEDI* [5].

In our present implementation of Anveshak, only one annotation per block is supported. In many scenarios, it is desirable to have multiple annotations per block, mainly in case of overlapping regions. In future, we plan to support more than one annotation per block. Present implementation of Anveshak has been made available online[1].

---

[1] http://www.facweb.iitkgp.ernet.in/~jay/anveshak/anveshak.html.

4   Generation of Groundtruth Using Anveshak

Anveshak is used to generate groundtruth for the dataset reported in [10]. The images in the dataset consist of various regions like logo, headers, text, signature, headline, bold text, etc. However, annotation of stamp regions is only available with the original dataset. The dataset consists of 425 scanned images in 600, 300, and 200 *dpi* resolutions. Out of these 425 images, 344 images contain non overlapping regions. Anveshak is used to annotate these 344 images of 300 *dpi* resolution, and the groundtruth data has been made available online[2]. These 344 images are annotated using Anveshak with the help of 6 users. There are on an average 5 labels, and 148 segments per image in the given dataset. Users involved in annotation are initially trained to annotate data with one random image. Average time taken by a user to annotate an image with Anveshak is about 3–4 min. The annotated dataset has been used in the works reported in [2,3].

5   Conclusion

The primary target of Anveshak is to annotate an input document image in an efficient manner. Our tool produces an XML file containing the metadata information, along with an annotated image. We have developed a user friendly groundtruth generation tool, with some semi-automatic modules which make the annotation process faster. We hope that Anveshak will serve the document analysis community in an effective manner by simplifying groundtruth generation procedure.

Acknowledgments. This work is partly funded by TCS research scholar program and partly by Ministry of Communications and Information Technology, Government of India; MCIT 11(19)/2010-HCC (TDIL) dt. 28-12-2010.

References

1. Bradski, G.: The OpenCV Library. Dr. Dobb's J. Softw. Tools **25**(11) (2000)
2. Dey, S., Mukherjee, J., Sural, S.: Stamp and logo detection from document images by finding outliers. In: 2015 Fifth National Conference on Computer Vision, Pattern Recognition, Image Processing and Graphics (NCVPRIPG), pp. 1–4, December 2015
3. Dey, S., Mukherjee, J., Sural, S.: Consensus-based clustering for document image segmentation. Int. J. Doc. Anal. Recogn. (IJDAR) **19**(4), 351–368 (2016)
4. Dey, S., Mukhopadhyay, J., Sural, S., Bhowmick, P.: Margin noise removal from printed document images. In: Workshop on Document Analysis and Recognition, pp. 86–93 (2012)
5. Doermann, D., Zotkina, E., Li, H.: GEDI - A Groundtruthing Environment for Document Images (2010). http://lampsrv02.umiacs.umd.edu/projdb/project.php?id=53

---

[2] http://www.facweb.iitkgp.ernet.in/~jay/anveshak_gt/anveshak_gt.html.

6. Douglas, D.H., Peucker, T.M.: Algorithm for the reduction of the number of points required to represent a digitized line or its caricature. Cartographica: Int. J. Geogr. Inf. Geovisualization **10**(2), 112–122 (1973)

7. Ford, G., Thoma, G.R.: Ground truth data for document image analysis. In: Proceedings of 2003 Symposium on Document Image Understanding and Technology, pp. 199–205, 9-11 April 2003

8. Gonzalez, R.C., Woods, R.E.: Digital Image Processing, 3rd edn. Prentice-Hall Inc., Upper Saddle River (2009)

9. Ha, L.C., Kanungo, T.: The architecture of trueviz: a groundtruth/metadata editing and VIsualiZing toolkit. Pattern Recogn. **36**(3), 811–825 (2003)

10. Micenkova, B., Beusekom, J.V.: Stamp detection in color document images. In: 11th International Conference on Document Analysis and Recognition, pp. 1125–1129 (2011)

11. Moll, M., Baird, H., An, C.: Truthing for pixel-accurate segmentation. In: The Eighth IAPR International Workshop on Document Analysis Systems, DAS 2008, pp. 379–385, September 2008

12. Otsu, N.: A threshold selection method from gray-level histograms. IEEE Trans. Syst. Man Cybern. **9**(1), 62–66 (1979)

13. Saund, E., Lin, J., Sarkar, P.: Pixlabeler: user interface for pixel-level labeling of elements in document images. In: 10th International Conference on Document Analysis and Recognition, pp. 646–650 (2009)

14. Shafait, F., Keysers, D., Breuel, T.: Pixel-accurate representation and evaluation of page segmentation in document images. In: 18th International Conference on Pattern Recognition, ICPR 2006, vol. 1, pp. 872–875 (2006)

15. Strecker, T., van Beusekom, J., Albayrak, S., Breuel, T.: Automated ground truth data generation for newspaper document images. In: 10th International Conference on Document Analysis and Recognition, pp. 1275–1279, July 2009

16. Suzuki, S., Abe, K.: Topological structural analysis of digitized binary images by border following. Comput. Vis. Graph. Image Process. **30**(1), 32–46 (1985)

17. Wahl, F.M., Wong, K.Y., Casey, R.G.: Block segmentation and text extraction in mixed text/image documents. Comput. Graph. Image Process. **20**(4), 375–390 (1982)

18. Wenyin, L., Dori, D.: A protocol for performance evaluation of line detection algorithms. Mach. Vis. Appl. **9**(5–6), 240–250 (1997)

19. Yacoub, S., Saxena, V., Sami, S.: Perfectdoc: a ground truthing environment for complex documents. In: 8th International Conference on Document Analysis and Recognition, pp. 452–456 (2005)

20. Yang, L., Huang, W., Tan, C.L.: Semi-automatic ground truth generation for chart image recognition. In: Bunke, H., Spitz, A.L. (eds.) DAS 2006. LNCS, vol. 3872, pp. 324–335. Springer, Heidelberg (2006). doi:10.1007/11669487_29

21. Yanikoglu, B., Vincent, L.: Pink panther: a complete environment for groundtruthing and benchmarking document page segmentation. Pattern Recogn. **31**(9), 1191–1204 (1998)

Writer Identification for Handwritten Words

Shilpa Pandey$^{(\boxtimes)}$ and Gaurav Harit

Indian Institute of Technology Jodhpur, Jodhpur 342011, Rajasthan, India
shilpaiitj@gmail.com, gharit@iitj.ac.in

Abstract. In this work we present a framework for recognizing writer for a handwritten word. We make use of allographic features at sub-word level. Our work is motivated by previous techniques which make use of a codebook. However, instead of encoding the features using the code-words, we exploit the discriminative properties of features that belong to the same cluster, in a supervised approach. We are able to achieve writer identification rates close to 63% on the handwritten words drawn from a dataset by 10 writers. Our work has application in scenarios where multiple writers write/annotate on the same page.

Keywords: Writer identification · Clustering · Allographic features

1 Introduction

The challenges for writer identification include the variation in writing style depending on the use of different pens, whether the writer has written in a hurry or not, and the inherent variability in human articulation so that one word is rarely written exactly the same way twice. The handwriting of a person may change over years and therefore makes further identification a harder task. Even in the presence of these challenges it can be seen that, at least for humans, the writing differs clearly for different writers.

In recent years, many different approaches have been proposed for writer identification for different writers. There have been a number of new and effective attempts to identify documents [1,5–7,11,15,19], textlines [17], words [3,17,18,21], and characters [4,12] penned by specific writer. Writer analysis can be studied under two levels: the Texture level [2,3,5,6,13,14,18,20,21] and Character level [10–12,15,16,19]. Features at texture level exhibit a global nature; they are informative for the habitual pen grip and the preferred writing slant [14]. Features at allograph level possess local nature and hence reveal the true character shapes [14]. For analyzing an allograph, first the handwriting has to be segmented. Thus, the writer identification process involves a segmentation method, which can introduce errors. After segmentation, features for individual writers can be calculated on these allographs. The writer identification methods, which use textural features, skip this segmentation step and calculate features directly on the image. They can be readily applied to any language without any prior knowledge of the letters or allographs [10]. They are fast because they encode a whole document or passage in a single feature vector.

© Springer International Publishing AG 2017
S. Mukherjee et al. (Eds.): ICVGIP 2016, LNCS 10481, pp. 265–276, 2017.
https://doi.org/10.1007/978-3-319-68124-5_23

The allographs are the smaller unit of handwritten text; they can be further studied at grapheme, bi-gram and character levels. Graphemes are small strokes of handwriting, which are extracted by applying a robust segmentation algorithm [11]. Bi-gram is a combination of a character with another adjacent character, and characters are the single alphabet of a word usually manually segmented. Figure 1 gives example of the three types of allographs.

Grapheme Level   **Graphemes of word Alas**   **Character Level**   **Bi–Grams Level**

Fig. 1. The three types of handwritten Word Allographs from CVL dataset

In this work, we exploit individual character shapes to identify the writers of handwritten words from a set of specified writers. So far, there have been few works that address offline writer identification for handwritten words [3,17,18, 21]. However, a proper exploration at allograph level is still lacking. We identify the writer of a particular word at allograph level, when multiple writers have penned a single document. In this paper, we examine the discriminability of writer identification at allograph level.

In this work, a codebook of graphemes is constructed after extracting the graphemes using a sliding window. In the following work, an assessment is made on 10 writers from CVL dataset [8]. The dataset includes handwritten words from a set of 4 documents of each writer. For each writer we use two of his document for training and the remaining two for testing. The grapheme level clusters are trained with 140 different words and further tested on 150 different words for each writer. We conduct two sets of experiments by building the codebook with overlapping and non-overlapping windows. The character level codebook is learned from 5698 characters from a total 10 writers it is tested upon 150 different words for each writer. K-means is used for codebook generation and one vs. rest SVM is used for further classification. In the end, majority voting decides the author of the given handwritten word.

The paper is organized as follows. In Sect. 2 we present a brief summary of writer identification at allograph level. Section 3 states the methodology that we adopted to identify the author of a word. In Sect. 4 we describe the experiments we conducted to investigate the performance of the various allograph level codebooks. We conclude this paper in Sect. 5.

2   Related Work

Numerous studies have attempted to study the writer identification problem at texture level, where the methods identify the writer of a document based on the overall look and feel of the writing. The problem has been attempted at the global features of complete document as well as at local level that deals with the various shapes of the handwritten text. We here present the past work of writer identification with a focus at the allograph level and word level writer identification.

2.1 Allographs Features

Grapheme level: Schomaker and Bulacu [1] worked at grapheme level for free handwriting in only lower case text. They claimed an improvement in writer identification rate by infusing both allographic and texture features. The Probability Distribution Function (PDF) was computed for features such as contour direction, contour hinge, contour co-occurrence, run length, and grapheme emission. The system yields a performance of 87% on 900 writers at document level, which is build by combining writers from Firemaker, IAM and ImUnipen datasets. For grapheme extraction, a cut at lower contour is made where the distance between the upper and lower contour of the image is comparable to the ink width. Siddiqi and Vincent [16] identified the writer with only grapheme features and reported an identification rate of 94% at document level. To extract graphemes, the handwritten text is divided into a large number of small windows of fixed size. Then a correlation similarity measure is used to cluster similar graphemes. Each document is then modeled as a Gaussian Mixture of grapheme codewords. Bayes decision theory is employed for document classification.

Quang et al. [19] claimed that for less than 150 writers in a system, grapheme-based method outperforms the character-based method but only for online handwritten text. They used both on-line and off-line features jointly to identify the writer and then recognize online handwritten text. This is termed as writer adaptive handwriting recognition system. Online graphemes are segmented using MyScript Builder and are classified into four groups depending on the initial writing direction. Further k-means is used to create several prototypes within each group and a similarity function is used to encode each writer's document into a weight matrix. The weight matrices are matched and the writers are identified for each document. In handwriting, the stroke thickness varies from pen to pen, ink to ink and paper to paper. In view of it, Paraskevas et al., [11] suggests to reduce the stroke thickness down to one pixel by skeletonizing the text. Using a fixed squared window size the graphemes are extracted and the codebook is build by Kohonen SOFM [9]. The main contribution of the system lies in introducing an improvement in edge directional features, which results in achieving an accuracy of 95.6% with Manhattan distance.

Character level: Sevilla et al., [4] proposed a writer identification scheme by manually segmenting offline handwritten characters. They performed two experiments on CEDAR database for 30 writers one with local codebook while the other with global codebook. The local codebook is composed of sub codebooks of 52 types of characters. K-means is used as a clustering scheme for creating the codebook. For each writer, the nearest codebook is searched using Euclidean distance. Therefore, for each writer one histogram (in the case of global code-book) or 52 histograms (one per character, in the case of local sub-codebooks) are obtained. A Probability Distribution Function (PDF) is computed from each whether common or sub codebooks, by histogram binning. This PDF is used to characterize each writer. Finally writer identification is done by a distance function. Their work concludes that (i) working with local sub codebook results in much better performance than using a unique single codebook, and (ii) when some of the sub codebooks are combined only slight difference in performance was seen.

Quang et al. [19] in their work found that character based method is relatively robust to character segmentation errors. They also claimed that grapheme level identification is computationally more expensive and less effective than character extraction based method, for an increasing number of writers. But these findings were restricted to only online handwritten text and their contribution lies in combining online features with offline features. PCA was applied to reduce the dimensions of the online and off-line features. Their work reported an accuracy of 93% on PSI database for 88 writers for online writer identification on documents.

Bi-gram level: Very few studies have investigated the impact of working with bigram level features on writer identification. The paper [12] presents a study of structural features of handwriting extracted from three characters "d", "y", and "f" and a bigram "th". They concentrated on the extraction of the micro level features like height, width, height to width ratio, relative height of ascender, slant of ascender, final stroke angle, fissure angle, relative height of descender, descender loop completeness, descender slant, final stroke angle, slant at point, slant of t-stem, slant of h-stem, position of t-bar. Neural network is used as a classifier and genetic algorithm is applied for searching an optimal feature set for writer identification. The paper claims that, the bigram possessed significantly higher discriminating power than any of the three single characters studied, which supports the opinion that a character form is affected by its adjacent characters. They reported an accuracy of 58% for 200 writers from 600 samples of the CEDAR letter dataset. A recent study by Newell [10] states that identification performance can be improved when bigrams are used for dictionary building. His work focused on the van der Maarten dataset comprising 251 writers with each writer writing a text passage. Each passage in the dataset contains only 32 types of characters in all. The test set contains only 20 characters. These characters are segmented from the text passage and histograms are formed either for each character for each writer or for group of characters. For the test passage these histograms are matched using NN classifier and on the majority voting the decision is built on the authorship of a particular writer. His work claimed that, in case when characters of a writér are bi-paired with each other, the one paired with the same character gives the best identification rate.

2.2   Handwritten Word Identification

Recognition of handwritten words is more challenging. Zhang and Srihari [21] used GSC (Gradient, Structural and Concavity) features on words and performed writer discrimination and verification. Their study majorly focused only on four characteristic words, "been", "Cohen", "Medical", and "referred". Their dataset comprises 1000 writers who wrote only these four words on three documents and reported an accuracy of 83%. Features are drawn only from these words by dividing their images in $n \times n$ blocks and are classified by applying k-NN based on Correlation measure as similarity function. Following this, Tomai et al. [18] used segmentation and segmentation-free feature extraction approaches to identify writer of a word image. Their dataset includes 75000 words images, representing 25 different words, written by more than 1000 writers. Their choice of features included GSC (Gradient, Structural and Concavity) features, WMR (Word Model Recognizer) features, SC (Shape Curvature) and SCON (Shape Context) features and reported an accuracy of 62% for identification with GSC feature. Further Aymen et al. [3] performed word level writer identification by combining the on-line and off-line features. For the same word the writer will form two images one offline and the other online. Then from both the word images high density of information points are identified and then they are surrounded by box. The points identified are called fractal and the features extracted from them are termed multi fractal features. The experiments are performed on 100 writers of ADAB database on 25 words and following conclusions were drawn:

1. The on-line fractal features (84.6%) over perform the off-line fractal features (80.9%).
2. The combination of online and offline fractal produces higher accuracies (93.2%).
3. To characterize the styles of writings online are better because they are more informative.

In a recent study, Fouad and Volker [17] claimed to achieve an accuracy of 23.03% at word level and 69.48% at line level for writer identification. They used sliding window approach to extract graphemes and avoided manual segmentation. A GMM is built for each writer of the AHTID dataset with 53 writers. Their work also states the comparison of using GMMs instead of HMMs for writer identification and also states that writer identification by a single word is more complex than by a single text line.

2.3 Our Contribution

Much of the work on handwritten word recognition has focused on a set of few words written by multiple writers. In this work we develop a framework that does not need to be trained on specific words. The handwritten words used for training need not be the same as the handwritten words used for testing. Our system is applicable to documents where multiple authors have annotated the same page. Instead of working with codewords, we work with the clusters of features. Writer-specific classifiers are then trained on each cluster. In this work, we examine grapheme and character level using sliding windows, and obtain a feature set on them. We also present an analysis of feature clustering applied to graphemes and characters for word level writer identification.

3   Methodology

Features are extracted from segments or windows defined on the word image. The features are then clustered using k-means clustering. We envisage that allographs that are similar will get grouped into the same cluster. The set of allographs that belong to a cluster may be coming from samples by several writers. For each cluster we train a suite of one-vs-rest SVM classifiers using samples that belong to that cluster. The feature vector extracted for each word segment (window) is associated with the closest cluster and is classified by the suite of SVMs trained for that cluster. A majority voting among the classification decisions for all the windows gives the final writer label assigned to the word.

3.1   Feature Extraction

We extract features from each segment of the word. A segment could either encompass a character or a grapheme. When we consider segments to be characters we do a manual segmentation of words into characters. For other allographs we use a sliding window, which encompasses a portion of the word – that could be a partial or complete character or even portions of multiple characters, depending on the position and width of the window. Allographic features extracted from a segment are considered to be at character level or grapheme level, depending on how wide is the segment. In this work we adopt features from the work reported in [17].

3.2   Classification of Segment Features

When using sliding windows we consider the two settings of overlapping or non-overlapping windows to identify the handwritten word segments. We use k-means to group the features to form clusters. Each cluster will have segments that may be coming from different writers. That is, similar allographs of various writers can be clustered together. The training phase involves analyzing each cluster. If in a given cluster there are allographs of n different writers then we train a set of n one-vs-rest SVM classifiers for that cluster. These n writers are said to be owning that cluster. Thus we learn a suite of classifiers: a set of one-vs-rest classifiers for each cluster. The decision making can be explained as follows. Consider that the features extracted for a given allographic segment α are closest to the cluster C_1 in terms of the Euclidean distance. Say the cluster C_1 has samples from k writers. On the execution of all one vs. rest SVM, a set of scores $W_{\alpha c1} = \{w_1, w_4, \ldots \ldots, w_k\}$ are computed which are the SVM decision scores for the writer classes or the "rest" class (unknown writer). From this set the writer with the highest decision score is selected as the label for the allograph α. There can be a possibility that an "unknown writer" is assigned to an allograph. This will be the case when all the one-vs-rest SVMs classify the allograph to the unknown (rest) class. This happens when the allogprah does not carry enough discriminative features to enable it to get classified to one of the writers owning that cluster.

After the assignment of writer labels to the allographs of segments in a hand-written word, the writer of the complete word is identified using the majority label. If the majority label is the unknown writer, the system refuses to classify the word.

4 Experiments

In order to assess the effectiveness of the proposed approach, we performed a series of experiment on the CVL dataset [8]. In this work, we experiment with 10 writers with four documents from each of them.

Experiments at Grapheme Level: Graphemes are extracted by means of a sliding window. Hence experiments are carried for both overlapping and non overlapping windows. Table 1 presents the accuracies obtained by sliding overlapping windows over a word. We varied the size of the codebook (number of clusters) from 100 to 1000. Table 2 provides the results obtained by sliding non-overlapping windows.

Experiments at Character Level: From manually segmented characters, the similar features are clustered together for training. The testing is carried for both overlapping and non overlapping sliding windows features. Table 3 presents the accuracies obtained by sliding overlapping windows over a word. We varied the size of the codebook (number of clusters) from 100 to 1000. Table 4 provides the results obtained by sliding non-overlapping windows.

It is apparent from Tables 1, 2, 3 and 4 that the overlapping window setting outperforms the non-overlapping approach for both the character and grapheme based feature clustering. Possibly the non-overlapping windows result in clusters

Table 1. Writer identification rate for an overlapping window at Grapheme level

Code book size	Window width		
	20	25	30
	Accuracies		
100	**66.40**	60.28	62.94
200	64.63	60.20	**63.30**
300	64.18	60.55	61.70
400	63.74	**61.44**	62.59
500	62.85	61.26	62.32
600	63.92	60.99	63.39
700	64.10	60.37	63.39
800	63.92	59.75	63.30
900	63.83	59.04	60.99
1000	63.56	60.20	62.15

Table 2. Writer identification rate for non-overlapping window at Grapheme level

Code book size	Window width		
	20	25	30
	Accuracies		
100	18.17	16.13	12.21
200	20.48	16.84	12.87
300	21.90	19.06	13.84
400	21.81	19.59	14.90
500	24.20	18.79	14.98
600	20.74	21.63	17.83
700	23.23	21.90	17.43
800	**24.47**	21.81	18.40
900	23.58	20.48	**19.54**
1000	22.52	**22.16**	17.59

Table 3. Writer identification rate for an overlapping window at Character level

Code book size	Window width		
	20	25	30
	Accuracies		
100	17.43	15.96	16.37
200	13.03	16.37	18.00
300	**18.81**	17.67	19.22
400	15.72	18.00	19.71
500	14.74	**19.06**	21.66
600	14.41	17.02	18.00
700	14.33	17.59	19.63
800	17.35	18.89	19.95
900	16.53	16.12	19.54
1000	18.49	18.40	**21.82**

Table 4. Writer identification rate for non-overlapping window at Character level

Code book size	Window width		
	20	25	30
	Accuracies		
100	3.66	4.40	3.42
200	7.49	8.31	5.94
300	5.70	8.55	4.89
400	10.10	10.34	8.88
500	10.34	9.93	8.55
600	11.89	11.07	10.50
700	11.56	11.97	9.85
800	13.52	**14.33**	12.54
900	**14.09**	13.27	11.48
1000	13.84	13.36	**12.62**

Table 5. Writer identification rate for an overlapping window based on [17]

Code book size	Window width		
	20	25	30
	Accuracies		
100	15.31	13.19	**24.02**
200	14.58	**20.28**	17.43
300	10.67	13.27	23.86
400	16.04	14.82	14.41
500	15.15	14.98	19.46
600	17.26	18.16	20.11
700	**19.71**	13.84	16.94
800	10.67	14.25	22.56
900	13.60	19.63	13.27
1000	12.79	10.59	12.87

Table 6. Writer identification rate for non-overlapping window based on [17]

Code book size	Window width		
	20	25	30
	Accuracies		
100	8.79	11.56	3.42
200	11.64	10.83	5.94
300	18.00	13.11	4.89
400	10.42	18.97	8.88
500	16.45	22.72	8.55
600	18.24	**24.10**	10.50
700	13.68	20.68	9.85
800	**20.03**	18.49	12.54
900	18.08	18.81	11.48
1000	14.50	18.73	**12.62**

that are compact and hence are unable to separate the writers properly in the feature space. Moreover, it is seen that smaller the size of the window the better is the accuracy achieved, irrespective of the number of clusters. The results show that the optimal size of the window for achieving the best classification accuracy is 20. From Figs. 2 and 3 it is clear that there is a major improvement in accuracy when using overlapping windows. It is because of the context that adds due to overlapping windows which makes the resulting clusters well populated and non-compact, thereby leading to better results.

Together these results provide an important insight into the fact that very small or very large window sizes lead to deterioration of classification results.

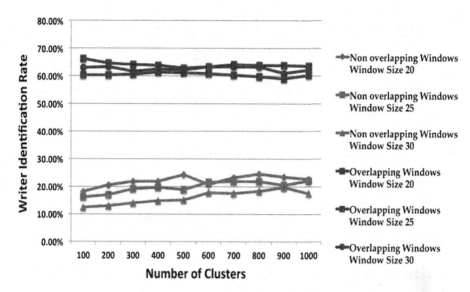

Fig. 2. Results for Grapheme based features with non overlapping and overlapping window.

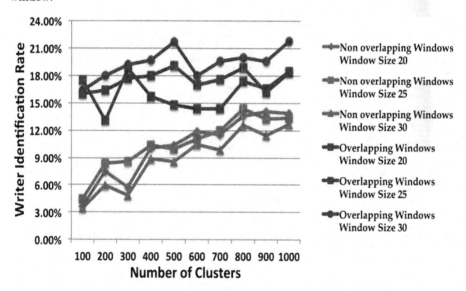

Fig. 3. Results for Character based features with non overlapping and overlapping window.

The classification accuracy is observed to be somewhat invariant to the number of clusters used for grapheme and character level allographic features. In the overlapping setting more windows are generated which increases the allographs extracted from the sample words. It is also found that the grapheme level outperforms the character level analysis irrespective of window size (see Fig. 4).

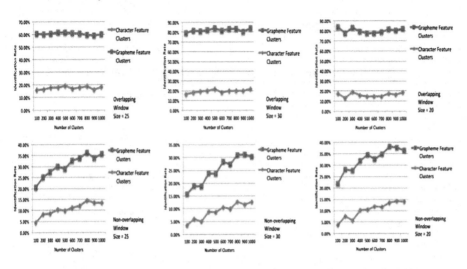

Fig. 4. Performance comparison between Grapheme and Character feature clusters

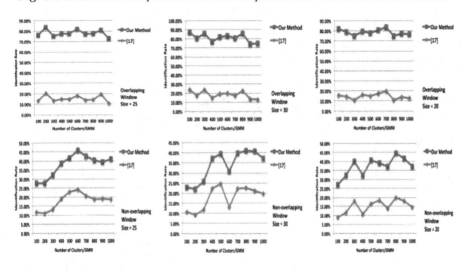

Fig. 5. Identification rate improvement between [17] and our method using Graphemes

Our methodology (using graphemes) which is a discriminative approach presents an improvement in identification accuracy over the generative approach described in [17] that uses window based features and models a GMM for each writer. Tables 1 and 5 illustrates an increase in the identification accuracy from 19% to 63% at grapheme level for overlapping windows. Tables 2 and 6 illustrates an increase in the identification accuracy from 18% to 22% at grapheme level for non-overlapping windows. It is observed that discriminative approach increases the offline writer identification rate at word level rather than generative approach, irrespective of window size (see Fig. 5).

5   Conclusions

In this work we exploit the allographic variations in the writing style at word level for writer identification. Allographic features at grapheme level exhibit discriminative properties when using overlapping windows. Our framework naturally allows to assign a test word to the unknown writer class in case the allographs in the word do not exhibit clear resemblance to any particular writer in the test set. Our future work involves working on feature selection strategies to select the best features that can discriminate the graphemes that are part of the same cluster.

References

1. Bulacu, M., Schomaker, L.: Combining multiple features for text-independent writer identification and verification, pp. 281–286 (2006)
2. Bulacu, M., Schomaker, L., Vuurpijl, L.: Writer identification using edge-based directional features. In: 7th International Conference on Document Analysis and Recognition (ICDAR 2003), 2-Volume Set, 3–6 August 2003, Edinburgh, Scotland, UK, pp. 937–941 (2003)
3. Chaabouni, A., Boubaker, H., Kherallah, M., Alimi, A.M., El Abed, H.: Combining of off-line and on-line feature extraction approaches for writer identification. In: 2011 International Conference on Document Analysis and Recognition, ICDAR 2011, Beijing, China, 18–21 September 2011, pp. 1299–1303 (2011)
4. Fernandez-de-Sevilla, R., Alonso-Fernandez, F., Fiérrez-Aguilar, J., Ortega-Garcia, J.: Forensic writer identification using allographic features. In: International Conference on Frontiers in Handwriting Recognition, ICFHR 2010, Kolkata, India, 16–18 November 2010, pp. 308–313 (2010)
5. Fiel, S., Sablatnig, R.: Writer identification and writer retrieval using the fisher vector on visual vocabularies. In: ICDAR, pp. 545–549. IEEE Computer Society (2013)
6. Jain, R., Doermann, D.: Combining local features for offline writer identification. In: 2014 14th International Conference on Frontiers in Handwriting Recognition (ICFHR), pp. 583–588, September 2014
7. Jain, R., Doermann, D.S.: Offline writer identification using k-adjacent segments. In: ICDAR, pp. 769–773. IEEE Computer Society (2011)
8. Kleber, F., Fiel, S., Diem, M., Sablatnig, R.: CVL-database: an off-line database for writer retrieval, writer identification and word spotting. In: 2013 12th International Conference on Document Analysis and Recognition, pp. 560–564, August 2013
9. Kohonen, T.: Self-organization and Associative Memory, 3rd edn. Springer, New York (1989)
10. Newell, A.J.: What should we be comparing for writer identification? In: 2013 12th International Conference on Document Analysis and Recognition, Washington, DC, USA, 25–28 August 2013, pp. 418–422 (2013)
11. Paraskevas, D., Gritzalis, S., Kavallieratou, E.: Writer identification using a statistical and model based approach. In: ICFHR, pp. 589–594. IEEE Computer Society (2014)
12. Pervouchine, V., Leedham, G.: Extraction and analysis of forensic document examiner features used for writer identification. Pattern Recogn. **40**(3), 1004–1013 (2007)

13. Said, H.E.S., Tan, T.N., Baker, K.D.: Personal identification based on handwriting. Pattern Recogn. **33**(1), 149–160 (2000)

14. Schomaker, L., Bulacu, M.: Automatic writer identification using connected-component contours and edge-based features of uppercase western script. IEEE Trans. Pattern Anal. Mach. Intell. **26**(6), 787–798 (2004)

15. Schomaker, L., Franke, K., Bulacu, M.: Using codebooks of fragmented connected-component contours in forensic and historic writer identification. Pattern Recogn. Lett. **28**(6), 719–727 (2007)

16. Siddiqi, I., Vincent, N.: Writer identification in handwritten documents. In: 9th International Conference on Document Analysis and Recognition (ICDAR 2007), 23–26 September, Curitiba, Paraná, Brazil, pp. 108–112 (2007)

17. Slimane, F., Margner, V.: A new text-independent GMM writer identification system applied to arabic handwriting. In: Proceedings of 14th International Conference on Frontiers in Handwriting Recognition, pp. 708–713 (2014)

18. Tomai, C.I., Zhang, B., Srihari, S.N.: Discriminatory power of handwritten words for writer recognition. In: 17th International Conference on Pattern Recognition, ICPR 2004, Cambridge, UK, 23–26 August 2004, pp. 638–641 (2004)

19. Visani, M., Ogier, J.-M., Prum, S., Bui, Q.A.: Writer identification using TF-IDF for cursive handwritten word recognition. In: 2011 11th International Conference on Document Analysis and Recognition (ICDAR 2011), pp. 844–848 (2011)

20. Wang, X., Ding, X., Liu, H.: Writer identification using directional element features and linear transform. In: 7th International Conference on Document Analysis and Recognition (ICDAR 2003), 2-Volume Set, 3–6 August 2003, Edinburgh, Scotland, UK, pp. 942–945 (2003)

21. Zhang, B., Srihari, S.N.: Analysis of handwriting individuality using word features. In: Proceedings of the Seventh International Conference on Document Analysis and Recognition - Volume 2, ICDAR 2003, p. 1142. IEEE Computer Society, Washington, DC (2003)

Kalanjiyam: Unconstrained Offline Tamil Handwritten Database

Faizal Hajamohideen and S. Noushath[✉]

Department of Information Technology, College of Applied Sciences – Sohar,
Sohar, Sultanate of Oman
{faizalh.soh,noushath.soh}@cas.edu.com

Abstract. In this paper, we present a new offline Tamil Handwritten database *Kalanjiyam*. This database serves dual purpose by providing isolated handwritten characters of varying writing styles (Phase-1) as well as handwritten text paragraphs (Phase-2). For both Phase-1 and Phase-2, we collect samples from 500 people of varying age groups, profession, different handedness etc. Each data collection form allows the volunteer to write 80 characters and two paragraphs of four sentences at least. Phase-1 of this work, involving data acquisition, processing and other protocols, has been reported in this paper for quick and timely dissemination of the ongoing work. The database is supplemented with essential ground-truth (GT) information and is made publicly available. To the best of our knowledge, this *Kalanjiyam* database when it is full-fledged (Phase-2 of the Database included), will be first of its kind to host comprehensive collection of offline handwritten characters as well text lines.

Keywords: Tamil offline database · Handwriting recognition · Writer identification · Document analysis

1   Introduction

Research in handwriting recognition analysis pertaining to Indic scripts has been receiving steady attention over the last couple of decades. This is evident through the existence of reasonably efficient machine recognition algorithms and publicly available handwritten database of few Indian scripts such as Oriya, Bengali, Telugu and Devanagari etc. [6].

Over the last decade, many machine learning algorithms have been proposed for the recognition of Tamil online characters. These algorithms have utilized mostly the Lipitk database developed by HP Labs, India for experimentation and evaluation purposes [4,7,11]. This database is publicly available [2] and is actually generated through simple piecewise interpolation of (x, y) pen coordinates of online data. Thus it does not capture inherent characteristics of offline samples such as sharp boundaries, stroke discontinuity (due to subsequent scanning and binarization processes), variable thickness due to the usage of pen,

© Springer International Publishing AG 2017
S. Mukherjee et al. (Eds.): ICVGIP 2016, LNCS 10481, pp. 277–287, 2017.
https://doi.org/10.1007/978-3-319-68124-5_24

pencil, sketch pens, gel pens etc. These variations are seldom perceived in the offline counterparts generated through online data.

There are many other works on Tamil offline handwriting recognition [1,10,12] but the underlying database used in respective works have several limitations such as *in-house* creation, unavailable publicly, not comprehensive, inadequate number of samples etc. It will incapacitate benchmarking and eventually impede the development of efficient algorithms for Tamil Handwriting recognition.

There are many handwritten databases that are available for scripts like Roman, Chinese and Arabic. This promoted widespread research in respective scripts and caused advancement in the development of handwriting recognition. For these scripts, the availability of databases also prompted organization of many competitions through dedicated document analysis conferences such as ICDAR, ICFHR, DAS, etc[1]. However, the Tamil script lacks a comprehensive offline database that can be used for research purposes such as handwriting recognition, script identification, text-line extraction, segmentation of touching characters, writer identification, forensic science etc. The aforementioned reasons motivated us to design a comprehensive offline Tamil database that could be utilized for performing many handwriting recognition tasks.

The creation of *Kalanjiyam* database is intended to serve many purposes: Enable research communities to objectively evaluate their algorithms, ascertain fundamental limitations/capabilities of some of the popular existing algorithms for Tamil script, benchmark many handwriting recognition tasks etc. Essentially, the availability of a comprehensive database publicly will foster research in Tamil Handwriting recognition and related other applications. With this we strongly believe that there would be a possibility of a paradigm shift in terms of enhanced accuracy and thus providing opportunity for real time applications involving Tamil scripts.

Rest of the paper is organized as follows: Sect. 2 provides overview of Tamil script and existing Tamil database. In Sect. 3, we present the overall process involved in the Phase-1 of the *Kalanjiyam* database development. Finally, some of the ongoing work and future avenues are reported in Sect. 4.

2   The Overview

2.1   Tamil Script

In addition to being an official language of India, Srilanka, and Singapore, it is also spoken in many other parts of the world. A sizable population speaks Tamil in the Fiji Islands, Mauritius, Trinidad, Madagascar, South Africa, Singapore and Malaysia. Even though the linguistic process of some minority languages such as Badaga, Irula, Paniya and Saurashtra are completely different from that of Tamil, they are written in Tamil scripts [5]. It is one of the 22 scheduled

---

[1] The 2006 edition of IWFHR conducted Tamil Handwritten Character Recognition competition but the emphasis was for Online data.

languages of India and was the first Indian language to be accorded a classical language status by the Government of India in 2004 [5]. Tamil language is also used widely by the majorities in social medias and by latest emerging technology which has a method of using Tamil scripts in Internet applications.

The Tamil script is made of 12 vowels, 18 consonants and one character the *aytam* [5]. There are five additional consonants which are known as *grantha letters* which are used to write consonants borrowed from Sanskrit and some words of English origin [3]. Overall, the complete script consists of 36 letters $(12 + 18 + 1 + 5)$ and additional 276 (12 vowels * 23 consonants) compound letters formed by the consonant-vowel combinations. We can represent all these characters through unique combination of only 156 symbols. Figure 1 shows the basic vowels, consonants and their transliteration in English. The last five letters in the first row of the Figure refers to the *grantha letters* [3]. The Fig. 2 shows the formation of various compound characters through different consonant and vowel combinations. For comprehensive details about script and its significance, refer [3,5].

அ	ஆ	இ	ஈ	உ	ஊ	எ	ஏ	ஐ	ஒ	ஓ	ஒள	ஃ	ஜ	ஷ	ஹ	ஸ	க்ஷ
a	ä	i	ī	u	ŭ	e	é	ai	o	ò	au	aytam	j	ṣ	h	s	kṣ
க	ச	ங	ஞ	ட	ண	த	ந	ப	ம	ய	ர	ல	ள	ற	வ	ழ	ன
k	c	ṅ	ṅ	ṭ	ṇ	t	n	p	m	y	r	l	ḷ	r	v	z	ṇ

Fig. 1. Set of vowels, consonants and granthas in Tamil

க்+அ	க்+ஆ	க்+இ	க்+ஈ	க்+உ	க்+ஊ	க்+எ	க்+ஏ	க்+ஐ	க்+ஒ	க்+ஓ	க்+ஒள
க	கா	கி	கீ	கு	கூ	கெ	கே	கை	கொ	கோ	கௌ

Fig. 2. Consonant + vowel combinations to form compound letters

2.2   Some Existing Handwritten Tamil Databases

Even though India is known as a multi-script and multi-lingual nation, the databases for handwritten recognition is sparingly available. The databases for offline handwritten Bangla and Devanagari numerals and characters has been developed by ISI Kolkata research teams [6]. As mentioned earlier, there is no comprehensive publicly available Tamil offline database even though there are sizable number of research papers has been published on Tamil handwriting recognition tasks. The HP Labs, India has not only provided a database for Tamil Handwritten Recognition purposes but has also published good number of papers as a benchmark for that database. However, this database is originally developed for

Table 1. The gist of some prominent Tamil handwriting database

Name of the database	Form	Features
1. The Lipitk isolated handwritten character database [2]	Online and offline	500 isolated samples each for 156 classes Collected using Tablet PCs offline samples synthetically created through on-line data Useful for offline/on-line handwriting character recognition
2. The Lipitk isolated handwritten word database [2]	Online	100 word samples each for 85 Tamil words Collected using Tablet PCs Useful for word recognition
3. Handwritten city name database [13]	Offline	Dataset of 265 Tamil city names Useful for postal automation Word recognition to some extent
4. Handwritten Tamil and Kannada word corpus [8]	Online	100000 words each in Kannada and Tamil collected from 500 writers Useful for online handwritten recognition

the online handwritten recognition task. Table 1 provides an overview of some of the existing Tamil handwritten databases.

The *Kalanjiyam* database can be seen as two independent repositories (Phase-1 and Phase-2) which can be used in various handwriting recognition and other related research pertaining to Tamil script (Refer Fig. 3). There are many salient features of this database (when it is full-fledged) compared to existing databases:

1. The Phase-1 of the database consists of offline isolated samples of 156 Tamil characters. Each class will contain variable number of samples (with at least 200 samples in each class). This database will be formed with the intended contribution of 500 volunteers of varying age group, profession, handedness etc. Each volunteer would contribute to writing 80 different characters and two paragraphs of 4 sentences at least. At the time of communicating this paper, we have accomplished this task by processing written form and subsequently segmenting individual characters.

2. In Phase-2 of the database, each volunteer writes two paragraphs: one fixed paragraph and one random paragraph. Fixed paragraph can be utlized for text-dependent writer identification while random paragraph could be utilized for text-independent writer identification. Apart from these, the Phase-2 of the database can be used for various other research purposes such as word recognition, word segmentation, touching character segmentation, text-line extraction and its skew estimation etc.

3. The unique paragraphs used in phase-2 are taken from 11 different sources and 500 such unique paragraphs are formed. Thus, Phase-2 would comprise hundreds of handwritten text lines and paragraphs.

4. Both Phase-1 and Phase-2 of the database would be supplemented with essential GT data.

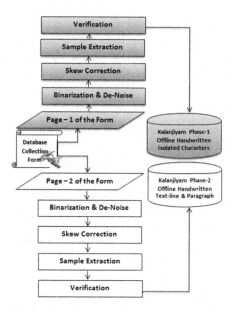

Fig. 3. Main steps involved in the overall *Kalanjiyam* database

3   The Kalanjiyam Database

The word *Kalanjiyam* is a Tamil word which means a repository. In this section, we describe brief statistics, data collection, subsequent data extraction, necessary post-processing and verification details related to Phase-1 of the *Kalanjiyam* database. The crucial steps performed here are shown as shaded boxes in Fig. 3.

3.1   Data Collection and Statistics

The whole process begins with a data collection form (Simple designed A4 sized paper) which consists of two pages. Page-1 and Page-2 are exclusively used for data collection in Phase-1 and Phase-2 of this database respectively. A sample handwritten data filled form is as shown in Fig. 4. In page-1, 10×8 grids are placed indicating the volunteer to write predefined Tamil characters. Each volunteer would fill both page-1 and page-2 of the same form. By this way, the complete set of Tamil character samples can be obtained by two volunteers[2]. In addition, letting a volunteer to write both characters and paragraph means we could exhaustively capture various writing styles in both Phase-1 and Phase-2 of the database. We did not impose any restrictions other than:

---

[2] Our preliminary experience with volunteers suggested that they were comfortable in providing 80 character samples and two separate paragraphs than providing 156 characters or two paragraphs alone. Also, letting the same volunteer to write complete 156 samples would be demanding and the volunteer might get hurried to fill the data. This may result in too much of deviation from normal writing style.

1. Asking the volunteer to write the characters and paragraphs within the pre-defined box as this would make our data extraction task relatively simpler.
2. Letting only those volunteer for whom Tamil was either primary/secondary language during their school. This would ensure that the writing style of the volunteer would not deviate too much from what is considered as normal or representative style of script.

Furnishing some personal data (which will be used for statistics about the participated volunteer) was also kept optional so as to keep the volunteer free from any stress before the data collection. At this stage, we have collected handwritten data from 500 forms (for both Phase-1 and Phase-2) and completed the data extraction for Phase-1. The Phase-2 work is currently an ongoing work. It is to be noted that Phase-1 and Phase-2 are independent repositories intended for specific document analysis tasks. Hence, scholars do not have to wait for Phase-2 work to get completed in order to work on handwriting character recognition tasks.

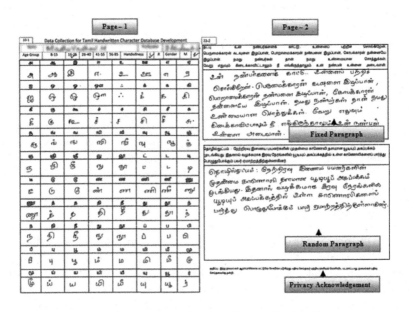

Fig. 4. A sample handwritten data collection form

The data has been collected from different age groups such as slabs of 8–15 (11.2), 16–25 (31.8), 26–40 (18.4), 41–55 (12) and 56–85 (1.6). The values in the parenthesis indicate the total percentage of volunteers in respective age groups (In 25% of forms, volunteer did not disclose their age). Finally, there were 5 forms written by left-handed volunteers and approximately 40:60 ratio of male-to-female volunteers respectively.

Fig. 5. Random samples of isolated handwritten characters

3.2 Data Acquisition and Needed Processing

The two pages of data collection form are digitized using multi functional HP flatbed scanner at a resolution of 300 DPI. During data collection, each form was assigned a unique three digit number (xxx) starting from 001 to 500. Each page of individual form was named xxx_1 and xxx_2 respectively. This would help us easily locate any inadvertently missed pages/forms during data collection stage.

Once digitized, we wrote specific Matlab modules to isolate the handwritten characters. As a first step, the scanned image was converted to binary format using simple global thresholding. We then applied median filtering to get rid of isolated pixels. We initially attempted a computationally inexpensive method to correct skew by detecting page edge pixels and subsequently performing linear regression analysis on those pixels to detect the skew. However, this method was susceptible to outliers along the actual page boundary. Hence, we resorted to using PCP algorithm [9]. Even though it was expensive, we were more concerned about accuracy of detected skew angle. We scanned each page with utmost attention so as to minimize page skew as much as possible and then restricted the profiling of PCP algorithm between −5 to +5° insteps of 0.1. This reduced unnecessary profiling computations involved in the PCP algorithm.

Since volunteers were asked to write characters within the boxes provided, we calculated pixel coordinates corresponding to each box and used them to extract individual characters. This seemed relatively simpler and accurate (than using Horizontal and subsequent vertical projection profiles) as all forms were uniformly designed and underwent similar preprocessing stages. Some sample isolated handwritten characters thus obtained are as shown in Fig. 5.

3.3 Verification Stages

Each isolated character included in the Phase-1 of *Kalanjiyam* has been verified at two different levels: prior-to-scanning and post-scanning during the

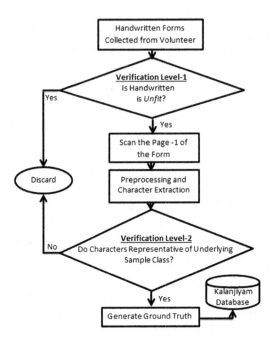

Fig. 6. The overall verification levels in phase-1 of *Kalanjiyam* database

GT review. This is to ensure that each sample is a representative Tamil character. As a result, there were many discarded samples which would be impossible
for computer algorithms (or even humans) to recognize. The overall verification
process is outlined in Fig. 6.

At level-1 verification, the page-1 of each form is manually examined in order
to classify as *Fit* or *Relatively fit* or *Unfit*. We followed the below simple strategies
to classify:

1. If there are more than 90% of characters whose writing style closely matches
   with usual handwriting style, those forms are classified as *Fit*.
2. If there are at least 50% of characters whose writing style matches with typical
   style of underlying character, then that form would be regarded as *Relatively
   Fit*.
3. If there are significant percentage of characters whose writing style deviates
   too much from that of a normal style or if they touch the bounding grid in
   data collection form, then that form would be considered as *Unfit*.

The remaining percentage of *Unfit/Relatively Fit* characters resulting from
above mentioned Step-1 and Step-2 classification would be either completely discarded or considered in an appropriate class whose normal writing style matches
the handwritten style of the character. All those forms which were deemed as
Unfit would be discarded from subsequent scanning process.

Finally, the remaining forms will undergo the steps mentioned in Fig. 3 before
the Level-2 verification takes place. The main objective of Level-2 verification

is to ensure that the GT data that we provide conforms with the handwritten samples in the database. In addition, we also countercheck previously deemed *Fit* samples individually for their appropriateness to be included in the database. Finally, the previously classified *Relatively Fit* and *Unfit* samples are carefully examined either to retain in a suitable class or to completely discard them. Some noteworthy cases we encountered during Level-2 verifications are:

- There were many samples that were not representative of Tamil script as shown in Fig. 7. It is impossible for a machine learning algorithm to recognize such sample and hence we eventually discarded them. This is to ensure that the database contains only those samples that captures various writing styles and at the same time get rid of badly written untypical samples.
- There are many letters in Tamil script which look almost the same except for slight inter-class variation due to the presence of tiny loops, dots, holes etc. Therefore, it is natural that the volunteer might have inadvertently wrote wrong character in the specified box. This may be partly due to negligence but mostly due to high degree of resemblance between samples of difference classes. In such cases the samples were considered in a more suitable class instead of being discarded.
- Some writers have the habit of elongating the tail/modifiers more than needed resulting in either improper or unwanted elongations. The improper elongation sometimes caused the character to be classified as *unfit* for inclusion in the database. In the unwanted elongation cases, we considered the sample in a class whose pattern includes the unwanted elongation as proper unit of letter. Some example cases are shown in Fig. 7.
- In few cases, unnecessary scratches were found (with and without) overlapping with characters. In such cases, we carefully removed those scratch marks instead of discarding otherwise a good sample.
- Although major portion of a character component is same, the presence of a tiny dot above or alongside a Tamil letter makes it different and significantly changes the way it gets pronounced compared to the one without a dot. Many writers follow unorthodox way of marking the presence of such dot by drawing semi circle, curved line, 'V' or inverted 'V' shapes etc. We replaced some of these *dot-like* components by a more suitable shape resembling the dot borrowed from good samples. We do this only if it is impossible for computer algorithm to recognize such shapes as a dot component and also if the remaining component of the letter comes under the purview of *fit* or *relatively fit* scenario.

4   Discussion and Future Work

Our futile search for a publicly available comprehensive offline Tamil database served as a prelude for the creation of *Kalanjiyam* database. The overall data collection for *Kalanjiyam* database is done through 500 volunteers of varying age, profession, handedness, gender etc. Each volunteer is supposed to fill two pages

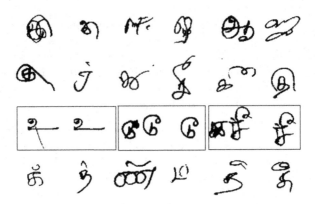

Fig. 7. Discarded, improper/unwanted elongation, scratch corrected and characters with improper dot components (From top-to-bottom rows)

of data collection form where page-1 will collect handwritten isolated characters and page-2 will let the volunteer to write two separate paragraphs (fixed and random) of four sentences atleast. As a result, the database would be available to document research communities as two separate repositories which we coined as Phase-1 and Phase-2. The Phase-1 is an exhaustive collection (at least 200 samples per class) of offline isolated Tamil characters and Phase-2 would be offline samples of hundreds of text lines and paragraph which could be used for many document analysis tasks. In this paper, we presented the overall process involved in the creation of Phase-1 *Kalanjiyam* database involving 500 volunteers.

The database has been hosted at https://kalanjyam.wordpress.com/. This website will be constantly updated as and when the data gets ready for the inclusion into the database. For optimal storage and ease of computational processing, the images are stored in bi-level TIFF format.

At present, we randomly formed a subset of 30% of samples per class as a test set and thus remaining 70% of samples can be used for calibrating the system. We are also contemplating to release another copy of Phase-1 wherein we divide the whole data into three sets: Training, Validation and Testing with split proportion of 50%, 25% and 25% respectively to be useful for many machine learning algorithms. Validation set can be combined with training set for those algorithms that does not need a validation set to tune the learning parameters. We wrote simple Matlab module to automate the process of GT data generation. This is done as a last step after each sample is manually verified and segregated in appropriated classes. The database is supplemented with two types of GT data: The Unicode standard 7.0 and English transliteration.

Our current target is to provide benchmarking on this Phase-1 samples by implementing existing state-of-the-art feature extraction algorithm (structural and statistical features) and testing them on various classifiers (Neural networks, SVMs, etc.). We would then embark on Phase-2 related work as benchmarking of Phase-1 may incite research communities to test their algorithms developed for handwriting recognition. Our initial experience with Phase-2 data suggests that it involves more tedious procedures than that of Phase-1 work. Providing GT data for individual text lines (which may have scribbling, overwriting, correction etc.) for hundreds of paragraphs is one such example that presents the drudgery involved.

We hope that existence of this database would serve as a bench mark and trigger wide spread research in offline Tamil handwriting recognition. Most of the procedures followed in this work are similar to some well known existing databases. This is to ensure that we do not make any major technical mistakes that nullifies the laborious effort that has undergone. It is worth noticing that this database when it is fully developed (including Phase-2) will be first of its kind to provide comprehensive offline samples of isolated characters, words, text-lines and paragraphs pertaining to Tamil script.

References

1. An Anonymous Online Article. airccj.org/CSCP/vol2/csit2213.pdf
2. Lipi Toolkit. http://lipitk.sourceforge.net/datasets/tamilchardata.htm
3. The Online Encyclopeadia of Writing Systems and Languages. www.uk.research. att.com/facedatabase.html
4. Research Papers Related to Lipi Toolkit. http://lipitk.sourceforge.net/about. htm#Research_Pubs
5. The Wikipedia Page. http://en.wikipedia.org/wiki/Tamil_language
6. Bharath, A., Madhvanath, S.: Online handwriting recognition for Indic scripts. In: Govindaraju, V., Setlur, S. (eds.) Guide to OCR for Indic Scripts Document Recognition and Retreival, pp. 209–236. Springer, London (2008). doi:10.1007/978-1-84800-330-9_11
7. Bharath, A., Madhvanath, S.: HMM-based lexicon driven and lexicon-free word recognition for online handwritten Indic scripts. IEEE Trans. Pattern Anal. Mach. Intell. **34**(4), 670–682 (2012)
8. Nethravathi, B., Archana, C.P., Shashikiran, K., Ramakrishnan, A.G., Kumar, V.: Creation of huge annotated database for Tamil and Kannada OHR. In: International Conference on Frontiers in Handwriting Recognition (ICFHR), pp. 415–420 (2010)
9. Chou, C.-H., Chu, S.-Y., Chang, F.: Estimation of skew angles for scanned documents based on piecewise covering by parallelograms. Pattern Recogn. **40**, 443–455 (2007)
10. Jagadeesh Kannan, R., Prabhakar, R.: Offline cursive handwritten Tamil character recognition. WSEAS Trans. Signal Process. **4**(6), 351–360 (2008)
11. Prasanth, L., Babu, J., Raghunath Sharma, K., Prabhakar Rao, G.V., Dinesh, M.: Elastic matching of online handwritten Tamil and Telugu scripts using local features. In: 9th International Conference on Document Analysis and Recognition, pp. 1028–1032 (2007)
12. Anlo Safi, L., Srinivasagan, K.G.: Offline Tamil handwritten character recognition using zone based hybrid feature extraction technique. Int. J. Comput. Appl. **65**(1), 12–16 (2013)
13. Thadchanamoorthy, S., Kodikara, N.D., Premaretne, H.L., Pal, U.: Tamil handwritten city name database development and recognition for postal automation. In: 12th International Conference on Document Analysis and Recognition, pp. 793–797 (2013)

Info-Graphics Retrieval: A Multi-kernel Distance Based Hashing Scheme

Ritu Garg[✉] and Santanu Chaudhury

Department of Electrical Engineering, Indian Institute of Technology Delhi,
Delhi, India
ritu2721a@gmail.com, schaudhury@gmail.com

Abstract. Information retrieval research has shown significant improvement and provided techniques that retrieve documents in image or text form. However, retrieval of multi-modal documents has been given very less attention. We aim to build a system for retrieval of documents with embedded information graphics (Info-graphics). Info-graphics are images of bar charts and line graphs appearing with textual components in magazines, newspapers, and journals. In this paper, we present multi-modal document image retrieval framework by learning an optimal fusion of information from text and info-graphics regions. The evaluation of the proposed concept is demonstrated on documents collected from various sources such as magazines and journals.

1 Introduction

The state-of-the-art document image retrieval systems exploit textual features for indexing document images. This not only requires reliable optical character recognition (OCR) systems but also semantically meaningful representation. The other category of document retrieval techniques rely on appropriate word image feature representation that helps in building a computationally inexpensive retrieval framework. Performance of existing retrieval techniques is limited as they provide uni-modal access to multi-modal documents. Moreover, such techniques fail to address the semantic relevance between the user query and actual information requirement.

A multi-modal document image represents information in multiple modalities including text, pictures and graphics in image form. The existing document image retrieval technique exploit either text or image modality for retrieval of multi-modal documents. For efficient access and management of such multi-modal documents efficient indexing techniques are required. We focus on building an indexing framework for retrieval of multi-modal documents that consists of text and info-graphics, where info-graphics are bar chart or line graphs that co-exist with textual portions in popular media such as newspaper, journals and magazines. Sample images are shown in Fig. 1. The information contained in info-graphics is often not repeated in the articles text or the info-graphics contain very less or no information about message it conveys. Thus, info-graphics

© Springer International Publishing AG 2017
S. Mukherjee et al. (Eds.): ICVGIP 2016, LNCS 10481, pp. 288–298, 2017.
https://doi.org/10.1007/978-3-319-68124-5_25

Fig. 1. Sample multi-modal document images where text and info-graphics coexists

in multi-modal documents cannot be ignored and combining information from both articles text and info-graphics can offer effective retrieval framework.

In this paper, we address the problem of combining information from different modalities i.e. text and info-graphics to present a more effective solution for retrieval allowing to exploit the underlying syntactic and semantic structure of multi-modal documents. In addition, due to distinct statistical properties of different modalities we employ MKL for optimal feature combination in kernel space. We present the application of multi-modal document indexing framework [5] that uses Multiple Kernel Learning (MKL) for generating composite hashing indexes using different modalities. The optimal fusion of multi-modal features in kernel space is formulated as a multi-objective formulation solved using Genetic Algorithm (GA) for building a retrieval framework that maximizes search accuracy with minimum search time.

The organization of the paper is as follows. Section 2 gives brief survey of existing literature in this area. The indexing framework and its application for retrieval of document images with info-graphics is discussed in Sects. 3 and 4 respectively. Finally, Sect. 5 concludes he paper and discusses the future directions for extension.

2   Related Work

Primarily the access to the multi-modal document image collections is via metadata. Traditional document image indexing systems rely on efficient image feature representation [2] schemes that performs reliably on document collection. However, the retrieval time is huge due to image matching in feature space which is computationally intensive and does not ensure semantic relevance of retrieved documents to user query. On the other hand, content level access to multi-modal document image collection can be provided by exploiting the textual attributes [10,11] of document and matching query words with words in documents or using related words or concepts observed using tf-idf or LDA [21] respectively.

Much of the research on info-graphics has focused on following: (1) classification of the type of bar graph or line chart [17], (2) extracting information and redesigns the info-graphics [19], and (3) convert info-graphics into tabular form [10]. Some work has been reported for summarization of info-graphics, majorly bar graphs and line charts [3,4]. To extract summary from info-graphic, the sample info-graphic is first segmented into visually distinguishable trends followed by extraction of communicative signals or features from the graph such as variation in colors on the bars, annotation of a point in line graph, whether labels on bars exists in the caption etc. These features are then fed as evidences to Bayesian network that hypothesizes the graphics intended message. Additional relevant propositions are observed using content identification rules [22] developed from human subject experiments that are combined to construct brief summary of info-graphic. In [14] author uses a set of heuristics to learn models that hypothesize information about the independent and dependent axis and the category of relevant graphics using the words that appears in the info-graphics caption and the semantics of the user query.

There has been very limited research for info-graphics retrieval. The summarization approach presented in [14,22] has been explored for retrieval of info-graphics as well. Li et al. [12,13] present a methodology for retrieving info-graphics relevant to user query by hypothesizing the structural content and high level intended message from info-graphics, followed by ranking the pre-selected pool of info-graphics using mixture model taking into account the textual content of info-graphic, relevance measure of the structural and intended message content in user query. Very little attention has been invested in the retrieval of multi-modal documents where text and info-graphics coexists in a document image. In [23], authors present a summarization technique for multi-modal documents that first constructs summary of the info-graphics in document followed by integration of the graphic summaries with the overall summary of the document. They present a methodology for retrieval of info-graphics that involves a mixture model using info-graphics intended message and textual components such as caption or accompanying text. They use KL divergence based metric to measure similarity between textual component and info-graphics and use appropriate paragraphs in mixture model to rank the info-graphics for retrieval in response to user query. Saleh et al. [18] present a method that learns style similarity metric for searching info-graphics. They consider info-graphics as complex overlaid design integrating text, images, sketches and charts. They use a combination of color histogram and HOG features.

Often text in the info-graphics is sparse and hence does not provide sufficient information for retrieval. Use of visual features such as color, texture or shape features has been primarily used for classification tasks, moreover they fail to capture the semantics of query for retrieval tasks. Thus, it is required to extract features from textual components within and surrounding the info-graphics and combine them with structural features of info-graphics for effective retrieval of multi-modal documents with embedded info-graphics that are not just visually similar but are in coherence with the user query. Combining information from multiple modalities and using it for retrieval has been reported in literature [8]. They demonstrate indexing of document images with embedded graphical components i.e. faces, buildings and natural scenes. They combine texture features extracted from word images and graphical components. In [5], author show indexing and retrieval of degraded document images by combining features from word in image and digitized form. We extend the framework for retrieval of multi-modal documents where text and info-graphics occur together. The indexing framework combines textual and structural features extracted from multi-modal document image collections. The framework uses MKL for optimal fusion of both text and info-graphics to generate composite indexing for improved retrieval. The retrieval results are ranked on kernel distance based similarity.

3 Multi-modal Document Indexing Framework

In this section, we present an overview of the multi-modal document image retrieval system. The document indexing methodology uses traditional hashing based indexing scheme. Figure 2 shows the block diagram that summarizes the indexing and retrieval framework. The framework shows fusion of multiple modalities, where each modality represents different component or feature representation. Finding optimal combination of multiple modalities is done using MKL, which is applied to distance based hashing (DBH) for generation of composite document indexing space. The scheme applies semi-supervised technique for learning the parameterized linear combination of modalities for composite indexing. Further, in this section we give a brief overview of the Kernel Distance based Hashing (KDBH) and how optimal kernel weights are learned for linear combination of features from multiple modalities using MKL.

Kernel DBH [7,8] is an extension to DBH, which applies MKL to learn optimal kernel K from a set of user define base kernels for generating composite

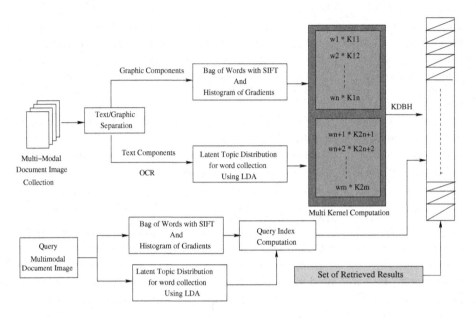

Fig. 2. Overall architecture for multi-modal document indexing

indicies for hashing in kernel space. KDBH defines line projection function in kernel space using pivot pair $(\phi(x_1), \phi(x_2))$ as:

$$G^{\phi(x_1),\phi(x_2)}\phi(x) = \frac{K(x_1,x_1) - K(x_1,x) + K(x_2,x) - K(x_1,x_2)}{\sqrt{(K(x_1,x_1) - 2K(x_1,x_2) + K(x_2,x_2))}} \qquad (1)$$

where kernel K is defined as a linear combination of weighted base kernels,

$$K(x_1,x_2) = \sum_{i=0}^{n} w_i K_i(x_1,x_2) \ with \ w_i \geq \forall i \qquad (2)$$

Multi-kernel DBH discussed in [5,6] is formulated as a multi-objective optimization problem for computing retrieval accuracy and time over validation set X_v, defined as:

$$\bar{x} = argmax_w F(X, X_v, w) F = fun(U, V) \qquad (3)$$

where X represents complete training set, X_v is the validation set on which function F is evaluated for different weights w. U and V compute the accuracy of retrieval obtained over X_v using weights w and the search complexity of the indexing scheme respectively. The measure used for evaluating U and V are:

1. First optimization objective is to improve *Retrieval Accuracy*, using Mean Average Precision (MAP) measure. MAP computes average precision for all relevant points in ranked results.

$$MAP(X_v) = \frac{1}{|X_v|} \sum_{j=1}^{|X_v|} \frac{1}{n_j} \sum_{k=1}^{n_j} Precision(R_{jk}) \qquad (4)$$

2. Second objective function aims to improve *Search Time Complexity*, using Entropy measure. Search time is determined by the number of objects in every bucket. In case of unbalanced buckets, the number of comparisons would be high as the probability of finding relevant documents in dense buckets is high. Thus, to reduce the average number of comparisons, every bucket must contain equal number of objects thereby maximizing the entropy.

$$Entropy(y) = -\sum_{i=1}^{2^m} \frac{N_i}{N} log \frac{N_i}{N} \tag{5}$$

where y is m-dimensional binary vector, N_i is the number of objects in bucket i and N is the total number of objects. Entropy is maximum for equal number of objects in each bucket.

The multi-objective formulation is solved using GA for finding optimal weights for linear combination of modalities using MKL, hence weights w are the optimization parameters.

The steps followed for application of KDBH for indexing and retrieval of document images are:

1. Identify text and non-text regions in document images. Here the non-text regions are info-graphics which can be either bar graphs or line charts. We use Tesseract OCR to digitize all the text in document image. We also identify text in the info-graphics using the scheme presented in [19] and eliminate them from indexing.
2. For each text term we compute latent topic distributions and use SIFT and HOG features for the info-graphics.
3. For defining the indexing scheme, we apply clustering using image and text features. This is done over the entire collection. The cluster centers are treated as pivot object set.
4. Next, we apply MKL in a GA based solution to learn optimal weights for kernel combination using both the modalities. For learning optimal kernel combination of features for indexing, kernels set is computed by ORing individual base kernel sets belonging to each feature. Gaussian kernel computed over different variances has been used as base kernel for the image components and for text terms, base kernel set is comprised of KL divergence based kernel.
5. Once we have the kernel weights, hash index computation and the generation of hash functions is done off-line for all the training samples.
6. For every query document we identify the text and info-graphics regions. Also we select a word from the document to retrieve other related document image. The hash index is computed using both the text and info-graphic features. The retrieved documents are ranked on basis of kernel distance based similarity.

MKL based indexing provides an ideal solution for combining text and info-graphic components for composite indexing of multi-modal documents. Subsequent section provide details for the dataset, feature extraction and associated parameters. Finally the retrieval performance is computed using MAP measure.

3.1   Data Description

As there does not exists any well known dataset for info-graphics, documents were collected by querying the web with keywords such as info-graphics or bar-charts or line-charts from four domains namely technology, stock exchange, health and tourism. We collected a total of 880 documents with embedded info-graphics. Text and graphics components are obtained by applying Tesseract OCR [20]. Segmentation resulted in 640 graphic images. The text component are digitized using Tesseract OCR [20], followed by elimination of stop-words, punctuation and numerals giving us 11850 text terms. The validation query set X_v consists of 100 text and 30 graphic queries. For evaluation of the indexing framework the test query set X_q consists of 80 text and 50 graphic queries. The proposed indexing framework generates unique indices by KDBH, where optimal kernels for indexing are learned by combining kernels computed for text and graphic features. For the given text or graphic query the framework computes indices on the hash table.

3.2   Features and Parameters

Features used to represent the text terms and graphic components are:

a. **Latent Topic Distribution** for text terms. The latent topic distribution for text terms as well as the text extracted from the info-graphics, i.e. $p(z|w)$ is used to represent the digitized documents in the indexing space using kernel distance based hashing. We learn topic distribution accompanying textual descriptions. Topic distribution based features possess distinct statistical characteristics, hence we need to apply a different set of kernels that compare probabilistic distributions. Symmetric Kullback-Leibler Divergence [16] based kernels as shown in Eq. (6) are used to represent the probabilistic distribution for indexing. Different values for scale (α) and shift (β) parameters are used for defining base kernel set. For our experiments, following values of $\alpha = (0.1, 0.5, 1, 2, 5)$ and $\beta = 0$ were selected. The topic distribution for the complete collection is learned for different number of topic, i.e. $z = (25, 50, 75, 100)$.

$$K(w_i, w_j) = K(p(z|w_i), p(z|w_j))$$
$$= \exp^{-\alpha D(p(z|w_i), p(z|w_j)) + \beta} \tag{6}$$

where D is symmetric KL divergence distance given as:

$$D(p(z|w_i), p(z|w_j)) = \int_{-\infty}^{\infty} p(z|w_i) \log(\frac{p(z|w_i)}{p(z|w_j)}) dz$$
$$+ \int_{-\infty}^{\infty} p(z|w_j) \log(\frac{p(z|w_j)}{p(z|w_i)}) dz$$

b. **Visual Features for info-graphics:** We have used SIFT and HOG for representing info-graphic images. A set of Linear and Gaussian kernels having variances from 2^{-5} to 2^5 with an increment of 0.5 at exponent are used to form the base kernel set.

b.1 **SIFT Features:** Bag-of-words computed with SIFT [15] features is applied for robust info-graphic representation. A visual vocabulary of 50 words was selected empirically. Thus the resulting 50 dimensional bag-of-words representation for the info-graphics segment.

b.2 **HOG Features** [1]: It is computed as the histogram of image derivatives with uniform bins. The histogram is weighted by the gradient magnitude. To capture finer details of the info-graphics we extract HOG features with cell size of 16.

4   Experimental Results

MKL is applied for optimal fusion of features from different modalities. It learns kernel K defined as a parametric linear combination of base kernels (2) for hashing. The kernel weights w_i are learned using multi-objective GA based framework. The kernel weight vector is encoded as a real valued vector of length 10. Other parameter settings of GA are (i) Initial population size = 40, (ii) Pareto fraction = 0.35, (iii) crossover probability = 0.8, (iv) GA iterations = 100. The experiments were carried out with variations in the number of hash tables ($L = 40, 60$) and hash function ($k = 12, 24$). One of the most important parameters for effective indexing is the pivot points, which are chosen using cluster centers found by applying DBSCAN over the complete dataset.

Similarity search is done based on the kernel distance k_{dis} computed as $\sum_{i=1}^{n} w_i K_i$. With graphic based queries the retrieval performance in terms of MAP score with hashing parameters $L = 40, k = 12$ is 25.24%, 78.14 with text based queries and the overall MAP score achieved on query set (X_q) is 81.27%. We compare our framework with one of the recent works in info-graphics retrieval by Li et al. [12]. We use Normalized Discounted Cumulative Gain (NDCG) [9] to evaluate the retrieval result and compare. In NDCG computation, as the length of the search varies depending on the query, performance evaluation from one query to another cannot be done using DCG alone. Hence, cumulative gain at each position for a chosen value of p (depicting the top p samples chosen from the list of retrieved results) should be normalized across queries. In order to do this, the documents in corpus is sorted as per their relative relevance and Ideal DCG (IDCG) is computed through position p. For our experiments we choose the value of $p = 10$. For a query the normalized discounted cumulative gain (NDCG) at p is computed as:

$$nDCG_p = \frac{DCG_p}{IDCG_p}$$

$$IDCH_p = \sum_{i=1}^{|REL|} \frac{2^{rel_i} - 1}{log_2(i + 1)} \tag{7}$$

$$DCG_p = \sum_{i=1}^{p} \frac{2^{rel_i} - 1}{log_2(i + 1)}$$

In Eq. 8, $|REL|$ is the list of relevant documents in corpus upto position p. Its value range between 0 and 1. It measure how well the ranked documents are retrieved using the proposed methodology vis-a-vis the rank given by the user. The Table 1 shows the evaluation of retrieval results using MAP and NDCG metric. The last row of the table shows the result obtained when text based feature and visual features from info-graphics in multi-modal documents are combined. We achieved $NDCG@10 = 0.6201$ on the given query set X_q for top 10 retrieved results. In comparison to the info-graphic retrieval technique presented in [12], our approach shows a slight improvement as the $NDCG@10$ achieved is 0.6201 on a similar data-set, while the maximum $NDCG@10$ obtained by their approach is 0.4866.

Table 1. Retrieval results for multi-modal document image retrieval

Features	MAP	NDCG@10
Image feature	25.24	0.1149
Text feature	78.14	0.4881
Image + text feature*	81.27	0.6201

5 Conclusion

In this paper we present a framework for retrieval of multi-modal documents where text and info-graphics coexists. The info-graphics we have focused on are bar graphs and line charts. The indexing methodology presented allows optimal fusion of features from text and info-graphics for multi-modal document image retrieval. We extract visual features such as Histogram of Gradients and SIFT from info-graphics and latent topic distribution for the text portions. The proposed indexing methodology is evaluated for retrieval performance in terms search accuracy and time, and shows significant improvement in comparison to the state-of-the-art. The experimental results are presented for English documents collected mostly from magazines, newspapers and books. In future we would like to experiment with with more complex information graphics.

References

1. Dalal, N., Triggs, B.: Histograms of oriented gradients for human detection. In: Proceedings of the 2005 IEEE Computer Society Conference on Computer Vision and Pattern Recognition (CVPR 2005), Washington, D.C., vol. 1, pp. 886–893. IEEE Computer Society (2005)
2. Datta, R., Joshi, D., Li, J., Wang, J.Z.: Image retrieval: ideas, influences, and trends of the new age. ACM Comput. Surv. **40**(2), 5:1–5:60 (2008)
3. Demir, S., Carberry, S., McCoy, K.F.: Generating textual summaries of bar charts. In: Proceedings of the Fifth International Natural Language Generation Conference, pp. 7–15 (2008)

4. Elzer, S., Carberry, S., Zukerman, I.: The automated understanding of simple bar charts. Artif. Intell. **175**(2), 526–555 (2011)
5. Garg, R., Hassan, E., Chaudhury, S.: Document indexing framework for retrieval of degraded document images. In: 13th International Conference on Document Analysis and Recognition, ICDAR 2015, Nancy, France, 23–26 August 2015, pp. 1261–1265 (2015)
6. Gaur, V., Hassan, E., Chaudhury, S.: Design of multi-kernel distance based hashing with multiple objectives for image indexing. In: ICPR, pp. 2637–2642 (2014)
7. Hassan, E., Chaudhury, S., Gopal, M.: Feature combination in kernel space for distance based image hashing. IEEE Trans. Multimedia **14**(4), 1179–1195 (2012)
8. Hassan, E., Chaudhury, S., Gopal, M.: Multi-modal information integration for document retrieval. In: ICDAR, pp. 1200–1204 (2013)
9. Järvelin, K., Kekäläinen, J.: Cumulated gain-based evaluation of IR techniques. ACM Trans. Inf. Syst. **20**(4), 422–446 (2002)
10. Lapata, M.: Image and natural language processing for multimedia information retrieval. In: Proceedings of the 32nd European Conference on Advances in Information Retrieval, p. 12 (2010)
11. Lew, M.S., Sebe, N., Djeraba, C., Jain, R.: Content-based multimedia information retrieval: state of the art and challenges. ACM Trans. Multimedia Comput. Commun. Appl. **2**(1), 1–19 (2006)
12. Li, Z., Carberry, S., Fang, H., McCoy, K.F., Peterson, K.: Infographics retrieval: a new methodology. In: Métais, E., Roche, M., Teisseire, M. (eds.) Natural Language Processing and Information Systems. LNCS, vol. 8455, pp. 101–113. Springer, Heidelberg (2014). doi:10.1007/978-3-319-07983-7_15
13. Li, Z., Carberry, S., Fang, H., McCoy, K.F., Peterson, K., Stagitis, M.: A novel methodology for retrieving infographics utilizing structure and message content. Data Knowl. Eng. **100**(PB), 191–210 (2015)
14. Li, Z., Stagitis, M., Carberry, S., McCoy, K.F.: Towards retrieving relevant information graphics. In: Proceedings of the 36th International ACM SIGIR Conference on Research and Development in Information Retrieval, SIGIR 2013, pp. 789–792 (2013)
15. Lowe, D.G.: Object recognition from local scale-invariant features. In: Proceedings of the Seventh IEEE International Conference on Computer Vision, vol. 2, pp. 1150–1157 (1999)
16. Moreno, P.J., Ho, P.P., Vasconcelos, N.: A Kullback-Leibler divergence based kernel for SVM classification in multimedia applications. In: Advances in Neural Information Processing Systems, pp. 1385–1392 (2004)
17. Prasad, V.S.N., Siddiquie, B., Golbeck, J., Davis, L.S.: Classifying computer generated charts. In: 2007 International Workshop on Content-Based Multimedia Indexing, pp. 85–92 (2007)
18. Saleh, B., Dontcheva, M., Hertzmann, A., Liu, Z.: Learning style similarity for searching infographics. In: Proceedings of the 41st Graphics Interface Conference, pp. 59–64. Canadian Information Processing Society (2015)
19. Savva, M., Kong, N., Chhajta, A., Fei-Fei, L., Agrawala, M., Heer, J.: ReVision: automated classification, analysis and redesign of chart images. In: Proceedings of the 24th Annual ACM Symposium on User Interface Software and Technology, pp. 393–402 (2011)
20. Smith, R.: An overview of the tesseract OCR engine. In: Proceedings of the Ninth International Conference on Document Analysis and Recognition, Washington, D.C., vol. 02, pp. 629–633. IEEE Computer Society (2007)

21. Wei, X., Croft, W.B.: LDA-based document models for ad-hoc retrieval. In: Proceedings of the 29th Annual International ACM SIGIR Conference on Research and Development in Information Retrieval, pp. 178–185 (2006)
22. Wu, P.: Recognizing the intended message of line graphs: methodology and applications. Ph.D. thesis, Newark, DE, USA (2012)
23. Wu, P., Carberry, R.: Toward extractive summarization of multimodal documents. In: Proceedings of the Canadian AI Workshop on Text Summarization, pp. 53–64 (2011)

MedImage

Neovascularization Detection on Retinal Images

Sudeshna Sil Kar[1], Santi P. Maity[1(✉)], and Seba Maity[2]

[1] Department of Information Technology,
Indian Institute of Engineering Science and Technology,
Shibpur, Howrah 711103, India
sudeshna.sil@gmail.com, santipmaity@it.iiests.ac.in
[2] Department of Electronics and Telecommunication Engineering,
College of Engineering and Management, Kolaghat, Kolaghat, India
seba.maity@gmail.com

Abstract. Proliferative Diabetic Retinopathy (PDR) is characterized by the growth of new abnormal, thin blood vessels called neovascularzation that spread along the retinal surface. An automated computer aided diagnosis system needs to identify neovasculars for PDR screening. Retinal images are often noisy and poorly illuminated. The thin vessels mostly appear to be disconnected and are inseparable from the background. This paper proposes a new method for neovascularization detection on retinal images. Blood vessels are extracted as thick, medium and thin types using multilevel thresholding on matched filter response. The total mutual information between the vessel density and the tortuosity of the thin vessel class is maximized to obtain the optimal thresholds to classify the normal and the abnormal vessels. Simulation results demonstrate that the proposed method outperforms the existing ones for neovascularization detection with an average accuracy of 97.54%.

Keywords: Neovascularization · Proliferative diabetic retinopathy · Mutual information · Compactness · Tortuosity

1 Introduction

Diabetic Retinopathy (DR) is a progressive ocular complication of diabetes melitus that may lead to severe vision loss and sometimes even blindness. There are two main stages of DR, the early stage known as non proliferative diabetic retinopathy (NPDR) and the advanced stage known as proliferative diabetic retinopathy (PDR) [3]. Different retinal lesions such as microaneurysms, dot hemorrhages etc. appear as the primary symptoms of NPDR. The blood vessels that nourish the retina sometimes get blocked and damaged with leakage of fluid (exudates) in this stage. PDR is characterized by the abnormal formation of the new, small, weak and the thin blood vessels along the surface of the retina, also referred to as neovascularization [11]. Being delicate and fragile, these blood vessels cause frequent bleeding that leads to blurred vision.

© Springer International Publishing AG 2017
S. Mukherjee et al. (Eds.): ICVGIP 2016, LNCS 10481, pp. 301–313, 2017.
https://doi.org/10.1007/978-3-319-68124-5_26

Retinal neovascularization most often appears on the optic disc (OD) known as neovascularization on OD (NVD) or on the retinal surface called neovascularization elsewhere (NVE) [5]. Generally these thin vessels are of low contrast, broken, disconnected with unsharp borders and almost inseparable from the background. Presence of noise along with poor illumination due to improper focusing of light during image acquisition, altogether make neovascularization detection and classification (segregation) from the normal blood vessels really a complicated and challenging task.

To this aim, this paper proposes a new method for neovascularization detection. Blood vessels are extracted separately as the thick, the medium and the thin vessels using multi-level thresholding on the maximum matched filter response (MFR). Detection of neovascularization from the entire vascular structure requires a number of features' extraction and the existing literature propose few techniques that suffer from the system complexity. Hence, a simple method that accurately detect the neovascularization is of utmost importance for screening of DR. Some of the features like vessel density and tortuosity are found to be unique for neovascularization with respect to its normal thin counterpart. To reduce the computational burden, the vessel density (compactness) and the tortuosity of the thin vessels are computed. Their mutual information (MI) is then maximized to obtain the thresholds that classify the thin vessels into the normal and the abnormal (neovascularization) class.

The rest of the paper is organized as follows: a detailed description of different state-of-the-art methods, their limitations and scope of this work are presented in Sect. 2. The proposed method of neovascularization detection is described in Sect. 3. Section 4 reports the experimental results and performance evaluation. Conclusions and scope of the future works are stated in Sect. 5.

2   Literature Review and Limitations

Detection of neovascularization, being a crucial stage prior to blindness, is of great importance for the diagnosis of PDR. A brief overview of the existing methods is presented in this section.

Vessel-like candidate segments are first detected and for each candidate segment, fifteen feature parameters are then calculated in [5]. Each segment is categorized as normal or abnormal type using a support vector machine (SVM) classifier. The main limitation of this method is that instead of detecting the entire abnormal vessel structure, the method is restricted to detect the abnormal vessels on the OD, i.e., NVD only. Agurto et al. [2] first manually selected a region of interest (ROI) from the image that contains the OD. The ROI is gradually reduced and textural features are extracted using amplitude-modulation frequency-modulation (AM-FM) techniques followed by granulometry to differentiate NVD from a normal OD. This method is restricted for NVD detection only. A multi-level m-mediod based classifier is used for abnormal blood vessel detection by Akram et al. [3]. This method is very efficient in detecting both NVD and NVE. However, this method involves extraction of a large number of features which increases the system complexity. A dual classification approach using the standard line operator and a novel modified line operator is implemented by Welikala et al. [13] to generate two different segmented vessel maps. Each of them is then classified independently as normal or abnormal using SVM classifier. Final decision is obtained by combining the individual classification outcomes. The vessel segmentation, straight vessel removal, feature extraction and classification of each of the two vessel maps make the system time consuming and complex.

Scope of present work- Detection of the entire retinal vessel map followed by their classification as the normal and the abnormal vessels in a single framework is very much essential for DR screening. This work suggests a new method for neovascularization detection using MI maximization which is not explored earlier to the best of our knowledge. The main contributions of the present work are as follows:

- First the vessels of the retinal image are extracted as the thick, the medium and the thin vessel class separately by conditional entropy optimization on maximum MFR to develop multi-level thresholds [9]. Since different properties like the width, the diameter, the density, the energy etc. of the thick and the medium vessels differ from the normal/abnormal thin vessels and neovascularization appears as thin microvascular nets, only the thin vessel class is considered for further processing.
- It is very difficult to obtain the optimal threshold that partitions the thin vessel class into the normal and the abnormal types due to their similar vascular properties. Also, thresholding on a singular property is not sufficient for neovascularization detection. Vessel density (compactness) and tortuosity are the two distinct features which are always high for the abnormal vessels as compared to the normal vessels. To obtain the optimal thresholds, these two features of the thin vessels are computed and their MI is maximized using Differential Evolution (DE).
- Proposed method is applied on a large set of images on different online databases [1, 7, 8, 12] and produces significantly improved results over the existing techniques.

Inclusion of all these attributes make the system efficient and robust enough to handle diverse types of diseased images for abnormal vessel detection. The main advantages of the proposed method are as follows:

- Most of the existing methods [2, 3, 5] involve a large set of features for abnormal vessel detection. This makes the method highly time consuming. Furthermore, inclusions of too many features sometimes results in poor performance on classification. On the contrary, less in number yet unique features may lead to even better performance at low computations. It is found in the proposed method that consideration of only two features, namely the compactness and the tortuosity are sufficient for accurate neovascularization detection. This reduces the time complexity to a large extent.

- Contrary to the state-of-the-art methods [2,5], where the scope is limited for NVD only, the proposed method addresses both the problem of NVD and NVE detection.
- Neovascularization detection methods, reported in the literature, mostly employ SVM [5] or linear regression classifier [2] based on supervised learning. For each and every new dataset the classifier needs to be trained separately with a large number of pre-classified data. This makes the classifier complex and time consuming. On the other hand, the proposed algorithm is completely unsupervised and no training set is required. Only a single pass is required which makes the entire process faster.

3   Proposed Method

The schematic diagram of the proposed method that consists of four steps is shown in Fig. 1.

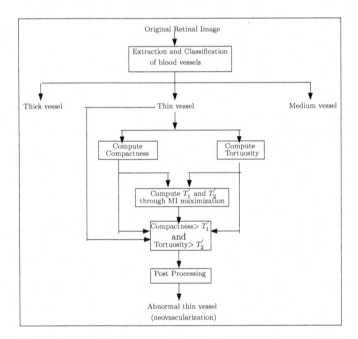

Fig. 1. Schematic diagram of the proposed method

3.1   Extraction and Classification of Retinal Vasculature

Accurate extraction of retinal blood vessels is very much necessary for neovascularization detection. This paper implements the DE based conditional entropy maximization algorithm for vessel extraction as reported in [9]. First green color plane from the RGB image is extracted as it shows the maximum vessel-background contrast. The different steps for vessel extraction are as follows:

Step 1: Curvelet denoising and edge enhancement: It is assumed that the retinal images are corrupted by additive white Gaussian noise with zero mean and some variance which is estimated. Curvelet transform with different scales and orientations are applied to decompose the retinal image into a number of subbands. Noise is then suppressed by hard thresholding of the curvelet coefficients. Next, the detailed subbands are amplified by a factor determined optimally through DE while coarse subband coefficients are set to zero. Inverse curvelet transform then offers background suppressed images with detailed edges enhanced.

Step 2: Sequential Bandpass filter (BPF) operation: The edge enhanced image thus obtained is then passed through a series of sequential BPFs (of bandwidth 10–15 Hz) determined optimally through DE to highlight the individual vessel segments. Each BPF output image is then weighted and superimposed on the edge enhanced image. The frequency band for each BPF varies from one image to another. The optimal gain (G), the lower and the upper cut-off frequencies f_L and f_U, respectively of the BPF is difficult to calculate analytically. For individual image, the gain and the two cut-off frequencies of each BPF is determined using DE through the maximization of Mean Structural Similarity Measure (M_{SSIM}), a standard measure of quantifying visual image quality.

Step 3: Matched filtering and fuzzy conditional entropy maximization: The blood vessels, in general, travel radially outward at different orientations after emerging from the OD. To track the vessels of multiple directions, the Gaussian filter kernel (with $\sigma = 1.5$) is rotated at an incremental angle of $12°$ and is matched (convolved) with the image under consideration. The maximum MFR corresponding to each rotation is retained to form the data set.

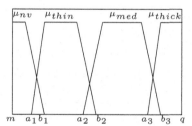

Fig. 2. Trapezoidal membership function for thresholding in 4 classes

Fuzzy conditional entropy maximization is then applied on the data set to partition it into the background, the thin, the medium and the thick vessel class using the standard trapezoidal membership functions $\mu_{nv}, \mu_{thin}, \mu_{med}$ and μ_{thick}, respectively as shown in Fig. 2. These fuzzy functions depend on the fuzzy parameters $a_1, b_1, a_2, b_2, a_3, b_3$, the optimal values of which are determined through DE based conditional entropy maximization. According to [4], suppose X is a discrete universe of discourse, and if $A,\ B \in \zeta(X)$ where $\zeta(X)$ contains all the fuzzy subsets of the discrete universe of discourse X and

$$X^+ = \{x\ |x \in X, \mu_A(x) \geq \mu_B(x)\} \tag{1}$$

$$X^- = \{x\ |x \in X, \mu_A(x) < \mu_B(x)\} \tag{2}$$

then fuzzy conditional entropy can be expressed as:

$$H(A|B) = -\frac{1}{n} \sum_{x \in X^+} \{\mu_A(x)log(\mu_A(x)) - \mu_B(x)log(\mu_B(x))$$

$$+[1 - \mu_A(x)]log\ [1 - \mu_A(x)] - [1 - \mu_B(x)]log\ [1 - \mu_B(x)]\} \tag{3}$$

$$H(B|A) = -\frac{1}{n} \sum_{x \in X^-} \{\mu_B(x)log(\mu_B(x)) - \mu_A(x)log(\mu_A(x))$$

$$+[1 - \mu_B(x)]log\ [1 - \mu_B(x)] - [1 - \mu_A(x)]log\ [1 - \mu_A(x)]\} \tag{4}$$

where n is the total number of points within X. Similarly the expression for conditional entropy between the non-vessel and the thin vessel class ($H(nv|thin)$), the thin and the medium vessel class ($H(thin|med)$), the medium and the thick vessel class ($H(med|thick)$) can also be obtained. The total fuzzy conditional entropy $H(nonvess|vess)$ can now be expressed as:

$$H(nonvess|vess) = H(nv|thin) + H(thin|med) + H(med|thick) \tag{5}$$

Equation (5) is maximized using DE to obtain the optimal values of a_n and b_n for $n = 1, 2, 3$. The thresholds that partition the maximum MFR into 4 classes, namely the non-vessel, the thin, the medium and the thick vessels are T_1, T_2 and T_3, respectively and can be calculated from the following equation.

$$T_n = \frac{a_n + b_n}{2} \quad for \quad n = 1, 2, 3 \tag{6}$$

Step 4: Post-processing in vessel extraction: Noise and other spurious components sometimes are detected as thin vessels due to their low MFR values. Hence, a post-processing operation is needed to exclude them from the vessel net structure. Connected components, based on 8-connectivity, is then used and the value of the same above a threshold value (determined experimentally) is identified as a vessel component. Classification of blood vessels for one sample image has been shown in Fig. 3.

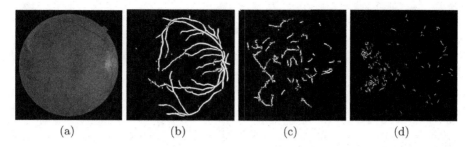

(a)   (b)   (c)   (d)

Fig. 3. Result of vessel classification (a) original image with neovascularization. Detected (b) thick, (c) medium and (d) thin vessels by [9]

3.2   Feature Extraction

After classification of vessels into different categories, the thin vessel class is selected for subsequent processing. A sub window of size $(w \times w)$ pixels is scanned through the image. For each candidate segment, within the sub-window, two distinct local features, namely the vessel density and the tortuosity are calculated. Vessel density (V_d) is computed by dividing the total number of vessel pixels within the region of neighborhood by the window size [3]. Equation (7) is used to measure tortuosity (V_t).

$$V_t = \frac{1}{p-1} \sum_{i=1}^{p-1} \mid \theta_{i+1} - \theta_i \mid \tag{7}$$

where θ_i is the tangential angle at the ith element and 'p' is the number of segment elements.

3.3   Mutual Information Maximization Using DE

MI measures the statistical dependence between two random variables or the amount of information that one variable conveys about the other [10]. For the two discrete random variables (A, B) with probability distributions $p(a)$ and $p(b)$, respectively MI is defined as

$$I(A, B) = H(A) + H(B) - H(A, B) \tag{8}$$

where $H(A), H(B)$ are the entropy of A and B, respectively, and $H(A, B)$ is their joint entropy.

Let the V_d and the V_t values of each candidate segment are stored in two arrays X and Y, respectively. Here $X = \{m_1, m_1 + 1, \ldots \ldots, q_1 - 1, q_1\}$ with m_1 and q_1 being the lowest and the highest vessel densities, respectively. Similarly, $Y = \{m_2, m_2 + 1, \ldots \ldots, q_2 - 1, q_2\}$ where m_2 and q_2 represent the lowest and the highest tortuosity values, respectively. Each of X and Y are then classified into the normal and the abnormal vessel (neovascularization) class. Let V_d and V_t are

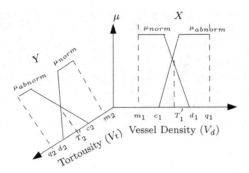

Fig. 4. Trapezoidal membership functions

the random variables denoted by x and y, respectively such that $x \in X$ and $y \in Y$. The optimal thresholds T_1' and T_2' that partition X and Y into the normal and the abnormal thin vessels are obtained through $I(X, Y)$ maximization. $I(X, Y)$ can be represented as

$$I(X, Y) = I(X, Y)_{norm} + I(X, Y)_{abnorm} \tag{9}$$

where $I(X, Y)_{norm}$ and $I(X, Y)_{abnorm}$ represent the MI of X and Y for the normal and the abnormal class, respectively. A 2-level standard trapezoidal membership function as shown in Fig. 4 is used in the present work to classify each of X and Y. The membership functions μ_{norm} and μ_{abnorm} for the normal and the abnormal class, respectively depend on the fuzzy parameters a_n and b_n and can be mathematically expressed as:

$$\mu_{norm}(k) = \begin{cases} 1 & k \leq c_n \\ \dfrac{k - c_n}{c_n - d_n} & c_n \leq k \leq d_n \\ 0 & k > d_n \end{cases} \tag{10}$$

$$\mu_{abnorm}(k) = \begin{cases} 0 & k \leq c_n \\ \dfrac{k - c_n}{d_n - c_n} & c_n \leq k \leq d_n \\ 1 & k > d_n \end{cases} \tag{11}$$

The expression for the optimal threshold T_n' is given by the following equation.

$$T_n' = \frac{c_n + d_n}{2} \tag{12}$$

$n = 1$ for X and $n = 2$ for Y.

Referring to Fig. 4, the 1st term of Eq. (9) can be expressed as:

$$I(X, Y)_{norm} = H(X)_{norm} + H(Y)_{norm} - H(X, Y)_{norm} \tag{13}$$

where $H(X)_{norm}$ and $H(Y)_{norm}$ are the entropy of X and Y, respectively that belong to normal vessel class.

$$H(X,Y)_{norm} = - \sum_{y=m_2}^{b_2} \sum_{x=m_1}^{b_1} p(x,y) log\, p(x,y) \qquad (14)$$

Similarly, the expression for $I(X,Y)_{abnorm}$ can also be obtained.

DE for Optimization: To obtain the optimal values of c_n and d_n, the objective function presented by Eq. (9) is maximized using DE. A population of 100 chromosomes are generated initially with random c_n and d_n. The maximum value of $I(X,Y)$ is considered to be the fitness value which is also randomly initialized. At every iteration, the values of c_n and d_n are updated through mutation and crossover subject to $I(X,Y)$ maximization. The chromosomes with better fitness value between the two successive iterations are allowed to survive in the next iteration. Finally, when the algorithm terminates (at iteration 100 for the present case), the best chromosome (chromosome with maximum fitness value within the pool) represents the optimal c_n and d_n values. Experiments over a large number of images show that DE converges within 100 iterations and the best solution remain unchanged with the increase in the iteration count. Therefore, the maximum iteration count is kept to be 100 (stopping criteria) which otherway ensures speed of convergence. The threshold T'_n is calculated according to Eq. (12). Since both V_d and V_t of the abnormal thin vessels are greater than the normal thin vessels, a pixel is classified as the abnormal if the corresponding $V_d > T'_1$ and $V_t > T'_2$.

3.4   Post-processing

Fragments of vessel segments may also be falsely detected as a candidate of abnormal vessel structure. These spurious components seem to be isolated in nature contrary to the abnormal vessels which appear as denser group of neovascular nets. Connected component analysis is then used to remove such isolated pixels. The 8-connected components, with area less than 8 pixels (which is selected empirically based on experiments over the images used in the present work) are then removed to obtain the final neovascularization structure. However, failure to select the proper threshold value may increase the false detection rate.

4   Experimental Results

Performance of the proposed method is evaluated on four publicly available retinal databases, namely STARE [7], DIARETDB1 [8] and MESSIDOR [1] database. From these databases, only 27 images with neovascularization structures are used in the present study. Three parameters, namely sensitivity (Sen), specificity (Spec) and accuracy (ACC) are used for evaluation purpose. The parameters are defined as follows:

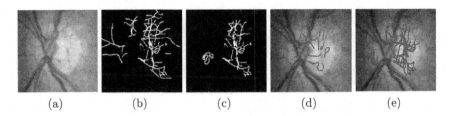

(a)   (b)   (c)   (d)   (e)

Fig. 5. Detection of NVD (a) original image. (b) Detected thin (both normal and abnormal) vessels by [9]. (c) Abnormal vessels (neovascularization) detected by proposed method. (d) Abnormal vessels detected by [5] (marked by red). (e) Ground-truth image. (Color figure online)

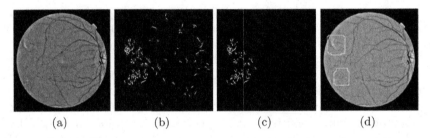

(a)   (b)   (c)   (d)

Fig. 6. Detection of NVE (a) original image with neovascularization. (b) Detected thin (both normal and abnormal) vessels by [9]. (c) Abnormal vessels (neovascularization) detected by proposed method. (d) Abnormal vessel regions marked by Welikala et al. [13]

1. $Sen = \dfrac{TP}{TP + FN}$

2. $Spec = \dfrac{TN}{TN + FP}$

3. $ACC = \dfrac{TP + TN}{TP + TN + FP + FN}$

where TP = correctly classified normal vessel pixels, FP = abnormal vessels detected as normal, TN = correctly classified abnormal vessels, FN = normal vessel segments wrongly classified as abnormal vessels. The proposed method is applied on a number of images of the different available databases. Detection of NVD and NVE by the proposed method is shown in Figs. 5 and 6, respectively. Comparing Fig. 5(c) and (d) with the ground-truth image presented in Fig. 5(e), it is observed that the present method accurately detects most of the NVD structures whereas [5] fails to detect these abnormal vessels. It can also detect the NVD and NVE structures collectively as depicted in Fig. 7.

Performance of the proposed method is compared with some state-of-the-art methods as shown in Table 1. Numerical values show that with 97.33% sensitivity and 97.54% accuracy, the proposed method outperforms the existing methods. The specificity value offered by the proposed method is 0.9623 which otherway indicates that on an average 3.77% of the background and/normal vessel

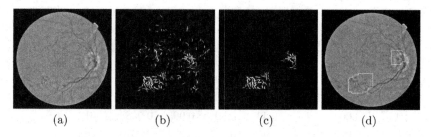

(a)   (b)   (c)   (d)

Fig. 7. Detection of neovascularization (a) original image with neovascularization. (b) Detected thin (both normal and abnormal) vessels [9]. (c) Abnormal vessels (neovascularization) detected by proposed method. (d) Abnormal vessel regions marked by [13].

pixels are falsely detected as neovascularization. After extraction and classification of vessels into different types, the features (vessel density and tortuosity) are extracted from the thin vessel structures. To suppress the effect of noise, the algorithm includes curvelet based denoising prior to vessel extraction. Furthermore, after vessel extraction, the isolated spurious components (noise) are removed through post processing. Simulations done on a number of images of the existing databases demonstrate that the proposed method is very efficient in neovascularization detection so long as the noise is within certain tolerable limit. To show the efficacy of the proposed method in presence of noise, the sensitivity, specificity and average ACC values for different noise variances (for one sample image shown in Fig. 5(a)) are reported in Table 2. Numerical results show that the method detects the neovascularization structures with an average sensitivity of 96.63% and accuracy of 96.24% in presence of noise.

Table 1. Comparison of neovascularization detection methods.

Sl. No	Method	Sen	Spec	Average ACC
1	Goatman et al. [5]	0.94	0.82	–
2	Hassan et al. [6]	0.6390	0.8940	–
3	Agurto et al. [2]	0.9600	0.8300	–
4	Akram et al. [3]	0.965	0.9300	0.95
5	**Proposed method**	**0.9733**	**0.9623**	**0.9754**

The proposed method shows improved performance over some existing methods. However, for some specific image regions (for extremely high pathological images) if the vessel density of the thin vessel nets and the thick vessels are similar, the proposed method may falsely detect some of the thick vessels. This may increase the false detection rate. Simulations are performed using MATLAB R2011b in a work station with P-III 1.5 GHz CPU and 512 MB RAM which takes less than 3 min (nearly 2.47 min for vessel extraction and 10.95 s for abnormal vessel classification) for neovascularization detection.

Table 2. Performance evaluation of the proposed method in presence of noise.

Sl. No	Noise variance	T_1'	T_2'	Sen	Spec	Average ACC
1	0.001	0.242	0.0037	0.9676	0.9612	0.9643
2	0.002	0.396	0.0037	0.9670	0.9600	0.9635
3	0.003	0.4225	0.004	0.9663	0.9592	0.9629
4	0.004	0.431	0.0043	0.9659	0.9588	0.9613
5	0.005	0.455	0.005	0.9648	0.9373	0.9602

5   Conclusions

Neovascularization is one of the prevalent symptoms of PDR. The use of MI (between the V_d and the V_t) maximization of the thin vessel structure is used for neovascularization detection. The proposed scheme achieves superior performance than the existing methods with 97.33% sensitivity and 96.23% specificity values. This method is equally efficient in detecting NVD and NVE separately or in a collective way. The ability of the present method to handle diverse types of images of multiple databases makes it well-suited as an automated CAD system for DR screening. Integrated with lesion detection algorithm, the proposed method may be extended for stage detection of DR.

References

1. Messidor. http://messidor.crihan.fr/index-en.php
2. Agurto, C., Yu, H., Murray, V., Pattichis, M.S., Barriga, S., Bauman, W., Soliz, P.: Detection of neovascularization in the optic disc using an AM-FM representation, granulometry, and vessel segmentation. In: 34th Annual International Conference of the IEEE Engineering in Medicine and Biology Society, pp. 4946–4949, August 2012
3. Akram, M.U., Khalid, S., Tariq, A., Javed, M.Y.: Detection of neovascularization in retinal images using multivariate m-mediods based classifier. Comput. Med. Imaging Graph. **37**, 346–357 (2013)
4. Ding, S., Shi, Z., Jin, F.: Studies on fuzzy information measures. In: 5th IEEE International Conference on Cognitive Informatics, vol. 1, pp. 292–296, July 2006
5. Goatman, K.A., Fleming, A.D., Philip, S., Williams, G.J., Olson, J.A., Sharp, P.F.: Detection of new vessels on the optic disc using retinal photographs. IEEE Trans. Med. Imaging **30**(4), 972–979 (2011)
6. Hassan, S.S.A., Bong, D.B.L., Premsenthil, M.: Detection of neovascularization in diabetic retinopathy. J. Digit. Imaging **25**(3), 437–444 (2012)
7. Hoover, A., Kouznetsova, V., Goldbaum, M.H.: Locating blood vessels in retinal images by piece-wise threshold probing of a matched filter response. IEEE Trans. Med. Imaging **19**(3), 203–210 (2000)
8. Kalesnykiene, V., Kamarainen, J.K., Voutilainen, R., Pietilä, J., Kälviäinen, H., Uusitalo, H.: DiaRetDB1 diabetic retinopathy database and evaluation protocol. http://www.it.lut.fi/project/imageret/diaretdb1

9. Kar, S.S., Maity, S.P.: Retinal blood vessel extraction using tunable bandpass filter and fuzzy conditional entropy. Comput. Methods Programs Biomed. **133**, 111–132 (2016)
10. Maes, F., Collignon, A., Vandermeulen, D., Marchal, G., Suetens, P.: Multimodality image registration by maximization of mutual information. IEEE Trans. Med. Imaging **16**(2), 187–198 (1997)
11. Mookiah, M.R.K., Acharya, U.R., Chua, C.K., Lim, C.M., Ng, E., Laude, A.: Computer-aided diagnosis of diabetic retinopathy: a review. Comput. Biol. Med. **43**(12), 2136–2155 (2013)
12. Staal, J., Abràmoff, M.D., Niemeijer, M., Viergever, M.A., van Ginneken, B.: Ridge-based vessel segmentation in color images of the retina. IEEE Trans. Med. Imaging **23**(4), 501–509 (2004)
13. Welikala, R., Dehmeshki, J., Hoppe, A., Tah, V., Mann, S., Williamson, T., Barman, S.: Automated detection of proliferative diabetic retinopathy using a modified line operator and dual classification. Comput. Methods Programs Biomed. **114**(3), 247–261 (2014)

Distribution Based EEG Baseline Classification

Gopika Gopan K.$^{(\boxtimes)}$, Neelam Sinha, and Dinesh Babu J.

International Institute of Information Technology Bangalore, Bangalore, India
gopika.gopank@iiitb.org, {neelam.sinha,jdinesh}@iiitb.ac.in

Abstract. Electrical signals generated in the brain, known as Electroencephalographic (EEG) signals, form a non-invasive measure of brain functioning. Baseline states of EEG are Eyes Open (EO) and Eyes Closed (EC) relaxed states. The choice of baseline used in an experiment is of critical importance since they form a reference with which other states are measured. In Brain Machine Interface, it is imperative that the system should be able to distinguish between these states and hence the need for automated classification of EEG baselines. In the proposed method, Statistical Moments are utilized. The Moment Generating Functions (MGFs) obtained using these moments are given as features to SVM and k-NN classifiers resulting in mean accuracies of 86.71% and 86.54%. The fact that MGF is able to differentiate between these states indicate that the two states have different source distribution parameters. A Smirnov test verified that the data of two classes indeed come from different distributions.

1 Introduction

Electroencephalographic (EEG) signals are electrical signals generated in the brain due to firing of neurons. EEG provides a non-invasive measure of brain functioning and can be used to assess and analyze any brain related disorders. EEG signals are separated into different frequency bands based on their occurrence related to various activities. Frequencies in the range 0–60 Hz are the significant frequencies used in any EEG based analysis. This range of frequencies is divided into bands as: Delta (0.1–3 Hz), Theta (4–8 Hz), Alpha (8–14 Hz), Beta (14–30 Hz) and Gamma (30–60 Hz). Some of the disorder characteristics are more prominent when EEG is analyzed using these bands.

In any EEG analysis, the following procedure is followed. The raw EEG is initially pre-processed to eliminate artifacts and noise. Depending on the problem being considered, the pre-processing may also include frequency band division. Next is feature extraction followed by classification by an optimal classifier. Features utilized in analysis of EEG, whether for disorder detection, sleep analysis, emotion recognition or Brain Machine Interface, are greatly dependent on the application being considered. For instance, Acharya et al. [1] has utilized nonlinear chaotic features for alcoholic EEG detection while Zhu et al. [22] utilized graph theoretic based approach. In epileptic EEG detection, wavelet based features [17], chaotic features [2] and time frequency analysis [19] were used. Sleep

© Springer International Publishing AG 2017
S. Mukherjee et al. (Eds.): ICVGIP 2016, LNCS 10481, pp. 314–321, 2017.
https://doi.org/10.1007/978-3-319-68124-5_27

stage analysis [7,8] and emotion recognition [15,21] also utilized a range of features from statistical features, wavelet based features and AR modelling.

An EEG baseline or resting condition (normally Eyes Open (EO) and Eyes Closed (EC) relaxed state) is utilized for some EEG analysis since it is considered as the lowest level of activation/arousal that could be achieved in an experimental setup. The baseline runs are required to analyze the change in the EEG from resting state when a task is performed [11] or emotions are analyzed [20] or in psychiatric analysis of the subject [9]. It is also imperative that the baseline should be chosen (whether EO or EC) depending on the problem being analyzed. This is because cognitive, emotional and motor processes can be associated with the individual differences in EEG baseline [4] and these baselines have EEG signals differing in topography as well as power levels [3]. In addition, it has been found that EO baseline can be viewed as 'activation' baseline and Eyes Closed baseline as 'arousal' baseline especially where tasks with visual processing (for instance, emotion recognition based on visual stimuli) are involved [3]. These differences should be taken into consideration when choosing the EEG baseline for different paradigms as they do not provide the same measure for baseline.

Several studies have been conducted on the differences between EO and EC baselines. Barry et al. [3] found that there is a topographical difference in these two baselines in addition to the difference in the power levels and suggests that EC baseline be used in all the paradigms that do not involve visual stimuli and EO baseline in all other paradigms. Li et al. [13] studied the differences in these two baselines using autoregressive modelling and concluded that the power of EC state is much higher than that of EO state. The differences in functional brain networks during these two baselines were analyzed by Tan et al. [18] using Graph theory based analysis. Their results depicted a decrease in connectivity of frontal theta and posterior alpha in EO compared to EC. In addition, they found topographical parameter differences between these two states. From these studies, it is evident that the EEG has significant differences in the two baseline states. In Brain Machine Interface system, the system needs to initially distinguish between these two baselines before utilizing and choosing the appropriate baseline for different tasks. Hence, an automated classification between these two baselines has become necessary.

EO and EC show topographical as well as connectivity differences in EEG. These differences are utilized in the automated classification of two baselines. Statistical analysis was carried out and it was found that the differences in the moments between the two classes were significant. This leads to the inference that the two states correspond to two different distributions. The two different distributions are captured by computing their respective MGF. The values of the MGF for a chosen range of real values are utilized as features. The popular off-the-shelf classifiers SVM and k-NN are used for classifying between EO and EC.

The paper is divided into various sections. Section 2 describes the dataset used in this experiment. Section 3 describes the proposed methodology. Section 4 provides the results obtained and Sect. 5 concludes the paper.

2   Dataset Description

The dataset was obtained from Physionet "EEG Motor Movement/Imagery Dataset" [10,16] where 64-channel EEG were recorded using the BCI2000 system. The 109 subjects performed two one-minute baseline runs and four two-minute tasks. For this experiment, only the two baseline runs were considered. The first baseline was EO and second EC. 9500 samples were obtained for each baseline run. Figure 1 shows sample EEG of EC and EO baselines. Visually, the difference is not observed.

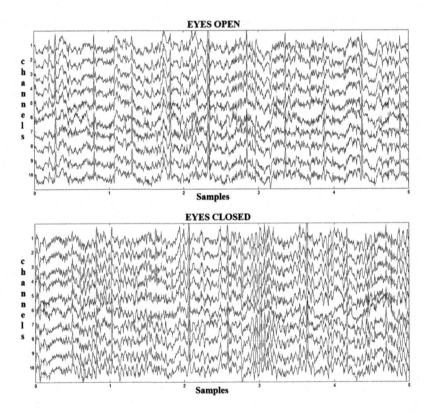

Fig. 1. Representative plots showing data from 10 channels, 9500 samples.

3   Proposed Approach

The approach introduced in this paper involves exploiting the difference in the probability distribution of data from the two classes, EO and EC, to distinguish between them. The proposed framework is shown in the Fig. 2. All the 64 channels are considered in this experiment since the aim is to distinguish between

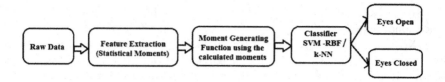

Fig. 2. Proposed methodology

the EO and EC baselines and not the EO and EC activity (where only Fp electrodes are required). The available data is preprocessed. Statistical moments are calculated upto seventh order. The moments are then used to obtain the respective MGF of the two different PDF of the two classes. The MGF of the baselines were utilized as features after normalization and given as input to the off-the-shelf classifiers, support vector machine and k-NN.

3.1 Feature Extraction

The Statistical Moments [14] are defined for a discrete random variable as:

$$E[X^n] = \sum_k x_k^n P_X(x_k). \tag{1}$$

where X is a discrete random variable, $E[.]$ is the expectation and $P_X(x_k)$ is the probability mass function of the random variable. The zero moment is 1 since it is the area under the PDF. The first moment is the mean and the second moment is the mean squared value.

Given a set of data $X = x_1, x_2, ..., x_N$, the kth moment can be calculated as

$$m_k = E[X^k] = \frac{\sum_{i=1}^{N} x_i^k}{N}. \tag{2}$$

The moments were then used to obtain MGF using the following equation [14]:

$$MGF(t) = 1 + tm_1 + \frac{t^2 m_2}{2!} + \frac{t^3 m_3}{3!} + ... + \frac{t^n m_k}{k!} + ... \tag{3}$$

where m_k is the kth moment and $t \in \mathbb{R}$. The choice of t determines the range of argument values for which MGF is calculated. The optimal range of argument values are those for which the MGF of the data from the two classes are easily distinguishable. Thus, appropriate range of t needs to be determined.

3.2 Classifier

Support Vector Machine (SVM) [6] with Radial Basis Function (RBF) kernel was used in this experiment. SVM works on the principle that if a data is not linearly separable, then the data can be separated when projected onto a higher dimensional plane.

K-NN classifier [12] works on the principle that a test data is assigned to the class to which majority of its 'k' neighbouring data belongs. It uses a non-parametric approach and ideally Euclidean distance is used as the distance measure. The choice of k is usually obtained by trial and error.

10 fold cross-validation was carried out ten times and mean accuracy was calculated.

4   Smirnov Test

In order to assert that data from the two classes indeed come from two distributions, Smirnov test was carried out. A Smirnov test [5] is a two sample, non-parametric test which analyzes whether the two samples given are from the same distribution. The intuition behind the test is the comparison of empirical cumulative distribution functions (CDF) of the two samples. The null hypothesis is that both the samples are from the same distribution.

The 64 channel data were concatenated to form a single vector. The empirical cumulative distribution of this vector was given for Smirnov test. EO and EC samples were compared against each other in all possible permutations to establish whether the data from EO and EC are from two different distributions.

5   Experimental Results

EEG baseline data were obtained from Physionet [10] and involved data from 109 subjects. Each performed EO and EC baselines for one minute each. The 64 channel raw data contained 9500 samples.

The 64 channel data was centered and moments upto the order of ten were calculated for each channel. The moments were then averaged across channels and hence each subject in each class was assigned a single set of moments. MGF was calculated using the computed moments for different ranges of t. It was found that t in the interval 2.5 to 3.2 was the most effective in distinguishing between the two classes. Figure 3 shows the MGF for two classes for $t = (2.5, 3.2)$. The obtained MGFs were normalized and given as features to classifiers using 10 fold cross-validation. SVM with RBF kernel was used for this classification. For k-NN classifier, $k = 13$ was found to be effective. Table 1 shows the mean accuracy of classification when MGF was calculated with different orders of moments. As observed from the table, MGF calculated using moments upto the seventh order were effective in distinguishing between the two classes. The classifiers both gave high accuracies for the same MGF values. This indicated the efficacy of the feature across both the classifiers. In addition, since the MGF was able to classify the two baseline states, it implies that the source distribution of the two states differ. Since SVM and k-NN performed well, it implies the data is class separable and is modelable.

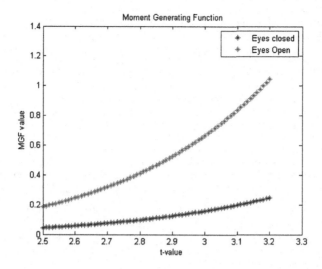

Fig. 3. Moment generating function of two classes for t = 2.5:0.01:3.2 (Color figure online)

Table 1. Mean accuracy for MGF calculated with different orders of moments using SVM-RBF with 10-fold cross validation

Moments used in calculation of MGF	Mean accuracy (SVM-RBF)(%)	Mean accuracy k-NN (k=13)(%)
0,1	39.64	16.6
0,1,2	57.88	54.1
0,1,2,3	77.13	76.64
0,1,2,3,4	75.4	77.31
0,1,2,3,4,5	79.66	78.52
0,1,2,3,4,5,6	80.44	78.03
0,1,2,3,4,5,6,7	**86.71**	**86.54**
0,1,2,3,4,5,6,7, 8	84.85	82.47
0,1,2,3,4,5,6,7,8,9	86.66	86.02

Since MGF values, as a features, was able to distinguish between the two classes, it indicated that the data from two classes belong to different distributions. Smirnov test was carried out to verify that the data of the two classes were indeed from two different distributions. The channels were concatenated and the empirical CDF was given for the test. The empirical CDF of two classes were tested with all permutations and it resulted in the rejection of null hypothesis which indicated that the data from two classes were indeed from two different distributions. This emphasizes the importance of appropriate choice of baseline used for various EEG experiments.

In comparison with other works [3,13,18] this work had quantified the ability of MGF in classifying the baselines. These works do not perform a classification of these states and the classification of baselines of EEG have not been carried out in any work to the best of our knowledge. Hence an effective comparison is not possible.

6   Conclusion

The choice of EEG baselines is important in various EEG based analyses. An automated classification of EO and EC is required in Brain Machine Interface system to accurately identify the baseline provided and hence the correct baseline for the task being considered. The proposed approach involves use of MGF as feature to SVM with RBF kernel and k-NN classifier with $k = 13$ to classify between EO and EC. Mean accuracies of 86.71% and 86.54% were obtained respectively for MGF values as features calculated using moments upto the seventh order. This also led to the conclusion that EC and EO baselines have different source probability distributions. Smirnov test is utilized to verify that the data of the two classes indeed came from different distributions. This difference enunciates the relevance of accurate choice of baseline for various EEG based experiments.

References

1. Acharya, U.R., Sree, S.V., Chattopadhyay, S., Suri, J.S.: Automated diagnosis of normal and alcoholic EEG signals. Int. J. Neural Syst. **22**(03), 1250011 (2012)
2. Adeli, H., Ghosh-Dastidar, S., Dadmehr, N.: A wavelet-chaos methodology for analysis of EEGs and EEG subbands to detect seizure and epilepsy. IEEE Trans. Biomed. Eng. **54**(2), 205–211 (2007)
3. Barry, R.J., Clarke, A.R., Johnstone, S.J., Magee, C.A., Rushby, J.A.: EEG differences between eyes-closed and eyes-open resting conditions. Clin. Neurophysiol. **118**(12), 2765–2773 (2007)
4. Bell, M.A., Fox, N.A.: Individual differences in object permanence performance at 8 months: locomotor experience and brain electrical activity. Dev. Psychobiol. **31**(4), 287–297 (1997)
5. Berger, V.W., Zhou, Y.: Kolmogorov-Smirnov test: Overview. Wiley StatsRef: Statistics Reference Online (2005)
6. Cortes, C., Vapnik, V.: Support-vector networks. Mach. Learn. **20**(3), 273–297 (1995)
7. Ebrahimi, F., Mikaeili, M., Estrada, E., Nazeran, H.: Automatic sleep stage classification based on EEG signals by using neural networks and wavelet packet coefficients. In: 2008 30th Annual International Conference of the IEEE Engineering in Medicine and Biology Society, pp. 1151–1154. IEEE (2008)
8. Estrada, E., Nazeran, H., Nava, P., Behbehani, K., Burk, J., Lucas, E.: EEG feature extraction for classification of sleep stages. In: 26th Annual International Conference of the IEEE Engineering in Medicine and Biology Society 2004, IEMBS 2004, vol. 1, pp. 196–199. IEEE (2004)

9. Fleck, J.I., Green, D.L., Stevenson, J.L., Payne, L., Bowden, E.M., Jung-Beeman, M., Kounios, J.: The transliminal brain at rest: baseline EEG, unusual experiences, and access to unconscious mental activity. Cortex **44**(10), 1353–1363 (2008)

10. Goldberger, A.L., Amaral, L.A., Glass, L., Hausdorff, J.M., Ivanov, P.C., Mark, R.G., Mietus, J.E., Moody, G.B., Peng, C.K., Stanley, H.E.: Physiobank, physiotoolkit, and physionet components of a new research resource for complex physiologic signals. Circulation **101**(23), e215–e220 (2000)

11. Janzen, T., Graap, K., Stephanson, S., Marshall, W., Fitzsimmons, G.: Differences in baseline EEG measures for add and normally achieving preadolescent males. Biofeedback Self Regul. **20**(1), 65–82 (1995)

12. Larose, D.T.: K-nearest neighbor algorithm. Discovering Knowledge in Data: An Introduction to Data Mining, pp. 90–106 (2005)

13. Li, L., Xiao, L., Chen, L.: Differences of EEG between eyes-open and eyes-closed states based on autoregressive method. J. Electron. Sci. Technol. China **7**(2), 175–179 (2009)

14. Miller, S., Childers, D.: Probability and Random Processes: with Applications to Signal Processing and Communications. Academic Press, Cambridge (2012)

15. Murugappan, M., Ramachandran, N., Sazali, Y., et al.: Classification of human emotion from EEG using discrete wavelet transform. J. Biomed. Sci. Eng. **3**(04), 390 (2010)

16. Schalk, G., McFarland, D.J., Hinterberger, T., Birbaumer, N., Wolpaw, J.R.: BCI 2000: a general-purpose brain-computer interface (BCI) system. IEEE Trans. Biomed. Eng. **51**(6), 1034–1043 (2004)

17. Subasi, A.: EEG signal classification using wavelet feature extraction and a mixture of expert model. Expert Syst. Appl. **32**(4), 1084–1093 (2007)

18. Tan, B., Kong, X., Yang, P., Jin, Z., Li, L.: The difference of brain functional connectivity between eyes-closed and eyes-open using graph theoretical analysis. Computational and mathematical methods in medicine 2013 (2013)

19. Tzallas, A.T., Tsipouras, M.G., Fotiadis, D.I.: Epileptic seizure detection in EEGs using time-frequency analysis. IEEE Trans. Inf Technol. Biomed. **13**(5), 703–710 (2009)

20. Valenzi, S., Islam, T., Jurica, P., Cichocki, A.: Individual classification of emotions using EEG. J. Biomed. Sci. Eng. **7**(8), 604 (2014)

21. Vijayan, A.E., Sen, D., Sudheer, A.: EEG-based emotion recognition using statistical measures and auto-regressive modeling. In: 2015 IEEE International Conference on Computational Intelligence and Communication Technology (CICT), pp. 587–591. IEEE (2015)

22. Zhu, G., Li, Y., Wen, P.P., Wang, S.: Analysis of alcoholic EEG signals based on horizontal visibility graph entropy. Brain Inf. **1**(1–4), 19–25 (2014)

Texture Based Person Identification Using Dental Radiographs and Photographs in Forensic Odontology

G. Jaffino[1]([⊠]), A. Banumathi[1], Ulaganathan Gurunathan[2], and J. Prabin Jose[3]

[1] Department of ECE, Thiagarajar College of Engineering, Madurai 625015, Tamilnadu, India
jaffino22@yahoo.com
[2] Best Dental Science College, Madurai 625015, Tamilnadu, India
[3] Kamaraj College of Engineering and Technology, Virudhunagar, Tamilnadu, India

Abstract. Forensic Odontology is the evaluation of dental information that includes ante-mortem (AM) and post-mortem (PM) radiographs for the purpose of identifying person in some grave situations such as mass fatalities, natural disasters and terrorist attacks etc. One of the key issues in using dental images is that, although both the AM and the PM radiographs belong to the same person, there may be a mismatch between those radiographs due to the missing tooth in either of the radiographs. In such a case, the missing tooth in the radiograph has to be identified prior to the matching in order to achieve accurate identification of an individual. Thus an automatic algorithm for person identification in dental radiographs and photographs is a more challenging one at present. In this paper, texture based shape extraction algorithm is taken for analysis. Distance measures and classifier based approaches are the shape matching algorithm which is used to match both AM and PM images in order to obtain exact person identification. A novel approach has to be introduced for the extraction of the missing tooth, and subsequently each tooth in the radiograph is classified using k-NN classifier with Hu's moment invariants as feature. Then each individual tooth is separated with pulp, enamel and dentine is applied to GLCM texture features. In this paper, a novel framework has been proposed to improve the identification performance. Moreover, the proposed algorithm achieves an overall accuracy of 98% than the existing approaches.

Keywords: Forensic Odontology · Tooth classification · Hu's moments · GLCM · k-NN classifier

1 Introduction

Dental identification plays a major role in the identification of ruins when the post-mortem changes, traumatic tissue injury or lack of a fingerprint record invalidate the use of visual or fingerprint methods. The identification of dental remains is a primary importance when the deceased person is decayed, burned or dismembered. The main advantage of dental evidence is that like other hard tissues the teeth can be preserved.

© Springer International Publishing AG 2017
S. Mukherjee et al. (Eds.): ICVGIP 2016, LNCS 10481, pp. 322–336, 2017.
https://doi.org/10.1007/978-3-319-68124-5_28

Dental pattern can be considered as a biometric if there is no other means of physiological information like DNA, palm print, Finger print, iris are not available. In some critical situations like severe bomb blast, fire accident and airplane crash all the other parts of the human body may smash. Only skeletal and dental patterns are remaining for this situation. In such a case, human identification using dental images has been proven to be best under these circumstances. In this work, different radiographic images of bitewing, periapical and panaromic radiographic images are used. Bitewing radiographs are taken for both left and right views with the inclusion of molar and premolar teeth contains both upper and lower jaws. Periapical images contain only three to four teeth in either of upper or lower jaws. Panaromic radiographs are an extra oral image which contains the entire teeth of the person and it is a challenging task to identify a person. There is many approaches used for dental image segmentation. Iterative thresholding technique is used to segment both pulp and teeth [1]. Jain and Chen dedicated a concept of semi-automatic contour extraction method for shape extraction and pattern matching [2]. The short comings in their approach are if the image is too blurred, their algorithm is not applicable and slight angle deviation in the ante-mortem and post-mortem images may not be handled with this approach. The poor quality of tooth contours is indiscernible. Gradient- based contour extraction technique has been proposed by Chen and Jain [3]. The main drawback of this method is that it is not able to discriminate edges in multiple objects. But in this technique, the result shows the edges overlie on boundary of the object. The basic idea of active contour model is to start with a curve around the object that is to be detected, and the curve move towards its interior normal and stops on the true boundary based on an energy minimizing model. Many methods have been introduced to improve the active contour model, but Osher and Seithian [4] have proposed the level set method. The level set method is based on active contour model and particularly designed to use deformable curve for approximating the boundary of an object. Enhanced matching is obtained by combined fusion approaches are explained by Nomir and Abdul Mottaleb [5]. Human identification using shape and appearance of tooth is explained by Nomir and Abdul Mottaleb [6]. Bhardwaj et al. [7] have proposed an active contour model with selective binary and Gaussian filtering regularized level set for contour extraction. Shape matching is done by both contour and skeleton based approaches. Rindhe and Shake [8] presented a method to recognize a tooth in dental x-ray images with Hu's moment invariants. Pushparaj et al. [9] have explained the concept of fast connected component-based contour shape extraction, and matching by Mahalanobis distance. Fast connected component labeling is used to connect the edges but the edges may show discontinuity in the outer contour and then matching is performed. Hierarchial distance [10] based matching of dental records proves to be efficient in terms of retrieval time. Classification and numbering based contour features are used to classify the teeth in terms of molars or premolars which are explained by Mahoor [11]. Numbering of teeth is based on universal numbering system, and bayesian classifier has been used to classify the teeth. In this case, the teeth numbering deviates from the universal numbering system which will, in turn, lead to difficulty in identification of individuals. Lin et al. [12] has explained the concept of classification and numbering. Teeth numbering is based on universal numbering system and then the contour of particular region of interest is extracted. Pushparaj et al. have been explaining the missing tooth detection logic [13]. The main drawback of this work is that, the missing tooth region extracted includes air gap also. The existing algorithms for the detection of missing tooth are less accurate. The key purpose of this work is to detect the missing tooth region automatically and identify the person correctly in the given dental radiograph.

2 Proposed Methodology

The concept map (c-map) of the proposed work is shown in Fig. 1. This research work is organized into five major sections. Preprocessing, Spline isolation, missing tooth detection, shape extraction and shape matching.

2.1 Preprocessing

The input image is preprocessed by using Butterworth high pass filter because it produces uniform edges due to its maximally flat response. It is used to provide uniform sensitivity to all the frequencies. The transfer function of Butterworth high pass filter is

$$H(u,v) = \frac{1}{1 + \left(\frac{D_0}{D(u,v)}\right)^{2n}} \tag{1}$$

where D_0 is the specified non-negative quantity, n is the order of the filter, here n is chosen as 2. If the order is too higher, the image is much brighter and the order is too lower, it is much darker and $D(u,v)$ is the distance from the point (u,v) to the origin in frequency plane and it is given by

$$D(u,v) = (u^2 + v^2)^{1/2} \tag{2}$$

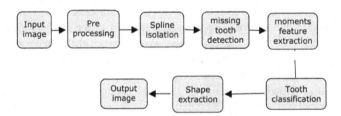

Fig. 1. Concept map (C-map) of the proposed work

2.2 Spline Isolation

In order to perform individual identification using dental images, the teeth in the dental structure have to be isolated to carry out the shape extraction and matching. The teeth isolation is done by using spline function and teeth can be partitioned as maxilla (upper jaw) and mandible (lower jaw) as well as a single tooth [14].

2.3   Missing Tooth Detection

Once the upper and the lower jaws are separated, centroids are calculated for each tooth. Binarization and morphological operations are used to separate each tooth in the given image to facilitate the calculation of centroids for the tooth. After centroid calculation, binarization is the process of thresholding the input image to convert it from gray scale image to binary image. Here, the pixel value at each location is compared with the threshold, and if the pixel value is less than the threshold, the corresponding pixel value in the output image is set to 1, else it is set to 0. The equation is given by

$$b(i,j) = \begin{cases} 1, & f(i,j) \le t \\ 0, & f(i,j) > t \end{cases} \tag{3}$$

Morphological erosion operation is performed for the binarized image. A line structuring element of length 10 and angle 90° is used for erosion. Then, morphological dilation is performed using the disk structuring element of size 5 for the eroded image. The series of morphological operations achieves tooth separation so that the centroids can be calculated for each tooth. A well-known distance measure which takes into account the covariance matrix is the Mahalanobis distance. The Mahalanobis distance can be observed by

$$D_i^{Maha} = \sqrt{D_i} = \sqrt{(X - \mu_i)^T \Sigma_i^{-1}(X - \mu_i)} \tag{4}$$

where μ_i is the covariance matrix, Σ_i^{-1} represents the inverse of the covariance matrix. The mahalanobis distance is also known as weighted Euclidean distance where the weight is determined by using the covariance matrix.

2.3.1   Moments Feature Extraction

Moment invariants have been widely applied to image pattern recognition in a variety of applications due to their invariant features on image translation, scaling and rotation. The image function $f(x, y)$ is a piecewise continuous bounded function, the moments of all orders exist, and the moment sequence $\{m_{pq}\}$ is uniquely determined by $f(x, y)$. Two-dimensional $(p + q)^{th}$ order moment is defined as

$$m_{pq} = \int_{-\infty}^{\infty} \int_{-\infty}^{\infty} x^p y^q f(x, y) dx dy, \quad p, q = 0, 1, 2. \ldots \tag{5}$$

The invariant features can be achieved using central moments, which are defined as follows

$$\mu_{pq} = \int_{-\infty}^{\infty} \int_{-\infty}^{\infty} (x - \bar{x})^p (y - \bar{y})^q f(x, y) dx dy \tag{6}$$

where $\bar{x} = \frac{m_{10}}{m_{00}}$ and $\bar{y} = \frac{m_{01}}{m_{00}}$

scale invariance can be obtained by normalization. The normalized central moments are defined as

$$\eta_{pq} = \frac{\mu_{pq}}{\mu_{00}^{\gamma}}, \gamma = (p+q+2)/2, \ p+q = 2,3,\ldots \tag{7}$$

The set of Hu's moments which are calculated for each individual tooth in the given radiographs and photographs which form the global shape descriptor [15]. These moment invariants are used as the feature for classification using k-NN classifier.

2.4 Tooth Classification

The algorithm used for k-NN classifier is defined as follows

Step 1: The value of k is set. In this work k value is set to 3.
Step 2: The distance between the test data and all the training data is calculated. In this work Euclidean distance is used.
Step 3: The distances are sorted, and the k- nearest neighbors are found based on the k-th minimum distance.
Step 4: The categories of those neighbors are found. The category to which the test data belongs is determined based on the majority vote. The test data is assigned either based on the minimum distance else they are assigned randomly. In this way, each tooth in the given radiograph is classified as molar or premolar.

The teeth arrangement without missing tooth should match one of these patterns (Fig. 2).

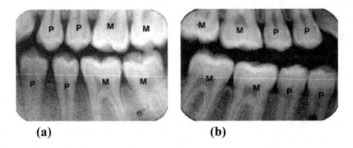

(a)   **(b)**

Fig. 2. Arrangement of teeth in dental bitewing images. (a) Left quadrant, (b) right quadrant, M: Molar, P: Premolar

PM, PMM, PMMM, PPM, PPMM and PPMMM (left quadrant image).
MP, MMP, MMMP, MPP, MMPP and MMMPP (right quadrant image).

3   Shape Extraction

Shape extraction is one of the more desirable feature in individual person identification. Texture based shape extraction plays an important role in human vision and for image segmentation. Initially the tooth layers are classified into pulp, enamel and dentine.

Threshold based classification may yields to differentiate the gray level values into pulp, enamel and dentine. The texture features were extracted from co-occurrence matrices of three different layers. Texture analysis is used to analyze the repeating structure in the image pattern. One of the statistical methods of Gray level Co-occurrence matrix (GLCM) contains information about the position of pixels having similar grey level values. GLCM is defined by specifying the displacement vector $dv = (dv_i, dv_j)$ and counting the pairs of pixels having grey level values x and y. The GLCM is given by

$$P_{dv}(x, y) = n_{x,y} \tag{8}$$

where $n_{x,y}$ is the number of occurrences of pixel values at a distance dv at co-ordinates (x, y) in the image.

3.1   Shape Matching

After extracting the shape of each individual tooth shape matching is the next evitable factor.

3.1.1   Texture Based Matching

Texture is one of the useful measures for image matching. The notable GLCM parameters for shape matching is

$$Contrast = \sum_{x,y} |x - y|^2 p_v(x, y) \tag{9}$$

$$Correlation = \sum_{x,y} \frac{(x - A_x)(y - A_y) \cdot p_v(x, y)}{B_x B_y} \tag{10}$$

$$Energy = \sum_{x,y} p_v(x, y)^2 \tag{11}$$

$$Homogeneity = \sum_{x,y} \frac{p_v(x, y)}{1 + |x - y|} \tag{12}$$

where A_x, A_y gives the mean value of row and column respectively, B_x, B_y corresponds to a standard deviation.

3.1.2   Fuzzy Classifier Based Matching

Fuzzy classifier is used to classify and match the images in both AM and PM images. Fuzzy logic is a power tool which makes decision based on if then rules. Fuzzy allows intermediate values of certainty to be defined between two conventional values such as yes/no, high/low or true/false. Intermediate values can be expressed degree to which an element belongs to a fuzzy set where 0 represents non membership and 1 represents membership. For the fuzzy set A in the space X is characterized by a membership function $fA(X)$, which associates each point of X is a real number in the interval $[0,1]$

with the value of $fA(X)$ at X representing the membership grade of X in A. One of the essential steps is to create the membership function (i.e.) fuzzy set that assume values in the range from 0 to 1 defined in universal space. The mathematical functions are expressed in linear, trapezoidal or Gaussian forms [16]. In this work, three variables pulp, enamel and dentine are used as input variables. The fuzzy membership functions are created based on the feature extraction. For each input variable, three fuzzy sets for the low, medium and high are defined and the triangular membership function used in this work shown in Fig. 3. For ease of understanding and simplicity, a graphic interpretation of the element and membership grade pairs which are created for the low, medium and high, using each variable.

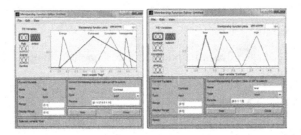

Fig. 3. Membership function of texture features

Taking the pulp, enamel and dentine of the labeled regions as fuzzy inputs, confidence score was built upon each individual tooth. The fuzzy rules used to build a confidence score are based on the fuzzy rules. The proposed fuzzy rules of the individual tooth separation texture features are shown in Fig. 4.

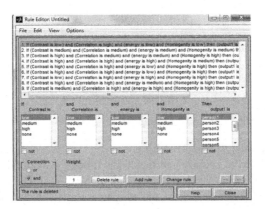

Fig. 4. Proposed fuzzy rules of tooth texture features

4   Results and Discussion

The radiograph images which are used in this work was collected from Dr.G. Ulaganathan, M.D.S, Vignesh dental clinic, Madurai. This algorithm is evaluated with a database containing quantitative radiographic dental images. The proposed algorithm was evaluated using Matlab 2013a software and it was tested with database radiographic images. This algorithm is evaluated with the database of 150 radiographic images. Out of the 150 images taken for analysis, only two sample radiograph images are shown in Fig. 3(a) of size 295×194, 265×210. This is initially preprocessed by using Butterworth high pass filter and it produces uniform edges in the image because of its maximally flat response which is shown in Fig. 5(b).

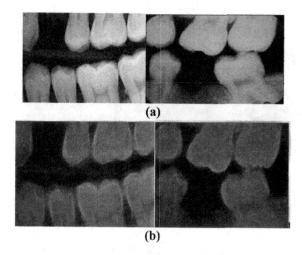

Fig. 5. (a) Sample radiographic images, (b) preprocessed result

Individual identification can give better result by considering the single tooth than the whole images. Hence in this work, spline isolation is used to separate each and every individual tooth. Out of the 150 radiographic images, 75 images are AM records and 75 are PM records. Normally, bitewing radiograph consists of 6 to 8 teeth and a periapical image consists of 3 to 4 teeth. The teeth separation in bitewing radiograph using spline function is shown in Fig. 6(a). Missing tooth region contains less intensity than the teeth region, hence by using the spline function the missing tooth region can be extracted. Then centroids are calculated for each individual tooth and it is shown in Fig. 6(b). After calculating the centroids, morphological operations are used to extract the missing tooth region and pseudocoloring was performed in this region and it is shown in Fig. 7. Then, k-NN classifier was used for tooth classification in order to categorize the missing tooth as molar or premolar.

The sample database of molar and premolar radiograph images is shown in Fig. 8(a). The Hu's moment invariants are calculated for each and every tooth in the database and query images. These features are used to identify whether the missing tooth is molar or

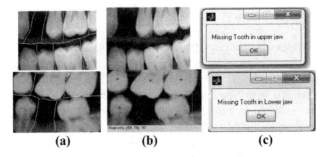

Fig. 6. (a) Spline isolation, (b) centroid calculation, (c) missing tooth location

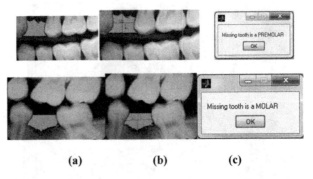

Fig. 7. (a) Pseudo coloring for the missing tooth region, (b) missing tooth parameter estimation, (c) tooth classification

premolar and it is shown in Fig. 8(b). By using the k-NN classifier the missing tooth in the given radiograph is found. After classification, the database is alienated into molar and premolar category for radiography images. It makes a healthy environment for decision making and reduces the computational time.

Contrast and energy parameters are different from pulp, enamel and dentine for a single tooth as well as for various teeth. Hence these are the desirable parameters for matching. From this table, it is evident that the best matching can be done by comparing both AM and PM images. The gray level co-occurrence matrix is different for radiographic and photographic images. In radiographic images it is easy to separate pulp, enamel, and dentine, and GLCM output is also different for all the three separations. Since in photographic images, are difficult to separate pulp, enamel and dentine, the structure of the whole tooth images are compared in the last row of Table 1. GLCM matrix is different even for the incisor of photographic images. The rank of matching is calculated based on this. The additional parameters are used to perform exact matching for individual person identification of missing tooth parameter is tabulated in Table 2. These measurements will be helpful for matching of missing tooth in addition with the matching distance, if the AM record consists of missing tooth.

The classification accuracy of individual missing tooth is tabulated in Table 3.

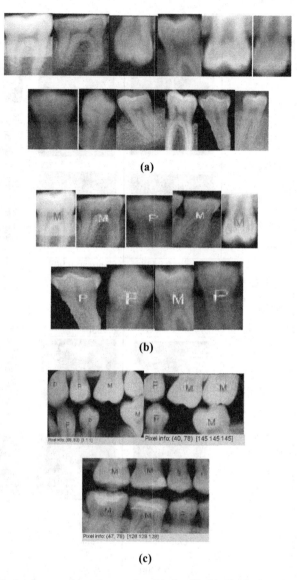

Fig. 8. (a) Sample database-molar and premolar, (b) classified Individual tooth, (c) classification of teeth

4.1 Performance Evaluation

The algorithm is evaluated by observing the accuracy, precision, recall or true positive rate, false positive rate, true negative rate and false negative rate. Precision is a correctness measure, recall is a completeness measure that the proportion of positive cases that were correctly identified.

Table 1. Texture parameters

Input tooth		Pulp	Enamel	Dentine
	Tooth separation			
	Texture output			
	GLCM parameters	Contrast: 0.2528 Correlation: 0.9681 Energy: 0.2652 Homogeneity: 0.9424	Contrast: 0.9072 Correlation: 0.8720 Energy: 0.4353 Homogeneity: 0.9330	Contrast: 0.7086 Correlation: 0.8621 Energy: 0.7696 Homogeneity: 0.9744
	Tooth separation			
	Texture output			
	GLCM parameters	Contrast: 0.3708 Correlation: 0.9253 Energy: 0.1000 Homogeneity: 0.8533	Contrast: 1.6070 Correlation: 0.8205 Energy: 0.2806 Homogeneity: 0.8716	Contrast: 0.6346 Correlation: 0.8318 Energy: 0.8575 Homogeneity: 0.9743
	Photographic Texture output			Contrast:0.0730 Correlation: 0.9669 Energy: 0.2860 Homogeneity: 0.9640

Table 2. Missing tooth parameter measurements

Images	Measurements		
	Length (pixels)	Width (pixels)	Area of missing tooth (pixels)
Missing tooth1	73	64	605
Missing tooth2	68	55	139
Missing tooth3	78	69	428
Missing tooth4	125	92	97
Missing tooth5	80	89	515

Table 3. Classification accuracy

Position	Molar (M)		Premolar (P)	
	Number	Accuracy (%)	Number	Accuracy (%)
Total number of images	140	99.2	120	97.5
Correctly classified	139		117	
Erroneously classified	01		03	

$$precision = \frac{S}{|S \cap T|} \qquad (13)$$

$$Recall = \frac{S}{|S \cap V|} \qquad (14)$$

False positive is the proportion of negative cases that were incorrectly classified as positive and it is given by

$$False\,positive = \frac{T}{|U \cap T|} \qquad (15)$$

True negative is defined as the proportion of negative cases that were classified correctly and it is obtained by

$$True\,negative = \frac{U}{|U \cap T|} \qquad (16)$$

False negative is the proportion of positive cases that were incorrectly classified as negative and the accuracy is the proportion of total number of predictions that were correct and it is given by

$$False\,negative = \frac{V}{|S \cap V|} \qquad (17)$$

$$accuracy = \frac{|S \cap U|}{|S \cap U| \cap |T \cap V|} \tag{18}$$

The confusion matrix of k-NN classifier is tabulated in Table 4 and the performance measures of k-NN classifier are tabulated in Table 5. From Table 5, it is observed that k-NN provides an accuracy of 90% for molar and 93% for premolar. This algorithm is evaluated based on the Cumulative Matching Characteristic curve (CMC). It is plotted between the number of matching is obtained for top-1 retrieval to the total number of images considered.

Table 4. Confusion matrix of k-NN classifier

Tooth	Confusion matrix			
	TP	FP	FN	TN
Molar	14	2	1	13
Premolar	16	1	1	11

Table 5. Performance measures of k-NN classifier

Performance measures	k-NN classifier (%)	
	Molar	Premolar
Accuracy	90	93
Precision	93.3	94.1
Recall	87.5	94.1
False positive	7.14	8.33
True negative	92.8	91.6
False negative	12.5	5.88

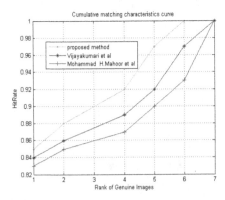

Fig. 9. Comparative performance analysis

Among the 150 query images, 128 genuine images were ranked first with the hit rate of 0.85 for similarity measure of ED in the radiographic images. Out of 22 images 15 images were top 2 priority and 4, 3 in the top 3 and top 4 respectively. Hit rate obtained in this algorithm is compared with the existing algorithms of Mohammad et al. and Vijayakumari et al. which is shown in Fig. 9. From this Figure, it is noticeable that the proposed method gives better results than the existing approaches.

5 Conclusion

An efficient algorithm is designed for the detection and identification of missing tooth in the radiographic images and photographic images. This algorithm initially checks if any tooth is missing in the given input image by calculating mahalanobis distance between the centroids of the tooth. Then the missing tooth identification is accomplished by using Hu's moment invariants and k-NN classifier. This work helps in better matching of both the AM and the PM radiographs and photographs which would otherwise be impossible without identifying the missing tooth in the given input images. By identifying the missing tooth, the accuracy of human identification is improved compared to the existing approaches. The proposed work is found to have an accuracy of 93% and this system is a novel one that identifies the missing tooth in the radiographs and photographs.

References

1. Chen, H., Jain, A.K.: Tooth contour extraction for matching dental radiographs, pp. 2128–2132. IEEE (2004)
2. Jain, A.K., Chen, H.: Matching of dental X-ray images for human identification. Pattern Recogn. Elsevier J. **35**, 1519–1532 (2004)
3. Chen, H., Jain, A.K.: Dental biometrics: alignment and matching of dental radiographs. IEEE Trans. Pattern Anal. Mach. Intell. **27**(8), 1319–1326 (2005)
4. Osher, S., Seithian, J.: Fronts propagating with curvature dependent speed: algorithm based Hamilton Jacob formulations. J. Comput. Phys. **79**(1), 12–49
5. Nomir, O., Abdul Mottaleb, M.: Fusion of matching algorithms for human identification using dental X-ray radiographs. IEEE Trans. Inf. Secur. **3**(2), 223–233 (2008)
6. Nomir, O., Abdul Mottaleb, M.: Human identification from dental X-ray images based on shape and appearance of teeth. IEEE Trans. Inf. Secur. **2**(2), 188–197 (2007)
7. Bhardwaj, A., Kaur, M., Kumar, A.: Recognition of plants by leaf image using moment invariant and texture analysis. Int. J. Innov. Appl. Sci. **3**(1), 237–248 (2013)
8. Rindhe, D., Shake, A.N.: A role of dental radiograph in human forensic identification. Int. J. Comput. Sci. Mob. Comput. **2**(12), 21–25 (2013)
9. Pushparaj, V., Gurunathan, U., Arumugam, B.: An effective shape extraction algorithm using contour information and matching by mahalanobis distance. J. Digit. Imag. **26**(2), 1–8 (2012)
10. Nomir, O., Abdul Mottaleb, M.: Hierarchial contour matching for dental X-ray radiographs. Pattern Recogn. **41**(1), 130–138 (2008)
11. Mahoor, M.H., Abdul Mottaleb, M.: Classification and numbering of teeth in dental bitewing images. J. Pattern Recogn. **38**(4), 577–586 (2005)

12. Lin, P.L., Lai, Y.H., Huang, P.W.: An effective classification and numbering system for dental bitewing radiographs using teeth region and contour information. Pattern Recogn. **43**(4), 1380–1392 (2010)
13. Pushparaj, V., Gurunathan, U., Arumugam, B.: Victim identification with dental images using texture and morphological operations. J. Electron. Imag. **23**(1), 1–8 (2014)
14. de Boor, C.: B-spline basics. In: Fundamental Developments of Computer Aided Geometric Modeling, pp. 27–49. Academic press, New York
15. Pattanachai, N., Covavisaruch, N., Sinthanayothin, C.: Tooth recognition in dental radiographs via Hu's moment invariants. In: IEEE International Conference on Electrical Engineering/Electronics, Computer Telecommunications and Information Technology (2012)
16. Akcam, M.O., Takada, K.: Fuzzy modeling for selecting head gear types. Euro. J. Orthod. **24**, 99–106 (2002)

Shearlet Based Medical Image Fusion Using Pulse-Coupled Neural Network with Fuzzy Memberships

Niladri Shekhar Mishra[1]([⊠]), Sudeb Das[2], and Amlan Chakrabarti[3]

[1] Department of Electronics and Communication Engineering,
Netaji Subhash Engineering College, Kolkata 700152, India
niladrimishra@gmail.com
[2] Videonetics Technology Private Limited,
B.P. Block, Sector V, Salt Lake City, Kolkata 700091, India
to.sudeb@gmail.com
[3] A.K. Choudhury School of Information Technology, University of Calcutta,
Kolkata 700009, India
amlanc@ieee.org

Abstract. In this article, we propose a novel multimodal Medical Image Fusion (MIF) method based on a neuro-fuzzy technique in the transform (Non-Subsampled Shearlet Transform (NSST)) domain for spatially registered, multi-modal medical images. The source medical images are first decomposed by NSST. The low-frequency subbands (LFSs) are fused using the Max-selection rule. Fuzzy triangular memberships are derived from a specific neighborhood-region of each high-frequency coefficient. Then they (high-frequency subbands, HFSs) are fused using a biologically inspired neural network (Pulse Coupled Neural Network (PCNN)) according to our newly proposed rule. Then inverse NSST (INSST) is applied to the fused coefficients to get the fused image. Visual and quantitative analysis and comparisons with state-of-the-art MIF techniques show the effectiveness of the proposed scheme in fusing multimodality medical images.

Keywords: Image fusion · Fuzzy triangular membership function · Non-Subsampled Shearlet Transform (i.e. NSST) · Pulse-coupled neural network

1 Introduction

By the advent of various modern imaging instruments and significant improvements in different technological domains, nowadays it is possible to represent the same body part (organ) by different types of images (known as multimodalities). This multi-modality approach is to extract different kind of information from the same human organ [6]. Different modalities of medical imaging provide diversified information of the same medical scene (of human body-part)

© Springer International Publishing AG 2017
S. Mukherjee et al. (Eds.): ICVGIP 2016, LNCS 10481, pp. 337–344, 2017.
https://doi.org/10.1007/978-3-319-68124-5_29

in different ways and have their respective application areas [1]. For example, Computed Tomography (CT), Magnetic Resonance Imaging (MRI), or Magnetic Resonance Angiography (MRA) provide the structural anatomical information whereas there are modalities to extract the functional information such as Position Emission Tomography (PET), Single-Photon Emission Computed Tomography (SPECT) etc. As a result, combining any two (or more than two) modalities of medical images we can have more useful information through image fusion (IF) which has become the focus of imaging research and processing [1].

In image processing and its application areas e.g. segmentation, clustering and fusion fuzzy sets and logics (introduced by Zadeh, 1965) have proved their significant contribution. The well known conjunctive, disjunctive and compromise properties of fuzzy sets are widely explored in the mentioned areas [6,14]. Fuzzy sets and logics are basically to represent ambiguities in real-world. It aims to deal in an ambiguous environment because it can handle the uncertainties caused by ill-posed data/information [2].

In Medical Image Fusion (MIF) researchers have started using NSST [5] due to its more directionality and less computation-intensiveness [9]. Over other type of transformations (e.g. wavelet, curvelet, contourlet etc.) it has already proved its usefulness [5,9]. NSST is advantageous over other transforms due to its capability of handling minute multidirectional changes while fusing two (or more than two) modalities (of same scene). It also highlights the different salient features through their (decomposed) sub-bands and its shift-invariance. These superiorities enhance the usage of NSST in various domains like image analysis (segmentation, clustering, extracting features from an image) and in the field of fusion [9].

MIF schemes based on PCNN [7] model when applied in spatial domain is generally suffers from various drawbacks (contrast reduction, finer detail loss) [4]. Thus to exploit the strength of PCNN, we have used it in transform (NSST) domain. Fuzzy logic is used as generator of the inputs to PCNN (derived from NSST coefficients) to catch-up the real-life uncertainties. Following human visual system (HVS) triangular-memberships (from the HFSs) are generated using a local window/neighborhood region as HVS is sensible to a region and not to a particular pixel/point. To prove the efficacy of the proposed technique we have compared it with various popular MIF techniques as in [4,10,12,13].

The rest of the paper is organized as follows: In Sect. 2 theoretical background is presented (Sects. 2.1 and 2.2 introduce the NSST and PCNN respectively). The proposed MIF scheme is described in Sect. 3. Experimental results and comparisons are in Sect. 4, and the conclusion is drawn in Sect. 5.

2   Theoretical Background

2.1   Non-subsampled Shearlet Transform

As mentioned earlier NSST can be more effective than the basic transformations (e.g. wavelet, contourlet). Though Non-Subsampled Contourlet Transform

(NSCT) [3] can overcome the major shortcoming (e.g. shift-variance) of the earlier ones (wavelet, contourlet, etc.) but it suffers from limited directionality and large computational complexity [9]. By employing Non-Subsampled Laplacian Pyramid (NSLP) and many shearing filters NSST is realized and can handle the slight changes in different directions (in an image) more efficiently.

To analyze an image through multi-scalability and multi-directionality property, in NSST firstly the NSLP is used to decompose an image into low and high-frequency components, and then direction filtering is employed to get the different subbands in different directions. The novelity of this type of transformation is to use Shear matrix (ShF) for direction filtering. At the decomposition level $m = 3$, an image is decomposed into $m + 1 = 4$ subbands (one LFS and 3 HFSs). The subbands are of same size of the source image (thus ensuring shift-invariance). How NSST decomposes an image using three levels is shown in Fig. 1(a).

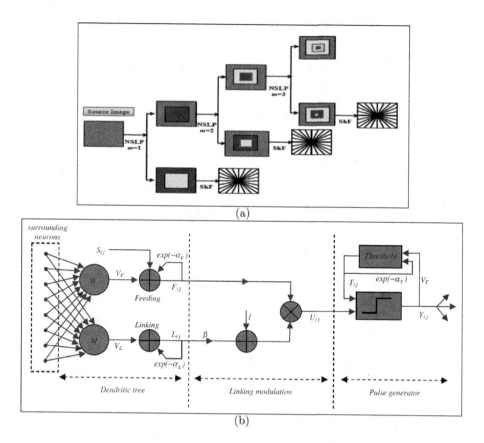

Fig. 1. Diagram representing (a) NSST decomposition and (b) structure of PCNN.

2.2   Pulse Coupled Neural Network

PCNN is a single layered, two-dimentional, laterally connected neural network of pulse coupled neurons [11]. As shown in Fig. 1(b) the network consists of three parts (an input known as dendritic tree, linking and a pulse generator). The neuron receives the input signals from feeding and linking inputs. The neighboring pixels of the corresponding pixel constitute the receptive area of the neuron (for detailing please see [4,11]).

3   Proposed Method

The notations used in this section are as follows: A, B, R represents the two source images and the fused image respectively. $C = (A, B, R)$. L_G^C indicates the LFS of the image C at the coarsest scale G. $D_{g,h}^C$ represents the HFS of the image C at scale g, $(g = 1, \ldots, G)$ and direction $h(i, j)$ denotes the spatial location of each coefficient. The method can be easily extended to more than two images.

Firstly the decomposition of the images (A and B) are done using NSST. Then we have fuzzified them using triangular membership function [8]. To do so we have considered a particular window (or sub-image of size 3×3) around each coefficient-location (contemporary to pixel-location). This yields the localized-memberships for each coefficient. These localized-memberships are input to PCNN. The fusion-scheme of LFS and HFSs are given below.

3.1   Fusing Low Frequency Subband

The LFSs coefficients (of two used modalities) are fused according to their (maximum of) absolute values. If the two coefficients under consideration are L_G^A and L_G^B with greater absolute value as the fused coefficients:

$$L_G^R(i, j) = \begin{cases} L_G^A(i, j), |L_G^A(i, j)| \geq |L_G^B(i, j)| \\ L_G^B(i, j), \text{otherwise.} \end{cases} \tag{1}$$

3.2   Fusing High Frequency Subband

Generation of Fuzzy memberships. We have used the following technique to generate the triangular memberships for the HFSs.

If a_1 be the maximum value of the local window under consideration, b_1 be the minimum of the same and if $c_1 = a_1 - 0.5(a_1 - b_1)$ then membership $mem_{i,j}^{g,h,C}$ is computed using the following formula:

$$mem_{i,j}^{g,h,C} = \begin{cases} \frac{1}{2}(\sin(\frac{1}{2} * \pi * (1 - \frac{a_1 - pix}{c_1})) + 1), \text{if } c_1 \neq 0.0 \\ 0.0, \text{otherwise.} \end{cases} \tag{2}$$

where pix is the corresponding high frequency coefficient under consideration. $mem_{i,j}^{g,h,C}$ is the derived triangular membership corresponding to a coefficient $D_{g,h}^C(i, j)$, where $C = (A, B)$.

Fusion using PCNN (*while derived memberships are input to it*). For MIF, PCNN has been used in literature slightly different from the standard model [4]. The following Eqs. (3)–(8) are presented here to describe the PCNN model for the present application:

$$F_{i,j}^{g,h,C}[n] = mem_{i,j}^{g,h,C} \tag{3}$$

$$L_{i,j}^{g,h,C}[n] = e^{-\alpha_L} L_{i,j}^{g,h,C}[n-1] + V_L \sum_{k,l} w_{i,j,k,l}^{g,h,C} Y_{i,j}^{g,h,C}[n-1] \tag{4}$$

$$U_{i,j}^{g,h,C}[n] = F_{i,j}^{g,h,C}[n](1 + \beta L_{i,j}^{g,h,C}[n]) \tag{5}$$

$$\theta_{i,j}^{g,h,C}[n] = e^{-\alpha_\theta} \theta_{i,j}^{g,h,C}[n-1] + V_\theta Y_{i,j}^{g,h,C}[n-1] \tag{6}$$

$$Y_{i,j}^{g,h,C}[n] = \begin{cases} 1, & U_{i,j}^{g,h,C}[n] > \theta_{i,j}^{g,h,C}[n] \\ 0, & \text{otherwise} \end{cases} \tag{7}$$

$$T_{i,j}^{g,h,C}[n] = T_{i,j}^{g,h,C}[n-1] + Y_{i,j}^{g,h,C}[n] \tag{8}$$

where $F_{i,j}^{g,h,C}$ and $L_{i,j}^{g,h,C}$ are feeding and linking inputs respectively. The current pixel (coefficient) location is (i, j). The corresponding linking range is $(k \times l)$. α_l, α_θ are the decay constants and β is the linking strength parameter. $w_{i,j,k,l}$ represents the gain strength. V_L, V_θ denote the amplitude gains. If $U_{i,j}^{g,h,C}$ (internal state of the neuron) greater than the $\theta_{i,j}^{g,h,C}$ (dynamic threshold), then a pulse ($Y_{i,j}^{g,h,C}=1$) is generated (this is known as one firing time). The summed up value of $Y_{i,j}^{g,h,C} = 1$ for N_1 iterations is used to represent the image information. Analysis is done on $T_{i,j}^{g,h,C}$ which is yielded after the N_1 number of iterations are over.

3.3   Algorithm

The medical images to be fused must be registered for proper alignment of the corresponding pixels. Here we outline the salient steps of the proposed MIF method:

1. Decompose the registered source medical images by NSST to get the LFSs and HFSs.
2. Fuse the coefficients of LFS using (1) as in Sect. 3.1.
3. Compute the triangular memberships for all the HFSs as in Sect. 3.2.
4. Apply the derived memberships as input to PCNN and generate pulse of neuron using (3)–(7). Also compute the firing times $T_{i,j}^{g,h,C}$ by (8) as in Sect. 3.2.
5. Stop iteration after a certain number [let it be N_1].

6. Fuse the HFSs according to the rule:

$$D_{g,h}^{R}(i,j) = \begin{cases} D_{g,h}^{A}(i,j), & T_{i,j}^{g,h,A}[N_1] \geq T_{i,j}^{g,h,B}[N_1] \\ D_{g,h}^{B}(i,j), & \text{otherwise} \end{cases} \qquad (9)$$

7. Apply inverse NSST on the fused LFS's and HFSs' coefficients to get the final fused medical image R.

4 Experimental Results and Comparisons

To evaluate the performance of the proposed MIF method, extensive experiments (over many datasets) were carried out on various modalities of medical images. Figure 2(a1)–(b1) and (a2)–(b2) show two different sets of source images used in our experiments, and are denoted by *ImSet1* and *ImSet2*, respectively. The CT image in Fig. 2(a1) shows the bones and the MRI image in Fig. 2(b1) displays the soft tissues information. The case is same for the second pair also (Fig. 2(a2)–(b2)). Figure 2(r1) and (r2) are the fused results by our proposed method. The shearing direction of NSST was chosen to be "1" to lower the computation cost. The selected quantitative measures used in the experiments are Spatial Frequency (*SF*), Entropy (*EN*) and Standard Deviation (*SD*) [4]. To measure the overall activity and clarity level of an image *SF* can be used. Larger *SF* value denotes better fusion result. The entropy of an image is a measure of information content. It is the average number of bits needed to quantize the intensities in the image. Higher *EN* would represent more fused information. *SD* is to measure the contrast in the fused image. Obviously an image with higher contrast (notion of better fusion) would have a higher standard deviation.

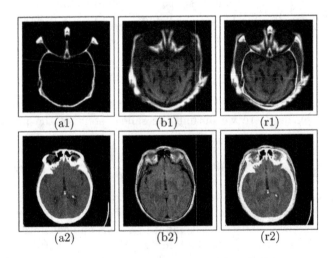

Fig. 2. Source images (first two column) with fusion results (last column). a1: CT, b1: MRI, a2: CT, b2: Proton density (PD) weighted MR; C_i: (a_i, b_i, r_i) is the particular combination, where r_i is the fused result by our proposed methodology.

By examining visually one can see that the fused images are of higher contrast and consisting of the combined characteristics (both, hard and soft tissue informations) from the two modalities. From the Tables 1 and 2 it can be seen that the proposed scheme is much more superior than the earlier ones. Our proposed technique performs best in terms of all the three quantitative criterions (*SF*, *EN* and *SD*) while compared with "Scheme [10,12,13]". While compared with "Scheme [4]" (a more recent one) our proposed technique provides better/comparable results. Because for *ImSet1* the proposed one provides better *EN* and *SD* and almost same *SF* (difference is only 0.01). For *ImSet2* it provides better *SF* and *SD* and slightly less *EN* (by 0.03 difference). That is why these two values are underlined in the mentioned tables. As our technique provides overall betterment, the corresponding results are shown in "**bold**".

Table 1. Performance comparisons using *ImSet1*

Schemes	SF	EN	SD
Scheme [10]	5.31	5.87	33.72
Scheme [12]	6.55	6.38	53.82
Scheme [13]	6.65	6.72	57.97
Scheme [4]	_6.94_	6.77	65.86
Proposed	**6.93**	**6.78**	**66.38**

Table 2. Performance comparisons using *ImSet2*

Schemes	SF	EN	SD
Scheme [10]	5.98	4.19	55.11
Scheme [12]	6.21	4.26	56.53
Scheme [13]	6.18	4.32	78.47
Scheme [4]	6.32	_4.36_	83.70
Proposed	**6.46**	**4.33**	**85.17**

5   Discussion and Conclusion

We propose a new shearlet based neuro-fuzzy technique. Pulse Coupled Neural Network is used effectively to fuse the high frequency subbands to ensure better reliability. Fuzzy memberships are used to capture the natural tendency of ambiguity in medical imaging. To show the effectiveness of the proposed technique, visual (*qualitative*) as well as quantitative analysis were carried out. From the analysis it has been seen that our method is overall superior than the selected methods for comparison purpose.

Acknowledgement. The authors would like to thank the anonymous referees for their constructive criticism and valuable suggestions. They also like to thank http://www.imagefusion.org/ and http://www.med.harvard.edu/aanlib/home.html for providing the source medical images. Prof. (Dr.) Amlan Chakrabarti likes to thank "CoE in Systems Biology and Biomedical Engineering, University of Calcutta supported by TEQIP-II Project" for supporting the research work.

References

1. Barra, V., Boire, J.Y.: A general framework for the fusion of anatomical and functional medical images. NeuroImage **13**(3), 410–424 (2001)
2. Bezdek, J.C.: Fuzzy models-what are they, and why? [editorial]. IEEE Trans. Fuzzy Syst. **1**(1), 1–6 (1993)
3. da Cunha, A.L., Zhou, J., Do, M.N.: The nonsubsampled contourlet transform: theory, design, and applications. IEEE Trans. Image Process. **15**(10), 3089–3101 (2006)
4. Das, S., Kundu, M.K.: NSCT-based multimodal medical image fusion using pulse-coupled neural network and modified spatial frequency. Med. Biol. Eng. Comput. **50**(10), 1105–1114 (2012)
5. Easley, G., Labate, D., Lim, W.Q.: Sparse directional image representations using the discrete shearlet transform. Appl. Comput. Harm. Anal. **25**, 25–46 (2008)
6. James, A.P., Dasarathy, B.V.: Medical image fusion: a survey of the state of the art. Inf. Fusion **19**, 4–19 (2014)
7. Johnson, J.L., Padgett, M.L.: PCNN models and applications. IEEE Trans. Neural Netw. **10**(3), 480–498 (1999)
8. Pedrycz, W.: Why triangular membership functions? Fuzzy Sets Syst. **64**(1), 21–30 (1994)
9. Singh, S., Gupta, D., Anand, R.S., Kumar, V.: Nonsubsampled shearlet based CT and MR medical image fusion using biologically inspired spiking neural network. Biomed. Sig. Process. Control **18**, 91–101 (2015)
10. Wang, Z., Ma, Y.: Medical image fusion using m-PCNN. Inf. Fusion **9**(2), 176–185 (2008)
11. Wang, Z., Ma, Y., Cheng, F., Yang, L.: Review of pulse-coupled neural networks. Image Vis. Comput. **28**(1), 5–13 (2010)
12. Yang, L., Guo, B.L., Ni, W.: Multimodality medical image fusion based on multiscale geometric analysis of contourlet transform. Neurocomputing **72**(1–3), 203–211 (2008)
13. Yang, Y., Park, D.S., Huang, S., Rao, N.: Medical image fusion via an effective wavelet-based approach. EURASIP J. Adv. Sig. Process. **2010**, 44:1–44:13 (2010)
14. Yue, S., Wu, T., Pan, J., Wang, H.: Fuzzy clustering based ET image fusion. Inf. Fusion **14**, 487–497 (2013)

MR Imaging via Reduced Generalized Autocalibrating Partially Parallel Acquisition Compressed Sensing

Sheikh Rafiul Islam[1(✉)], Seba Maity[2], Santi P. Maity[3], and Ajoy Kumar Ray[3]

[1] Neotia Institute of Technology Management and Science,
Jhinga, Amira, 24 Pgs.(S), Kolkata 743368, India
sk.rafiul@gmail.com
[2] College of Engineering and Management, Kolaghat 721171, India
seba.maity@gmail.com
[3] Indian Institute of Engineering Science and Technology, Shibpur,
Howrah 711103, India
santipmaity@it.iiests.ac.in, ajoy_ray2004@yahoo.com

Abstract. Magnetic Resonance Imaging (MRI) system in recent times demands a high rate of acceleration in data acquisition to reduce the scanning time. The data acquisition rate can be accelerated to a significant order through Parallel MRI (pMRI) approach. An additional improvement in low sensing time for data acquisition can be achieved using Compressed Sensing (CS) or Compressive Sampling that enables reconstruction of a sparse signal from sub-sample (incomplete) measurements. This paper proposes an efficient pMRI scheme by combining CS with Generalized Auto-calibrating Partially Parallel Acquisitions (GRAPPA) to produce an MR image at high data acquisition rate. A kernel of reduced size is used within GRAPPA for estimating the unobserved encoded samples. Instead of all the unobserved samples, a certain number of the same are estimated randomly. Now, an l_1-minimization based CS reconstruction technique is used in which the observed and the estimated unobserved samples are taken as measurements to reconstruct the final MR images. Extensive simulation results show that a significant reduction in artifacts and thereby consequent visual improvement in the reconstructed MRIs are achieved even when a high rate of acceleration factor is used. Simulation results also demonstrate that the proposed method outperforms some state-of-art pMRI methods, both in terms of subjective and objective quality assessment for the reconstructed images.

Keywords: Compressed sensing · GRAPPA · Parallel imaging · pMRI · Image reconstruction

1 Introduction

In recent times, Magnetic Resonance Imaging (MRI) is considered to be a widely used biomedical imaging modality due to its ability to provide global anatomic

© Springer International Publishing AG 2017
S. Mukherjee et al. (Eds.): ICVGIP 2016, LNCS 10481, pp. 345–357, 2017.
https://doi.org/10.1007/978-3-319-68124-5_30

assessment over soft-tissue characterization without using any harmful ionizing radiation or X-rays [1]. Even MRI is the best choice as imaging modality for a patient when frequent imaging is required in diagnosis or therapy, especially in the brain [2,3]. However, it is sometime difficult to get an MR image with good quality for a child or the patient suffering from claustrophobia due to intolerance of long scan time inside the imaging equipment. An open or upright MRI scanner is often suggested for these patients. However, the open MRI scanner is unable to produce good quality images compared to the closed scanner due to the use of permanent magnets [4]. In this situation, Compressed Sensing or Compressive Sampling (CS) based parallel imaging approach can be adopted to provide the fast and the robust MRI with significantly reduced scanning time. The CS framework enables reconstruction of a sparse signal from a very less numbers of random linear projections known as measurements, compared to the number of samples required in conventional signal processing technique dictated by the Nyquist rate [5–7]. MRI scanners acquire the encoded samples instead of direct pixel samples [2,8]. The encoded samples are naturally sparse in some appropriate transform domain like Fourier transform (FT), discrete cosine transform (DCT), wavelet transform (WT) etc. [9]. Random acquisition of a certain number of the encoded samples make the acquisition system incoherence with the certain sparsifying basis [5,9]. The properties of compressibility of the k-space data as well as possible incoherence of the sparsifying basis with the sensing basis persuade the CS framework as a successful application to the MRI system.

An integration of Parallel MRI (pMRI) system and CS thus looks promising as a new data acquisition and reconstruction approach to achieve high acceleration rate. The natural sparsity property of an MR encoded data samples by combining Generalized Autocalibrating Partially Parallel Acquisitions (GRAPPA) with CS can then be exploited. The novelty of the imaging system lies in acquisition of a very few data samples through the multiple coils by using a cartesian sampling pattern. The data samples are then increased through an estimation technique as adopted in GRAPPA and then a CS reconstruction technique can be used to provide the full field of view (FOV) data samples.

The rest of the paper is organized as follows: Sect. 2 presents a brief review on related works that include limitations and scope of the present work. In Sect. 3, the proposed rGRAPPA-CS scheme for pMRI system is presented. Section 4 presents simulation results and discussion. Finally, conclusions and scope of the future work are stated in Sect. 5.

2   Related Work

Recently, several pMRI schemes are reported to accelerate data acquisition by considering reduced FOV [10–14]. The acquisition speed can be increased significantly using sensitivity encoding (SENSE) based pMRI [10,11,15–17]. In this method, the data acquisition rate is improved by neglecting certain number of samples along phase-encoding direction [10]. MRIs can be reconstructed from these data samples as the spatial sensitivities of multiple coils are distinct [10].

However, the method fails to reconstruct good quality images when the coil sensitivity maps are not available accurately. Griswold et al. [11] present an alternative approach for pMRI, popularly known as GRAPPA. The method uses a number of auto-calibration signal (ACS) to determine the weights for a linear combination of the acquired under-sampled k-space data [11]. Some aliasing artifacts, along the under-sampled direction, are observed in the reconstructed image if the number of ACS lines are insufficient.

The method in [18] proposed an MR imaging by combining sparsity with GRAPPA. The scheme enables high acceleration in data acquisition for MRI. However, reconstruction quality to an extent depends on the accuracy of the sensitivity profiles of the coils. Miao et al. [19] present a partially pMRI method that combines CS with GRAPPA to reconstruct high-resolution images from measurements captured at high acceleration rate. This method provides the full k-space data by performing joint-sparsity guided multiple CS reconstructions to determine coil weights that used in GRAPPA reconstruction for calibration purpose. This method is able to reconstruct MRI by exploiting sparsity of multi-coil images in a significant manner. But the quality of the reconstructed image often depends on the estimation accuracy of coil weights. In [20], a sparsity-promoting nonlinear GRAPPA scheme is proposed to reconstruct MRIs with capability of reducing noise and errors. The method uses fully sampled ACS lines at the central k-space for GRAPPA calibration. Weller et al. [13] propose another method to accelerate the image reconstruction by limiting ACS data. The method applies sparsity before performing the calibration. However, the method still requires a set of ACS to provide high quality MRIs at high acceleration rate. Moreover, these methods may not be able to reconstruct a superior quality MRIs when the samples are degraded during acquisition.

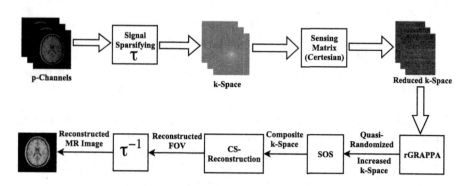

Fig. 1. Proposed rGRAPPA-CS scheme.

2.1   Scope and Contributions of Present Work

The brief literature review shows that the use of multiple coils in MRI improves the acquisition speed along with improvement in clinically detailed information.

A simple combining effect of CS with reduced size of GRAPPA kernel expects to provide an MRI with all useful spatial information at higher acceleration rate and is the focus of the present work. To this aim, a simple yet effective pMRI acquisition and reconstruction scheme is proposed here to achieve high rate of data acquisition. The proposed method combines GRAPPA with CS for a significant reduction in scanning time and called as reduced GRAPPA-CS (rGRAPPA-CS). This scheme provides almost an artifacts-less reconstructed MRI from multiple copies of incomplete observations (or measurements) in two steps. In the first step, a cartesian sampling patter with high rate of acceleration factor is used to acquire the encoded samples in multiple coils. The number of the encoded samples are increased by a certain amount through the estimation of some missing samples using the reduced-GRAPPA kernel. The positions of the estimated missing samples are chosen randomly such that the sensing matrices become nearly orthogonal. Then, a square-of-sum (SOS) scheme is performed over the multi-coil observed samples and the estimated samples to provide the composite measurements. These composite measurements are now used in a relaxed OrthoNormal Expansion l_1 minimization (rONE-L1) framework [21] to get the full FOV k-space data in second step. The rONE-L1 algorithm is able to reconstruct a sparse signal even if the sensing matrix is nearly orthonormal [21].

The overall contributions of the present work are as follows:

- A reduced size GRAPPA Kernel is used to estimate some of the missing encoded samples that are used as the increased measurements for CS reconstruction. The estimation process uses the most C-number of significant coefficients in GRAPPA kernel to increase the encoded data samples randomly as measurements. A significant improvement in the reconstructed image quality is achieved due to the use of C-number of most significant coefficients in reduced GRAPPA kernel.
- The number of ACS lines required for calculating the global weighting factors can be reduced significantly. The weight factors are used for estimating the missing encoded samples.
- The actual encoded samples, along with the estimated samples, are then used as measurements in an l_1-minimization based CS reconstruction process. This produces the final full FOV k-space data for the required MRI.
- This rGRAPPA-CS reconstruction approach provides a highly informative MRI even if the input observations are degraded due to any inappropriate coil profiles. Extensive simulation results show the efficiency of the proposed method in terms of improved subjective and quantitative quality measuring parameters when compared with the several existing methods [11,13,16,19].

3   Proposed rGRAPPA-CS Reconstruction Scheme

The block diagram of the proposed rGRAPPA-CS scheme is shown in Fig. 1. An equal-spaced highly under sampled phase encoding certesian sampling patterns are used in multiple coils to acquire M_f number coefficients from an equivalent sparse representation of input encoded samples. Any suitable transform τ can be used to sparsify the input encoded samples. It uses GRAPPA for estimating random positioned M_g number of missing k-space samples. However, the total number of measurements $M = M_f + M_g$, must be much less than the number of samples required at Nyquist rate. The GRAPPA kernel as shown in Fig. 2 is used in the proposed method while considering 'C' number of most significant neighbors only. The size of the GRAPPA kernel depends on choosing the value of C which reduces with increasing the number of coils used by the acquisition system. Equation 1 is used to determine M_g number of missing k-space data using linear weighted coil sensitivity profile [11].

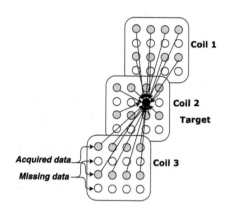

Fig. 2. Schematic description of determining missing samples through GRAPPA for an undersampling scheme (here r = 2)

$$y_j^{M_g}(k_y + m\Delta k_y) = \sum_{l=1}^{L}\sum_{b=1}^{N_b} \omega(j,b,l,m)S_l(k_y + br\Delta k_y) \qquad (1)$$

where

$y_j^{M_g}$: the estimated missing coefficients through GRAPPA
$k_y + m\Delta k_y$: line offset
L: total number of input coils
N_b: number of blocks used in the reconstruction
ω: global weights used in GRAPPA
S: coil sensitivity profiles
r: acceleration factor (rate)

Every block, used in the estimation process, is constructed using C number of random positioned missing encoded samples from $r - 1$ missing lines and a single acquired line. In this step, a total M_g number of missing samples are estimated. Now the composite measurements 'y^M' are formed by performing SOS over all coils' under-sampled known and the estimated k-space data, as shown in Fig. 1. The rONE-L_1 [21] is used as CS reconstruction algorithm to develop the full FOV k-space data from the composite measurements. A modified iterative soft thresholding (IST) approach with an aggressive continuation strategy is used by the rONE-L_1 algorithm. In this approach, the well known augmented Lagrange multiplier method [22,23] is used with a heuristic simplification. The reconstruction of the sparse or approximately sparse signal 'x' is carried out by the following iterative formula.

$$x_{t+1} = S_{\mu_t^{-1}} \left(\Phi \left(p_t + \mu_t^{-1} \psi_t \right) \right) \qquad with\ t = 0, 1, 2, \ldots \qquad (2a)$$

$$p_{t+1} = \begin{bmatrix} y^M \\ \overline{\Gamma}(x_{t+1} - \mu^{-1}\psi_t) \end{bmatrix} \qquad (2b)$$

where

   Φ: the ortho-normalized sensing matrix
   $\mu_t \in R^+$ and $\psi_t \in R^N$: the Lagrange multipliers

The Lagrange multiplier μ_t is considered as an exponentially increasing numerical value which ensures faster convergence by finding an acceptable solution. The soft thresholding operator $S_{\mu^{-1}}(.)$, used in Eq. 2a, can be defined on a variable $\omega \in R$ with a threshold $\mu^{-1} \in R^+$ as

$$S_{\mu^{-1}}(\omega) = sgn(\omega).(|\omega| - \mu^{-1})^+$$

where

$$(.)^+ = max(., 0)$$

and

$$sgn(\omega) = \begin{cases} \frac{\omega}{|\mu^{-1}|}, & \omega \neq 0 \\ 0, & \omega = 0 \end{cases}$$

The operator $\overline{\Gamma}(.)$, used in Eq. 2b, determines the projections of variable to its last $N - M$ entries. Finally, the inverse transform τ^{-1} is done on the reconstructed k-space data to provide the final MRI.

3.1   Algorithm

The proposed rGRAPPA-CS reconstruction approach is presented in Algorithm 1. This algorithm completes the MRI process in two stages. The method takes highly under-sampled phase encoded data y^{M_f} from the different input coils and acceleration rate 'r' as inputs. In the first stage, a set of random positioned unobserved encoded samples are estimated from the observed encoded samples and different coil sensitivity profile as stated Stage A in Algorithm 1. A reduced size of GRAPPA kernels and less number of ACS lines are used in the estimation process. The size of GRAPPA kernel is reduced by considering C-number of most significantly observed encoded samples as neighbors.

The positions of unknown encoded samples are guided by a random sensing matrix A as stated in Step A(III). A normal SOS is used to combine all the coils' sensed samples as well as estimated increased k-space samples to form the composite measurements y^M.

In the second stage, the iterative soft-thresholding based CS reconstruction algorithm rONE-L_1 [21] is used to provide full FOV k-space data from the composite measurements y^M. This is shown as Step B in Algorithm 1. The reconstruction of the equivalent sparse representation 'x' of the MRI is carried out till the convergence condition achieves. Finally, the inverse transform on the reconstructed sparse signal 'x' is performed to yield the final MRI.

Input: Multi-coils k-space observations, $y_i^{M_f}$ for $i = 1$ to L
  Rate of acceleration, r

Output: The reconstructed MRI, $\tau^{-1}(x)$

A. Estimating M_g number of missing k-space data using rGRAPPA
  I. Compute a 2D kernel, G, for estimating the missing k-space data from 3D kernel.
  II. Compute a reduced 2D kernel, G_C such that $C-$number of most significant k-space data is used as neighbors for determining missing k-space data.
  III. Construct sensing matrix A by choosing M_g- number of missing positions randomly.
  IV. Determine the M_g- number of missing k-space data using Eq. 1.
  V. Perform SOS on multi-coils observed and estimated k-pace data to form composite measurements, y^M.

B. Reconstructing the MRI from the composite measurements
  I. Initialize $x_0 = 0$, $\mu_0 = 0$, $\psi_0 = 0$ and $p_0 = \begin{bmatrix} y^F \\ 0 \end{bmatrix}$; t=0
  II. Expand the sensing matrix A, as orthonormal matrix Φ

$$\Phi^T = AA + B^T B = 1$$

where, B is a partially orthonormal matrix.
  III. Execute Eq. 2 for $t \geq 1$

Algorithm 1. Proposed rGRAPPA-CS reconstruction algorithm

---

4 Simulation Results and Discussion

This section presents some simulation results to evaluate the performance of the proposed method. Two popular objective measures, namely Peak-Signal-to-Noise-Ratio (PSNR) and mean Structural SIMilarity (SSIM) are used to quantify the quality of the reconstructed images with respect to the corresponding original (full scaled) images. The effectiveness of the proposed rGRAPPA-CS method is shown through the performance comparison with some state-of-art methods like standard GRAPPA [11], CS-GRAPPA [19], CS-GRAPPA [13] and CS-SENSE [16] based pMRI schemes. Different multi-coil input measurements are also considered to be degraded due to the imperfect coil sensitivities. This work used Fourier transform as coefficient of sparse transforms in different input coils. However, any other appropriate transform may also be used as equivalent sparse transform of multi-coil sensitivities.

Figure 3 demonstrates perceptual comparison of the reconstructed images for the proposed rGRAPPA-CS method and other methods [11,13,16,19] as well as multi-coil input images. The axial brain MRIs of (256 × 256), 8 bits/pixel for different coil sensitivities used as four coil input images, are shown in Fig. 3(a–d). The reconstructed axial brain MRIs using standard GRAPPA [11], CS-GRAPPA [19], CS-GRAPPA [13], CS-SENSE [16] and proposed rGRAPPA-CS, for the value of rate of acceleration (r) = 2, are shown in Fig. 3(f–j), respectively. Figure 3(k–o) are the reconstructed images for r = 4 using the existing [11,13,16,19] and the proposed method, respectively. In this simulation, the proposed method considers 50% most significant coefficients (C) in GRAPPA kernel for estimating 10% random-positioned unobserved coefficients that used in CS reconstruction. All the simulations of this work use total 32 number of ACS lines. The values of PSNR and SSIM for the reconstructed MRIs averaged over 100 images are presented in Table 1. An improved visual information in term of salient features in Fig. 3(j) and (o) compared to Fig. 3(f–i) and (k–n) validate better reconstruction quality of the proposed rGRAPPA-CS scheme over the other methods [11,13,16,19]. The reconstructed MRIs using the proposed rGRAPPA-CS maintain superior quality for a high acceleration rate which enables reduction in scanning time for MRI systems.

Table 1. PSNR and SSIM of the reconstructed MR images

Quality metrics	r	GRAPPA [11]	CS-GRAPPA [19]	CS-GRAPPA [13]	CS-SENSE [16]	rGRAPPA-CS
PSNR (dB)	2	39.88	40.02	40.52	41.19	**43.23**
SSIM		0.94	0.95	0.95	0.96	**0.98**
PSNR (dB)	4	30.80	32.57	33.08	34.33	**36.02**
SSIM		0.81	0.83	0.84	0.85	**0.87**

Performance of the proposed rGRAPPA-CS method, in terms of average PSNR and SSIM values of a large number (100) of reconstructed images, over other methods [11,13,16,19] is presented in Fig. 4. The variation of average PSNR and SSIM values of the reconstructed images on increasing rate of acceleration from 2 to 8 are demonstrated graphically in Fig. 4(a) and (b), respectively while four number of coils are considered. The average PSNR and SSIM values of the reconstructed MRIs on increasing number of coils from 2 to 8 with r = 2 using different methods are presented in Fig. 4(c) and (d), respectively. The proposed method uses 10% random-positioned unobserved coefficients as increased measurements using GRAPPA by considering C = 50% in the kernel. As expected,

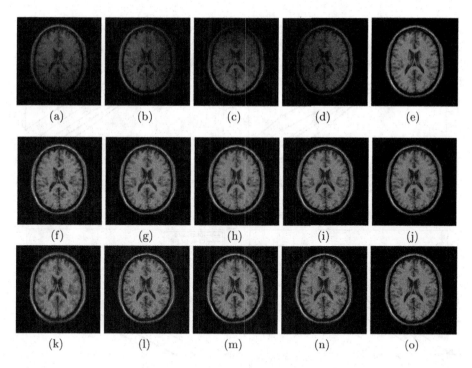

Fig. 3. Performance studies: (a–d) are Axial MRI slices of different input coils. (e) Original full scale image (f–j) are reconstructed Axial MRI slices using standard GRAPPA [11], CS-GRAPPA [19], CS-GRAPPA [13], CS-SENSE [16] and the propose r-GRAPPA-CS method for rate = 2, respectively. (k–o) are reconstructed Axial MRI slices using standard GRAPPA [11], CS-GRAPPA [19], CS-GRAPPA [13], CS-SENSE [16] and the propose r-GRAPPA-CS method for rate = 4, respectively.

the average values of PSNR and SSIM are decreased with the increase in rate of acceleration for all the methods. Initially, the average values of PSNR and SSIM are increased notably with the increase in the number of coils for all the methods. Later the average values of PSNR and SSIM are increased slightly for a value of number of coils 6 onwards. However, PSNR and SSIM values for the reconstructed images in the proposed rGRAPPA-CS method are relatively high compared to the other methods [11,13,16,19].

Performance of the proposed scheme is also studied on noisy encoded data samples. Some reconstructed MRIs for a four-coils pMRI system are presented in Fig. 5. A set of reconstructed axial brain MRI of (256 × 256), 8 bits/pixel and sagittal brain MRI of (256 × 256), 8 bits/pixel with r = 2 using the existing [11,13,16,19] and the proposed methods are shown in Fig. 5(a–e) and (f–j), respectively. In this study, the proposed rGRAPPA-CS uses $C = 60\%$ as reduced GRAPPA kernel and estimates 10% random-positioned unobserved coefficients that are used in CS reconstruction with the observed coefficients as measurements. Figure 5(e) and (j) show some significant visual improvement with respect

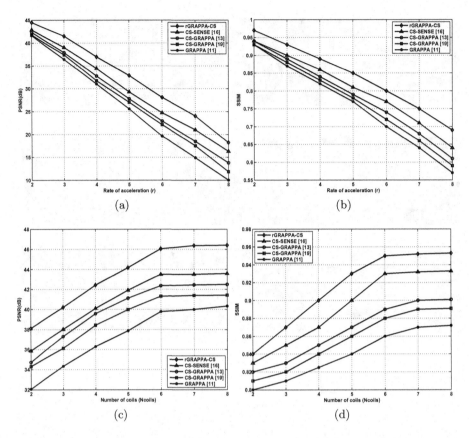

Fig. 4. Performance comparison: (a) Average PSNR (in dB) vs. Rate of acceleration (r), (b) Average SSIM vs. Rate of acceleration (r), (c) Average PSNR (in dB) vs. Number of coils and (d) Average SSIM vs. Number of coils.

to the corresponding individual input images shown in Fig. 5(a–d) and (f–i). The respective PSNR and SSIM values of the two types of reconstructed images of Fig. 5 are shown in Table 2. Improvement in the reconstructed image quality in terms of both subjective as well as objective measures justify the efficiency of the proposed rGRAPPA-CS scheme.

The execution time taken by the proposed method is also reported to show the efficiency in terms of computational cost. The proposed method takes 3.22 to 4.73 s time to reconstruct the MR images at $r = 2$ when 4 number of coils are used, considering $C = 60\%$ as reduced GRAPPA kernel and 10% random-positioned estimated coefficients. In this study, the program executed in MATLAB 2013a on a PC with an Intel Pentium dual-core 1.60 GHz processor and 1 GB of RAM under Windows 7 service pack1.

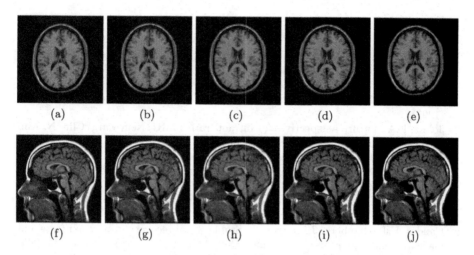

Fig. 5. Performance studies: (a–e) are reconstructed axial brain MRI slices noisy encoding samples using standard GRAPPA [11], CS-GRAPPA [19], CS-GRAPPA [13], CS-SENSE [16] and the propose rGRAPPA-CS method for rate = 2, respectively. (f–j) are reconstructed sagittal brain MRI slices for noisy encoded samples using standard GRAPPA [11], CS-GRAPPA [19], CS-GRAPPA [13], CS-SENSE [16] and the propose r-GRAPPA-CS method for rate = 2, respectively.

Table 2. PSNR and SSIM of the reconstructed MR images

MRI name	Quality metrics	GRAPPA [11]	CS-GRAPPA [19]	CS-GRAPPA [13]	CS-SENSE [16]	rGRAPPA-CS
Axial Brain	PSNR (dB)	34.82	36.04	36.85	37.71	**39.06**
	SSIM	0.85	0.87	0.88	0.90	**0.93**
Sagittal Brain	PSNR (dB)	34.20	35.75	36.10	37.33	**38.84**
	SSIM	0.83	0.86	0.88	0.89	**0.92**

5   Conclusions and Future Works

This paper proposes a pMRI scheme to provide MR images with high rate of acceleration during data acquisition. The proposed method uses GRAPPA with reduced kernel to estimate some unobserved encoded samples that are used as measurements with the observed samples in CS reconstruction to provide full FOV. Simulation results show that the proposed rGRAPPA-CS method is found to be effective in terms of reduction in scanning time by observing less encoded samples compared to other state-of-art methods. The overall quality of the reconstructed MRI is also improved significantly using the proposed method. An average improvement in PSNR value by 2 ± 0.40 dB and SSIM value by 0.2 ± 0.07 for 4 number of input coils with rate of acceleration as 4 are obtained using 50% reduced kernel with 32 ACS lines to estimate 10% unobserved coefficients, compared to the other methods.

The proposed method may be extended as calibration-less pMRI scheme to reduce extra computational cost and hardware complexity. This method may also be explored as a generalized multi-channel imaging application for bandwidth efficient transmission over radio mobile communication systems.

References

1. Semelka, R.C., Armao, D.M., Elias, J., Huda, W.: Imaging strategies to reduce the risk of radiation in CT studies, including selective substitution with MRI. J. Magn. Reson. Imaging **25**(5), 900–909 (2007)
2. Wright, G.: Magnetic resonance imaging. IEEE Sig. Process. Mag. **14**(1), 56–66 (1997)
3. Jolesz, F.A.: Future perspectives for intraoperative MRI. Neurosurg. Clin. N. Am. **16**(1), 201–213 (2005)
4. Sasaki, M., Ehara, S., Nakasato, T., Tamakawa, Y., Kuboya, Y., Sugisawa, M., Sato, T.: MR of the shoulder with a 0.2-t permanent-magnet unit. Am. J. Roentgenol. **154**(4), 777–778 (1990)
5. Donoho, D.L.: Compressed sensing. IEEE Trans. Inf. Theory **52**(4), 1289–1306 (2006)
6. Candes, E.J., Romberg, J.K., Tao, T.: Stable signal recovery from incomplete and inaccurate measurements. J. Commun. Pure Appl. Math. **59**(8), 1207–1223 (2006)
7. Baraniuk, R.G.: Compressive sensing. IEEE Sig. Process. Mag. **24**(4), 118–120 (2007)
8. Edelman, R.R., Warach, S.: Magnetic resonance imaging. N. Engl. J. Med. **328**(10), 708–716 (1993)
9. Lustig, M., Donoho, D.L., Santos, J.M., Pauly, J.M.: Compressed sensing MRI. IEEE Sig. Process. Mag. **25**(2), 72–82 (2008)
10. Pruessmann, K.P., Weiger, M., Scheidegger, M.B., Boesiger, P., et al.: Sense: sensitivity encoding for fast MRI. Magn. Reson. Med. **42**(5), 952–962 (1999)
11. Griswold, M.A., Jakob, P.M., Heidemann, R.M., Nittka, M., Jellus, V., Wang, J., Kiefer, B., Haase, A.: Generalized autocalibrating partially parallel acquisitions (GRAPPA). Magn. Reson. Med. **47**(6), 1202–1210 (2002)
12. Weller, D., Polimeni, J., Grady, L., Wald, L., Adalsteinsson, E., Goyal, V.: Combining nonconvex compressed sensing and GRAPPA using the nullspace method. In: 18th Annual Meeting of ISMRM, p. 4880 (2010)
13. Weller, D.S., Polimeni, J.R., Grady, L., Wald, L.L., Adalsteinsson, E., Goyal, V.K.: Sparsity-promoting calibration for GRAPPA accelerated parallel MRI reconstruction. IEEE Trans. Med. Imaging **32**(7), 1325–1335 (2013)
14. Xie, G., Song, Y., Shi, C., Feng, X., Zheng, H., Weng, D., Qiu, B., Liu, X.: Accelerated magnetic resonance imaging using the sparsity of multi-channel coil images. Magn. Reson. Imaging **32**(2), 175–183 (2014)
15. Schmidt, R., Baishya, B., Ben-Eliezer, N., Seginer, A., Frydman, L.: Super-resolved parallel MRI by spatiotemporal encoding. Magn. Reson. Imaging **32**(1), 60–70 (2014)
16. Zhou, J., Li, J., Gombaniro, J.C.: Combining sense and compressed sensing MRI with a fast iterative contourlet thresholding algorithm. In: 12th IEEE International Conference on Fuzzy Systems and Knowledge Discovery (FSKD), pp. 1123–1127 (2015)
17. Chun, I.Y., Adcock, B., Talavage, T.M.: Efficient compressed sensing sense pMRI reconstruction with joint sparsity promotion. IEEE Trans. Med. Imaging **35**(1), 354–368 (2016)
18. Fischer, A., Seiberlich, N., Blaimer, M., Jakob, P., Breuer, F., Griswold, M.: A combination of nonconvex compressed sensing and GRAPPA (CS-GRAPPA). In: Proceedings of the International Society for Magnetic Resonance in Medicine, vol. 17, p. 2813 (2009)

19. Miao, J., Guo, W., Narayan, S., Wilson, D.L.: A simple application of compressed sensing to further accelerate partially parallel imaging. Magn. Reson. Imaging **31**(1), 75–85 (2013)

20. Chang, Y., King, K.F., Liang, D., Ying, L.: Combining compressed sensing and nonlinear GRAPPA for highly accelerated parallel MRI. In: Proceedings of the International Society for Magnetic Resonance in Medicine, p. 2219 (2012)

21. Yang, Z., Zhang, C., Deng, J., Lu, W.: Orthonormal expansion l1-minimization algorithms for compressed sensing. IEEE Trans. Sig. Process. **59**(12), 6285–6290 (2011)

22. Daubechies, I., Defrise, M., De Mol, C.: An iterative thresholding algorithm for linear inverse problems with a sparsity constraint. Commun. Pure Appl. Math. **57**(11), 1413–1457 (2004)

23. Bredies, K., Lorenz, D.A.: Linear convergence of iterative soft-thresholding. J. Fourier Anal. Appl. **14**(5–6), 813–837 (2008)

Tracking of Retinal Microsurgery Tools Using Late Fusion of Responses from Convolutional Neural Network over Pyramidally Decomposed Frames

Kaustuv Mishra, Rachana Sathish, and Debdoot Sheet[✉]

Indian Institute of Technology Kharagpur, Kharagpur, India
debdoot@ee.iitkgp.ernet.in

Abstract. Computer vision and robotic assistance are increasingly being used to improve the quality of surgical interventions. Tool tracking becomes critical in interventions viz. endoscopy, laparoscopy and retinal microsurgery (RM) where unlike open surgery the surgeons do not have direct visual and physical access to the surgical site. RM is performed using miniaturized tools and requires careful observation through a surgical microscope by the surgeon. Tracking of surgical tools primarily provides robotic assistance during surgery and also serves as a means to assess the quality of surgery, which is extremely useful during surgical training. In this paper we propose a deep learning based visual tracking of surgical tool using late fusion of responses from convolutional neural network (CNN) which comprises of 3 steps: (i) training of CNN for localizing the tool tip on a frame (ii) coarsely estimating the tool tip region using the trained CNN and (iii) a finer search around the estimated region to accurately localize the tool tip. Scale invariant tracking of tool is ensured by incorporating multi-scale late fusion where the CNN responses are obtained at each level of the Gaussian scale decomposition pyramid. Performance of the proposed method is experimentally validated on the publicly available retinal microscopy instrument tracking (RMIT) dataset (https://sites.google.com/site/sznitr/code-and-datasets). Our method tracks tools with a maximum accuracy of 99.13% which substantiates the efficacy of the proposed method in comparison to existing approaches.

1 Introduction

Retinal microsurgery (RM) is a critical intervention procedure for the treatment of age-related macular degeneration, diabetic retinopathy, glaucoma, etc. [13]. The small size of the tools used, sensitiveness of the target area and observing the target via a microscope makes the task of performing RM quite challenging. Intraoperative Optical Coherence Tomography (iOCT) [3] based microscopes have been introduced recently that provide the surgeons with the depth information for better manipulation of the surgical tools. However, it burdens the surgeon with the additional task of manually positioning an additional

© Springer International Publishing AG 2017
S. Mukherjee et al. (Eds.): ICVGIP 2016, LNCS 10481, pp. 358–366, 2017.
https://doi.org/10.1007/978-3-319-68124-5_31

imaging device along with the surgical microscope over the region of interest. On the other hand, visual tracking of tools provides the surgeon with an effortless means for observing the tool trajectory.

Challenge: High variability in inter subject and intra-device appearance of the surgical tools and background throughout the surgery, shadow of the tools and variation in illumination in the video are major challenges to precisely tracking the tool.

Approach: We propose a method based on late fusion CNN responses [7] over pyramidally decomposed video frames for supervised learning to localize the tool tip in each frame of a surgical video, thus tracking the movement of the tool. The response of the CNN for pyramidally decomposed instances of each frame is fused to roughly localize the tool tip. The exact location of the tool tip is then identified by feeding forward a set of image patches around the earlier localized region through the trained CNN for fine grained accurate localization.

Related works: Classical methods of object tracking using features like color [1] and geometry [2] have been employed for the task of surgical tool tracking. These methods require prior knowledge of geometry of the tool. Learning based methods have also been used to effectively track the tools in surgical videos. Spiking neural networks have also been used in another such approach [4] which makes use of the natural appearance features associated with the tool. The learning based approach proposed by Sznitman et al. [13] uses deformable feature learning and a simple gradient tracker. An online learning approach for tool tracking in RM has been proposed by Li et al. [8] which learns a target specific detector gradually from appearance samples of the tool on the go. Regression forests [10] have also been proposed to track tools in surgical videos.

This paper is organized as follows. The challenge at hand is formally defined in Sect. 2. The methodology is explained in Sect. 3. The experiments are detailed with the results in Sect. 4. The conclusion is presented in Sect. 5.

2   Problem Statement

The problem of localizing the tool tip in each of the tth frame $\mathcal{F}(t)$ in the video of RM can be formulated as a classification problem each patch p_i of size $m \times m$ is assigned a class label $\omega \in \{tooltip, background\}$ with probability $P(\omega|p_i)$. The point $\mathbf{t}$ indicting the tool shaft end can then be located as the centroid of estimated tool tip region. A window of size $n \times n$ centered at $\mathbf{t}$ encompasses the tool tip.

3   Exposition to the Solution

The solution to the problem is achieved in two steps by (i) training the CNN to localize the tool tip region in the given frame $\mathcal{F}(t)$ of the video and (ii) fine grained search to locate the junction of the shaft and tip of the tool also referred to as the tool shaft end, while tracking. Figure 1 shows the scheme adopted for training the CNN.

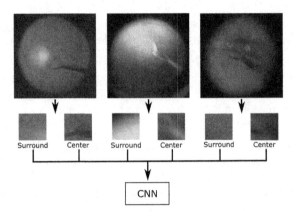

Fig. 1. Figure shows the training framework for the CNN. Patches of size 32×32 are selected and a few samples are presented as examples.

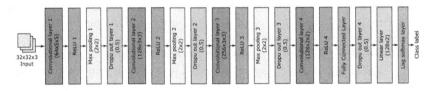

Fig. 2. Figure shows the architecture of the CNN used in the proposed method.

3.1 Convolutional Neural Network

A modified version of LeNet [6] CNN architecture is trained by stochastic gradient descent to learn a hypothesis space $\mathcal{H}(.) \longmapsto \arg\max P(\omega|p)$ that assigns a class label ω to a patch p of a frame with a using a train set $\{p_{\text{train}}, \omega_{\text{train}}\}$, where $P(.)$ denotes probability, p_{train} denotes patches from both the classes and ω_{train} denotes their corresponding class label. Figure 2 shows the architecture of the network used. It comprises of 4 main blocks namely, convolutional layer, rectified linear unit (ReLU), pooling stage and fully connected layer (FCN). The output of the convolutional layer for an input z is given as,

$$y(i, j) = \sum_{k,l} w(k, l) z(i - k, j - l) \tag{1}$$

where, $w(.)$ is the convolution kernel learnt by the CNN. This layer extracts meaningful features from the input that aids in learning the hypothesis $\mathcal{H}(.)$. Each convolution layer is associated with a specific number of kernels (N), size of the kernel ($k \times k$), and stride of the kernel (S). The number of features extracted for each input corresponds to the number of filters. The ReLU follows the convolutional layer applies a rectified linear transformation on the output of convolutional layer. The output of ReLU for an input z is given as,

$$f(z) = \max(0, z) \tag{2}$$

Compared to other common activation functions like sigmoid(.) and tanh(.), ReLU is computationally less expensive and have been demonstrated to ensure faster convergence of stochastic gradient descent. Pooling layers are introduced to reduce the spatial dimension of the representations learnt by the CNN. This effectively reduces the number of parameters to be tuned in the network thereby controlling overfitting. In the architecture used, max pooling is employed. Like convolutional kernels, pooling kernels are also associated with a size and stride which dictates the reduction of dimension. As the name suggests, the neurons in FCN are connected to all the activations of the previous layer. A linear layer which follows the FCN maps the learnt representations to a lower dimension. The output softmax layer is given as,

$$P(y = \omega | \mathbf{z}) = \frac{e^{\mathbf{z}^T \mathbf{w}_j}}{\sum_{k=1}^{K} e^{\mathbf{z}^T \mathbf{w}_k}} \tag{3}$$

where ω is the class label, $\mathbf{w}$ is the weights learnt by the network and $\mathbf{z}$ is the input.

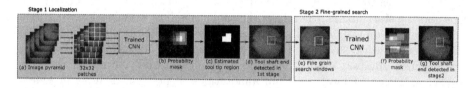

Fig. 3. Figure shows the framework for detecting the tool shaft end point in the given frame. The pyramidally decomposed frames (a) of the region of interest in the frame is divided into tiles of size 32×32 and fed into the CNN. The obtained probability mask (b) is threshold to estimate the probable tool tip region as shown in (c). The predicted shaft end point is marked by a green colored '+' and ground truth annotation in red in (d). In the second stage of prediction, a fine grained search is done centered around the predicted tool shaft end to locate the shaft end with better accuracy as shown in (g). (Color figure online)

3.2 Multi-scale Late Fusion

To ensure scale invariant detection of tools, late fusion of responses of CNN has been executed while testing a video frame for tool presence. We construct a multi-resolution pyramid for each frame by decimating it at factors of $1, 0.9, 0.8, 0.7, 0.6$. The image at each level is sub-divided into non-overlapping patches of size 32×32 and fed-forward through the trained CNN to obtained a probability of tool presence in the patch which are mapped to corresponding coordinates on the image at each level, and then up-scaled by a matching factor to match the size of the original frame. The predictions are then summed up to obtain the frame level response, and the tool is localized at the coordinate with highest probability. This process is referred as Stage 1 in Fig. 3. Early fusion technique which involves concatenating multi-scale information of the input prior to training is avoided since it increases the size of the input data thereby increasing computational complexity.

3.3 Fine Grained Search for Tool Tip

Localization of the tool tip region is followed by a finer search [14] for the shaft end location within the estimated region. An exhaustive search using sliding window method [5] for the shaft end point within this region of interest is computationally expensive. Therefore, we select a set of patches of 32×32 pixels size by shifting its centroid in steps of 5, 10, 15, 20 pixels along the left-right, up-down, diagonal and cross-diagonal directions from the centroid of tool predicted in Stage 1. The set of 33 patches are fed-forward through the CNN and the centroid of the patch receiving highest response is the shaft end. This is referred to as the Stage 2.

4   Experiments, Results and Discussions

Dataset: The proposed method is validated by training and testing the network on the publicly available RMIT dataset[1]. The dataset comprises of 1171 frames of size 480×640 pixels from 3 different surgeries. The ground truth annotations for the tool location is provided in the form of coordinate location of the two tool tips and the start and end points of the tool shaft. The illumination, tool used and magnification is different in the 3 sequences provided ensuring robustness of the trained network. 90% of the frames from each sequence are used for training and the rest 10% are used for testing. Currently, RMIT dataset is the only publicly available dataset with full annotations of position of tools in videos of retinal microsurgery. This prevents validation of the proposed method on a larger dataset to claim generality. However, the accuracy of state of the art methods with which the comparisons have been made is reported on the same dataset. The large number of parameters associated with the network requires huge amount of training data to achieve a good fit. Considering the small size of the dataset for training a CNN from scratch, data augmentation is incorporated.

Training: Since each video frame of 480×640 pixels has only a smaller area with the surgical view, we process only the valid region which is obtained by ROI selection using Otsu's method of binary thresholding [9]. Image patches of size $32 \times 32 \times 3$ centers around the shaft end coordinate provided in the ground truth annotation of the dataset is labeled as *tooltip* class. The patches are rotated by $\pi/4$ to obtain eight views per positive (tool) patch per frame. Eight negative (background) patches are randomly selected per frame. We train our model using a set of such positive (P)/negative (N) patches from 90% of the starting frames from all videos amounting to $2,896P + 2,896N$ patches from 362 of 402 frames in Video 1, $1,600P + 1,600N$ patches from 200 of 222 frames in Video 2, and $3,824P + 3,824N$ patches from 478 of 531 frames in Video 3. The network was trained over 25 epochs with a learning rate of 0.01, weight decay of 10^{-4}, momentum of 0.9, dropout of 0.5 and batch size of 125.

Baselines: The performance of the proposed method is validated by comparing it with the following baselines. The proposed method is compared with state of

---

[1] https://sites.google.com/site/sznitr/code-and-datasets.

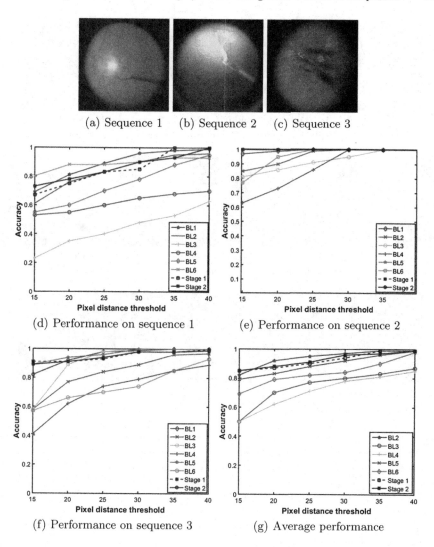

Fig. 4. Figure illustrates (a), (b), (c) the sample images from the three different sequences in the RMIT dataset, (d), (e), (f) the performance of the proposed method on individual sequences and (g) the average performance.

the art methods proposed by Li et al. [8] (**Baseline 1 (BL1)**) and Sznitman et al. [13] (**Baseline 2(BL2)**). **Baseline 3 (BL3)** is defined where frames are fed forward through the pre-trained (ImageNet[2]) GoogLeNet [12] truncated at 2nd inception module to extract the features. These features are then used to train a random forest to detect the tool. **Baseline 4 (BL4)** is similar as BL3 by using the pretrained CNN VGGNet [11] (ImageNet). The fully connected

---

[2] http://www.image-net.org/.

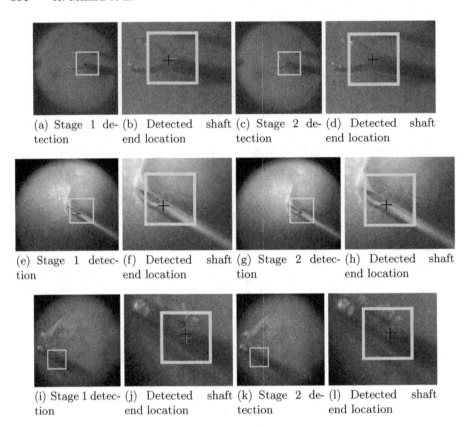

(a) Stage 1 detection (b) Detected shaft end location (c) Stage 2 detection (d) Detected shaft end location

(e) Stage 1 detection (f) Detected shaft end location (g) Stage 2 detection (h) Detected shaft end location

(i) Stage 1 detection (j) Detected shaft end location (k) Stage 2 detection (l) Detected shaft end location

Fig. 5. Figure shows the predicted tool shaft end location as a cyan colored '+' and ground truth annotation as a red colored '+' in a sample frame from (a) sequence 1, (e) sequence 2 and (i) sequence 3 after the first stage of detection that localizes the tool tip region. (b), (f) and (j) shows the magnified view of the detected locations of stage 1. The shaft end locations detected after the stage 2 finer grain search for the sample image from sequence 1 is shown in (c), for sequence 2 in (g) and for sequence 3 in (k). The corresponding magnified view of detections are shown in (d), (h) and (l) respectively. (Color figure online)

layer is modified to in accordance with the 32×32 pixel input patches. Feature extraction is followed by classification using random forest. **Baseline 5 (BL5)** has a logsoftmax decision layer is added to the truncated GoogLeNet of BL3 and fine-tuned. In **Baseline 6(BL6)** a VGG-Net trained on ImageNet is fine-tuned using the RMIT dataset.

During testing, the localized centroid is said true-positive (TP) if it is within a distance 'd' from the annotated centroid in ground truth. If the localized centroid is beyond d then its marked as false-negative (FN). This approach is based on prior-art [13] and d ranges 15–40 pixels. Performance of the proposed method is shown in Fig. 4, where the stage 1 outperform prior-arts at $d = 15$.

As d increases the accuracy intuitively increases as is observed for our approach and comparisons. In case of stage 2, interestingly, as d increases from 15 to 40 pixels to become more liberal, other methods outperform our approach in the intermediate range of 20–30 pixels, and asymptotically reach similar performance limits. Figure 5 illustrates sample predictions of the proposed method. We further experimented to utilize the temporal information in the videos while testing. Stage 1 of testing was performed on every 10th frame and for the intermediate frames, finer search around the prediction of Stage 1 i.e., Stage 2 was performed. This yielded an average accuracy of $0.56, 0.32$, and 0.19 for video sequences 1, 2 and 3 respectively for $d = 15$ over the entire length of the video. The average tool shaft diameter in the dataset is 20 pixels [13]. Thus, the higher accuracy of our method in the pixel distance range of 15 pixels shows that its performance is superior to the baselines.

Implementation: Our implementation is based on Torch, CUDA using Nvidia GTX Titan X GPU accelerator, with training and testing times of 3 sec/epoch and 12 ms/frame for stages $1 + 2$. Since the movement of the tools is not fast, it is sufficient that the tool tip be re-localized in every 25th frame of the video. The tool tracking framework should thus be fast enough to process 1 frame every second. The proposed method meets this requirement and therefore is suitable for real time deployment.

5 Conclusion

We have presented a scale invariant deep learning based approach for tool tracking in retinal microsurgery videos that is capable of tracking tools with high level of accuracy. A CNN is trained to locate the tool tip in static frames of the surgical video. In deployment stage, multi-scale information of the video frame is fed into the CNN for estimating the tool tip location. Spatially shifted patches from this region is then fed into the CNN to obtain a more accurate location of the tool shaft end that marks the tool tip. The efficacy of the proposed method is experimentally verified by comparing with existing approaches and other baselines. It is observed that our method outperforms the different baselines in terms of locating the tool shaft end with high accuracy.

Acknowledgments. We thank NVIDIA Inc. for donating the GTX TitanX GPU used in this work.

References

1. Allan, M., Ourselin, S., Thompson, S., Hawkes, D.J., Kelly, J., Stoyanov, D.: Toward detection and localization of instruments in minimally invasive surgery. IEEE Trans. Biomed. Eng. **60**(4), 1050–1058 (2013)
2. Baek, Y.M., Tanaka, S., Kanako, H., Sugita, N., Morita, A., Sora, S., Mochizuki, R., Mitsuishi, M.: Full state visual forceps tracking under a microscope using projective contour models. In: International Conference on Robotics and Automation, pp. 2919–2925. IEEE (2012)

3. Balicki, M., Han, J.-H., Iordachita, I., Gehlbach, P., Handa, J., Taylor, R., Kang, J.: Single fiber optical coherence tomography microsurgical instruments for computer and robot-assisted retinal surgery. In: Yang, G.-Z., Hawkes, D., Rueckert, D., Noble, A., Taylor, C. (eds.) MICCAI 2009. LNCS, vol. 5761, pp. 108–115. Springer, Heidelberg (2009). doi:10.1007/978-3-642-04268-3_14

4. Chen, C.J., Huang, W.S.W., Song, K.T.: Image tracking of laparoscopic instrument using spiking neural networks. In: International Conference on Control Automation and Systems, pp. 951–955. IEEE (2013)

5. Felzenszwalb, P.F., Girshick, R.B., McAllester, D., Ramanan, D.: Object detection with discriminatively trained part-based models. IEEE Trans. Patt. Anal. Mach. Intell. **32**(9), 1627–1645 (2010)

6. LeCun, Y., Bottou, L., Bengio, Y., Haffner, P.: Gradient-based learning applied to document recognition. Proc. IEEE **86**(11), 2278–2324 (1998)

7. LeCun, Y., et al.: Generalization and network design strategies. J. Connect. Perspect. 143–155 (1989)

8. Li, Y., Chen, C., Huang, X., Huang, J.: Instrument tracking via online learning in retinal microsurgery. In: Golland, P., Hata, N., Barillot, C., Hornegger, J., Howe, R. (eds.) MICCAI 2014. LNCS, vol. 8673, pp. 464–471. Springer, Cham (2014). doi:10.1007/978-3-319-10404-1_58

9. Otsu, N.: A threshold selection method from gray-level histograms. Automatica **11**(285–296), 23–27 (1975)

10. Rieke, N., Tan, D.J., Alsheakhali, M., Tombari, F., di San Filippo, C.A., Belagiannis, V., Eslami, A., Navab, N.: Surgical tool tracking and pose estimation in retinal microsurgery. In: Navab, N., Hornegger, J., Wells, W.M., Frangi, A.F. (eds.) MICCAI 2015. LNCS, vol. 9349, pp. 266–273. Springer, Cham (2015). doi:10.1007/978-3-319-24553-9_33

11. Simonyan, K., Zisserman, A.: Very deep convolutional networks for large-scale image recognition. arxiv preprint arXiv:1409.1556 (2014)

12. Szegedy, C., Liu, W., Jia, Y., Sermanet, P., Reed, S., Anguelov, D., Erhan, D., Vanhoucke, V., Rabinovich, A.: Going deeper with convolutions. In: Conference on Computer Vision and Pattern Recognition, pp. 1–9 (2015)

13. Sznitman, R., Ali, K., Richa, R., Taylor, R.H., Hager, G.D., Fua, P.: Data-driven visual tracking in retinal microsurgery. In: Ayache, N., Delingette, H., Golland, P., Mori, K. (eds.) MICCAI 2012. LNCS, vol. 7511, pp. 568–575. Springer, Heidelberg (2012). doi:10.1007/978-3-642-33418-4_70

14. Zhang, Y., Sohn, K., Villegas, R., Pan, G., Lee, H.: Improving object detection with deep convolutional networks via Bayesian optimization and structured prediction. In: Proceedings of Conference on Computer Vision and Pattern Recognition, pp. 249–258 (2015)

Cardiac Ultrasound Image Enhancement Using Tissue Selective Total Variation Regularization

Deepak Mishra[1]([✉]), Santanu Chaudhury[1], Mukul Sarkar[1],
and Arvinder Singh Soin[2]

[1] Indian Institute of Technology Delhi, New Delhi, India
deemishra21@gmail.com
[2] Medanta Hospital, Gurgaon, India

Abstract. Speckle reduction is desired to improve the quality of ultrasound images. However, a uniform speckle reduction from the entire image results in loss of important information, especially in cardiac ultrasound images. In this paper, a tissue selective total variation regularization approach is proposed for the enhancement of cardiac ultrasound images. It measures the pixel probability of belonging to blood regions and uses it in the total variation framework. As a result, the unwanted speckle from the blood chamber regions is removed and the useful speckle in the tissue regions is preserved. This helps to improve the visible contrast of the images and enhances the structural details. The proposed approach is evaluated using synthetic as well as real images. A better performance is observed as compared to the state-of-the-art filters in terms of speckle region's signal to noise ratio, structural similarity measure index, figure of merit, and mean square error.

Keywords: Ultrasound image · Total variation · Speckle · Blood region

1 Introduction

Echocardiography is a well-known application of medical ultrasound. It is used in the diagnosis of the patients with heart diseases. The cardiac ultrasound images provide useful information about heart function, heart capacity, and tissue damage [6]. However, it is not easy to extract the desired information due to the presence of speckle. For example, the measurement of blood chamber size requires the delineation of chamber boundaries which is a difficult task in the presence of speckle. Therefore, speckle should be removed from the blood regions for an accurate boundary delineation. On the other hand, the procedures like measurement of the extent of damaged tissues, are benefited from the speckle patterns, therefore, speckle should be preserved in tissue regions.

Speckle is a tissue-dependent phenomenon which is generated from constructive and destructive interferences of reflecting echoes of ultrasound pulses [13]. In the tissue regions, the speckle pattern is repeatable and depends on tissue

© Springer International Publishing AG 2017
S. Mukherjee et al. (Eds.): ICVGIP 2016, LNCS 10481, pp. 367–379, 2017.
https://doi.org/10.1007/978-3-319-68124-5_32

characteristics whereas such repeatability is not certain in blood regions. Therefore, in this paper, the speckle reduction problem is considered from the selective filtering perspective.

Speckle reduction is a well-studied problem. Several speckle reducing filters are reported in the literature. Spatially adaptive filters like Lee filter [12] and Kuan filter [11] are some of the well-known traditional speckle reducing filters. More advanced filters or filtering approaches are based on anisotropic diffusion. For example speckle reducing anisotropic diffusion (SRAD) [19] and detail preserving anisotropic diffusion (DPAD) [1]. These filters use local image statistics to control the diffusion process and reduce noise while preserving the edges. As reported in [15], these filters suffer from the oversmoothing problem and result in piece-wise smooth images. Some other well-known approaches are local and non-local neighbourhood averaging, for example, speckle reducing bilateral filter (SRBF) [3] and optimized Bayesian non-local mean (OBNLM) filter [5]. Transformation based approaches are also popular for speckle reduction [20,21]. These approaches work on the basis that the noise gets separated from the signal in transform domain where it can be easily removed using the methods like anisotropic diffusion.

Apart from these, variational approaches using the total variation (TV) regularizer have also been reported for speckle reduction [2,4,9,17]. The variational approaches are optimization problems which minimize the objective functions with two terms: a data fidelity term and a regularization term. The speckle is considered as a multiplicative noise and the fidelity term is formulated with respect to the logarithm of the input. The approaches are designed for piece-wise smooth outputs and result in the oversmooth images similar to the diffusion approaches.

In this paper, a tissue selective total variation (TSTV) regularization approach is proposed. The paper focuses on regularization term, instead of the fidelity term. Although, there have been works in the past to make the regularizer more adaptive to the image structural details, to our knowledge this is the first attempt to make it tissue selective. The existing works, for example [7] and reference therein, try to make the regularization parameter locally adaptive to solve the problem of over regularization. However, the present scenario of cardiac ultrasound image filtering is different. The objective here is to preserve the speckle in the tissue regions while filtering the blood regions. The proposed approach uses the probability of a pixel belonging to the blood region in the regularization term. The pixels with high probability of belonging to the blood region are filtered and remaining pixels are preserved. The probability values are measured using Gaussian mixture model (GMM) based clustering. The experiments are also performed with k-means and hierarchical clustering, however, best results are observed with GMM. The performance evaluation of the proposed TSTV regularization is done using synthetic as well as real ultrasound images. The obtained results show that the proposed approach outperforms the state-of-the-art filters.

Rest of the paper is organized as follows: Sect. 2 provides the technical details of the proposed approach. Section 3 contains the experimental results and the performance evaluation. The paper is finally concluded in Sect. 4.

2   Proposed Approach

The objective function of the fundamental TV minimization is defined as [16]:

$$J(u) = \frac{||g - u||_2^2}{2} + \lambda\phi(u) \tag{1}$$

where $g : \Omega \to \mathbb{R}_+, \Omega \subset \mathbb{R}^2$ and $u : \Omega \to \mathbb{R}_+, \Omega \subset \mathbb{R}^2$ represent the input/noisy and output/filtered images, respectively. λ is the regularization parameter which controls the amount of filtering. $||u||_2$ gives L_2 norm of u and $\phi(u)$ is the regularization term, defined as:

$$\phi(u) = \sum_{(i,j)\in\Omega} \sqrt{(u_{i+1,j} - u_{i,j})^2 + (u_{i,j+1} - u_{i,j})^2} \tag{2}$$

where $(i, j) \in \Omega$ represents the location of a pixel. The term $\frac{||g-u||_2^2}{2}$ in (1) is the fidelity term. Though it is generally used in case of uncorrelated additive noise, it is considered here for three reasons:

1. In contrast to the other fidelity terms like in [2], $\frac{||g-u||_2^2}{2}$ is absolutely convex.
2. It keeps the output very close to the input for vanishing regularizer, therefore, is suitable to preserve information in selective filtering.
3. Ultrasound imaging system generally uses logarithm compression to cover a large display range. The logarithm operation converts the multiplicative part of the speckle into an additive noise, therefore, the considered fidelity term is a suitable choice.

The filtered image is obtained as:

$$u^* = \min_u J(u) \tag{3}$$

The definition of $J(u)$ in (1) results in the piece-wise smooth images where the speckle is removed from the entire image. To facilitate the selective filtering, u is replaced with p in (2) where p represents a probability image and $p_{i,j}$ is the pixel probability of belonging to the blood region. The blood region pixels with $p_{i,j} \to 1$, experience noise filtering and the pixels having $p_{i,j} \to 0$ are preserved. The probability images representing different classes of tissues have been used earlier in [18] to improve the object boundary definitions. In contrast to [18], which uses multiple probability images representing different classes of tissues, only one probability image representing the blood is used in this work.

The probability image p can be calculated in many different ways. The best choice is to use a supervised learning scheme with a large size dataset and train a network to result in the desired probability values. However, the biggest bottleneck is the unavailability of any benchmark dataset. An alternative way is to use unsupervised clustering techniques. These techniques do not require information about the priors. Three well-known unsupervised clustering techniques, GMM based clustering, k-means clustering and hierarchical clustering, are considered for probability estimation.

GMM assumes the image to be a mixture of Gaussian distributions. The rationale behind the suitability of GMM in the proposed scenario is that the pixels belonging to different classes of tissues depict heavy tail distributions where most of the values lie near to the mean value. Further, the works reported in [8] and references therein, describe that the log-transformed speckle noise shows a distribution very close to the Gaussian distribution.

The distribution parameters, mean and standard deviation, of the class representing blood region are denoted by μ_m and σ_m respectively. These parameters are estimated using the expectation-maximization (EM) algorithm and $p_{i,j}$ is calculated as:

$$p_{i,j} = \frac{1}{Z_{i,j}} \left\{ \frac{exp\left\{ \frac{-(u_{i,j}-\mu_m)^2}{2(\sigma_m)^2} \right\}}{\sigma_m} \right\} \tag{4}$$

$$Z_{i,j} = \sum_{c=1}^{N_c} \left\{ \frac{exp\left\{ \frac{-(u_{i,j}-\mu_c)^2}{2(\sigma_c)^2} \right\}}{\sigma_c} \right\} \tag{5}$$

where N_c represents the number of classes. The blood regions appear as lowest echogenicity regions in the ultrasound images, therefore, μ_m can be obtained as:

$$\mu_m = min\{\mu_1, \mu_2, ..., \mu_{N_c}\} \tag{6}$$

The μ_m is used to identify the blood regions and calculate the corresponding pixel probabilities. Further, as reported in [18], the pre-processing of probability images improves the performance of the filtering. Therefore, a 5×5 median filter is applied on the obtained probability image p. The median filter uses the contextual information to reduce the effect of noise and improve the clustering results.

Apart from GMM, the other two considered techniques are k-means and hierarchical clustering. GMM has the flexibility of estimating discrete values of probability whereas the other two can only provide the binary values. In k-means clustering, all the pixels belonging to the cluster representing blood region are assigned the probability 1 and rest of pixels are assigned the value 0. A similar procedure can be used with hierarchical clustering, however, the technique is highly susceptible to noise therefore, an intuitive approach is followed. Initially, the whole image is divided into a large number of clusters and then the cluster representing similar regions are clubbed together.

To compare the utility of the clustering techniques, a synthetic phantom image is created, as shown in Fig. 1(a). The image contains cysts of variable size, shape, and echogenicity. The noisy ultrasound image is generated by multiplying

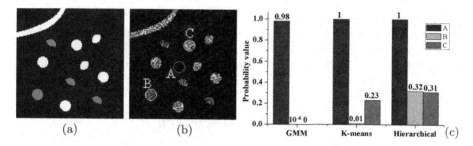

Fig. 1. (a) Synthesized cyst image, (b) noisy image with three marked regions, (c) comparison of clustering methods for the three regions A, B and C. (Color figure online)

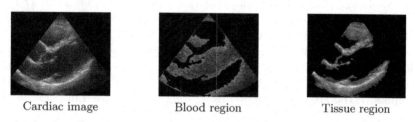

Cardiac image   Blood region   Tissue region

Fig. 2. The blood and tissue regions extracted from a real cardiac ultrasound image using GMM clustering.

the Rayleigh distribution based noise of the variance 0.1, as shown in Fig. 1(b). Three regions of different echogenicity (A, B, and C) are marked in the noisy image. Region A represents the blood region whereas region B and C represent high echogenicity cyst or tissue regions. These regions are used to compare the clustering performance. To obtain the desired selective filtering, $p_{i,j}$ should be close to 1 in region A and should be close to 0 in region B and C. The average values of pixel probabilities for the three regions are shown using the bar diagram in Fig. 1(c). The probability values are also shown on top of the bars. As can be observed, the k-means and hierarchical clustering are not as effective as GMM over the regions B and C. In region A, the value resulted by GMM is slightly lower than the other two techniques, however, it is very close to one. Hence, the GMM is most suitable choice to generate probability image for TSTV regularization.

A real cardiac ultrasound image, shown in Fig. 2, is considered for the probability image generation using GMM. The obtained probability images are used to extract the tissue and blood regions, shown in Fig. 2. As can be seen, the regions are accurately extracted with minor details.

The probability image p obtained using GMM, as in (4), is a complex function of u. It is difficult to obtain an optimized solution with the regularizer $\phi(p)$, therefore, it is approximated with $p.\phi(u)$. The probability image p is obtained using only the input image and assumed to be independent of the optimization process. $p.\phi(u)$ is obtained with element-wise multiplication. The rationale behind this approximation is that $p.\phi(u)$ will have the same effect on the optimization process as $\phi(p)$. The intensity variations in blood regions, where the pixels attain high probability values, are suppressed and remaining are preserved. The proposed TSTV filtering is implemented using the well-known Chambolle's fixed point algorithm [22]. It provides the ability to obtain the desired solution in a time efficient manner.

3   Experimental Results and Discussion

The proposed approach is tested to denoise synthetic as well as real ultrasound images. The performance of TSTV is compared with the state-of-the-art filters, DPAD [1], OBNLM [5] and MIDAL [4]. The working codes of the considered filters are obtained from the webpages of the respective authors. The TSTV is implemented in MATLAB. The evaluations are done based on speckle region's signal to noise ratio (SSNR), mean square error (MSE), structural similarity measure (SSIM), and figure of merit (FoM). The SSNR measures the amount of speckle present in a region. It is the ratio between mean and standard deviation of the considered region. The definitions of MSE and SSIM are borrowed from [15]. Similarly, the FoM is calculated using the definition given in [19].

3.1   Experiments with Synthesized Images

The first synthesized image considered for the experiment is the cyst phantom image which is included in Sect. 2 and shown in Fig. 1(a). Similar to the cardiac ultrasound images, the considered phantom image is dominated by low intensity regions representing blood. The noisy image, shown in Fig. 1(b), is filtered using the existing and the proposed methods. Implementation parameters of the considered filters are optimized based on the recommendations provided in the corresponding articles. The three regions marked in the noisy image shown in Fig. 1(b) are used to compare the selective filtering performances. For an ideal filter, the SSNR over region A should be as high as possible whereas it should be very close to noisy image over the other two regions. Filtered images obtained using DPAD, OBNLM, MIDAL, and TSTV are shown in Fig. 3(a)–(d) respectively.

The DPAD shows blurring and oversmoothing effects. OBNLM and TSTV remove speckle from region A. However, the speckle over the desired regions (B and C) is best preserved by the proposed TSTV regularization. MIDAL gives a mixed response. It partially preserves speckle near the object boundaries but results in inefficient filtering over the low intensity region. SSNR is measured over the three regions to compare the performances of the considered methods. For more analysis, the noise variance is varied from 0.1 to 1.0 and the SSNR values are measured for region A. The measured SSNR is normalized with the SSNR of the noisy image and plotted in Fig. 4(a). Similarly for region B and C, the difference between the SSNR values of noisy and filtered images, termed as SSNR error, is plotted in Fig. 4(b) and (c) respectively. The TSTV provides better performance as compared to the existing filters. As observed in Fig. 1(c),

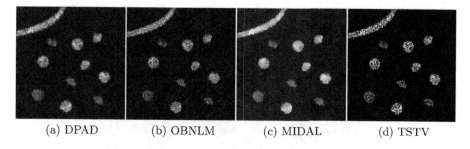

(a) DPAD   (b) OBNLM   (c) MIDAL   (d) TSTV

Fig. 3. (a)–(d) Noisy cyst image filtered by DPAD, OBNLM, MIDAL, and TSTV minimization.

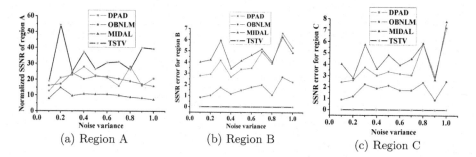

(a) Region A   (b) Region B   (c) Region C

Fig. 4. (a) Normalized SSNR values with respect to the noise variance for region A, (b)–(c) SSNR error variation with respect to the noise variance for region B and C.

Table 1. Comparison of filtering time for considered filters

Filter	DPAD	OBNLM	MIDAL	TSTV
Time (sec)	4.43	9.07	0.56	0.86

$p_{i,j}$ is very close to 1 in region A and 0 in regions B and C. Thus, the TV regularizer term dominates in region A and the region is filtered to result in high SSNR values. On the other hand, the fidelity term dominates over regions B and C, and the speckle is preserved efficiently.

Further, the considered filters are compared for their time complexity. The total computation time in filtering the noisy cyst image (Fig. 1(b)) is measured and listed in Table 1. The proposed TSTV regularization takes smaller time as compared to the other filters except MIDAL.

Rayleigh distribution based noise multiplication is used to generate noisy cyst image (first synthesized image). This procedure is simple but not very accurate. It is unable to replicate the behaviour of the real ultrasound scanners. More realistic simulators [10,14] use random walk model for speckle simulation. A synthetic image with the noise simulated using Field-II simulator [10] is shown in Fig. 5(a). Similar to the synthetic cyst image, two regions of

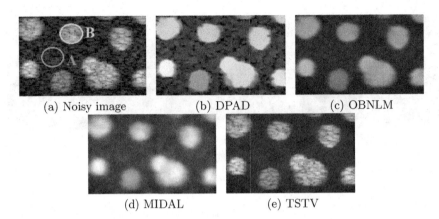

(a) Noisy image   (b) DPAD   (c) OBNLM

(d) MIDAL   (e) TSTV

Fig. 5. (a) Noisy image with marked regions, (b)–(e) filtered image obtained using DPAD, OBNLM, MIDAL, and TSTV minimization.

Table 2. SSNR values observed from the filtered outputs shown in Fig. 5

Filter	$SSNR_{regionA}$	$SSNR_{regionB}$
Noisy image	3.32	4.61
DPAD	5.64	6.72
OBNLM	26.84	6.00
MIDAL	17.01	5.77
TSTV	**49.07**	**4.67**

different echogenicity, A and B, are marked in this image also. The image is filtered using the considered filters and the outputs are also shown in Fig. 5. The implementation parameters are optimized to remove speckle from the region A and preserve it in the region B. Accordingly, the filtered image should have the SSNR value as high as possible in the region A and a value close to the noisy image in region B. The observed values for different filters are listed in Table 2. The proposed approach outperforms the existing filters in both regions.

A kidney phantom is used as the third synthesized image. The noisy image is generated using the method reported in [14]. A uniform variation of the number of scatterers in the range 3 to 15 is considered with 275 angular and 275 radial samples. The simulated kidney phantom and the corresponding noisy image are shown in Fig. 6(a) and (b), respectively. Although the image is not a heart image, it shows closeness with real ultrasound kidney images.

The implementation parameter values for the considered filters are optimized for the best visual quality. Figure 7(a)–(d) show the filtered images obtained using DPAD, OBNLM, MIDAL and TSTV, respectively. For quantitative analysis, the filtered outputs are compared using SSIM, FoM, and MSE. The calculated values are listed in Table 3. The TSTV results in the best values of all performance measures, which shows that the proposed approach not only

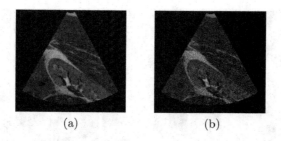

Fig. 6. (a) Kidney phantom image, (b) noisy image.

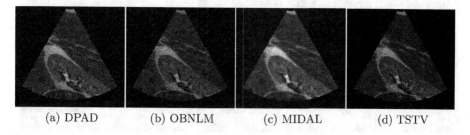

(a) DPAD   (b) OBNLM   (c) MIDAL   (d) TSTV

Fig. 7. (a)–(d) Filtered output of noisy kidney image obtained using DPAD, OBNLM, MIDAL and TSTV.

Table 3. Quantitative evaluation of speckle filtering methods for kidney phantom

Method	SSIM	FoM	MSE
Noisy image	0.79	0.70	101.2
DPAD	0.82	0.74	68.65
OBNLM	0.857	0.77	73.21
MIDAL	0.40	0.70	354
TSTV	**0.886**	**0.802**	**67.8**

removes noise but also preserves the structural details. The visual quality of the filtered output also supports the quantitative analysis. DPAD and MIDAL result in oversmooth images. MIDAL has been designed for multiplicative noise reduction, therefore, in this experiment its performance is not upto the mark. OBNLM produces better outputs than DPAD and MIDAL, however, the visual quality of the output is comparatively inferior to TSTV.

3.2   Experiments with Real Cardiac Ultrasound Images

The experiments with synthesized images show better performance using TSTV regularization as compared to the existing filters. However, it is also necessary to validate the performance on real data. Therefore, multiple real images of heart are considered for the experiment. The images are acquired using GE Healthcare

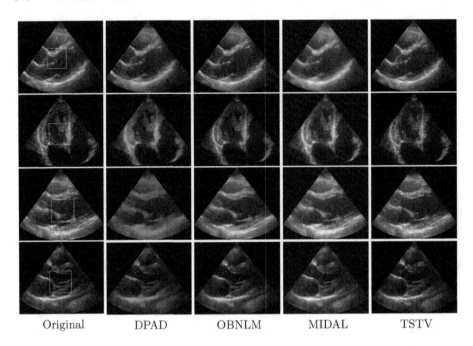

Original   DPAD   OBNLM   MIDAL   TSTV

Fig. 8. Original cardiac ultrasound images are shown in the first column. Filtered images obtained using the considered methods, second column: DPAD, third column: OBNLM, fourth column: MIDAL, fifth column: TSTV regularization.

Vivid ultrasound system. The original images are shown in the first column of Fig. 8. The filtered images obtained using DPAD, OBNLM, MIDAL, and TSTV are also shown in Fig. 8 from second column to fifth column, respectively. For the qualitative analysis of the obtained results, zoomed views of the regions marked in original images are shown in Fig. 9.

The zoomed views show that the quality of the enhanced ultrasound images obtained using TSTV is better than the other filters. For example, in the images shown in the first row, speckle is completely removed from the blood chambers without tempering the details over septum wall. On the other hand DPAD, MIDAL and OBNLM fail to preserve the septum wall details. Similar observations can be made for other images also.

To complement these observations, SSIM values for the filtered outputs are calculated. SSIM is considered to be robust against the noise generated spurious edges, therefore, the original image can be considered as reference [15]. The SSIM values for all the images are calculated and the mean SSIM values corresponding to all the filters are listed in Table 4. The TSTV results in the best value, which shows the robustness and suitability of the approach for ultrasound image enhancement.

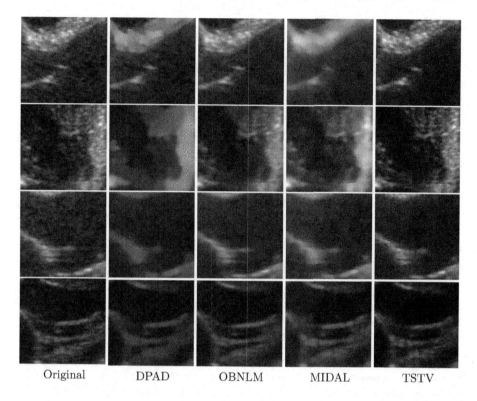

Original   DPAD   OBNLM   MIDAL   TSTV

Fig. 9. Zoomed views of the original and filtered images shown in Fig. 8.

Table 4. Mean SSIM values of the outputs obtained using considered filters

Filter	DPAD	OBNLM	MIDAL	TSTV
Mean SSIM	0.77	0.86	0.47	**0.91**

4   Conclusions

The modification proposed in this paper enables the TV regularization to perform selective filtering. For every pixel, the probability of being a part of blood regions is measured using the GMM based clustering. The pixels are selectively filtered according to the measured probability values. The proposed TSTV regularization approach is low time consuming. It provides efficient speckle reduction and tissue detail preservation. The experiments performed with synthetic and real images manifest the better performance of the proposed approach. Further, it has been observed during the experiment that the multiplicative noise reduction based methods are comparatively less suitable for speckle reduction in ultrasound images.

References

1. Aja-Fernández, S., Alberola-López, C.: On the estimation of the coefficient of variation for anisotropic diffusion speckle filtering. IEEE Trans. Image Process. **15**(9), 2694–2701 (2006)

2. Aubert, G., Aujol, J.F.: A variational approach to removing multiplicative noise. SIAM J. Appl. Math. **68**(4), 925–946 (2008)

3. Balocco, S., Gatta, C., Pujol, O., Mauri, J., Radeva, P.: SRBF: speckle reducing bilateral filtering. Ultrasound Med. Biol. **36**(8), 1353–1363 (2010)

4. Bioucas-Dias, J.M., Figueiredo, M.A.: Multiplicative noise removal using variable splitting and constrained optimization. IEEE Trans. Image Process. **19**(7), 1720–1730 (2010)

5. Coupé, P., Hellier, P., Kervrann, C., Barillot, C.: Nonlocal means-based speckle filtering for ultrasound images. IEEE Trans. Image Process. **18**(10), 2221–2229 (2009)

6. Finn, S., Glavin, M., Jones, E.: Echocardiographic speckle reduction comparison. IEEE Trans. Ultrason. Ferroelect. Freq. Control **58**(1), 82–101 (2011)

7. Grasmair, M.: Locally adaptive total variation regularization. In: Tai, X.-C., Mørken, K., Lysaker, M., Lie, K.-A. (eds.) SSVM 2009. LNCS, vol. 5567, pp. 331–342. Springer, Heidelberg (2009). doi:10.1007/978-3-642-02256-2_28

8. Gupta, N., Swamy, M.N., Plotkin, E.: Despeckling of medical ultrasound images using data and rate adaptive lossy compression. IEEE Trans. Med. Imaging **24**(6), 743–754 (2005)

9. Huang, Y.M., Ng, M.K., Wen, Y.W.: A new total variation method for multiplicative noise removal. SIAM J. Imaging Sci. **2**(1), 20–40 (2009)

10. Jensen, J.A., Svendsen, N.B.: Calculation of pressure fields from arbitrarily shaped, apodized, and excited ultrasound transducers. IEEE Trans. Ultrason. Ferroelect. Freq. Control. **39**(2), 262–267 (1992)

11. Kuan, D.A., Sawchuk, A.L., Strand, T.I., Chavel, P.: Adaptive restoration of images with speckle. IEEE Trans. Acoust. Speech Sig. Process. **35**(3), 373–383 (1987)

12. Lee, J.S.: Speckle analysis and smoothing of synthetic aperture radar images. Comput. Graph. Image Process. **17**(1), 24–32 (1981)

13. Loizou, C.P., Pattichis, C.S., Christodoulou, C.I., Istepanian, R.S., Pantziaris, M., Nicolaides, A.: Comparative evaluation of despeckle filtering in ultrasound imaging of the carotid artery. IEEE Trans. Ultrason. Ferroelect. Freq. Control **52**(10), 1653–1669 (2005)

14. Perreault, C., Auclair-Fortier, M.F.: Speckle simulation based on B-mode echographic image acquisition model. In: Fourth Canadian Conference on Computer and Robot Vision, pp. 379–386. IEEE (2007)

15. Ramos-Llordén, G., Vegas-Sánchez-Ferrero, G., Martin-Fernandez, M., Alberola-López, C., Aja-Fernández, S.: Anisotropic diffusion filter with memory based on speckle statistics for ultrasound images. IEEE Trans. Image Process. **24**(1), 345–358 (2015)

16. Rudin, L.I., Osher, S., Fatemi, E.: Nonlinear total variation based noise removal algorithms. Phys. D: Nonlinear Phenom. **60**(1), 259–268 (1992)

17. Shi, J., Osher, S.: A nonlinear inverse scale space method for a convex multiplicative noise model. SIAM J. Imaging Sci. **1**(3), 294–321 (2008)

18. Vegas-Sanchez-Ferrero, G., Aja-Fernandez, S., Martín-Fernández, M., Frangi, A.F., Palencia, C.: Probabilistic-driven oriented speckle reducing anisotropic diffusion with application to cardiac ultrasonic images. In: Jiang, T., Navab, N., Pluim, J.P.W., Viergever, M.A. (eds.) MICCAI 2010. LNCS, vol. 6361, pp. 518–525. Springer, Heidelberg (2010). doi:10.1007/978-3-642-15705-9_63

19. Yu, Y., Acton, S.T.: Speckle reducing anisotropic diffusion. IEEE Trans. Image Process. 11(11), 1260–1270 (2002)

20. Yue, Y., Croitoru, M.M., Bidani, A., Zwischenberger, J.B., Clark, J.W.: Nonlinear multiscale wavelet diffusion for speckle suppression and edge enhancement in ultrasound images. IEEE Trans. Med. Imaging 25(3), 297–311 (2006)

21. Zhang, F., Yoo, Y.M., Koh, L.M., Kim, Y.: Nonlinear diffusion in Laplacian pyramid domain for ultrasonic speckle reduction. IEEE Trans. Med. Imaging 26(2), 200–211 (2007)

22. Chambolle, A.: An algorithm for total variation minimization and applications. J. Math. Imaging Vis. 20(1–2), 89–97 (2004)

Methods and System for Segmentation of Isolated Nuclei in Microscopic Breast Fine Needle Aspiration Cytology Images

Hrushikesh Garud[1]([✉]), Sri Phani Krishna Karri[1], Debdoot Sheet[1],
Ashok Kumar Maity[2], Jyotirmoy Chatterjee[1], Manjunatha Mahadevappa[1],
and Ajoy Kumar Ray[1]

[1] Indian Institute of Technology Kharagpur, Kharagpur 721301, India
hrushikesh.garud@ti.com
[2] Midnapur Medical College and Hospital, Midnapur 721101, India

Abstract. Computer vision systems for automated breast cancer diagnosis using Fine Needle Aspiration Cytology (FNAC) images are under development for a while now. Accurate segmentation of the nuclei in microscopic images is crucial for functioning of these systems, as most quantify and analyze nuclear features for diagnosis. This paper presents a nucleus segmentation system (NSS) involving pre-processing, pre-segmentation and refined segmentation stages. The NSS includes a novel pixel transformation step to create a high contrast grayscale representation of the input color image. The grayscale image gives NSS the capability- to disregard elements that mimic nuclear morphological and luminescence characteristics, and to minimize effects of non-specific staining of cytoplasm by Hematoxylin. Experimental results illustrate generalizability of the NSS to use multiple refined segmentation techniques and particularly achieve accurate nucleus segmentation using active contours without edges(F-score > 0.92). The paper also presents the results of experiments conducted to study the impact of image pre-processing steps on the NSS performance. The pre-processing steps are observed to improve accuracy and consistency across tested refined segmentation techniques.

Keywords: Breast FNAC · Nucleus segmentation · Active contour models

1 Introduction

Automated nuclei detection and segmentation are well-studied problems in digital pathology and cytology. Where, many methods have been discussed in the related works, and new methodologies continue to be investigated [8,13,19]. Though detection and segmentation of nuclei in cytology images are considered

H. Garud—Special Thanks: Texas Instruments Inc. and Dr. Arindam Ghosh for their continued support.

© Springer International Publishing AG 2017
S. Mukherjee et al. (Eds.): ICVGIP 2016, LNCS 10481, pp. 380–392, 2017.
https://doi.org/10.1007/978-3-319-68124-5_33

to be simpler than in histology [8], they still are the challenging problems due to high variability in images of breast FNAC. The variability is present due to the composition of the aspirated sample, underlying disease condition, quality and variability of slide preparation, and the imperfection of data acquisition process. The specific challenges are due to (i) other tissue elements, and nuclear cluster topology mimicking visual and morphological characteristics of nuclei; (ii) closely separated, touching or overlapping nuclei; (iii) loss of contrast between nuclei and their background; (iv) slide preparation artifacts like over/under staining of the samples, and non-specific staining of the cytoplasm by Hematoxylin (in commonly used Hematoxylin and Eosin (H&E) staining technique).

This paper presents a multistage process for segmentation of isolated and closely separated nuclei from high magnification breast fine needle aspiration cytology (FNAC) images. The method proposes a new technique to create a grayscale representation of chromatic and contrast staining properties of the nuclear material that enables accurate segmentation of the nuclei. The grayscale representation also enables the process to minimize effects of other tissue components mimicking nuclear characteristics on the detection and segmentation of nuclei. Additionally, the grayscale representation efficiently incorporates into segmentation process the ability to handle the challenging situation of non-specific staining of cytoplasm by Hematoxylin. The segmentation process thus includes stages of (i) image pre-processing; (ii) pixel transformation to create a grayscale nuclear differential image (NDI); (iii) pre-segmentation of nuclear regions by automatic thresholding [14]; (iv) morphological filtering for suppression of the regions inconsistent with morphological properties of the isolated nuclei [16]; and (v) refined segmentation of the remaining objects by active contours without edges [1].

The remainder of this paper is organized as follows - Sect. 2 presents details of the process for segmentation of nuclei. Section 3 presents details of the experimental setup used to validate and benchmark performance of the segmentation system. Results of the experiments are discussed in Sect. 4 and concluding remarks presented in Sect. 5.

2   Proposed Segmentation Process

A block diagrammatic representation of the proposed multi-stage segmentation process is depicted in Fig. 1 and detailed description of the functional steps is provided in the following sub-sections.

2.1   Image Pre-processing

Most of the images acquired in digital microscopy systems include defects present due to the imperfections and limitations of the system elements such as light source, optics, and camera electronics. Additionally, external factors like fungal growth or dust accumulation on the optics also affect the quality of acquired

Fig. 1. Block diagrammatic representation of the multi-stage isolated nuclei segmentation process. The image preprocessing block consists of vignetting correction and auto white balance procedures. The refined segmentation of the pre-segmented nuclei can be performed using various techniques like Snakes, Level sets, Fast marching technique, Randoms walker, etc.

images. Thus, before segmentation of nuclei in an image, the image is conditioned for non-uniform luminance correction [20] and fast auto white balance correction for color constancy [2,3].

2.2   Creation of the Nuclear Differential Image

This section presents a simple method of NDI creation by combining the visual characteristics of color saturation and stain quantity information. In the H&E staining technique, Hematoxylin binds with nucleic acids and gives the nuclear region its characteristic deep blue-purple color whereas Eosin stains proteins non-specifically and gives magenta-red color to the cytoplasm [17]. Thus, the differential image creation process is defined based on the knowledge that presence of Hematoxylin stain at a point in the smear and high color saturation in its image imply the presence of nuclear material at the point. In many cell samples, using only the Hematoxylin stain separated images for segmentation can not provide desired contrast between the nuclei and their background especially in the case of non-specific staining of the cytoplasm. To handle this scenario we define a nonlinear combination of the quantity of Hematoxylin stain, quantity of Eosin stain, and color saturation information to assign gray level value to the pixels in NDI as

$$f_D(i,j) = \min((f_{QH}(i,j) - \varepsilon f_{QE}(i,j)), f_s(i,j)) \qquad (1)$$

where $f_{QH}(i,j)$[1], $f_{QE}(i,j)$ and $f_s(i,j)$ represent the quantity of Hematoxylin stain, quantity of Eosin stain, and color saturation at location (i,j) and ε is a factor which is used to define the fraction of measured Eosin stain quantity that should be subtracted from the measured Hematoxylin stain quantity to compensate for the nonspecific staining of the cytoplasm by Hematoxylin. The values of stain quantities $f_{QH}(\cdot)$, $f_{QE}(\cdot)$ and color saturation $f_s(\cdot)$ are defined in the range of $[0, 255]$.

For a microscopic image $\mathbf{f}$ of the stained cytological sample, acquired under known illumination (in this case a white balanced image), presence of the stains

---

[1] In this paper symbols f and **f** are used to represent single channel and multi-channel images.

Color input Grayscale ver- $f_D, \varepsilon = 0.0$ $f_D, \varepsilon = 0.5$
image   sion of input
image

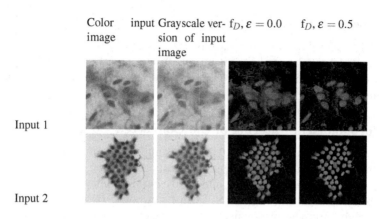

Input 1

Input 2

Fig. 2. Comparison of NDIs obtained using different values of ε with input and its grayscale version are presented here. The first example illustrates advantage of combining Hematoxylin, Eosin and color saturation information over using just the Hematoxylin and color saturation information when the non-specific staining of cytoplasm by Hematoxylin is suspected. The second example illustrates the condition when just the Hematoxylin and color saturation information are sufficient to obtain a high contrast NDI. (Color figure online)

can be quantified by stain separation method described in [17], and presented in equation form as

$$\mathbf{f}_Q(i,j) = \mathbf{D} \times \mathbf{f}_{OD}(i,j) \qquad (2)$$

where $\mathbf{f}_Q(i,j)$ is a column vector representing quantity of the constituent stains, $\mathbf{D}$ is the deconvolution matrix for stain separation, and $\mathbf{f}_{OD}(i,j)$ is a column matrix depicting optical densities of red, green and blue wavelengths at location (i,j).

The NDI thus created represents nuclei as high-intensity regions with a dark background, such that contrast across the nuclear boundary is larger than input color image or its grayscale version. This method effectively extends the ability of stain separation methods of handling the presence of tissue elements like red blood cells and overlapping cellular components to handle non-specific staining of the cytoplasm. In the system, the value of ε can be set heuristically for a tissue sample based on the expectation of non-specific staining. Illustrative examples comparing results for the differential image generation process are shown in Fig. 2.

2.3   Noise Filtering

The process of NDI creation described here works only on pixel level information thus commonly leads to the presence of noisy local variations. To avoid local minima that can affect the segmentation process and to aid accurate segmentation, the luminance similarity-aware weighted-local-difference median filter (LAWLDMF) [5] is employed. The filtered NDI is then used for the segmentation of nuclei.

2.4   Pre-segmentation of Nuclei

In the NDI, nuclei show up as bright blobs with a darker background. In this scenario, the nuclei can be easily segmented by use of thresholding techniques. For this purpose, the segmentation system uses Otsu's automatic threshold selection technique [14].

2.5   Morphological Filtering of the Connected Components

A pre-segmented image contains multiple connected components representing region masks for single, touching and overlapping nuclei present in the input image. The pre-segmented image may also contain some objects that do not belong to the real nuclear regions and can be removed by use of morphological filtering. Here, only the pre-segmented objects that closely match the size and shape (round/elliptical) of isolated nuclei are retained using a method, similar to the one proposed by Pietka et al. [16]. The rules for filtering and selection of the objects can be presented as

(i) Remove all connected components on the edge of an image
(ii) From the remaining connected components, retain all those who have the size within the probable range of isolated nuclei or are larger in size but closely match the shape of isolated nuclei (i.e. retain compact, less eccentric rounded objects).

Here, the size of objects is measured in number of pixels, eccentricity is defined as the ratio of the distance between foci of the ellipse and its major axis length, and the compactness is defined as the area (size) upon squared object perimeter in pixels.

2.6   Active Contour Models Based Refined Segmentation

It is observed that, though close to the actual nuclear regions, pre-segmentation of nuclei is not accurate and requires further refinement. The segmentation system described here uses the 'active contour without edges', or Chan-Vese level sets technique [1] for refinement of pre-segmentation. Here, the output of morphological filtering process provides initialization masks which are then evolved by Chan-Vese model to obtain refined segmentation.

Active contour without edges: The level sets model introduced by [1] is an energy minimization approach to segmentation, where, the model assumes that a grayscale image f is formed by two regions of approximatively piecewise-constant intensities having distinct values f^{in} and f^{out}. Thus, if C_0 is the boundary of the object of interest, then $f \approx f^{in}$ inside C_0 and $f \approx f^{out}$ outside of C_0. The level sets approach then tries to optimize the fitting function $\mathbb{E}(c_1, c_2, C)$ defined below to find C_0

$$\mathbb{E}(c_1, c_2, C) = \begin{array}{l} \mu \cdot \text{Length}(C) \ + \ \nu \cdot \text{Area}(\text{inside}(C)) \\ + \ \lambda_1 \cdot \int_{\text{inside}(C)} |f(i,j) - c_z 1|^2 \, di \, dj \\ + \ \lambda_2 \cdot \int_{\text{outside}(C)} |f(i,j) - c_2|^2 \, di \, dj \end{array} \qquad (3)$$

where C is a variable curve that can be initialized arbitrarily or to an initial estimate of the region boundary obtained by pre-segmentation; c_1, and c_2 are the average intensities inside and outside of C respectively.

2.7 Post-segmentation Morphological Filtering of the Connected Components

The connected components obtained after refined segmentation process are filtered based on the morphological attributes as defined in Sect. 2.5. Figure 3 shows the processed images at different stages of the complete segmentation process.

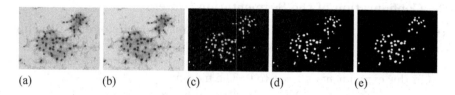

(a)   (b)   (c)   (d)   (e)

Fig. 3. The images on right depict different stages of the segmentation process (a) input image, (b) preprocessed image, (c) NDI, (d) pre-segmented image after morphometric filtering, and (e) nuclear regions mask obtained after entire segmentation process.

3 Experimental Setup

The focus of experimentation in this paper is on the evaluation of refined segmentation strategies. The segmentation quality of various algorithms can be evaluated by comparing their results with suitably defined ground truth using objective measures, and by visual evaluation by experts. The objective measures based benchmarking of Chan-Vase level sets model is performed against *three* nucleus segmentation methods of Snakes [10], Fast marching method [18], and Random walks [6] commonly used in digital pathology applications. This is followed by visual verification by a cytopathologist. The experimentation strategy also studies the impact of pre-processing and noise filtering techniques on segmentation quality, results for which are provided along with the other results presented in Sect. 4.

3.1 Image Dataset and Ground Truth Segmentation

For development and experimental validation of the image segmentation system, an image dataset was prepared from the slide archives of our institute. The cell samples used for imaging were obtained from routine FNAC performed on the patients with breast masses by an expert cytologist. The slides were prepared by wet fixation and H&E staining methods commonly used for primary diagnosis from FNAC [4]. The slides were imaged using Leica DM750 microscope with 40× magnification objective having the numerical aperture of 0.65. The microscope comes fitted with Leica DFC295 camera via a 0.5× optocoupler and housing a 1024 × 768 pixel resolution color image sensor. During image acquisition, the camera was programmed to provide RGB coded pixel data without any image pre-processing. Focus and field illumination settings were user defined, with variations within the acceptable range, over which images retain their diagnostic value for a human expert. The performance of segmentation techniques is tested using a set of 21 randomly selected benign/malignant breast FNAC sample images of size 1024 × 768 pixels. Since each image contains a large number of nuclei and manual segmentation of all is impractical, 213 nuclear regions were manually marked by an expert to create ground truth for objective evaluation.

3.2   Configuration of the Segmentation System

Preprocessing, NDI generation, noise, and morphological filtering: When integrating the auto white balance and LAWLDMF for noise filtering, the best settings presented in the relevant literature were applied, for NDI creation in this experiments ε is set to 0. The morphological filtering step discards the connected components within 20 pixels from the nuclear boundary, retains nuclei having area in the range of [40, 700] pixels and any shape or nuclei having area >700 pixels and eccentricity less than 0.9.

Refined segmentation algorithms: Each of the compared refined segmentation methods has multiple configuration parameters that can be tuned to get the best performance for individual test images. However, this is undesirable as it is impossible to tune a segmentation technique for each image in real life. Thus, during this study, all methods use the same set of parameters for the entire dataset (specific for each technique), and aggregate values for objective measures are compared. For this study, our implementation of Snakes and Chan-Vese level sets have been used, along with the publicly available segmentation program for Random walks technique [7]. The fixed settings of each algorithm were determined so as to produce visually and objectively most accurate segmentation results on the dataset. In this regard during experimentation, the behavior of compared methods was studied on following parameters to select the best settings that achieve best F-score value (averaged over dataset)- (i) number of iterations for Snakes and Chan-Vese level sets (4 to 104 iterations at interval of 4, 26 experiments each) while setting other parameters constant ($\mu = 0.9$, $\nu = 0$, $\lambda_1 = \lambda_2 = 1$), (ii) threshold value used for computation of gradient difference weight for Fast marching method (varied between range 4 to 24 at the interval of 4, 6 experiments), and (iii) Weighting parameter used in Random walks method (varied between 10 to 100 at interval of 10, 10 experiments).

3.3   Objective Measures for Performance Evaluation

If the marked ground truth is available for a connected component segmented by a technique, the two regions are compared to measure the statistical measures of precision [12,15], recall [12,15], F-Score and Jaccard similarity coefficient [9,11].

4   Results and Discussion

Figures 4 and 5 show the F-Score and Jaccard coefficient (J) respectively obtained over the parameter set described in Sect. 3.2. The tuning curves describe the behavior of algorithms as input parameters change, and can be used to determine the appropriate input parameters to be used. The F-Score and Jaccard coefficient curves of the Chan-Vese level sets and Snakes, show an almost monotonic increase in the segmentation accuracy over initial increments in the number of iterative steps and saturate after that. The curves of Fast marching and Random walks methods show very small change with variation of the objective parameters. The best performance for Chan-Vese level sets algorithm was obtained at 76 iterations, for Snakes at 104 iterations, for Fast marching method at gray level difference threshold of 12, and Random walks method for weighting parameter function value of 90. The figures do not show an experiment-wise comparison between various configurations of the compared methods.

Objective measure results for configurations leading to the best performance for the compared methods is given in Table 1. It can be observed that Snakes technique has the lowest performance both regarding over (precision) and under (recall)-segmentation. Comparison of Chan-Vese level sets and Random walks method reveals that later has the lower rate of over-segmentation than the former, but under-segmentation rates show inverted behavior. Overall, Chan-Vese level sets method has more balanced performance and higher F-Score among all the compared methods. The same behavior is exhibited on the Jaccard coefficient as well.

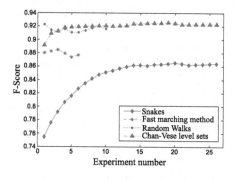
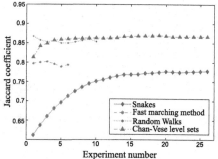

Fig. 4. Plot for average F-score for different configurations of the compared refined segmentation algorithms.

Fig. 5. Plot for average Jaccard coefficient for different configurations of the compared refined segmentation algorithms

Figure 6 shows segmentation results for the compared algorithms on multiple nuclear regions from *three* sample images from the test dataset for which ground truth is available. The settings used for each of the segmentation techniques correspond to the configurations leading to the highest F-Score values.

Table 1. Accuracy for the compared fine-segmentation techniques with respective optimal configuration parameters

Segmentation technique	Precision	Recall	F-Score	Jaccard coefficient
	Average (Variance)			
Snakes	0.9158 (0.0161)	0.8430 (0.0229)	0.8642 (0.0150)	0.7775 (0.0245)
Fast marching method	0.9237 (0.0113)	0.8740 (0.0182)	0.8846 (0.0069)	0.8021 (0.0147)
Random walks	0.9625 (0.0061)	0.8926 (0.0080)	0.9207 (0.0055)	0.8599 (0.0104)
Chan-Vese level sets	0.9483 (0.0127)	0.9179 (0.0079)	0.9256 (0.0079)	0.8697 (0.0148)

The images also show the comparison of obtained segmentations with ground truth. It can be observed that Snakes, and Fast marching segmentation techniques, as observed through objective measures, have the tendency to both over and under segment, greater than that of Chan-Vese level sets, and Random walks methods. Random walks method though has the performance comparable with that of Chan-Vese method, it commonly produces jagged nuclear boundary and can potentially affect performance of the feature extraction techniques that quantify the state of nuclear membrane. Chan-Vese level sets method, on the other hand, includes the boundary length (Length) term in the energy minimization function, that results in smoother region boundary, which is desirable at least for small lengths.

Results for segmentation of the nuclei by level sets method in various breast FNAC conditions are shown in Fig. 7 where boundaries of the segmented nuclei are overlaid on the input images. The images highlight performance of the proposed segmentation system in various types of cell samples including benign and malignant conditions and difficult to segment cell clustering and cytoplasm conditions. The results of the segmentation technique have been visually verified by an expert cytopathologist.

4.1   Impact of Pre-processing and Noise Filtering Techniques

To study the impact of pre-processing and noise filtering techniques on segmentation quality, these pre-processing steps are bypassed and segmentation accuracy noted for the algorithm configurations that lead to the best performance with those steps enabled. The aggregate results over the dataset are presented in Table 2. All the compared methods except Fast marching method show the degradation in segmentation accuracy and increased variance in the objective measures. Chan-Vese level sets method remains the best performing segmentation algorithm.

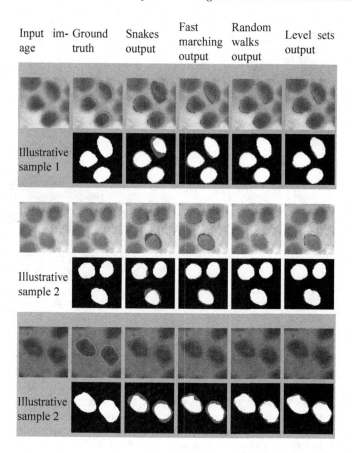

Fig. 6. Visualizations of the outputs for compared methods, highlighting over and under-segmentation with respect to ground truth. Visualizations for the inputs and corresponding outputs are shown in shaded rectangular boxes with the column-wise left to right arrangement of input, ground truth, and output visualizations for the compared methods. The cropped out regions of *three* test images are shown in the first column. Ground truth segmentation for the nuclear regions is depicted in the second column, where inside boundary is shown as a green colored closed contour overlaid on the input image shown on the top; the bottom image in the same column shows corresponding binary nuclear region mask. Here, (white) pixels in the ground truth image are the pixels that belong to a nuclear region, and black pixels are the pixels that belong to the background region. The top image in a results column of a compared method shows the over-segmented (red colored pixels) and under-segmented (blue colored pixels) pixels in the segmentation mask overlaid on the input image. The bottom image in the column shows the corresponding segmentation mask with the color coding as described above. (Color figure online)

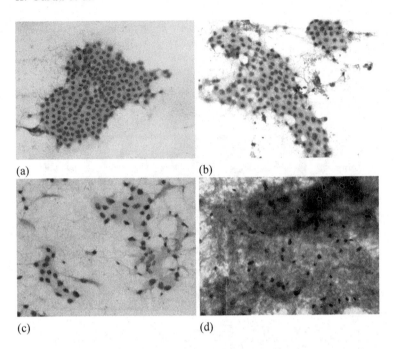

(a)   (b)

(c)   (d)

Fig. 7. Results for segmentation of the nuclei by level sets method in various breast FNAC conditions are shown in this figure. The inside boundaries of the segmented nuclei are overlaid in green color on the input image. The images (a) and (b) present the high magnification images of benign samples, with image (a) showing a sheet of benign looking nuclei and the image (b) shows the segmentation performance in the presence of debris present on the slide. The images (c) and (d) correspond to malignant samples with scattered nuclei of variable size and shape with the image (d) showing segmentation performance in a sample with abundant eosinophilic cytoplasm. (Color figure online)

Table 2. Accuracy for the compared fine-segmentation techniques without pre-processing of the images

Segmentation technique	Precision	Recall	F-Score	Jaccard coefficient
	Average (Variance)			
Snakes	0.9212 (0.0137)	0.8321 (0.0217)	0.8588 (0.0121)	0.7667 (0.0218)
Fast marching method	0.9281 (0.0082)	0.8750 (0.0188)	0.8884 (0.0062)	0.8075 (0.0134)
Random Walks	0.9449 (0.0144)	0.8775 (0.0132)	0.9022 (0.0110)	0.8338 (0.0162)
Chan-Vese level sets	0.9411 (0.0139)	0.9033 (0.0102)	0.9111 (0.0095)	0.8479 (0.0160)

5   Conclusions

This paper presented a two-stage segmentation process (pre-segmentation followed by refined segmentation) in the high magnification microscopy images of H&E stained breast FNAC samples. The system integrates image pre-processing, and segmentation techniques to achieve desired high segmentation accuracy for application in CAD systems. Though the segmentation process can use various segmentation techniques, Chan-Vese level sets method provides more balanced performance among all the compared methods with Random walks method process being the close second. Due to the inclusion of Length in the energy minimization function, Chan-Vese level sets method provides smoother region boundary than Random walks method and is more suitable for estimation of nuclear morphometric features. The pre-processing steps used here contribute to the improvement of accuracy and consistency across tested refined segmentation techniques. Beyond complete integration of the pre-processing and segmentation techniques, novelty of the system lies in combining image color properties and Hematoxylin and Eosin stain separated images to synthesize the NDI and using it for accurate segmentation of the nuclei. The NDI simplifies the problem of nucleus segmentation into a simpler problem of separation of bright high-intensity regions with a dark background. The use of NDI also gives the system ability to handle the presence of tissue elements like red blood cells, voluminous Eosinophilic cytoplasm covering nuclei, and other common debris. The use of NDI further augments capability of the system to handle non-specific staining of the cytoplasm by Hematoxylin.

References

1. Chan, T.F., Vese, L.A.: Active contours without edges. IEEE Trans. Image Process. **10**(2), 266–277 (2001)
2. Garud, H., Pudipeddi, U.K., Desappan, K., Nagori, S.: A fast color constancy scheme for automobile video cameras. In: 2014 International Conference on Signal Processing and Communications (SPCOM), pp. 1–6, July 2014
3. Garud, H., Ray, A.K., Manjunatha, M., Chatterjee, J., Mandal, S.: A fast auto white balance scheme for digital pathology. In: 2014 IEEE-EMBS International Conference on Biomedical and Health Informatics (BHI), pp. 153–156, June 2014
4. Garud, H.T., Sheet, D., Mahadevappa, M., Chatterjee, J., Ray, A.K., Ghosh, A.: Breast fine needle aspiration cytology practices and commonly perceived diagnostic significance of cytological features: a pan-India survey. J. Cytol. **29**(3), 183 (2012)
5. Garud, H., Sheet, D., Ray, A., Mahadevappa, M., Chatterjee, J.: Adaptive weighted-local-difference order statistics filters, US Patent 9,208,545 (2015)
6. Grady, L.: Random walks for image segmentation. IEEE Trans. Pattern Anal. Mach. Intell. **28**(11), 1768–1783 (2006)
7. Grady, L., Schwartz, E.: The graph analysis toolbox: image processing on arbitrary graphs. CAS/CNS Technical Report Series (021) (2010)
8. Irshad, H., Veillard, A., Roux, L., Racoceanu, D.: Methods for nuclei detection, segmentation, and classification in digital histopathology: a review- current status and future potential. IEEE Rev. Biomed. Eng. **7**, 97–114 (2014)

9. Jaccard, P.: Étude comparative de la distribution florale dans une portion des Alpes et des Jura. Bulletin del la Société Vaudoise des Sciences Naturelles **37**, 547–579 (1901)

10. Kass, M., Witkin, A., Terzopoulos, D.: Snakes: active contour models. Int. J. Comput. Vis. **1**(4), 321–331 (1988)

11. Levandowsky, M., Winter, D.: Distance between sets. Nature **234**(5323), 34–35 (1971)

12. Martin, D., Fowlkes, C., Tal, D., Malik, J.: A database of human segmented natural images and its application to evaluating segmentation algorithms and measuring ecological statistics. In: Proceedings of the 8th International Conference on Computer Vision, vol. 2, pp. 416–423, July 2001

13. Obuchowicz, A., Hrebień, M., Nieczkowski, T., Marciniak, A.: Computational intelligence techniques in image segmentation for cytopathology. In: Smolinski, T.G., Milanova, M.G., Hassanien, A.E. (eds.) Computational Intelligence in Biomedicine and Bioinformatics. SCI, pp. 169–199. Springer, Heidelberg (2008). doi:10.1007/978-3-540-70778-3_7

14. Otsu, N.: A threshold selection method from gray-level histograms. IEEE Trans. Syst. Man Cybern. **9**(1), 62–66 (1979)

15. Perry, J.W., Kent, A., Berry, M.M.: Machine literature searching X. Machine language; factors underlying its design and development. Am. Doc. **6**(4), 242–254 (1955). doi:10.1002/asi.5090060411

16. Pietka, D., Dulewicz, A., Jaszczak, P.: Removing artefacts from microscopic images of cytological smears. A shape-based approach. In: Kurzyński, M., Puchała, E., Woźniak, M., żołnierek, A. (eds.) Computer Recognition Systems. Advances in Soft Computing, vol. 30, pp. 661–669. Springer, Heidelberg (2005). doi:10.1007/3-540-32390-2_78

17. Ruifrok, A.C., Johnston, D.A.: Quantification of histochemical staining by color deconvolution. Anal. Quant. Cytol. Histol. **23**, 291–299 (2001)

18. Sethian, J.A.: Level Set Methods and Fast Marching Methods: Evolving Interfaces in Computational Geometry, Fluid Mechanics, Computer Vision, and Materials Science, vol. 3. Cambridge University Press, Cambridge (1999)

19. Xing, F., Yang, L.: Robust nucleus/cell detection and segmentation in digital pathology and microscopy images: a comprehensive review. IEEE Rev. Biomed. Eng. **9**, 234–263 (2016)

20. Young, I.T.: Shading correction: compensation for illumination and sensor inhomogeneities. In: Current Protocols in Cytometry. John Wiley & Sons, Inc. (2001). ISBN 9780471142959. doi:10.1002/0471142956.cy0211s14

Segmentation of Lumen and External Elastic Laminae in Intravascular Ultrasound Images Using Ultrasonic Backscattering Physics Initialized Multiscale Random Walks

Debarghya China[1], Pabitra Mitra[2], and Debdoot Sheet[3(✉)]

[1] Advanced Technology Development Centre,
Indian Institute of Technology Kharagpur, Kharagpur, India
[2] Department of Computer Science and Engineering,
Indian Institute of Technology Kharagpur, Kharagpur, India
[3] Department of Electrical Engineering,
Indian Institute of Technology Kharagpur, Kharagpur, India
`debdoot@ee.iitkgp.ernet.in`

Abstract. Coronary artery disease accounts for a large number of deaths across the world and clinicians generally prefer using x-ray computed tomography or magnetic resonance imaging for localizing vascular pathologies. Interventional imaging modalities like intravascular ultrasound (IVUS) are used to adjunct diagnosis of atherosclerotic plaques in vessels, and help assess morphological state of the vessel and plaque, which play a significant role for treatment planning. Since speckle intensity in IVUS images are inherently stochastic in nature and challenge clinicians with accurate visibility of the vessel wall boundaries, it requires automation. In this paper we present a method for segmenting the lumen and external elastic laminae of the artery wall in IVUS images using random walks over a multiscale pyramid of Gaussian decomposed frames. The seeds for the random walker are initialized by supervised learning of ultrasonic backscattering and attenuation statistical mechanics from labelled training samples. We have experimentally evaluated the performance using 77 IVUS images acquired at 40 MHz that are available in the IVUS segmentation challenge dataset (http://www.cvc. uab.es/IVUSchallenge2011/dataset.html.) to obtain a Jaccard score of 0.89 ± 0.14 for lumen and 0.85 ± 0.12 for external elastic laminae segmentation over a 10-fold cross-validation study.

Keywords: External elastic laminae segmentation · Intravascular ultrasound · Lumen segmentation · Random forests · Random walks · Signal confidence

1 Introduction

Coronary artery diseases cause partial or total restriction of blood supply due to formation of hard or soft plaques that lead to a condition of constrained blood

© Springer International Publishing AG 2017
S. Mukherjee et al. (Eds.): ICVGIP 2016, LNCS 10481, pp. 393–403, 2017.
https://doi.org/10.1007/978-3-319-68124-5_34

circulation around the heart. The outcome of this disorder leads to myocardial cardiac infarction (heart attack) and may even lead to death. There are several imaging techniques for *in vivo* estimation of atherosclerotic plaques viz. X-ray computed tomography or magnetic resonance imaging. One of the commonly used *in vivo* adjunct imaging techniques is intravascular ultrasound (IVUS) which provides detailed information about the lumen wall, compositing tissues, plaque morphology and pathology imaging is performed using a catheter is inserted in the blood vessel, with the transducer usually positioned at the tip of the catheter. A signal of high frequency (20–40 MHz) ultrasonic signal is transmitted and the beam reflected as it passed through different layers. The received signal is used for image formation and the combination of constant speed catheter's pullback and the reflection of ultrasonic waves from the material, generates sequence of images along the length of the artery. This modality also provides information about the constituent component of plaque which clinically assist to identification of likelihood lesion of a rupture.

2   Prior Art

Methods for automated identification and segmentation of the lumen from media adventitia and from media externa for assessing the pathology and morphology of plaques for assisting clinicians for better diagnosis and treatment planning. Manual delineation of lumen and external elastic luminae for segmenting these layers is tedious and time consuming process. Prior art includes active surface segmentation algorithm for 3D segmentation in assessment of coronary morphology [13,23]. Deformable shape models with energy function minimization using a hopfield neural network [16], 3D IVUS segmentation model based on the fast-marching method and using Rayleigh mixture model [4] are amongst others. A combination of implicit anisotropic contour closing (ACC) and explicit snake model for detection of media adventitia and lumen was proposed [8]. A shape-driven method was proposed for segmentation of arterial wall in the rectangular domain [26]. A knowledge based system for IVUS image segmentation was introduced which minimizes inter- and intra-observer variability [2]. There are few IVUS border detection algorithms developed based on edge tracking and gradient based techniques [10,24]. A new approach based on 3-D optimal graph search was developed for IVUS image segmentation [7]. A fully automated segmentation method based on graph representation was introduced for delineation of luminal and external elastic lamina surface of coronary artery [25]. A probabilistic approach for delineation of luminal border was presented based on minimization of the probabilistic cost function [14]. A holistic approach for media-adventitia border detection was introduced in [5]. An automated *in vivo* delineation of lumen wall had done using graph theoretic random walk method [15].

3   Problem Statement

Let us considered an IVUS frame I where $i(x)$ is the intensity at location x. The lumen and external elastic luminae borders split the image I in to three disjoint set as I_{lumen}, I_{media} and $I_{externa}$ such that $I_{lumen} \cap I_{media} \cap I_{externa} = \emptyset$ and $I_{lumen} \cup I_{media} \cup I_{externa} = I$. Image I can be represented as an equivalent graph $\mathcal{G}$ such that the nodes of the graph can be represented as $n \in I$ and the edges connecting nodes of graph $\mathcal{G}$ are modeled by physics of acoustic energy propagation and attenuation within highly scatteering biological tissues. The probability of the each node $n \in \mathcal{G}$ to belong to either of $\{I_{lumen}, I_{media}, I_{externa}\}$ can be solved using the random walks for image segmentation approach [17]. The class posterior probability at a $x \in I$ is the probability of the corresponding node $n \in \mathcal{G}$. A pixel at location x is labeled as $\arg\max\{p(lumen|x, I), p(media|x, I), p(externa|x, I)\}$.

A set of seeds S constituting some of the marked nodes of graph $\mathcal{G}$ such that $S \subseteq \{(S \in I_{lumen}) \cup (S \in I_{media}) \cup (S \in I_{externa})\}$ and $(S \in I_{lumen}) \cap (S \in I_{media}) \cap (S \in I_{externa}) = \emptyset$ is define for initialization of the random walker. Ultrasonic backscattering physics based model is used to achieve the solution of the random walker. Hence, class posterior probability would be assign to the unmarked nodes $U_m = \mathcal{G} - S$ of the graph to achieve the lumen and media adventitia border such that $\mathcal{G} \subseteq \{S \cup U_m\}$ and $S \cap U_m = \emptyset$. Different stages of our proposed method have been shown in Fig. 1 and that are detailed in the subsequent sections.

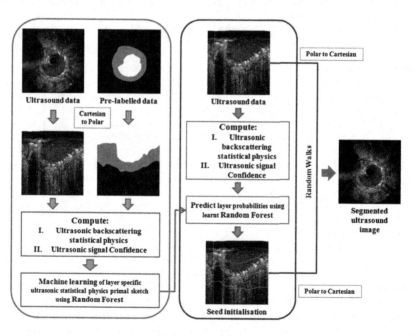

Fig. 1. Flow diagram of our proposed method for lumen and external elastic luminae segmentation from intravascular ultrasound images

4   Exposition to the Solution

Ultrasonic acoustic pulse travelling through tissues are either backscattered, attenuated or absorbed. Ultrasonic images are formed using the returned echos caused by backscattering acoustic pulse. The main cause of backscattering are the scatteres present in the tissue where there nature varies with the tissue types. The statistical nature of the envelope of ultrasonic echo (R) depends on the nature of the scatterers. The Scatterers' contribution is normally treated as random walk on account of their random location within the resolution limit of the range cell of the propagating ultrasonic backscattering pulse. Let r be the value of the sensed signal at an instant and $R = \{r\}$ represents the set of values recorded by the transducer array, where R is purely stochastic in nature. Let y be a type of tissue and $y \in Y$ represents the set of tissue type. Probability of a tissue type y, characterized by ultrasonic echo envelop r, can be written in Bayesian paradigm as

$$p(y|r) = \frac{p(r|y)P(y)}{p(r)} \tag{1}$$

where $p(r|y)$ is the conditional likelihood of received signal r from a known tissue type y; $P(y)$ is the prior probability of tissue type y, and $p(r)$ is the evidence of r. Since there are three tissue types viz. Lumen, Media and Externa, thus $Y \in \{Lumen, Media, Externa\}$.

Let $f_1(r; \dots |y)$ be the parametric stochastic model of ultrasonic backscattering echos and $f_2(r; \dots |y)$ be the model of signal attenuation of ultrasonic propagation. Hence we can write

$$p(r; \dots |y) \propto \left\{ \quad \underbrace{f_1(r; \phi_1|y)}_{backscattering\ stats.} \quad , \quad \underbrace{f_2(r; \phi_2|y)}_{signal\ attenuation} \quad \right\} \tag{2}$$

The properties of the tissues can be denoted using statistical physics model $\Theta = \{\phi_1, \phi_2\}$. So, each type of tissue is characterized by a unique set of statistical physics model $\{\Theta|y\} \forall Y$.

Accordingly (1) can be re-written by taking (2) into consideration

$$p(y|\Theta; r) = \frac{p(\Theta; r|y)P(y)}{p(\Theta; r)} \tag{3}$$

where $p(y|\Theta; r)$ is the posterior probability of predicting the type of tissue y, and $p(\Theta; r|y)$ is the conditional likelihood of tissue specific backscattering and ultrasonic pulse propagation model as modeled in (2). In order to solve this problem we would have to (i) estimate the backscattering statistical physics of ultrasonic echos, (ii) estimate signal attenuation of received ultrasonic echos and (iii) machine learning of the primal $(\Theta; r)$ for solution of (3).

4.1   Statistical Physics of Ultrasonic Backscattering

The conditional distribution of the random variable $r \in R$ is Nakagami distributed [19] such that $p(r|y) \propto N(r|m, \Omega)$ represented as

$$N(r|m, \Omega) = \frac{2m^m r^{2m-1}}{\Gamma(m)\Omega^m} exp(-\frac{m}{\Omega}r^2)U(r) \qquad (4)$$

where m and Ω are known as the Nakagami shape and scale factors respectively. $\Gamma(.)$ is the mathematical Gamma distribution function and $U(.)$ is the unit step response. The parameters are estimated from the moments of the enveloped signal R as

$$m = \frac{(E[R^2])^2}{E[R^2 - E[R^2]]^2} \quad \text{and} \quad \Omega = E[R^2] \qquad (5)$$

where $E(.)$ is the mathematical expectation operator. Since in a B-mode image, the image intensity i is a log-compressed version of the signal r, the intensity $i \in I$ is accordingly Fisher-Tippett distributed [20,22] such that $p(i|y) \propto F(i|\sigma)$ and

$$F(i|\sigma) \propto exp([2i - ln(2\sigma^2)] - exp[2i - ln(2\sigma^2)]) \qquad (6)$$

where σ is the standard deviation of intensity [20].

The parameters of i and σ are estimated through a nonlinear multiscale estimation. According to our proposition, these parameter are estimated at different scales $\tau = (\tau_{trans}, \tau_{axial})$ where τ_{trans} is the number of neighboring scan lines and τ_{axial} is the number of samples along each scan line, with $(\tau_{trans}, \tau_{axial}) \in \{(3,3), (3,5), (3,7), \ldots, (3,30)\}$ such that estimation holds true for the strong law of large numbers [18]. Thus an ordered vector of $(i, \sigma) \subset \Theta$ forms part of the information required for solving (3).

4.2   Ultrasonic Signal Confidence Estimation

Ultrasonic signal attenuation measured as signal confidence in (3) is estimated using the method of random walks [11,12,21]. The backscattered ultrasonic echos from randomly distributed scatterers can be treated as a random walk walking from a point in space to the transducer [19]. According to that concept, backscattered echo and ultrasonic pulse are travelling through the same path of a heterogeneous media are subjected to the same attenuation. The confidence of the ultrasonic signal has been estimated as the probability of a random walker starting at a node on the scan-line and reaching to the origin of each scan line where the virtual transducer element placed. Thus the signal confidence is represented as

$$p(r; \ldots |y) \propto f_2(r; \phi_2|y) \qquad (7)$$

where ϕ_2 is the received ultrasonic signal confidence associated with backscattered echo r by a tissue type y.

4.3   Learning of Statistical Mechanics of Ultrasonic Backscattering for Initial Seed Selection

The parameters of $f_1(r; \ldots | y)$ and $f_2(r; \ldots | y)$ constitute subspaces of jointly model for prediction of the tissue specific posterior probability. Non-parametric machine learning framework of random forest [3,6] has been employed for this purpose. The prediction model of random forest can be represented as

$$p(y|\Theta; r) = H(y|\Theta; r) \tag{8}$$

where $H(.)$ is the learnt random forest model. A random forest $H(y|\Theta; r)$ is formally defined as a classifier consisting of a collection of tree-structured decision maker $\{h(y|\Theta, \Phi_k), k = 1, \ldots\}$ where $\{\Phi_k\}$ are independent identically distributed random vectors which represent sample features and each tree $h(y|\Theta, \Phi_k)$ casts a unit vote for the most popular class y at input Θ [3]. At the time of learning of the model, each tree is a binary tree and trained on the independent random vector Φ_k. There are $nTrees \in \mathbb{N}$ number of trees constituting the forest model. We employ $nPercentToSample \in \mathbb{R}_+$ random samplingwith replacement from complete observation space for generating Φ_k. Depending on the response of the $weakLearner$ each of the nodes split to two children. If the number of observation at the node is less than $minLeaf \in \mathbb{N}$ or if all the observations at the node belong to a single class then the splitting test on a node stop. During prediction, the vote casted by the forest is the class specific mean response of each of the trees such that $p(y|\Theta; i) = E[h(\ldots, \Phi_k)]$. Initial segmentation is done using this random forest model to obtain seeds for each tissue type $Y \in \{lumen, media, externa\}$. This initial labels are considered as the seed points of those individual labels. Final label of segmentation has been done with graph theoretic random walk method using the initial label seed points.

4.4   Random Walks for Lumen and External Elastic Luminae Segmentation

The graph G is represented as a combinatorial Laplacian matrix L for achieving an analytically convergent solution [9,17].

$$L_{pq} = \begin{cases} d_p & \text{if } p = q \\ -w_{pq} & \text{if } v_p \text{ and } v_q \text{ are adjacent nodes} \\ 0 & \text{otherwise} \end{cases} \tag{9}$$

where L_{pq} is indexed by vertices v_p and v_q. The set of vertices or nodes V can be divided into two, V_M consisting of marked seeded nodes and V_U consisting of unmarked or unseeded nodes such that $V_M \cup V_U = V$ and $V_M \cap V_U = \emptyset$. Thus the Laplacian matrix can be decomposed as

$$L = \begin{bmatrix} L_M & B \\ B^T & L_U \end{bmatrix} \tag{10}$$

where L_M and L_U are Laplacian submatrices corresponding to V_M and V_U, respectively. We denote the probability of a random walker starting at a node v_q to reach a seeded point belonging to tissue type $\omega \in \{lumen, media, externa\}$ as x_q^w s.t. $\sum_\omega x_q^w = 1$. Further, to achieve a solution, the set of labels defined for all the seeds in $V_M \in S$ is specified using a function

$$Q(v_q) = \omega \quad and \quad \forall v_q \in V_M \tag{11}$$

where $\omega \in \mathbb{Z}, 0 < \omega < 3$ s.t. $\omega = 1$ is the set of label corresponding to $I_{lumen}, \omega = 2$ is the set of labels corresponding to I_{media}, and $\omega = 3$ is the set of labels corresponding to $I_{externa}$. This helps us in defining $M \in S$ is a 1-D vector of $|V_M| \times 1$ elements corresponding to each label at a node $v_q \in V_M$ constituted as

$$m_q^\omega = \begin{cases} 1 & \text{if } Q(v_q) = \omega \\ 0 & \text{if } Q(v_q) \neq \omega \end{cases} \tag{12}$$

Therefore, for label ω, the solution can be obtained by solving

$$L_U x_q^\omega = -B^T m_q^\omega \tag{13}$$

$$L_U X = -B^T M \tag{14}$$

where solving for $\omega = 1$ yields $X = \{x_q \forall q | v_q \in V\}$ as the set of solution probabilities of a random walker originating at a node $q \in G$ and reaching the lumen and is associated and solved accordingly

$$p(lumen|x, I) = x_q^\omega \forall \{q \in G \Leftrightarrow x \in I\}, \omega = 1 \tag{15}$$

$$p(media|x, I) = x_q^\omega \forall \{q \in G \Leftrightarrow x \in I\}, \omega = 2 \tag{16}$$

$$p(externa|x, I) = x_q^\omega \forall \{q \in G \Leftrightarrow x \in I\}, \omega = 3 \tag{17}$$

5   Experiments, Results and Discussions

The data used in this experiment is acquired from the Lumen + External Elastic Laminae (Vessel Inner and Outer Wall) Border Detection in IVUS Challenge dataset[1]. There are two dataset (dataset **A** and dataset **B**) where we only took dataset **A** for this experiment. The data set A is composed of 77 groups of five consecutive frames, obtained from a 40 MHz IVUS scanner, acquired from different patients. Manually labeled data was also provided with this set of data and a MATLAB script for evaluating the results in a unified way. At the time of random forest learning, the D dimentional ordered vector Θ consisting of multiscale estimated Fisher-Tippett parameter and ultrasonic signal confidence is computed and represented as $\{(\Theta; r) \forall r \in \mathcal{G}\}$. In this experiments we have

---

[1] http://www.cvc.uab.es/IVUSchallenge2011/dataset.html.

tissue specific labels $y \in Y$ and $Y = \{lumen, media, externa\}$ corresponding to the ultrasound echo measurements at a grid points $r \in \mathcal{G}$. We train a random forest model $H(y|\Theta; r)$ using the ordered vector in training case $\{(\Theta; r)\forall r \in \mathcal{G}\}$. The random forest parameter is used in this work are $nTrees$ is 50 where $treeDepth$ is $\infty, minLeaf$ is 50 and $splitObj$ is Gini Diversity Index (GDI) maximization. This trained model is finally tested on selected number unknown test images(not used during training). This experiments is performed using a k-fold cross-validation technique. In this particular experiment we have considered 10 fold cross-validation where 9 sets of images are used for training the model and remaining one set is used for testing. The random forest is trained using 500 randomly drawn samples for the each tissue type from an image.

After testing of the unkhown images, the classified data would taken as initial segmented layer and finally random walks algorithm has been employed for calculation of layer specific prosterior probability. Using this 10-folded cross-validation experiments we obtain an average Jaccard coefficient value for lumen is 0.89 ± 0.14 and for external elastic luminae is 0.85 ± 0.12, the Hausdorff distances for lumen is 0.81 ± 0.53 and for external elastic luminae 0.95 ± 0.48 and the percentage of area difference value is 0.12 ± 0.10 for lumen and 0.10 ± 0.09 for external elastic luminae. The scores are competitively better from the prior art of the challenge [1]. The results are approximately same as the inter- and intra-observer [1]. In Table 1, the comparison is clearly drawn with the existing approaches. $Appr1$ shows the performance of initially segmented layer obtained from Sect. 4.3. Figure 2 shows that, in the left side in Fig. 2(a), (c), (e) are shows three different sizes of lumen on the right side in Fig. 2(b), (d), (f) shows three different size of media adventitia.

Table 1. Performance evaluation metric with the dataset and comparison with existing approaches. $P1$ and $P4$ has no experimental results with dataset A in the challenge

Methods	JCC		HD		PAD	
	Lumen	Media	Lumen	Media	Lumen	Media
$P2$ [1]	0.75 ± 0.11	–	1.78 ± 1.13	–	0.19 ± 0.12	–
$P3$ [1]	0.85 ± 0.12	0.86 ± 0.11	1.16 ± 1.12	1.18 ± 1.02	0.10 ± 0.12	0.10 ± 0.11
$P5$ [1]	0.72 ± 0.12	–	1.70 ± 1.09	–	0.22 ± 0.14	–
$P6$ [1]	–	0.76 ± 0.11	–	1.78 ± 0.83	–	0.17 ± 0.14
$P7$ [1]	0.83 ± 0.12	–	1.20 ± 1.03	–	0.14 ± 0.17	–
$P8$ [1]	0.80 ± 0.14	0.80 ± 0.13	1.32 ± 1.18	1.57 ± 1.03	0.11 ± 0.12	0.14 ± 0.16
$Intra\text{-}obs$ [1]	0.86 ± 0.10	0.87 ± 0.11	1.04 ± 0.95	1.14 ± 1.00	0.10 ± 0.10	0.11 ± 0.14
$Inter\text{-}obs$ [1]	0.92 ± 0.06	0.91 ± 0.07	0.67 ± 0.52	0.85 ± 0.60	0.05 ± 0.06	0.06 ± 0.07
$Appr1$[a]	0.72 ± 0.18	0.69 ± 0.13	1.35 ± 1.14	1.49 ± 1.21	0.26 ± 0.19	0.29 ± 0.17
$Appr2$	0.89 ± 0.14	0.85 ± 0.12	0.81 ± 0.53	0.95 ± 0.48	0.12 ± 0.10	0.10 ± 0.09

[a]Initially segmentation using random forest

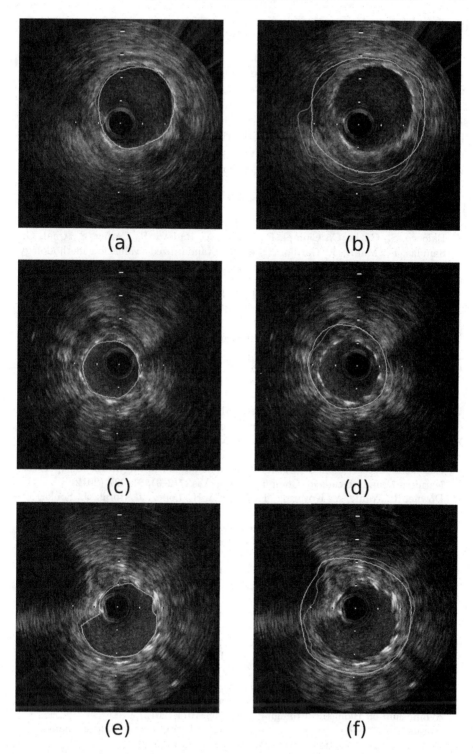

Fig. 2. First column is the lumen segmentation and second column is the external elastic laminae segmentation where YELLOW - ground truth data generated by the experts and RED - result of our proposed method (Color figure online)

6 Conclusion

The approach to layer characterization or boundary detection using ultrasonic backscattered signal from the heterogeneous atherosclerotic tissue is a very crucial task. In this paper, we have proposed a method for lumen and external elastic laminae segmentation in IVUS using: (i) ultrasonic backscattering physics and signal confidence estimation (ii) joint learning of these estimatesusing technique like random forests for initial layer localization and (iii) employing random walks for fine segmentation of boundaries. Our proposed algorithm is competitively more accurate and less time consuming than prior art.

References

1. Balocco, S., Gatta, C., Ciompi, F., Wahle, A., Radeva, P., Carlier, S., Unal, G., Sanidas, E., Mauri, J., Carillo, X., et al.: Standardized evaluation methodology and reference database for evaluating IVUS image segmentation. Comput. Med. Imaging Graph. **38**(2), 70–90 (2014)
2. Bovenkamp, E.G., Dijkstra, J., Bosch, J.G., Reiber, J.H.: User-agent cooperation in multiagent IVUS image segmentation. IEEE Trans. Med. Imaging **28**(1), 94–105 (2009)
3. Breiman, L.: Random forests. Mach. Learn. **45**(1), 5–32 (2001)
4. Cardinal, M.H.R., Meunier, J., Soulez, G., Maurice, R.L., Therasse, É., Cloutier, G.: Intravascular ultrasound image segmentation: a three-dimensional fast-marching method based on gray level distributions. IEEE Trans. Med. Imaging **25**(5), 590–601 (2006)
5. Ciompi, F., Pujol, O., Gatta, C., Alberti, M., Balocco, S., Carrillo, X., Mauri-Ferre, J., Radeva, P.: HoliMAb: a holistic approach for media-adventitia border detection in intravascular ultrasound. Med. Image Anal. **16**(6), 1085–1100 (2012)
6. Criminisi, A., Shotton, J., Konukoglu, E.: Decision forests: a unified framework for classification, regression, density estimation, manifold learning and semi-supervised learning. Found. Trends®. Comput. Graph. Vis. **7**(2–3), 81–227 (2012)
7. Downe, R., Wahle, A., Kovarnik, T., Skalicka, H., Lopez, J., Horak, J., Sonka, M.: Segmentation of intravascular ultrasound images using graph search and a novel cost function. In: Proceedings of the Medical Image Computing and Computer Assisted Intervention Workshop, Computer Vision for Intravascular and Intracardiac Imaging, pp. 71–79 (2008)
8. Gil, D., Hernández, A., Rodriguez, O., Mauri, J., Radeva, P.: Statistical strategy for anisotropic adventitia modelling in IVUS. IEEE Trans. Med. Imaging **25**(6), 768–778 (2006)
9. Grady, L.: Random walks for image segmentation. IEEE Trans. Pattern Anal. Mach. Intell. **28**(11), 1768–1783 (2006)
10. Herrington, D.M., Johnson, T., Santago, P., Snyder, W.E.: Semi-automated boundary detection for intravascular ultrasound. In: Proceedings of the Computers in Cardiology Conference, pp. 103–106 (1992)
11. Karamalis, A., Katouzian, A., Carlier, S., Navab, N.: Confidence estimation in IVUS radio-frequency data with random walks. In: Proceedings of the International Symposium on Biomedical Imaging, pp. 1068–1071 (2012)
12. Karamalis, A., Wein, W., Klein, T., Navab, N.: Ultrasound confidence maps using random walks. Med. Image Anal. **16**(6), 1101–1112 (2012)

13. Klingensmith, J.D., Shekhar, R., Vince, D.G.: Evaluation of three-dimensional segmentation algorithms for the identification of luminal and medial-adventitial borders in intravascular ultrasound images. IEEE Trans. Med. Imaging **19**(10), 996–1011 (2000)
14. Mendizabal-Ruiz, E.G., Rivera, M., Kakadiaris, I.A.: Segmentation of the luminal border in intravascular ultrasound b-mode images using a probabilistic approach. Med. Image Anal. **17**(6), 649–670 (2013)
15. Nag, M.K., Mandana, K., Sadhu, A.K., Mitra, P., Chakraborty, C.: Automated in vivo delineation of lumen wall using intravascular ultrasound imaging. In: Proceedings of the International Conference on Engineering in Medicine and Biology Society, pp. 4125–4128 (2016)
16. Plissiti, M.E., Fotiadis, D.I., Michalis, L.K., Bozios, G.E.: An automated method for lumen and media-adventitia border detection in a sequence of IVUS frames. IEEE Trans. Inf. Tech. Biomed. **8**(2), 131–141 (2004)
17. Roy, A.G., Conjeti, S., Carlier, S.G., Dutta, P.K., Kastrati, A., Laine, A.F., Navab, N., Katouzian, A., Sheet, D.: Lumen segmentation in intravascular optical coherence tomography using backscattering tracked and initialized random walks. IEEE J. Biomed. Health Inf. **20**(2), 606–614 (2016)
18. Sen, P.K., Singer, J.M.: Large Sample Methods in Statistics: An Introduction with Applications, vol. 25. CRC Press, Boca Raton (1994)
19. Shankar, P.M.: A general statistical model for ultrasonic backscattering from tissues. IEEE Trans. Ultrason. Ferroelectr. Freq. Control **47**(3), 727–736 (2000)
20. Shankar, P.: Estimation of the Nakagami parameter from log-compressed ultrasonic backscattered envelopes (L). J. Acoust. Soc. Am. **114**(1), 70–72 (2003)
21. Sheet, D., Karamalis, A., Eslami, A., Noël, P., Chatterjee, J., Ray, A.K., Laine, A.F., Carlier, S.G., Navab, N., Katouzian, A.: Joint learning of ultrasonic backscattering statistical physics and signal confidence primal for characterizing atherosclerotic plaques using intravascular ultrasound. Med. Image Anal. **18**(1), 103–117 (2014)
22. Sheet, D., Karamalis, A., Kraft, S., Noël, P.B., Vag, T., Sadhu, A., Katouzian, A., Navab, N., Chatterjee, J., Ray, A.K.: Random forest learning of ultrasonic statistical physics and object spaces for lesion detection in 2D sonomammography. In: Proceedings of the SPIE Medical Imaging, p. 867515 (2013)
23. Shekhar, R., Cothren, R., Vince, D.G., Chandra, S., Thomas, J., Cornhill, J.: Three-dimensional segmentation of luminal and adventitial borders in serial intravascular ultrasound images. Comput. Med. Imaging Graph. **23**(6), 299–309 (1999)
24. Sonka, M., Zhang, X., Siebes, M., Bissing, M.S., DeJong, S.C., Collins, S.M., McKay, C.R.: Segmentation of intravascular ultrasound images: a knowledge-based approach. IEEE Trans. Med. Imaging **14**(4), 719–732 (1995)
25. Sun, S., Sonka, M., Beichel, R.R.: Graph-based IVUS segmentation with efficient computer-aided refinement. IEEE Trans. Med. Imaging **32**(8), 1536–1549 (2013)
26. Unal, G., Bucher, S., Carlier, S., Slabaugh, G., Fang, T., Tanaka, K.: Shape-driven segmentation of the arterial wall in intravascular ultrasound images. IEEE Trans. Inf. Tech. Biomed. **12**(3), 335–347 (2008)

Author Index

Babu J., Dinesh   314
Banerjee, Samik   180
Banerji, Sugata   168
Banumathi, A.   322
Bhattacharya, U.   120

Chakrabarti, Amlan   337
Chanda, Bhabatosh   97, 192
Chatterjee, Jyotirmoy   380
Chaudhury, Santanu   109, 157, 288, 367
Chebiyyam, M.   109
Chetan, K.R.   3
China, Debarghya   393

Das, Sudeb   337
Das, Sukhendu   75, 180
Devarapalli, Koteswara Rao   243
Dey, Soumyadeep   255

Gad, M.D.   15
Gad, R.S.   15, 27
Gaonkar, A.A.   15
Garg, Ritu   288
Garud, Hrushikesh   380
Ghorai, Mrinmoy   97
Gopan K., Gopika   314
Gurunathan, Ulaganathan   322

Hajamohideen, Faizal   277
Harit, Gaurav   265

Ishii, Idaku   157
Islam, Sheikh Rafiul   345

Jaffino, G.   322
Jampana, P.V.   204

Kar, I.N.   109
Kar, Sudeshna Sil   301
Karri, Sri Phani Krishna   380
Karthikeyan, S.   88
Kumar, P.U. Praveen   204

Lalitha, K.S.   75

Mahadevappa, Manjunatha   380
Maity, Ashok Kumar   380
Maity, Santi P.   301, 345
Maity, Seba   301, 345
Medhi, Moushumi   145
Menon, Arun   75
Mishra, Deepak   367
Mishra, Kaustuv   358
Mishra, Niladri Shekhar   337
Mitra, Pabitra   393
Mitra, Suman K.   133
Mohamed Mansoor Roomi, S.   63
Mondal, Sounak   192
Mukherjee, Jayanta   219, 231, 255

Nagarajan, Pitchandi   50
Naik, G.M.   27
Nandedkar, Amit Vijay   219, 231, 255
Negi, Atul   243
Nirmala, S.   3
Noushath, S.   277

Pal, Soumyajit   192
Pandey, Shilpa   265
Parui, S.K.   120
Phophalia, Ashish   133
Prabin Jose, J.   322
Prasad, T.   204

Raghavendra, R.   27
Raju, Kota S.   157
Rameshan, Renu   39
Ray, Ajoy Kumar   345, 380

Saha, Rupsa   133
Saha, Sanjoy Kumar   192
Sahay, Rajiv Ranjan   145
Saini, Anil K.   157
Saini, Ravi   157
Samanta, Soumitra   97
Sanofer, I.   63

Sanyal, A.   120
Saravana Perumaal, S.   50
Sarkar, Mukul   367
Sasithradevi, A.   63
Sastry, C.S.   204
Sathish, Rachana   358
Sathyabama, B.   88
Saurav, Sumeet   157
Sharma, Krishan   39
Sheet, Debdoot   358, 380, 393
Singh, Sanjay   157
Sinha, Atreyee   168
Sinha, Neelam   314

Sinha, Shubham   145
Soin, Arvinder Singh   367
Sural, Shamik   219, 231, 255
Synthiya Vinothini, D.   88

Tanwar, Pramod   157
Tilve, Vithal Shet   15

Varghese, Koshy   75
Vetrekar, N.T.   15, 27

Yogameena, B.   50

Printed in the United States
By Bookmasters